Female Entrepreneurship as a Driving Force of Economic Growth and Social Change

Ana Dias Daniel
Universidade de Aveiro, Portugal

Cristina Fernandes
Universidade da Beira Interior, Portugal

A volume in the Advances in Human Resources Management and Organizational Development (AHRMOD) Book Series

IGI Global
PUBLISHER of TIMELY KNOWLEDGE

Published in the United States of America by
IGI Global
Business Science Reference (an imprint of IGI Global)
701 E. Chocolate Avenue
Hershey PA, USA 17033
Tel: 717-533-8845
Fax: 717-533-8661
E-mail: cust@igi-global.com
Web site: http://www.igi-global.com

Library of Congress Cataloging-in-Publication Data

Names: Daniel, Ana Dias, editor. | Fernandes, Cristina I., editor.
Title: Female entrepreneurship as a driving force of economic growth and social change / edited by Ana Daniel, Cristina Fernandes.
Description: Hershey, PA : Business Science Reference, [2023] | Includes bibliographical references and index. | Summary: "This book aims to compile what we have learned so far about female entrepreneurship, namely the main motivations that lead women to undertake and the characteristics of this type of business, as well as the impact of context and technology on the promotion and management of companies by women. In doing so, it is intended to contribute to a better understanding of this phenomenon and how it is different from male entrepreneurship, allowing a better delimitation of this field of research"-- Provided by publisher.
Identifiers: LCCN 2022054956 (print) | LCCN 2022054957 (ebook) | ISBN 9781668476697 (hardcover) | ISBN 9781668476703 (paperback) | ISBN 9781668476710 (ebook)
Subjects: LCSH: Businesswomen. | Entrepreneurship. | Women in development.
Classification: LCC HD6053 .F394 2023 (print) | LCC HD6053 (ebook) | DDC 658.1/1082--dc23/eng/20230327
LC record available at https://lccn.loc.gov/2022054956
LC ebook record available at https://lccn.loc.gov/2022054957

This book is published in the IGI Global book series Advances in Human Resources Management and Organizational Development (AHRMOD) (ISSN: 2327-3372; eISSN: 2327-3380)

British Cataloguing in Publication Data
A Cataloguing in Publication record for this book is available from the British Library.

Advances in Human Resources Management and Organizational Development (AHRMOD) Book Series

Patricia Ordóñez de Pablos
Universidad de Oviedo, Spain

ISSN:2327-3372
EISSN:2327-3380

Mission

A solid foundation is essential to the development and success of any organization and can be accomplished through the effective and careful management of an organization's human capital. Research in human resources management and organizational development is necessary in providing business leaders with the tools and methodologies which will assist in the development and maintenance of their organizational structure.

The **Advances in Human Resources Management and Organizational Development (AHRMOD) Book Series** aims to publish the latest research on all aspects of human resources as well as the latest methodologies, tools, and theories regarding organizational development and sustainability. The **AHRMOD Book Series** intends to provide business professionals, managers, researchers, and students with the necessary resources to effectively develop and implement organizational strategies.

Coverage

- E-Human Resources Management
- Diversity in the Workplace
- Recruitment Process
- Coaching and Mentoring
- Personnel Policies
- Employee Benefits
- Corporate Governance
- Organizational Behavior
- Employee Evaluation
- Performance Improvement

IGI Global is currently accepting manuscripts for publication within this series. To submit a proposal for a volume in this series, please contact our Acquisition Editors at Acquisitions@igi-global.com or visit: http://www.igi-global.com/publish/.

The Advances in Human Resources Management and Organizational Development (AHRMOD) Book Series (ISSN 2327-3372) is published by IGI Global, 701 E. Chocolate Avenue, Hershey, PA 17033-1240, USA, www.igi-global.com. This series is composed of titles available for purchase individually; each title is edited to be contextually exclusive from any other title within the series. For pricing and ordering information please visit http://www.igi-global.com/book-series/advances-human-resources-management-organizational/73670. Postmaster: Send all address changes to above address.

Titles in this Series

For a list of additional titles in this series, please visit: http://www.igi-global.com/book-series/advances-human-resources-management-organizational/73670

Developing Diversity, Equity, and Inclusion Policies for Promoting Employee Sustainability and Well-Being
Sónia P. Gonçalves (ISCSP, Universidade de Lisboa, Portugal) Paula Cristina Nunes Figueiredo (Universidade Lusófona, Portugal) Eduardo Luis Soares Tomé (ULHT, Universidade Lusófona, Portugal) and José Baptista (ISCSP, Universidade de Lisboa, Portugal)
Business Science Reference • © 2023 • 333pp • H/C (ISBN: 9781668441817) • US $240.00

Valuing People and Technology in the Workplace Ethical Implications and Imperatives for Success
Claretha Hughes (University of Arkansas, USA)
Business Science Reference • © 2023 • 367pp • H/C (ISBN: 9781668453216) • US $205.00

Talent Acquisition and Retention Strategies in Global Startups
Neetima Agarwal (Symbiosis International University, India) Leo Paul Dana (Kingston University, UK) and Sujata Khandai (Amity University, India)
Business Science Reference • © 2023 • 305pp • H/C (ISBN: 9781668475140) • US $250.00

Strategic Human Resource Management in the Hospitality Industry A Digitalized Economic Paradigm
Kannapat Kankaew (Suan Sunandha Rajabhat University, Thailand)
Business Science Reference • © 2023 • 309pp • H/C (ISBN: 9781668474945) • US $250.00

Corporate Sustainability as a Tool for Improving Economic, Social, and Environmental Performance
Bartolomé Marco-Lajara (University of Alicante, Spain) Javier Martínez-Falcó (University of Alicante, Spain & Stellenbosch University, South Africa) and Luis A. Millán-Tudela (University of Alicante, Spain)
Business Science Reference • © 2023 • 337pp • H/C (ISBN: 9781668474228) • US $250.00

Handbook of Research on Dissecting and Dismantling Occupational Stress in Modern Organizations
Adnan ul Haque (Yorkville University, Canada)
Business Science Reference • © 2023 • 559pp • H/C (ISBN: 9781668465431) • US $315.00

Managing Technology Integration for Human Resources in Industry 5.0
Naman Sharma (Indian Institute of Foreign Trade, India) and Kumar Shalender (Chitkara University, India)
Business Science Reference • © 2023 • 294pp • H/C (ISBN: 9781668467459) • US $215.00

IGI Global
PUBLISHER of TIMELY KNOWLEDGE

701 East Chocolate Avenue, Hershey, PA 17033, USA
Tel: 717-533-8845 x100 • Fax: 717-533-8661
E-Mail: cust@igi-global.com • www.igi-global.com

Table of Contents

Detailed Table of Contents

Despite the growth of female entrepreneurship over the last decade, research in this area is still at an embryonic stage. Its development is essential to understand how this phenomenon can be leveraged, allowing to achieve a more inclusive and developed society. Social media platforms have been recognized as a relevant tool in promoting female entrepreneurship, but studies in this area are still limited. Through a bibliometric analysis combined with a literature review, this study concluded that the studies published in this area essentially focus on one of three perspectives: a business creation perspective, a business strategy and performance perspective, and a women's empowerment perspective. Moreover, articles analysed used a diverse range of research methodologies and focused mainly on developing countries. Therefore, future research should include different research perspectives, as well as the analysis of different economic and social contexts to better understand the phenomenon of female entrepreneurship

Entrepreneurship is the engine of economic, cultural, and social development. In a reality where equal opportunities between men and women in business are not yet verifiable, we would benefit from an adequate understanding of female entrepreneurship's impact. This chapter explores the concept of female entrepreneurship in a systematic literature review. Based on Web of Science database articles, it uses bibliometric analysis to analyze the drivers influencing female entrepreneurial intentions, performance, and outcomes. This study enables the systematization of the existing literature into four themes: 1) gender-specific entrepreneurial intention factors, 2) women´s entrepreneurial success factors, 3) women´s entrepreneurial performance, and 4) gender-specific entrepreneurial performance. The results provide insights into the triggering factors of female entrepreneurship intention and help to develop a more profound understanding of the factors affecting their entrepreneurial performance and outcomes. An agenda for further research was laid out based on the existing literature.

Social entrepreneurship (SE), which aims to solve social problems of deprived groups, has become a popular area of research and practice. The recent investigation on SE has been characterized by a greater focus on gender differences, emphasizing that the role and characteristics of females are more suitable for social entrepreneurial initiatives. This chapter investigates the predominant themes on females in SE and identifies further research opportunities. On the one hand, the main macro (e.g., sociocultural values) and micro (e.g., personality traits) levels determinants are examined. On the other hand, the macro (e.g., social change) and micro (e.g., women economic empowerment) levels outcomes of females in SE are analyzed. Furthermore, directions for future research are suggested which will enable future authors to focus their studies more effectively.

The purpose of this chapter is to provide a methodological framework for assessing digital entrepreneurial competencies (DEC) of university students and to point out the importance of different socio-demographic, institutional, and contextual factors as drivers of DEC levels. The chapter provides a roadmap for measuring DEC levels of university students along with the detailed corresponding methodology. The preliminary results of the pilot study targeting the first competence area of the corresponding DEC framework (EmDigital) and conducted simultaneously in Kuwait and Serbia are also presented in this chapter, demonstrating the perceived DEC levels and exact DEC levels of university students in two countries. Those results indicate that different factors drive the DEC levels of university students. This is the first research of this kind in academic literature.

Two phenomena are described in this chapter. The inclusion of women in executive and administrative positions is, on the one hand, a crucial problem in diversity management. On the other side, there are more and more successful female business owners. Therefore, the main research issue guiding this work is whether female entrepreneurs' success stories might encourage the hiring of more female managers in organizations. The authors apply a qualitative technique based on several case studies that have been used in prior research on entrepreneurs. Five case studies of successful female entrepreneurs were chosen in order to create study findings with management and theoretical implications.

Preface

Female entrepreneurship is currently considered a driving force of economic growth and social change, contributing for poverty reduction and social exclusion. While female entrepreneurship is growing, recent studies show that women entrepreneurs still face several challenges on a social, economic, or cultural level that are specific to their status as women. In addition, there is the stigma that entrepreneurship is a male job, as it is associated with male characteristics, such as aggressiveness and high-risk propensity. Due to these distinctive features, some researchers suggest that the study of female entrepreneurship should be an area of investigation distinct from entrepreneurship.

In fact, in the last decade, female entrepreneurship has gained considerable attention from both academics and policymakers. Despite the proliferation of studies, this field of research is characterized by being a highly multidisciplinary and dispersed, encompassing studies from a wide range of disciplines such as business and management, education, political science, technology, and innovation. In order to legitimize female entrepreneurship as a distinct field of research, it is important to deepen the scientific reasoning regarding women entrepreneurs while promoting the theoretical consolidation of this area of knowledge.

This book aims to compile what we have learned so far about female entrepreneurship, namely the main motivations that lead women to undertake and the characteristics of this type of business, as well as the impact of context and technology on the promotion and management of companies by women. In doing so, it is intended to contribute to a better understanding of this phenomenon and how it is different from male entrepreneurship, allowing a better delimitation of this field of research.

The book is mainly intended to support an academic audience (academics, university teachers, researchers, and post-graduate students – both Master and Doctorate levels). In addition, this book pretends to be a benefit to the general public and private institutions, developers, and researchers within the fields of Entrepreneurship, Innovation, Regional Development and Gender issues.

Ana Dias Daniel
Universidade de Aveiro, Portugal

Cristina Fernandes
Universidade da Beira Interior, Portugal

Chapter 1
Female Entrepreneurship in the Age of Social Media: A Research Agenda

Adriana Coutinho Gradim
University of Aveiro, Portugal

Ana Isabel Dias Daniel
University of Aveiro, Portugal

ABSTRACT

Despite the growth of female entrepreneurship over the last decade, research in this area is still at an embryonic stage. Its development is essential to understand how this phenomenon can be leveraged, allowing to achieve a more inclusive and developed society. Social media platforms have been recognized as a relevant tool in promoting female entrepreneurship, but studies in this area are still limited. Through a bibliometric analysis combined with a literature review, this study concluded that the studies published in this area essentially focus on one of three perspectives: a business creation perspective, a business strategy and performance perspective, and a women's empowerment perspective. Moreover, articles analysed used a diverse range of research methodologies and focused mainly on developing countries. Therefore, future research should include different research perspectives, as well as the analysis of different economic and social contexts to better understand the phenomenon of female entrepreneurship

INTRODUCTION

Although research in the field of entrepreneurship has grown significantly in the last 30 years (Alvarez et al., 2011; Walby et al., 2012), the relationship between gender and entrepreneurship has been an unsolved issue in the field (Quagrainie, 2016). Entrepreneurship is usually associated with male characteristics, such as ambition and risk tolerance, which leads women and men to differ in their entrepreneurial intention and behaviour (Merza, 2019; Verheul et al., 2006). In fact, according to the Global Entrepreneurship

DOI: 10.4018/978-1-6684-7669-7.ch001

Monitor 2021/2022 report "15 of the 47 economies have two or more men running established businesses for every woman doing so" (Global Entrepreneurship Monitor, 2022, p. 63).

Nevertheless, in the last decade there has been an increase in female entrepreneurship in some countries, often supported by government initiatives (Global Entrepreneurship Monitor, 2022). Female entrepreneurship can be defined as women "who solely or with partners started a business, and are willing to undertake risk, responsibilities, and managerial activities of an organisation" (Hossain & Rahman, 2018, p.99).

While women face different challenges depending on the context which they start a business (e.g., developed or developing country), there are some challenges common to all women, such as access to external capital, lack of family support and the need to balance work and family responsibilities, particularly in the case of motherhood (Al-Dmour & Abuhammad, 2021; Basaffar et al., 2018; Plazibat & Renko, 2020).

In turn, the increased use of social media has drastically changed the business environment (Mulkowe & Korir, 2016) as, on the one hand, allowed customers to become more active in their relationship with businesses, and on the other hand, fostered the development of new types of businesses (Aboutaleb, 2020). Between 2021 and 2022, social media users increased by 10% which represents a social media reach of 4.62 billion which in turn represents 93,4% of internet connected people. It is even expected that in 2027 4.4 billion people will be on social media (Schaffer, 2022). Moreover, social media as an internet-based channel, increased opportunities for female entrepreneurs as it allowed for a better work-life balance (Basaffar et al., 2018; Hossain & Rahman, 2018; Mamodu et al., 2019). Although the use of social media seems promising, there are a limited number of studies that analyse the influence of social networks on female entrepreneurship, namely studies that assess the factors that may or may not lead women to seek this type of activity, as well as clarification on how social media can contribute to overcoming barriers to female entrepreneurship (Cesaroni et al., 2017; Plazibat & Renko, 2020). The present study aims to clarify the main topics investigated in this area, through a literature review combined with a bibliometric analysis, to identify which topics, need to be further analysed and, thus, contribute to enhancing research in female entrepreneurship. In this paper, social media includes the use of online platforms that enable the interaction between customers and businesses, such as Instagram, Facebook, and WhatsApp.

The remainder of this paper is organized as follows. In section 2, the methodology followed to select and analyse the sample article is described. In turn, section 3 presents the main findings regarding the bibliometric analysis and literature review. Finally, in section 4, the main conclusions are presented, highlighting key implications and limitations in our study.

METHODOLOGY

In this study, a literature review combined with a bibliometric analysis was used, based on the two most important research databases, namely the Scopus by Elsevier and the ISI Web of Science by Clarivate Analytics. The search was carried out on the 17th of January 2022, using the following query ("wom* entrepreneur*" OR "female entrepreneur*" AND "social media"), which allowed the collection of a total of 62 articles in Scopus and 40 articles in ISI Web of Science, without any limitation imposed due to the reduced number of articles found.

RIS files documents were retrieved from both databases to allow the bibliometric analysis using the VOSviewer software. By using the VOSviewer software it is possible to obtain a graphical image of the connection between the keywords that were used in the search.

Both files were imported to the Mendeley Reference Manager and analysed using the PRISMA method (Liberati et al., 2009). This method allows to systematically reduce the number of articles to be analysed to increase the focus of the research. Initially, duplicates were removed, and the remaining articles were analysed considering the title and abstract. This allows to eliminate those who are not focused on the topic this paper aims to analyse, namely the influence of social media on female entrepreneurship and the factors that can lead women to pursue or not this type of activity. This screening provided a total of 62 documents. From these, three additional references were removed since they were conference proceedings abstracts. Therefore, a total of 59 documents were considered for analysis.

RESULTS AND DISCUSSION

Descriptive Analysis

The first publication from this sample is dated from 2014 and it was published by the Mediterranean Journal of Social Sciences. It is related to the use of social media by female entrepreneurs and how to unlock their potential for success. Figure 1 present the number of publications between 2014 and 2021, showing an increasing trend in publications after 2019, which reveals the growing interest of researchers in this field of research.

Figure 1. Number of publications per year

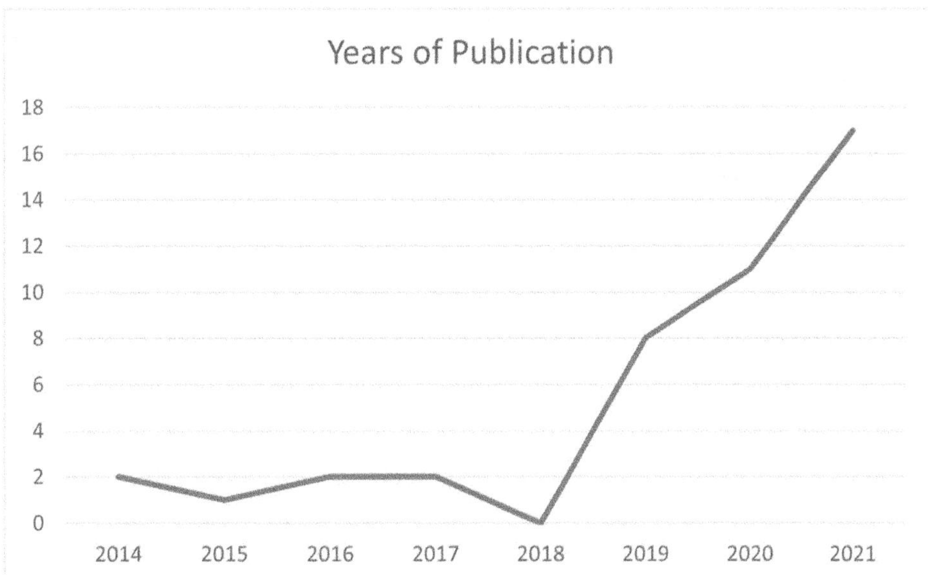

In terms of the publishing journals, the *International Journal of Entrepreneurship and Small Business* and the *Mediterranean Journal of Social Sciences* stand out.

VOSviewer Analysis

VOSviewer analysis enable the identification of the main authors and the main topics of research in the field. In terms of the co-occurrence of keywords, a minimum of occurrence of two for each keyword was defined. From the results, names of countries and general words were removed to reduce the bias. Figure 1 presents the results obtained and it is possible to observe that from a total of 45 items, 7 clusters emerged with 232 links and a total link strength of 377. Table 1 presents the results from the main clusters.

Figure 2. Co-occurrence of keywords

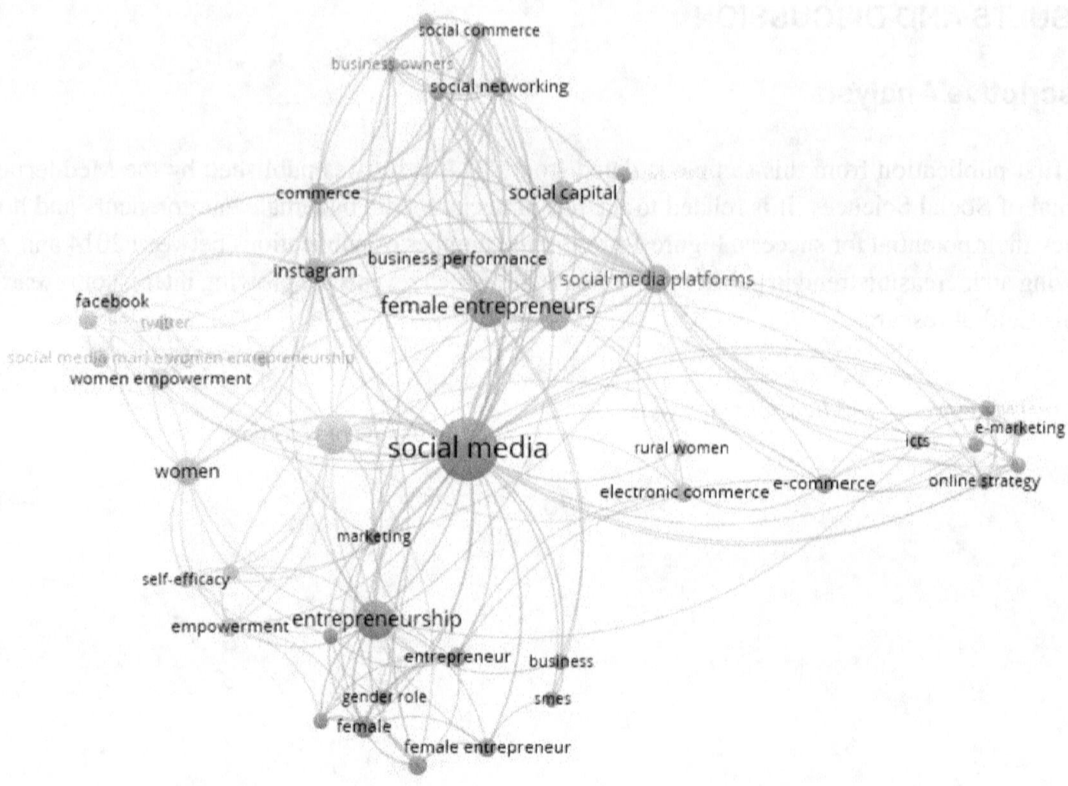

Table 1. Cluster description (1 to 5)

Cluster	Title	Total items	Main topics (minimum of 2 occurrences)	Occurrences	Links
Cluster 1 (red)	Social media and entrepreneurship	12	Social media	30	42
			Entrepreneurship	12	17
			Entrepreneur	3	10
			Female entrepreneurship	3	6
			Marketing	2	11
			Gender role	2	8
			Intersectionality	2	7
Cluster 2 (green)	Social media commerce	8	Social media platforms	6	23
			Instagram	5	18
			Commerce	4	17
			Business owners	2	10
			Social commerce(s)	2	10
Cluster 3 (blue)	Online commerce strategies	7	E-commerce	3	11
			E-marketing	2	8
			Online social networking	2	8
			Online strategy	2	8
Cluster 4 (yellow mustard)	Social media platforms for female entrepreneurship	7	Women entrepreneurs	12	20
			Facebook	4	8
			WhatsApp	3	8
			Twitter	2	8

Clusters 5 (purple, 6 items), 6 (baby blue, 4 items) and 7 (orange, 3 items) are related to business performance in female entrepreneurship. Therefore, it can be grouped as one cluster designated as "female entrepreneurship and business performance".

In terms of authors, Figure 2 shows that there is not a strong relationship among the authors on the topic with a minimum of two occurrences per author. These results show that, in general it is not an area of investigation where there is great collaboration between researchers.

Figure 3. Co-occurrence of authors

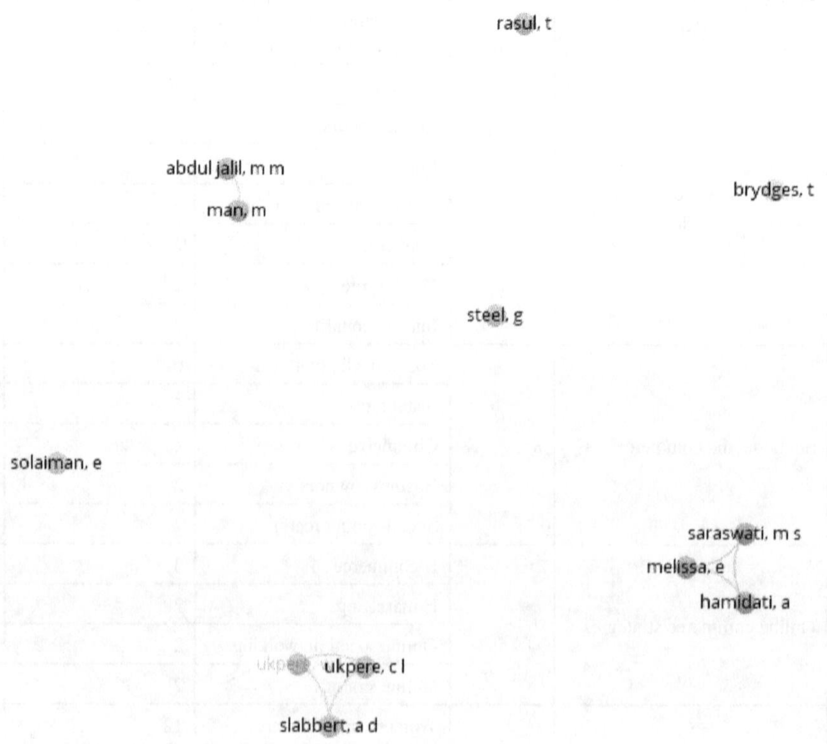

Cluster Analysis and Literature Review

This section is divided into three subsections. The first concerns the analysis of the main topics covered within each cluster. The second subsection describes the analysis of the methods and contexts used in the articles, which is useful for understanding if there is a need to improve the methodologies applied. The third subsection refers to the analysis of the main results and future research suggestions mentioned in the sample articles, which can be grouped into different categories.

Cluster's Analysis

The **'social media and entrepreneurship cluster'** (red) encompasses the articles that follow a business creation perspective and address the role of gender in the promotion of new businesses, and how social media influences the female entrepreneurship process. Female entrepreneurship activities have been growing for the past years and must be seen as a fundamental aspect for economic growth. According to the Global Entrepreneurship Monitor there is a stable increase in the number of women-owned businesses (Global Entrepreneurship Monitor, 2022), which could lead to the decrease of unemployment and secure gender equality by breaking the "glass-ceiling" through increasing diversity in the workforce (Jiménez-Zarco et al., 2021; Olamide & Ogbechie, 2021).One of the most relevant topic addressed concerns how social media has changed, not only the business environment, but also the entrepreneurial activity. In 2020, 43% of consumers increased their use of social media to discover and buy new products (Cover, 2021).

There is no doubt that there is an increase in the use of communication technologies and social media platforms which has led to the creation of new ventures (Hashim et al., 2021; Jose, 2018; Steel, 2017, 2021). On the one hand, social media can facilitate the access to resources and allow reaching broader markets to improve sales, as well as promoting partnerships, collaborations and co-creation processes with customers and end-users, and, on the other hand, it can foster the development of innovative ideas and approaches to conducting business (Camacho & Barrios, 2021; Chaudhry & Paquibut, 2021). However, literature on social media and female entrepreneurship remains scarce with four main streams of research being identified: social media as a boost for entrepreneurial learning; social media as a tool for entrepreneurial marketing; social media to identify and pursue entrepreneurial opportunities and; social media as a tool for women to engage in entrepreneurial networks and ecosystems (Secundo et al., 2021).

The articles in clusters **'social media commerce'** (green) and **'online commerce strategies'** (blue) focus on business strategy perspective, as they address topics related to the use of social media to enhance business development, as well as the development of commercial strategies based on social media platforms, respectively. In this case, the use of social media is relevant for women who aim to create new business ventures since social media is widely used by businesses in engagement strategies with their customers (Olsson & Bernhard, 2020). Although female entrepreneurship is often associated with activities typically related to women (e.g., makeup), social media enables small businesses to develop and grow, as it facilitates their entry into global business networks through digital marketing strategies (Melissa et al., 2013). It is agreed over the years that these networks can provide women access to new alliances by ending their isolation and giving them access to strategic information (Myers, 1998). Moreover, entering social media allows women to explore existing skills and developing new ones which allows them to engage in larger projects overtime (Chaker & Zouaoui, 2022).

According to the articles belonging to the cluster **'social media platforms for female entrepreneurship'**, platforms such as Facebook, WhatsApp and Twitter are the main platforms used by women to develop their entrepreneurial ventures. It is believed that there is a positive connection between the use of these platforms and the sustainable development of small businesses owned by women. Furthermore, these articles advocate a women's empowerment perspective and show that social networks empower women both on a personal and relational level, and that women can even be more empowered than men after using social media to conduct their business (Miniesy et al., 2021). In this case, the education of women in the use of social media and online commerce strategies is considered a key instrument in helping them promoting business sustainability (Clark & Tomos, 2020; Vivakaran & Maraimalai, 2017). For example, in Oman, young girls are receiving education in social media, allowing them to have an online business, while performing their activities at home (Chaudhry & Paquibut, 2021). Nevertheless, a country's context, such as their level of freedom, may influence women to use different social media platforms to promote their businesses (Jose, 2018). For example, in the case of the Arab countries, several policies were promoted to support female entrepreneurship as a way of generating income and creating new jobs, while contributing to the country's economy (Chaudhry & Paquibut, 2021; Melissa et al., 2013). This led to a rise to 17,7% of women entrepreneurial activity in Saudi arabia (Mastercard, 2022). However, some main barriers remain such as access to capital and funding support with majority of women relying in their savings as their primary or only source of capital, with a study showing that these represents 60% of the analysed participants. Moreover, the same study concludes that 30% of its participants believe that there is a lack of specialisation regarding services for women entrepreneurs and that they fell uncomfortable while approaching banks for loans if alone (Mounzer, 2022).

According to the cluster articles **'female entrepreneurship and business performance'**, social media commerce allows women to showcase their products or services, while increasing the visibility and financial performance of their business (Bedarkar et al., 2020). Thus, these articles follow mainly a business performance perspective. In addition, it is argued that female entrepreneurship can increase women's sense of empowerment, self-realization, and freedom (Brydges & Sjöholm, 2019; Frankel et al., 2021; Miniesy et al., 2021; Steel, 2017). In this case, women experience a feeling of achieving work-life balance while becoming an entrepreneur using social media, since it enables women to balance their work commitments and family responsibilities (Steel, 2017). This raises the question of whether social media is really helping women become more empowered and freer or is it pushing them back into the traditional stay-at-home role of women. Steel (2017), argues that it depends on the desire of women, because there are those who want to assume the traditional role while others no, but what is true is that social media allows all to go beyond home market while establishing their business.

Also, the Covid-19 pandemic is a topic discussed in some articles, as it posed serious challenges to the way businesses were being managed, with most of them turning to social media to thrive. At the same time, as people were at home due to lockdown measures, social media usage increased, providing the perfect context for businesses to change their marketing and delivery services (Alessa et al., 2021). Therefore, this pandemic was also an opportunity for women to develop new ideas and launch their businesses (Jiménez-Zarco et al., 2021; Kézai & Szombathelyi, 2021). According to Mastercard Index of Women Entrepreneurs from 2022, the pandemic reshaped business for all, especially women. Although the world is still facing the challenges from the pandemic and an emerging economic crisis, governments in some economies are taking more into account the long-term effect of the pandemic on gender equality by reshaping public policies to help women thrive in business. The implementation of

Table 2. Summary of methodologies

Methodologies	References
Case studies (in-depth interviews and observation)	Baulch & Pramiyanti, 2018; Brydges & Sjöholm, 2019; Dam & Pillai, 2021; Frankel et al., 2021; Hashim et al., 2021; Jia et al., 2021; Jose, 2018; Mehtap et al., 2019; Olsson & Bernhard, 2020; Tuite, 2021
In-depth interviews	Hashim et al., 2021; Jia et al., 2021; Melissa et al., 2013
Focus group	Ghouse et al., 2017
Surveys	Al-Dmour & Abuhammad, 2021; Chaudhry & Paquibut, 2021; Ghouse et al., 2017; Hashim et al., 2021; Jia et al., 2021; Jiménez-Zarco et al., 2021; Kargwell, 2021; Melissa et al., 2015; Olamide & Ogbechie, 2021; Shahzad et al., 2021
Literature review	Steel, 2021; Swartz et al., 2016; Zainuddin et al., 2017.
Netnography	Chakraborty & Biswal, 2021
Document analysis	Sarpong et al., 2021

these policies is important because women can help to recover the economy and drive societal health and wealth while innovation and inclusion are promoted (Mastercard, 2022).

Methods and Contexts

Regarding the methods applied in the sample articles, there is a variety of approaches that were used which are summarised in Table 2.

The articles analysed used a diverse range of research methodologies, namely qualitative and quantitative research, as well as mixed methods research approach. In the case of qualitative research, case study analysis was the most used approach, while a survey was the most used methodology for quantitative research. In terms of mixed methods research, the most common approaches were in-depth surveys and interviews.

In terms of the local/national context, most of the articles focus on developing countries, namely Nigeria (Olamide & Ogbechie, 2021; Sarpong et al., 2021), Egypt (Miniesy et al., 2021), Indonesia (Baulch & Pramiyanti, 2018; Melissa et al., 2013), Oman (Chaudhry & Paquibut, 2021; Ghouse et al., 2017), Sudan (Steel, 2017, 2021), Jordan (Al-Dmour & Abuhammad, 2021; Mehtap et al., 2019) and the Gulf States (Hashim et al., 2021).These latter Arabic countries have reported an increase in female-led businesses as a result of the implementation of policies to promote female entrepreneurship on social media. Other countries analysed in the articles include China (Jia et al., 2021), United Arabs Emirates (Kargwell, 2021), United States of America (Brydges & Sjöholm, 2019) and several European countries (Olsson & Bernhard, 2020).

Further Research Avenues

This section provides a summary of the main results and future research suggestions of the articles analysed. For policy makers, namely governments and authorities, there is the need to define more clearer the role of government support in promoting female entrepreneurship. For example, access to bank capital should be facilitated, especially in case of developing countries were women have less freedom (Ghouse et al., 2017).

In terms of the lack of skills to use social media, there is the need to promote training opportunities for women to improve their digital and business skills (Brydges & Sjöholm, 2019; Chaudhry & Paquibut, 2021). For example, social media platforms can be used for networking and learning (Frankel et al., 2021; Ghouse et al., 2017; Olamide & Ogbechie, 2021; Steel, 2017) and social media communities can encourage female entrepreneurship activities (Kézai & Szombathelyi, 2021)

Regarding motivations and challenges, most studies agree that all the factors that influence female entrepreneurship have not yet been exhaustively identified (Mehtap et al., 2019; Olsson & Bernhard, 2020). Zainuddin et al. (2017) argue that challenges should also be seen as opportunities, but more research is needed to identify what the specific challenges are and how they can be overcome in order for a woman to become a successful entrepreneur.

In the case of methodologies and context of analysis, there is a need to carry out studies in different social and economic contexts (Swartz et al., 2016), not just to fully understand the nature of entrepreneurship, but also the differences between male and female entrepreneurship (Brydges & Sjöholm, 2019). In particular, it is important to understand how social media has contributed to the development of female entrepreneurship in different contexts and how these tools have affected the development of women's own businesses (Olsson & Bernhard, 2020; Steel, 2021). For example, comparative studies between different countries are relevant to understand the impact of public policies in promoting female entrepreneurship, as well as analysing the influence of the level of freedom on women's intention to become entrepreneurs. This can also help to identify different types of female entrepreneurship (Ghouse et al., 2017; Zainuddin et al., 2017).

Table 3. Future research field

Future research topic	References
Definition of female entrepreneurship	Clark & Tomos, 2020
Use of different research methodologies	Brydges & Sjöholm, 2019; Swartz et al., 2016
How women conduct business using social media	Ghouse et al., 2017; Swartz et al., 2016
Training of women to use social media	Chaudhry & Paquibut, 2021
Female entrepreneurship barriers and motivations	Mehtap et al., 2019; Melissa et al., 2013; Olsson & Bernhard, 2020b; Zainuddin et al., 2017
Changing nature of entrepreneurship through the use of social media	Brydges & Sjöholm, 2019; Jose, 2018
Analysis of female entrepreneurship in different countries	Ghouse et al., 2017; Jose, 2018; Zainuddin et al., 2017

Finally, there is a need to develop more studies to clearly identify the challenges and motivations of female entrepreneurs, as these differ from previous studies that adopt a predominant male perspective (Zainuddin et al., 2017). Also, there is the need to consider that women differ among themselves and that a generalisation about women entrepreneurship should not be made (Stone, 2004). The motivations to use a specific social media platform by women entrepreneurs can also be different than male entrepreneurs, which could also be influenced by the social and economic context of the entrepreneur, as well as type of business (Jose, 2018). Table 3 provides a summary of future research topics considering the above analysed.

CONCLUSION

In the last decade, female entrepreneurship has attracted the attention of both the scientific and political communities, as it is a relevant instrument for promoting a more inclusive and developed society. As a result, the literature on female entrepreneurship has been growing, although there is still a need for more studies to better understand this phenomenon.

The role of social media platforms in the promotion of female entrepreneurship has been studied mainly from three different perspectives: a business creation perspective, a business strategy and performance perspective, and a women's empowerment perspective. First, social media platforms are relevant in the entrepreneurial process, as they allow them to overcome many of the social and cultural barriers imposed on women. Second, they have an impact on business strategy and performance, as they contribute to showcase products and services to a wider target market and, consequently, increasing brand recognition and sales. Finally, social media platforms contribute to women's empowerment through self-realization and freedom.

Moreover, sample articles used a diverse range of research methodologies (in-dept interviews, observation, surveys, literature review and netnography) and focused mainly on developing countries.

This work is not without limitations. One of the main limitations is related to the use of only two online databases and the reduced number of articles derived from them. Therefore, future researchers can expand this work by incorporating articles from other databases. In addition, the sample articles only covered peer-reviewed articles that were published in English in the areas of business management, ignoring other types of publication and areas of research.

Implications

The present study has implications at both a practical and theoretical level. In terms of practical implications, this study highlights the role of governments in raising awareness of the opportunities that social media can offer women as drivers of economic growth. in this case, governments should develop and implement initiatives to specifically support female entrepreneurship, as women entrepreneurs have different needs than men and these needs must be addressed differently to promote access to equal opportunities for both sexes.

In terms of theoretical implications, this study stresses the need to promote further research in the field of female entrepreneurship through the identification of existing research gaps. Moreover, researchers need to consider new perspectives that would provide a clearer understanding of the female entrepreneurship phenomenon, as well as the need to use different research methodologies (e.g., netnography) and explore different social and economic contexts. This can enhance the development of new theories in the area, as well as a better understanding of the factors that distinguish female from male entrepreneurship.

REFERENCES

Abdul Jalil, M. M., Mohd, F., Man, M., Ali, N., & Muhamad, S. (2019). Social media application usage and women entrepreneurship achievement through e-business model: Case of Setiu wetland. *ACM International Conference Proceeding Series, Part F1479*, (pp. 505–509). ACM. 10.1145/3316615.3316709

Aboutaleb, G. A. (2020). *Social Media Potentials in Supporting Women Entrepreneurship: The Case of Egypt*. The American University in Cairo.

Al-Dmour, R. H., & Abuhammad, H. (2021). The extent of use of social media networks by the female entrepreneurs in Jordan: Empirical study. *International Journal of Business and Globalisation, 29*(3), 406–427. doi:10.1504/IJBG.2021.118684

Alessa, A. A., Alotaibie, T. M., Elmoez, Z., & Alhamad, H. E. (2021). Impact of COVID-19 on Entrepreneurship and Consumer Behaviour: A Case Study in Saudi Arabia. *Journal of Asian Finance Economics and Business, 8*(5), 201–210. doi:10.13106/jafeb.2021.vol8.no5.0201

Alvarez, C., Urbano, D., Coduras, A., & Ruiz-Navarro, J. (2011). Environmental conditions and entrepreneurial activity: A regional comparison in Spain. *Journal of Small Business and Enterprise Development, 18*(1), 120–140. doi:10.1108/14626001111106460

Anwar, M., Bingley, S., & Burgess, S. (2018). Understanding ICT strategy of women small business owners in developing countries: Linking social media use, business strategy and well-being. *ACIS 2018 Proceedings*. IEEE.

Basaffar, A. A., Niehm, L. S., & Bosselman, R. (2018). Saudi Arabian women in entrepreneurship: Challenges, opportunities and potential. *Journal of Developmental Entrepreneurship*, *23*(2), 1850013. doi:10.1142/S1084946718500139

Baulch, E., & Pramiyanti, A. (2018). Hijabers on Instagram: Using Visual Social Media to Construct the Ideal Muslim Woman. *Social Media + Society*, *4*(4). doi:10.1177/2056305118800308

Bedarkar, M. M., Mishra, M., & Khatwani, R. A. (2020). Leveraging social media in facilitating women entrepreneurs in India: A case study of pune ladies (PULA). *International Journal of E-Entrepreneurship and Innovation*, *10*(2), 76–90. doi:10.4018/IJEEI.2020070105

Brydges, T., & Sjöholm, J. (2019). Becoming a personal style blogger: Changing configurations and spatialities of aesthetic labour in the fashion industry. *International Journal of Cultural Studies*, *22*(1), 119–139. doi:10.1177/1367877917752404

Camacho, S., & Barrios, A. (2021). Social commerce affordances for female entrepreneurship: The case of Facebook. *Electronic Markets*. doi:10.100712525-021-00487-y

Cesaroni, F. M., Paola, D., & Paola, P. (2017). Women in business and social media: Implications for female entrepreneurship in emerging countries. *African Journal of Business Management*, *11*(14), 316–326. doi:10.5897/AJBM2017.8281

Chaker, H., & Zouaoui, S. (2022). Meeting the Challenge of Entrepreneurship with social media: The Case of Tunisian Women Entrepreneurs. *Journal of Entrepreneurship and Innovation in Emerging Economies*, *9*(1), 33–61. doi:10.1177/23939575221138439

Chakraborty, U., & Biswal, S. K. (2021). Psychological empowerment of women entrepreneurs: A netnographic study on twitter. *Management Research Review*. doi:10.1108/MRR-01-2021-0046

Chaudhry, I. S., & Paquibut, R. Y. (2021). Women Empowerment through Micropreneurship in Online Businesses in the Sultanate of Oman. *Academy of Entrepreneurship Journal*, *27*(1), 1–14. https://www.scopus.com/inward/record.uri?eid=2-s2.0-85103106690&partnerID=40&md5=74db46e6d48a8ebf3a99fdfa2a24d862

Clark, A., & Tomos, F. (2020). Entrepreneurial learning and the success of Welsh businesswomen. *Journal Women's Entrepreneurship and Education*, *2020*(1–2), 87–102. doi:10.28934/jwee20.12.pp87-102

Cover, L. (2021, June 17). *7 statistics that prove the importance of social media marketing in business*. Sprout Social.

Dam, L. B., & Pillai, D. (2021). Crafting Virtual Community of Indigenous Entrepreneurs: Case in Social Entrepreneurship. *South Asian Journal of Business and Management Cases*. doi:10.1177/2277977921991916

Frankel, S., Cuevas, L., Lim, H., & Benjamin, S. (2021). Exploring Tattooed Presentation on YouTube: A Case Study of Kat von D. *Fashion Theory*, *0*(0), 1–21. doi:10.1080/1362704X.2021.1882769

Ghouse, S., McElwee, G., Meaton, J., & Durrah, O. (2017). Barriers to rural women entrepreneurs in Oman. *International Journal of Entrepreneurial Behaviour & Research*, *23*(6), 998–1016. doi:10.1108/IJEBR-02-2017-0070

Global Entrepreneurship Monitor. (2022). *Global Entrepreneurship Monitor 2021/2022 Global Report Opportunity Amid Disruption Global Entrepreneurship Monitor 2021/2022 Global Report Key GEM Definitions and Abbreviations 6*. http://www.witchwoodhouse.comBBRDesignhttps://bbrdesign.co.uk

Hashim, S., Naldi, L., & Markowska, M. (2021). "The royal award goes to ... ": Legitimacy processes for female-led family ventures .... *Journal of Family Business Strategy*, *12*(3), 100358. doi:10.1016/j.jfbs.2020.100358

Hossain, M., & Rahman, M. F. (2018). Social Media and the Creation of Entrepreneurial Opportunity for Women. *Management*, *8*(4), 99–108. doi:10.5923/j.mm.20180804.02

Jia, H., Xu, Z., Lin, S., & Jiang, F. (2021). Does persistence make you healthy? An empirical study on female entrepreneurs from China. *BMC Women's Health*, *21*(1), 327. Advance online publication. doi:10.118612905-021-01471-6 PMID:34496817

Jiménez-Zarco, A. I., Clemente-Almendros, J. A., González-González, I., & Aracil-Jordà, J. (2021). Female Micro-Entrepreneurs and Social Networks: Diagnostic Analysis of the Influence of Social-Media Marketing Strategies on Brand Financial Performance. *Frontiers in Psychology*, *12*, 630058. doi:10.3389/fpsyg.2021.630058 PMID:33912108

Jose, S. (2018). Strategic use of digital promotion strategies among female emigrant entrepreneurs in UAE. *International Journal of Emerging Markets*, *13*(6), 1699–1718. doi:10.1108/IJoEM-10-2016-0268

Kargwell, S. (2021). The impact of horizontal revolution on small and medium size enterprises owned by women: The context of the UAE. *International Journal of Entrepreneurship and Small Business*, *44*(3), 256–273. doi:10.1504/IJESB.2021.119230

Kézai, P. K., & Szombathelyi, M. K. (2021). Factors Effecting Female Startuppers in Hungary. *Economia e Sociologia*, *14*(4), 186–203. doi:10.14254/2071-789X.2021/14-4/11

Liberati, A., Altman, D. G., Tetzlaff, J., Mulrow, C., Gøtzsche, P. C., Ioannidis, J. P. A., Clarke, M., Devereaux, P. J., Kleijnen, J., & Moher, D. (2009). The PRISMA statement for reporting systematic reviews and meta-analyses of studies that evaluate health care interventions: Explanation and elaboration. *Journal of Clinical Epidemiology*, *6*(7), 1–28. doi:10.1016/j.jclinepi.2009.06.006 PMID:19631507

Mamodu, C., Moses, C., Ekeagbara, J., & Peter, D. (2019). Effects Of Instagram Marketing on Female Entrepreneurial Performance in Lagos Nigeria: An Exploratory Study. *Covenant Journal of Entrepreneurship, 3*(2), 60–75. https://journals.covenantuniversity.edu.ng/index.php/cjoe

Mastercard. (2022). The Mastercard Index of Women Entrepreneurs.

Mehtap, S., Ozmenekse, L., & Caputo, A. (2019). "I'm a stay-at-home businesswoman": An insight into informal entrepreneurship in Jordan. *Journal of Entrepreneurship in Emerging Economies*, *11*(1), 44–65. doi:10.1108/JEEE-10-2017-0080

Melissa, E., Hamidati, A., Saraswati, M. S., & Flor, A. (2015). The internet and indonesian women entrepreneurs: Examining the impact of social media on women empowerment. In *Impact of Information Society Research in the Global South* (pp. 203–222). Springer Singapore, doi:10.1007/978-981-287-381-1_11

Melissa, E., Hamidati, A., Saraswati, M. S., & Flor, A. G. (2013). Investigating the potentials of social media to support women entrepreneurship in Indonesian urban areas. *ACM International Conference Proceeding Series,* (pp. 92–95). ACM. 10.1145/2517899.2517921

Merza, Z. (2019). The role and importance of social media on women entrepreneurship. SSRN *Electronic Journal*. doi:10.2139/ssrn.3408414

Miniesy, R., Elshahawy, E., & Fakhreldin, H. (2021). Social media's impact on the empowerment of women and youth male entrepreneurs in Egypt. *International Journal of Gender and Entrepreneurship*. doi:10.1108/IJGE-06-2021-0085

Mounzer, L. (2022, March 8). *Overview of Female Entrepreneurship in the Middle East and North Africa Region*. Wilson Center.

Mulkowe, E., & Korir, J. (2016). Social Media and Entrepreneurship: Tools, Benefits, and Challenges. A Case Study of Women Online Entrepreneurs on Kilimani Mums Marketplace on Facebook. *International Journal of Humanities and Social Science*, *6*(8), 248–256.

Myers, B. (1998). *Women entrepreneurs: key messages*. Purdue.

Strategic Direction. (2019). Getting the most out of Facebook and WhatsApp: social media strategies by female entrepreneurs in the UAE. *Strategic Direction, 35*(4), 18–20. doi:10.1108/SD-01-2019-0008

Olamide, A., & Ogbechie, R. (2021). Social capital and business performance: A study of female-owned SMEs in the Nigerian informal sector. *Small Enterprise Research*, *28*(2), 190–205. doi:10.1080/13215906.2021.1901140

Olsson, A. K., & Bernhard, I. (2020a). Keeping up the pace of digitalization in small businesses–Women entrepreneurs' knowledge and use of social media. *International Journal of Entrepreneurial Behaviour & Research*, *27*(2), 378–396. doi:10.1108/IJEBR-10-2019-0615

Olsson, A. K., & Bernhard, I. (2020b). Keeping up the pace of digitalization in small businesses–Women entrepreneurs' knowledge and use of social media. *International Journal of Entrepreneurial Behaviour & Research*, *27*(2), 378–396. doi:10.1108/IJEBR-10-2019-0615

Plazibat, I., & Renko, S. (2020). Social Media as a Channel for Boosting Female Entrepreneurship in Retailing. In T. Kovačević & I. Akrap (Eds.), *Contemporary issues in economy & technology* (pp. 84–97). University of Split.

Quagrainie, F. A. (2016). Institutional approach and competitive behaviours of informal Ghanaian women entrepreneurs. *International Journal of Entrepreneurship and Small Business*, *28*(2–3), 323–338. doi:10.1504/IJESB.2016.076648

Sarpong, D., Nyuur, R., & Torbor, M. K. (2021). Careers of commercially successful female entrepreneurs in context of underdeveloped markets and weak institutions. *International Journal of Entrepreneurial Behaviour & Research*. doi:10.1108/IJEBR-06-2021-0526

Schaffer, N. (2022, December). *55 Compelling Social Media Marketing Statistics You Need To Know For 2023*. Sprout Social.

Secundo, G., del Vecchio, P., & Mele, G. (2021). Social media for entrepreneurship: Myth or reality? A structured literature review and a future research agenda. *International Journal of Entrepreneurial Behaviour & Research*, *27*(1), 149–177. doi:10.1108/IJEBR-07-2020-0453

Shahzad, F., Abbas, A., Fateh, A., Kasim, R. S. R., Akram, K., & Ashraf, S. F. (2021). Late-Night Use of social media and Cognitive Engagement of Female Entrepreneurs: A Stressor–Strain–Outcome Perspective. *SAGE Open*, *11*(3). doi:10.1177/21582440211037652

Steel, G. (2017). Navigating (im)mobility: Female entrepreneurship and social media in Khartoum. *Africa*, *87*(2), 233–252. doi:10.1017/S0001972016000930

Steel, G. (2021). Going global – going digital. Diaspora networks and female online entrepreneurship in Khartoum, Sudan. *Geoforum*, *120*(July 2019), 22–29. doi:10.1016/j.geoforum.2021.01.003

Stone, A. (2004). Essentialism and Anti-Essentialism in Feminist Philosophy. *JMP*, *1*(2), 135–153.

Swartz, E., Amatucci, F. M., & Coleman, S. (2016). Using a multiple method and mixed mode approach to examine women entrepreneur negotiating styles. *International Journal of Gender and Entrepreneurship*, *8*(1), 48–68. doi:10.1108/IJGE-09-2013-0060

Tuite, A. (2021). Gendered Entrepreneurialism and the Labour of Online Consumption in the Independent Fashion Sector. *Fashion Theory*, *25*(3), 419–438. doi:10.1080/1362704X.2019.1633831

Verheul, I., van Stel, A., & Thurik, R. (2006). Explaining female and male entrepreneurship at the country level. *Entrepreneurship and Regional Development*, *18*(2), 151–183. doi:10.1080/08985620500532053

Vivakaran, M., & Maraimalai, N. (2017). Feminist pedagogy and social media: A study on their integration and effectiveness in training budding women entrepreneurs. *Gender and Education*, *29*(7), 869–889. doi:10.1080/09540253.2016.1225008

Walby, S., Armstrong, J., & Strid, S. (2012). Intersectionality: Multiple inequalities in social theory. In Sociology, 46(2), 224–240)s SAGE Publications Ltd. doi:10.1177/0038038511416164

Zainuddin, A., Ahmad, J., Puteh, F., Chandran, S. D., Hassim, A. A., & Ismail, T. N. T. (2017). The 21st century challenges among women entrepreneurs: Revisiting the literature. *Advanced Science Letters*, *23*(8), 7845–7848. doi:10.1166/asl.2017.9591

Chapter 2
Female Entrepreneurship Drivers:
Entrepreneurial Intention, Performance, and Outcomes

Natália Figueiredo
Research Centre in Digital Services, Instituto Politécnico de Viseu, Viseu, Portugal

Lurdes D. Patrício
Research Unit in Business Sciences, Universidade da Beira Interior, Covilhã, Portugal

João J. Ferreira
Universidade da Beira Interior, Portugal & NECE, University of Beira Interior, Portugal

ABSTRACT

Entrepreneurship is the engine of economic, cultural, and social development. In a reality where equal opportunities between men and women in business are not yet verifiable, we would benefit from an adequate understanding of female entrepreneurship's impact. This chapter explores the concept of female entrepreneurship in a systematic literature review. Based on Web of Science database articles, it uses bibliometric analysis to analyze the drivers influencing female entrepreneurial intentions, performance, and outcomes. This study enables the systematization of the existing literature into four themes: 1) gender-specific entrepreneurial intention factors, 2) women´s entrepreneurial success factors, 3) women´s entrepreneurial performance, and 4) gender-specific entrepreneurial performance. The results provide insights into the triggering factors of female entrepreneurship intention and help to develop a more profound understanding of the factors affecting their entrepreneurial performance and outcomes. An agenda for further research was laid out based on the existing literature.

DOI: 10.4018/978-1-6684-7669-7.ch002

1. INTRODUCTION

Entrepreneurship drives innovation, contributes to economic recovery, and creates employment opportunities (Miranda, Sergio, & Jesús, 2017). Entrepreneurship consists of exploring opportunities, developing new business models, and innovating in production processes (Agarwal & Lenka, 2015). Despite categorizing entrepreneurship as a "man's job" (Agarwal & Lenka, 2015), women are emerging as successful entrepreneurs locally and internationally (Chipfunde, Yahaya, & Othman, 2021).

Female entrepreneurship refers to the activity of women who create, manage, and own businesses (Martini, Malacarne, Pederzolli Giovanazzi, & Buffa, 2020). It is a form of economic empowerment for women, allowing them to gain financial independence and contribute to the economy's growth (Chipfunde et al., 2021). This phenomenon substantially impacts society because businesses owned by women have a positive impact on their countries and communities (Isa, Jaganathan, Ahmdon, & Ibrahim, 2019; Martini et al., 2020; Sidratulmunthah, Hussain, & Imran Malik, 2018).

Despite the benefits, female entrepreneurship still faces significant challenges (Thébaud, 2015). Women face numerous barriers in entrepreneurship, including limited access to resources and opportunities compared to men, such as funding and mentorship (Brixiová, Kangoye, & Tregenna, 2020). Additionally, societal stereotypes and biases can represent significant challenges for women seeking to establish themselves as successful entrepreneurs (Van Emmerik, Euwema, & Wendt, 2008).

The study of female entrepreneurship has increased in recent years, leading to a deeper understanding of the subject. Researchers include the reasons behind women's difficulty in developing an entrepreneurial career (Cardella, Hernández-Sánchez, & Sánchez-García, 2020), the contribution of female entrepreneurs in sustainable development (Martini et al., 2020), and the impacts of various factors affecting the performance (Chipfunde et al., 2021).

The existing Systematic Literature Reviews (SLR) contribute to the concept and development of female entrepreneurship. Although contributions have already analyzed female entrepreneurship, they do so by addressing specific aspects rather than in a more holistic way. The researchers are more specifically approaching a particular theme, like theories, a particular geographic area, or a specific type of entrepreneurship, such as rural or sustainable entrepreneurship.

As expected, and given the importance of female entrepreneurship, we find multiple SLR about the subject. Some of them are very recent, for instance, Fernandes, Ferreira, Veiga, Kraus, & Dabić (2022) analyzed digital entrepreneurship platforms, and Akter, Rahman, & Radicic (2022) focused on gender and international women's entrepreneurship. The work developed by Ferreira, Fernandes, & Ratten (2019) addresses entrepreneurship and the different theories associated. However, no SLR explored the concept of female entrepreneurship more broadly, analyzing the drivers influencing female entrepreneurship intentions, performance, and outcomes. Thus, this systematic approach contributes to the literature by mapping more streams, areas, contributions, and locations associated with female entrepreneurship. This SLR also provides a comprehensive framework to understand the process and impact of female entrepreneurship on the development of organizations and countries. This framework illustrates how the identified thematic groups are interrelated. The results of this SLR can inform and support women entrepreneurs, leaders, and governments in promoting and enhancing female entrepreneurship. This research also responds to a gap that calls for further studies on female entrepreneurship, which is why it is still understudied (Chipfunde et al., 2021; Palalic, Ramadani, & Dana, 2017).

The current research follows the following structure. First, the study provides an overview of the literature on female entrepreneurship. Second, it exhibits materials, methods, and a conceptual framework. The results and discussion based on bibliometric analysis are presented, providing insights into the current state of knowledge in this field. Finally, the study presents the conclusions and proposes an agenda for future research.

2. THEORETICAL BACKGROUND

The growth of economies is characterized by introducing innovative combinations in the circular flow, disrupting its recurring patterns. Entrepreneurship is a driver of innovation and economic development (Fernandes et al., 2022; Miranda et al., 2017), contributing to economic and social stability (Isa et al., 2019; Martini et al., 2020; Sidratulmunthah et al., 2018). As a result, entrepreneurs play a pivotal role in boosting economic growth by introducing new production methods, products, technologies, organizational models, markets, and resources (Schumpeter, 1942).

Entrepreneurship has traditionally been seen as male-dominated, with women facing barriers and biases that discourage them from pursuing entrepreneurial ventures (Agarwal & Lenka, 2015). However, promoting gender equality provides societies with a greater opportunity for economic and human growth and development (Shaw, 2006). The performance of female entrepreneurship has been a topic of increasing interest in recent years (Chipfunde et al., 2021; Sidratulmunthah et al., 2018). There are significant differences in entrepreneurial performance between women and men (Palalic et al., 2017), and women are breaking through as successful entrepreneurs (Agarwal & Lenka, 2015).

Several factors contribute to the development of the entrepreneurship intention of women. One of the main factors is women's unique skills and qualities (Kruse, Wach, Costa, & Moriano, 2019; Shahin, Ilic, Gonsalvez, & Whittle, 2021). Women entrepreneurs are often highly motivated and innovative and have strong problem-solving skills, which are essential for success in business (Palalic et al., 2017; Shahin et al., 2021). Additionally, women are often more risk-averse than men, which can lead to more cautious and sustainable business strategies (Palalic et al., 2017). Another factor appointed is entrepreneurial education's influence on young women's entrepreneurial intention (Alonso-Galicia, Fernández-Pérez, Rodríguez-Ariza, & del Mar Fuentes-Fuentes, 2015; Entrialgo & Iglesias, 2018; Sidratulmunthah et al., 2018). In this sense, universities play a fundamental role (Entrialgo & Iglesias, 2018); they must empower students, providing entrepreneurial education and support to develop and improve them with the tools they need (Sidratulmunthah et al., 2018).

The relationship between a company's knowledge management practices and entrepreneurial performance must be established to drive business development and fuel economic growth (Qader et al., 2022). The management practices that women entrepreneurs adopt as innovation, proactivity, and risk-taking decisions, impact their entrepreneurial and organizational performance (Palalic et al., 2017). Since governments, business organizations, and other institutions recognize female entrepreneurship's value (Akter et al., 2022), it is essential that they establish support mechanisms, provide advisory services, and offer entrepreneurship education to encourage women to leap into entrepreneurship. These initiatives will help to create a more conducive environment for women to start and grow their businesses (Entrialgo & Iglesias, 2018).

Despite the evidence of women's entrepreneurial capabilities, the number of women participating in entrepreneurial activities remains lower compared to men, owing to the various challenges they face (Thébaud, 2015). The lack of several factors as funding and mentorship (Brixiová, Kangoye, & Tregenna, 2020); attitudes, resources, skills, knowledge, regulatory, institutional, and social barriers (Dawson &

Henley, 2015); societal stereotypes and biases complex the entrepreneurial activities of women (Van Emmerik et al., 2008).

3. METHODS

This research on female entrepreneurship follows a SLR based on pre-defined procedures, allowing the advancement of knowledge, minimization of deviations, and the possibility of replication (Tranfield, Denyer, & Smart, 2003). The research was based on collecting articles considered representative through the Web of Science database without a timeframe. This database is adopted because it is a multidisciplinary, comprehensive, and quality database, thus ensuring the articles' validity (Gasparyan, Ayvazyan, & Kitas, 2013).

A search by topics was made in the *WoS Core Collection*, with no time restriction, using the keywords: "female entrep*" AND ("entrep* intention" OR "entrep* performance" OR "entrep* outcomes"), and it was carried out on 02 January 2023. The filters applied were "type of document" and "language", restricting the analysis to articles written in English. The search yielded 67 articles that, after the application of the respective filters, were reduced to 50. The research protocol is shown in Figure 1.

Figure 1. Research protocol

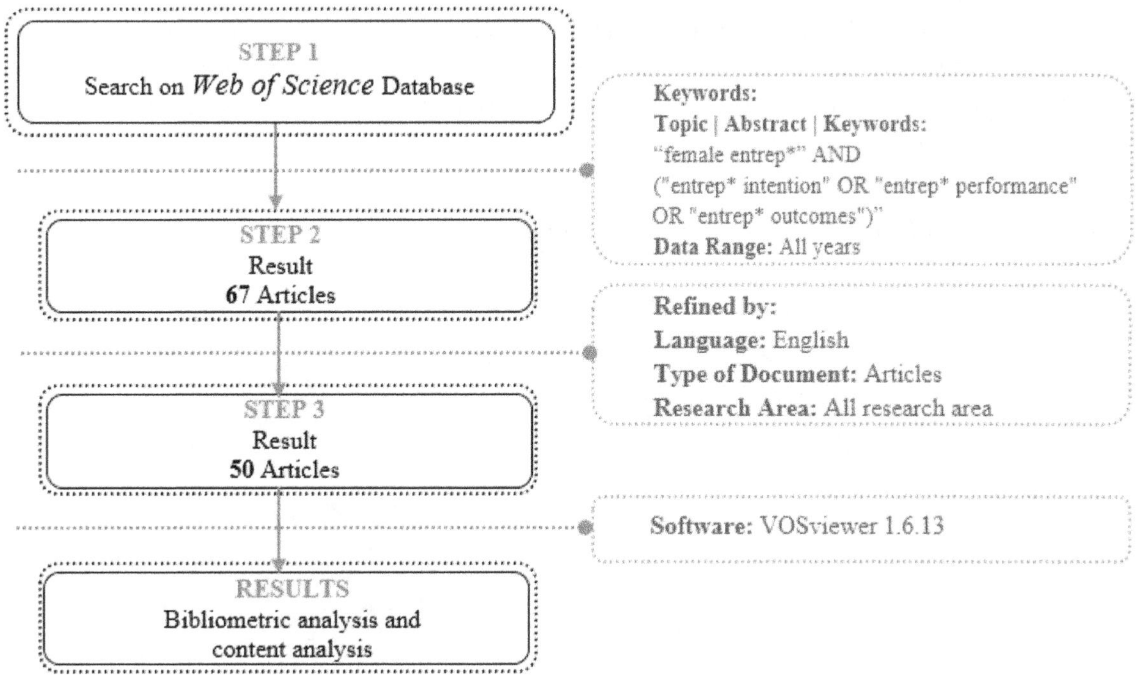

The 50 articles were subject to different bibliometric analyses (Cobo, López-Herrera, Herrera-Viedma, & Herrera, 2011) using *VOSviewer*, version 1.6.13 software, as it allows for mapping and processing the articles with reliability and suitability (van Eck & Waltman, 2010). According to O'Connor & Voos (1981), bibliometric techniques contribute to the development of scientific knowledge by helping explain the causes of bibliographic phenomena related to scientific interest. The various bibliometric analyses performed are complementary, allowing a wide-ranging view of the evolution and different dynamics of the literature on the topic analyzed (Marchiori & Franco, 2020). Thus, the following complementary bibliometric techniques were applied: (i) bibliographic coupling of documents and (ii) co-occurrence analysis of keywords.

The bibliographic coupling of documents method uses citation analysis to establish a similarity relationship between documents. Thus, this technique groups articles according to references shared by two articles (Kessler, 1963). The relations between keywords of all the documents were analyzed based on their co-occurrences. The co-occurrence of keywords allows us to examine the relationship between them, which is determined by the number of articles in which they occur together (van Eck & Waltman, 2010). This technique highlights the main concepts addressed in the analyzed topic, allowing the identification of conceptual structures (Marchiori & Franco, 2020).

4. RESULTS

4.1. Descriptive Analysis

Figure 2 shows the evolution of the number of publications and citations of the 50 articles obtained for analysis from 1995 to 2022. The information is by year, and it is possible to verify that the number of citations has evolved, reaching its maximum in 1995, with 201 citations, and posteriorly in 2002, with 131 citations. The number of articles increased over the years, and 2022 was the year that reached the highest peak, with 14 publications.

Figure 2. Evolution of the number of publications/citations

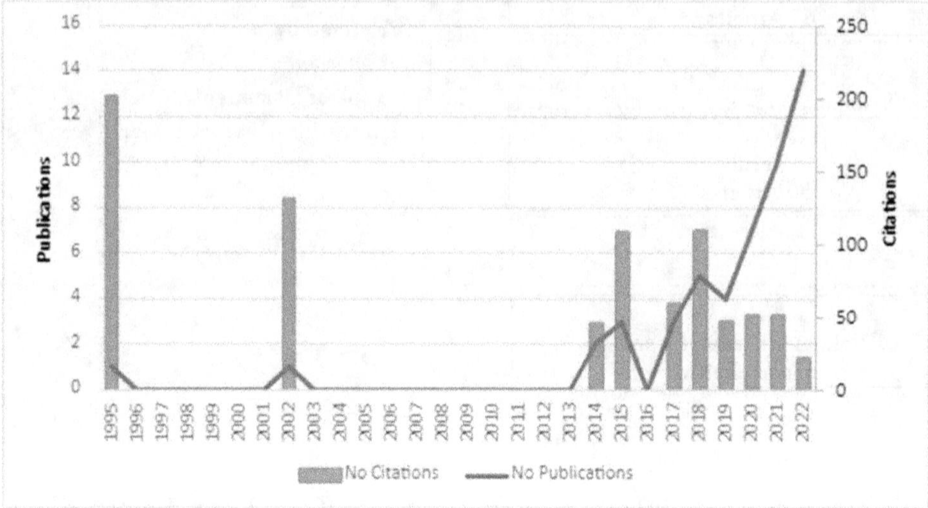

Of the 50 articles obtained in the survey, 10 (20%) have no citations, possibly because they are very recent articles from 2022, and 29 (58%) have less than 10 citations. The first study identified was Cooper & Artz (1995) is also the most cited article, which analyses entrepreneurial satisfaction as a measure of performance.

Table 1 shows the main journals contributing to the theme.

Table 1. Main journals contributing to the theme

Journals	Number of articles	Total of citations (in *WoS Core Collection*)
Sustainability	4	11
International Journal of Gender and Entrepreneurship	3	40
Gender in Management	3	8
Journal of Business Venturing	2	220
Small Business Economics	2	142
International Entrepreneurship and Management Journal	2	15

The remaining 34 articles are distributed over 34 different journals, with 1 article per journal.

The distribution of articles by area of research is presented in Figure 3. There is a concentration of articles in the areas of business (52%), management (26%), and economics (22%).

Figure 3. Main research areas

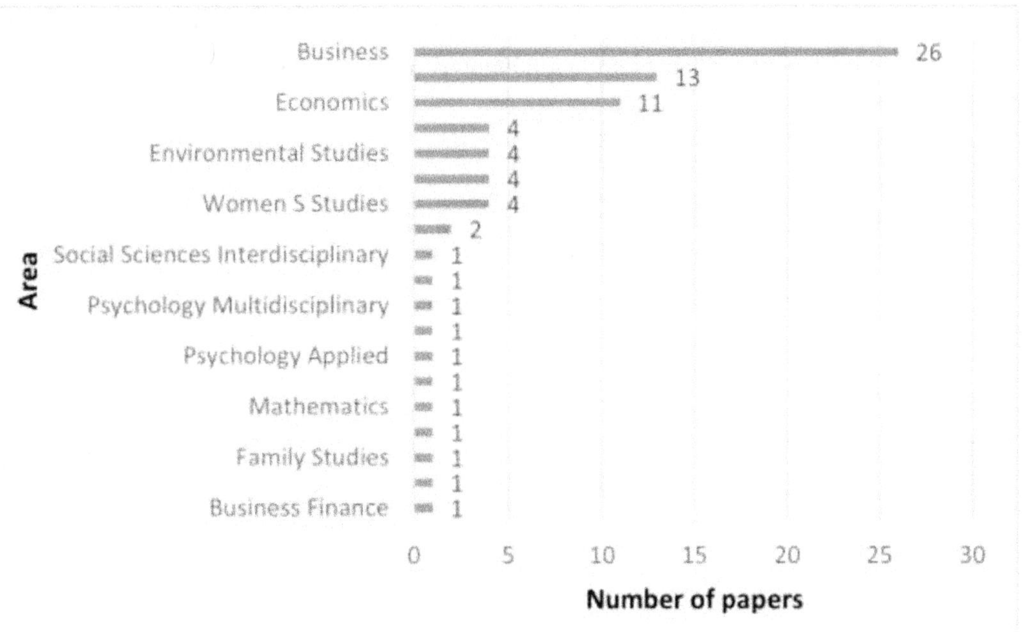

The distribution of publications by region is presented in Figure 4, and we can observe that Spain was the top publishing region, accounting for 16% (8 articles), followed by the USA with 14% (7 articles) and India with 10% (5 articles).

Figure 4. Number of Publications by region

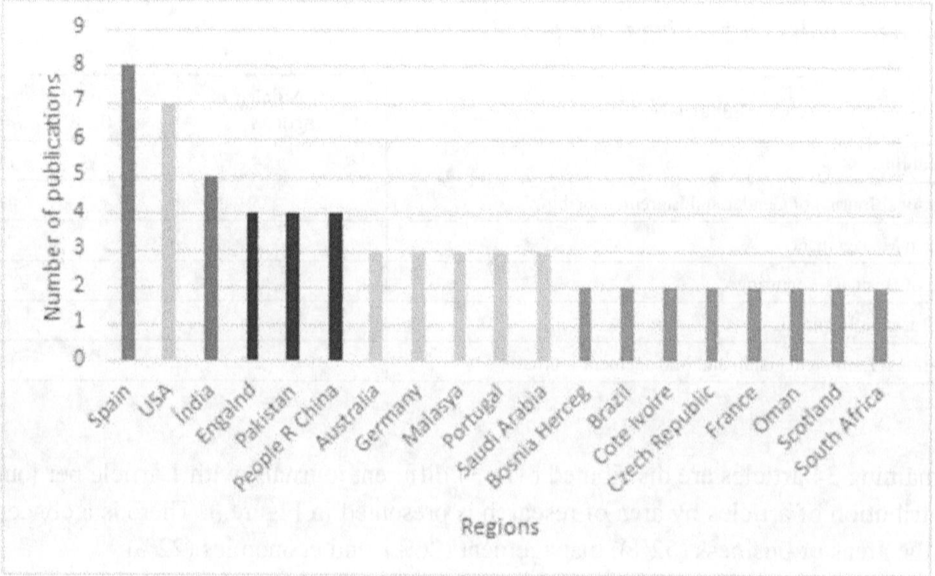

Table 2 shows the top ten of the most cited articles. We observe that the most cited articles are published in different journals and that mainly follow a quantitative methodology, which may highlight the need to understand and explain a particular phenomenon (Sánchez-Algarra and Anguera, 2013), in this case, female entrepreneurship.

Table 2. Top 10 of the most cited articles

Article	Authors	Journal	Total Citations (in *WoS Core Collection*)	Methodology
Déterminants of Satisfaction for Entrepreneurs	Cooper & Artz (1995)	Journal of Business Venturing	201	Quantitative analysis
Self-employment wealth and job creation: The roles of gender, non-pecuniary motivation and entrepreneurial ability	Burke, FitzRoy, & Nolan (2002)	Small Business Economics	131	Quantitative analysis
Tourism Entrepreneurship Performance: The Effects of Place Identity, Self-Efficacy, and Gender	Hallak, Assaker, & Lee (2015)	Journal of Travel Research	68	Quantitative analysis
Values Matter, Don't They? - Combining Theory of Planned Behavior and Personal Values as Predictors of Social Entrepreneurial Intention	Kruse, Wach, Costa, & Moriano (2019)	Journal of Social Entrepreneurship	46	Quantitative analysis
The Myth of Female Credit Discrimination in African Manufacturing	Hansen & Rand (2014)	Journal of Development Studies	36	Quantitative analysis
Are the Intentions to Entrepreneurship of Men and Women Shaped Differently? The Impact of Entrepreneurial Role-Model Exposure and Entrepreneurship Education	(Entrialgo & Iglesias, 2018)	Entrepreneurship Research Journal	34	Quantitative analysis
Towards nurturing the entrepreneurial intentions of neglected female business students of Pakistan through proactive personality, self-efficacy and university support factors	Sidratulmunthah, Hussain, & Imran Malik (2018)	Asia Pacific Journal of Innovation and Entrepreneurship	24	Quantitative analysis
Academic entrepreneurial intention: the role of gender	Miranda, Sergio, & Jesús (2017)	International Journal of Gender and Entrepreneurship	23	Quantitative analysis
Entrepreneurship in Bosnia and Herzegovina: focus on gender	Palalic, Ramadani, & Dana (2017)	European Business Review	21	Quantitative analysis
Entrepreneurial cognitions in academia: exploring gender differences	Alonso-Galicia, Fernández-Pérez, Rodríguez-Ariza, & del Mar Fuentes-Fuentes (2015)	Journal of Managerial Psychology	21	Quantitative analysis

4.2. Bibliometric Analysis

This study used different bibliometric analysis techniques to provide a comprehensive and integrated view of the various dimensions of this research area. Thus, all bibliometric analyses were performed using the VOSviewer software, version 1.6.13 (van Eck & Waltman, 2010).

4.2.1. Bibliographic Coupling of Documents

To identify trends, in the literature, on leadership in the public sector, the research on this topic was divided into clusters based on a bibliographic coupling of 50 articles. The analysis unit is considered "documents," with a minimum of 2 documents in each cluster, resulting in 49 papers divided into 4 clusters (see figure 5 - VOSviewer output).

Figure 5. Network of documents based on bibliographic coupling analysis

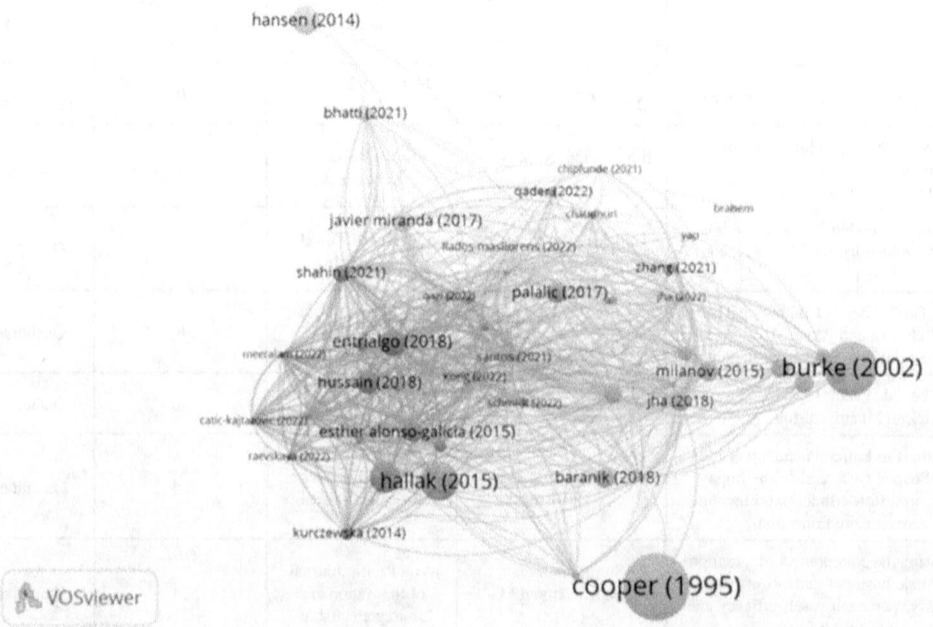

Table 3 systematizes the articles in each of the 4 clusters and respective citations, formed according to the bibliographic coupling of documents.

Table 3. Constitution of clusters

Cluster 116 Articles	Citation (in *WoS Core Collection*)	Cluster 215 Articles	Citation (in *WoS Core Collection*)	Cluster 310 Articles	Citation (in *WoS Core Collection*)	Cluster 48 Articles	Citation (in *WoS Core Collection*)
Ali, Shabir, & Shaikh (2021)	7	Baranik, Gorman, & Wales (2018)	**18**	Chaudhuri, Agrawal, Chatterjee, & Hussain (2022)	0	Ali, Jabeen, & Burhan (2023)	0
Castelló-Sirvent & Pinazo-Dallenbach (2021)	3	Batjargal et al. (2019)	10	Hallak et al. (2015)	**68**	Bhatti, Al Doghan, Saat, Juhari, & Alshagawi (2021)	**12**
Ćatić-Kajtazović, Glavaš, & Kljajić-Dervić (2022)	0	Brixiová, Kangoye, & Said (2020)	**19**	Huang, Li, Wang, & Li (2022)	1	Brahem & Boussema (2022)	0
Entrialgo & Iglesias (2018)	**34**	Brixiová, Kangoye, & Tregenna (2020)	12	Palalic et al. (2017)	**21**	Chipfunde et al. (2021)	**1**
Alonso-Galicia et al. (2015)	**21**	Burke et al. (2002)	**131**	Qader et al. (2022)	**6**	Hansen & Rand (2014)	**36**
Gomes et al. (2022)	1	Cooper & Artz (1995)	**201**	Qazi, Qazi, Raza, & Yousufi (2022)	0	Miranda et al. (2017)	**23**
Sidratulmunthah et al. (2018)	**24**	Dutta & Mallick (2018)	17	Santos, Marques, & Ferreira (2021)	2	Llados-Masllorens & Ruiz-Dotras (2022)	**2**
Kong & Kim (2022)	2	Echchabi, Omar, & Ayedh (2020)	4	Schmidt, Bohnenberger, Nodari, & Da Silva (2022)	0	Yap, Keling, & Ho (2022)	0
Kruse et al. (2019)	**46**	Jha, Makkad, & Mittal (2018)	16	Yoopetch (2021)	**5**		
Kurczewska & Białek (2014)	9	Jha & Alam (2022)	1	Zhang & Zhou (2021)	**6**		
Meeralam & Adeinat (2022)	1	Milanov, Justo, & Bradley (2015)	**19**				
Pelegrini & Moraes (2022)	7	Murphy, Ferreira, Fernandes, & do Paço (2021)	1				
Raevskaya, Anastasia, & Tatarko (2022)	0	Oppedal Berge & Garcia Pires (2020)	11				
Shahin et al. (2021)	**14**	Perez-Quintana, Hormiga, Martori, & Madariaga (2017)	15				
Sweida, Sherman, Duranso, & Berkley (2022)	0	Faiza, Saeed, & Muhammad (2022)	0				
Vodă, Haller, Anichiti, & Butnaru (2020)	1						

The 4 clusters formed, revealing distinct characteristics in size (number of articles), influence (total article citations), and research focus, confirm the wide range of themes in this area of investigation. The different research focuses within each cluster led to assigning a descriptive name: 1) Gender-specific Entrepreneurial Intention Factors, 2) Women´s Entrepreneurial Success Factors, 3) Women's Entrepreneurial Performance, and 4) Gender-specific Entrepreneurial Performance.

4.2.2. Keyword co-occurrence

The co-occurrence of all keywords was performed to identify the most critical concepts in female entrepreneurship. Figure 6 shows the keyword network for female entrepreneurship based on co-occurrence. The main keywords used in the articles were "gender", "female entrepreneurship", "entrepreneurial intention", and "self-efficacy". In this way it is possible to identify four main groups of keywords through co-occurrence analysis of the articles on this subject.

Cluster 1, grouping 30% of the keywords analyzed. The main keyword, due to its more significant number of co-occurrences, is "performance" associated with the words "access", "barriers", "business

Figure 6. Networks of keywords based on co-occurrence

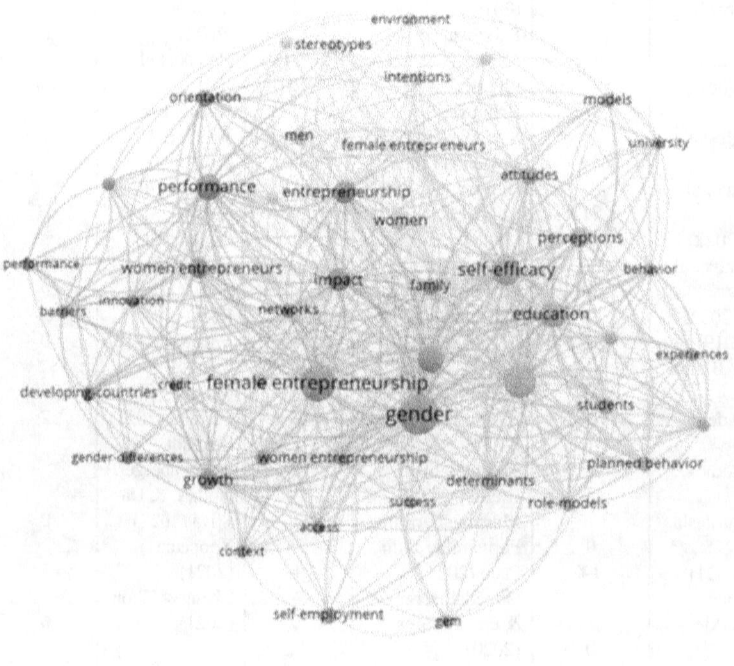

performance", "credit", "developing-countries", "entrepreneurship", "firm performance", "gender-differences", "growth", "impact", "innovation", "networks", "orientation", and "women entrepreneurs".

Cluster 2 presents 30% of the keywords. The keyword with the most significant number of co-occurrence is "entrepreneurial intention" associated with the words "attitudes", "behavior", "determinants", "education", "entrepreneurial education", "experiences", "models", "perceptions", "planned behavior", "role models", "self-efficacy", "students", "theory of planned behavior", and "university".

Cluster 3 groups 22% of the keywords analyzed. The main keyword is "gender" associated with the words "business", "competence", "context", "family", "female entrepreneurship", "GEM" (Global Entrepreneurship Monitor), "motivations", "self-employment", "success", and "women entrepreneurship".

Finally, cluster 4 has the smallest number of keywords, presenting 18%. The keyword with the most significant number of co-occurrences is "women" associated with the words "entrepreneurial performance", "environment", "female entrepreneurs", "gender stereotypes", "intentions", "management research", "men", and "stereotypes".

Table 4 presents the main keywords associated with the four clusters, and each cluster was named with the keyword with the most co-occurrences.

Table 4. Clusters of keywords

Cluster Number	Color	Cluster Name	Main Keywords
1	Red	Performance	Access, barriers, business performance, credit, developing-countries, entrepreneurship, firm performance, gender-differences, growth, impact, innovation, networks, orientation, women entrepreneurs
2	Green	Entrepreneurial intention	Attitudes, behavior, determinants, education, entrepreneurial education, experiences, models, perceptions, planned behavior, role models, self-efficacy, students, theory of planned behavior, university
3	Blue	Gender	Business, competence, context, family, female entrepreneurship, GEM, motivations, self-employment, success, women entrepreneurship
4	Brown	Women	Entrepreneurial performance, environment, female entrepreneurs, gender stereotypes, intentions, management research, men, stereotypes

Figure 7 shows that the most influential keywords emerge between 1990 and 2000, where "gender" and "entrepreneurship" stand out. The words occurring more recently, in 2020, show the recent interest in the area such as self-efficacy, education, and women entrepreneurs.

Figure 7. Evolution of the networks of keywords based on co-occurrence

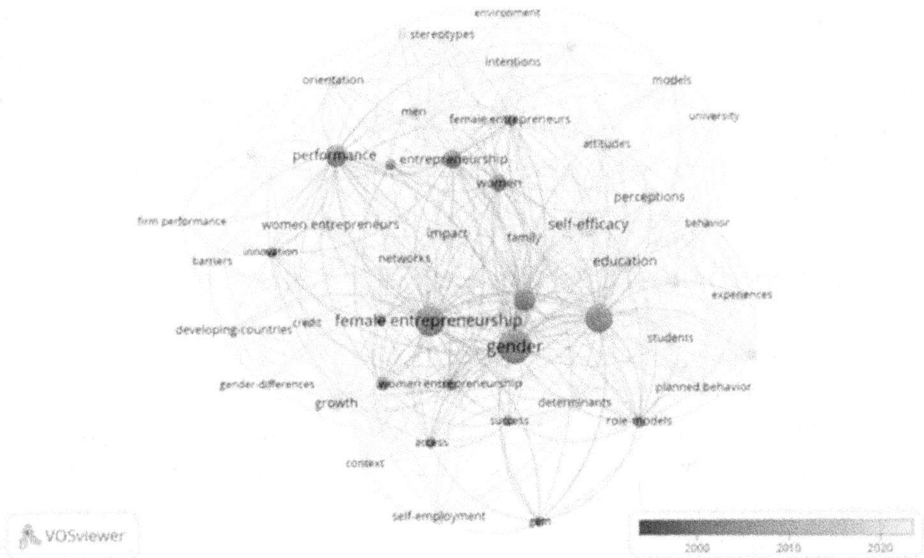

5. DISCUSSION

According to the results obtained from the bibliographic coupling of documents (see figure 5), four clusters (see table 3) were identified. In this section, we will discuss the main themes approached in each of the four clusters.

5.1 Gender-specific Entrepreneurial Intention Factors (Cluster 1)

Cluster 1 (red) is the largest, with 16 articles analyzed. This cluster contains recent articles, 7 from 2022 and 3 from 2021. According to the analysis of the five most cited articles, this cluster addresses the impact that some different factors play in shaping entrepreneurial intention.

A critical factor in developing entrepreneurial attitudes in young women is associated with developing interpersonal skills, particularly in creative thinking, risk-taking, problem-solving, and leadership development (Shahin et al., 2021). Kruse et al. (2019) state that the main personality traits related to people's cognition, openness to change, and self-improvement values significantly impact entrepreneurial intention. Also focusing on the analysis of entrepreneurial intention in young women, Sidratulmunthah et al. (2018) highlight the importance of a proactive personality, entrepreneurial self-efficacy, and university support factors. Furthermore, it is essential to analyze the influence of close social groups, perceived differently by men and women, especially concerning entrepreneurial education on attitudes (Alonso-Galicia, Fernández-Pérez, Rodríguez-Ariza, & del Mar Fuentes-Fuentes, 2015), and how human connections, including positive role modeling and peer learning, promote entrepreneurial intention, (Shahin et al., 2021).

Adopting another perspective, Entrialgo & Iglesias (2018)(Entrialgo & Iglesias, 2018) focus on analyzing the prior influence of exposure to external factors - parental role models and education in entrepreneurship - on the attitudes and perceptions of women and men to generate entrepreneurial behavior. In keeping with their findings, verifying that these external factors influence it is more significant in women than in men. Nevertheless, young women's entrepreneurial intention must be focused on solving relevant societal problems and has a broader global purpose with an overall positive impact on the world (Shahin et al., 2021).

5.2 Women´s Entrepreneurial Success Factors (Cluster 2)

Formed of 15 articles, Cluster 2 (green) contains the most influential article (according to total citations number) developed by Cooper & Artz (1995). This cluster addresses drivers or inhibitors for developing female entrepreneurship. Entrepreneurial satisfaction is a way to measure a company's performance. In this sense, objectives, attitudes, and backgrounds bring higher entrepreneurial satisfaction and, consequently, better performance (Cooper & Artz, 1995). According to Cooper & Artz (1995), women entrepreneurs were more satisfied with business ownership.

Social capital refers to opportunities from social networks, such as those found in organizations, elite institutions, and personal contacts (Baranik et al., 2018). So, relationships and networks are critical to business results (Milanov et al., 2015). Individual and group characteristics of the female entrepreneur influence the number of ties created and the group's performance (Milanov et al., 2015). Baranik, Gorman, & Wales (2018) highlight two critical factors likely to explain the success of female entrepreneurship, namely social capital and religiosity. Thus, it was possible to verify that social capital is a driving factor while religiosity does not present any statistically significant relationship. Burke et al. (2002) explored and compared the influence of education and inheritance on the propensity of men and women to become entrepreneurs. This analysis verified that these factors are not determinants of boosting female entrepreneurship. Another critical and fundamental factor for developing female entrepreneurship is access to credit. However, access to it can, in many cases, is regarded as a barrier due to the difficulty of access compared to men (Brixiová, Kangoye, & Tregenna, 2020).

5.3. Women´s Entrepreneurial Performance (Cluster 3)

Cluster 3 (blue) has 10 articles that address knowledge management practices and how they influence female entrepreneurship, specifically their performance and success. Entrepreneurial self-efficacy and company performance should be the main entrepreneurial capabilities and the differentiating factors that separate entrepreneurs from managers (Hallak et al., 2015). Entrepreneurial self-efficacy refers to individual's belief in their ability to successfully carry out entrepreneurship tasks (Hallak et al., 2015; Yoopetch, 2021). These positively affect performance, perceptions of performance, growth, and innovation (Hallak et al., 2015).

Entrepreneurial performance is directly associated with company knowledge management practices (Qader et al., 2022) and families (Zhang & Zhou, 2021), which boost business development and economic growth. Palalic et al. (2017) found that women entrepreneurs make better innovation, proactivity, and risk-taking decisions. This knowledge management influences entrepreneurship and organizational performance (Palalic et al., 2017; Qader et al., 2022).

The family positively and negatively affects women's entrepreneurial success, impacting the performance obtained. The demands of family and work can generate conflicts of interest and prevent higher performance. But on the other hand, the resources provided by the family can generate precious resources in the case of female entrepreneurship, namely in the form of encouragement, attention, and positive attitudes, which in this case will lead to high performance (Zhang & Zhou, 2021).

5.4. Gender-specific Entrepreneurial Performance (Cluster 4)

Cluster 4 (brown), formed by 8 articles, addresses women's entrepreneurial behavior and intention regarding factors like training and education. Entrepreneurial intention is lower in women than in men due to implicit barriers that hinder the female entrepreneurial attempt, which is not directly attended to by gender (Miranda et al., 2017).

Recent studies, like those prepared by Llados-Masllorens & Ruiz-Dotras (2022), Bhatti, Al Doghan, Saat, Juhari, & Alshagawi (2021), and Chipfunde, Yahaya, & Othman (2021) analyzed which factors effectively affect the intention and performance of women entrepreneurs. As stated by Bhatti et al. (2021), the impact of training and education play an essential role in improving women's entrepreneurial intention behavior. Furthermore, financial and numerical skills significantly boost entrepreneurial culture (Llados-Masllorens & Ruiz-Dotras, 2022). In turn, Chipfunde et al. (2021) conclude that individual characteristics, family support, access to loans and financial support, gender inequality, and orientation significantly influence the performance of women entrepreneurs. However, when compared to enterprises owned by males, female entrepreneurs are less likely to be credit-constrained (Hansen & Rand, 2014).

6. CONCEPTUAL FRAMEWORK AND FUTURE RESEARCH AGENDA

The different bibliometric analyses allow understanding of trends in the literature on female entrepreneurship. The results obtained with the various techniques complement and corroborate the systematization of literature, allowing the development of an integrative framework (Figure 8), and articulating the main themes found in the literature.

Figure 8. An integrative framework on female entrepreneurship: entrepreneurial intention, performance, and outcomes

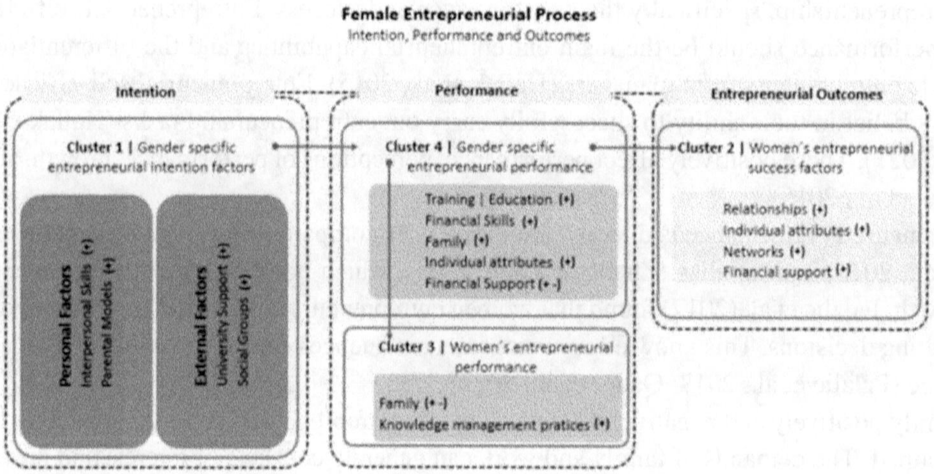

The conceptual model helps to assess favorable and unfavorable factors to female entrepreneurship, namely entrepreneurial intention, performance, and outcomes. Gender-specific Entrepreneurial Intention Factors theme (theme 1) addresses entrepreneurial intention, which refers to an individual's desire to start a business and the level of preparation to undertake the business. This theme includes personal factors and external factors. Personal factors refer to interpersonal skills and parental models, which positively affect women's entrepreneurial intentions, and external factors include university support and the social group, which, if they existed, would encourage women to undertake.

Women's Entrepreneurial Success Factors (theme 2) are related to access to relationships, networks, and individual attributes. Networking and relationships are essential for women entrepreneurs because it allows women access to valuable resources such as business advice, market information, and growth opportunities. One of the most critical factors is access to capital; providing women entrepreneurs access to financial resources, such as loans and grants, can help overcome many barriers. Finally, interpersonal attitudes are also a success factor for female entrepreneurship due to the objectives that lead to greater satisfaction and, consequently, better performance.

Women's Entrepreneurial Performance (theme 3) includes knowledge management practices and family influence. Women entrepreneurs tend to be better at innovation, proactivity, and risk-taking decisions, leading to the growth of their businesses. Therefore, women-led businesses can achieve high-performance levels with adequate support and resources. The impact of family on women's entrepreneurial success has both positive and negative. Family support through encouragement, attention, and positive attitudes can provide valuable resources contributing to high performance in female entrepreneurship. However, family demands can create conflicts with work and hinder high performance.

Gender-specific Entrepreneurial Performance (theme 4) involves training, education, financial skills, family, individual attributes, and financial support. Women entrepreneurs need knowledge and skills to manage their businesses better and achieve success, and training must include financial management, marketing, and strategic planning. Furthermore, they often face difficulties obtaining finance and investments, limiting their growth and potential. Factors like capital, networks, entrepreneurship education and training, and a supportive environment could promote diversity and equality by addressing these factors, women entrepreneurs succeed and contribute to the growth and development of the economy.

From the framework analysis, it is possible to perceive that entrepreneurial intention will influence the performance of an entrepreneur, regardless of gender. Thus, through their measures, policies, and even government support, the government and educational institutions play a fundamental role as a driver of entrepreneurial activity, especially concerning female entrepreneurship. Only then female entrepreneurs will achieve the desired performance and success.

Thus, future research should be developed to understand the influence of gender on psychological attributes and entrepreneurial intention before and after an entrepreneurship program (Bhatti et al., 2021). Table 5 summarizes the future research agenda for each one of the clusters.

Table 5. Future research agenda

Cluster/Theme	Future Research Suggestions
Gender-specific Entrepreneurial Intention Factors	- More research on sociodemographic and educational variables that can interact with and influence entrepreneurial attitude. - Longitudinal studies that allow analyzing the role of gender in the perceptions of academics. - Studies that analyze the variations in entrepreneurial intentions before and after entrepreneurship education.
Women Entrepreneurial Success Factors	- Longitudinal studies to examine the difference between women in the relationship size-performance of the network. - Comparative cross-country analysis of how land ownership and access to financing affect company performance.
Women Entrepreneurial Performance	- More research should deepen this theme by conducting qualitative studies, such as in-depth interviews. - Studies in different countries to explore the interaction between family and female entrepreneurial performance.
Gender-specific Entrepreneurial Performance	- Determine the contribution of financial skills to entrepreneurial intentions among women in different universities. It is also interesting studies with a comparison with potential male entrepreneurs. - Studies that understand the influence of gender on psychological attributes and entrepreneurial intention before and after an entrepreneurship program.

It was possible to conclude that the performance of female entrepreneurship is a topic of growing importance, and the evidence suggests that women-led businesses are thriving and contributing to economic growth. By providing continued support and resources, women entrepreneurs overcome their challenges and continue to succeed in the entrepreneurial world.

To promote and support female entrepreneurship, governments must implement policies and programs that give women access to the resources they need to start and grow their businesses. These can include funding, mentorship, and networking opportunities. On the other hand, educational institutions should promote the type of support women entrepreneurs need by designing entrepreneurship programs and courses. Additionally, it is vital for society to recognize the value and potential of female entrepreneurs and to work towards dismantling stereotypes and biases that impede their success. In this sense, a conceptual model was proposed that could contribute to future analysis of the theme. However, by the present SLR, it is possible to perceive the need to carry out further studies on this theme as there is still much to be investigated.

7. CONCLUSION AND LIMITATIONS

The phenomenon of female entrepreneurship has garnered significant attention in recent years, with an increasing number of women starting their businesses and significantly impacting economic growth. This study is a systematic female entrepreneurship review in which, through a bibliometric analysis, four thematic groups (clusters) were identified: 1) Gender-specific Entrepreneurial Intention Factors, 2) Women's Entrepreneurial Success Factors, 3) Women's Entrepreneurial Performance, and 4) Gender-specific Entrepreneurial Performance.

From the analyzed literature on the first thematic group (gender-specific entrepreneurial intention factors), we concluded that it refers to the different variables influencing the entrepreneurial intention of women and men. Female entrepreneurship aims to empower women, give them opportunities to express their creativity and entrepreneurial skills, and improve their financial stability. In this sense, it is fundamental to know these factors to support and promote female entrepreneurship effectively. By addressing them, it is possible to create a more equitable and inclusive entrepreneurial environment that supports the growth and success of women-led businesses. Thus, for future research, it would be interesting to develop more research on sociodemographic and educational variables that can interact with and influence entrepreneurial attitude (Shahin et al., 2021). On the other hand, future research should focus on longitudinal studies that allow analyzing the role of gender in the perceptions of academics (Alonso-Galicia et al., 2015). Finally, it will be fundamental to develop studies that explore the variations in entrepreneurial intentions before and after entrepreneurship education (Entrialgo & Iglesias, 2018).

Regarding the second thematic group (Women´s Entrepreneurial Success Factors), it was possible to see that female entrepreneurship is a force for economic growth and development driven by several key factors. It was possible to see that women's entrepreneurial success factors include relationships, networks, individual attributes, and financial support. Thus, for future research, the elaboration of longitudinal studies would be interesting to examine the difference between women in the relationship size-performance of the network (Milanov et al., 2015). Since access to credit can be a critical success factor, it would be vital to investigate how land ownership and access to financing affect firm performance, namely by comparing countries (Brixiová, Kangoye, & Tregenna, 2020).

The third thematic approach (Women´s Entrepreneurial Performance) analyzed knowledge management practices for Female Entrepreneurial Performance, and it may be helpful for the government to know the main barriers to women's engagement in entrepreneurial activities. Thus, future research should deepen this theme by conducting qualitative studies, such as in-depth interviews (Palalic et al., 2017). On the other hand, it also approaches the family's impact on women's performance, whether positive or negative. In this sense, it will be crucial the development of studies in different countries that explore the interaction between family and female entrepreneurial performance (Zhang & Zhou, 2021).

Finally, the fourth thematic group (Gender-specific Entrepreneurial Performance), focuses on training, education, financial skills, family, individual attributes, and financial support. Training and education are essential in improving women's entrepreneurial intention behavior. Thus, future research should determine the contribution of financial skills to entrepreneurial intentions among women in different universities. On the other hand, it might also be interesting to compare potential male entrepreneurs (Llados-Masllorens & Ruiz-Dotras, 2022). Attitudes and skills must be developed through business simulation experiences in a school context.

Although this article brings meaningful collaborations to the literature on female entrepreneurship, namely through the systematization of research areas and, due to these, articulating possible lines of future research, it is not free of some limitations. One of the study's limitations is that it resorted to using a single database to collect literature (WoS), and a systematic review could be reductionist. As defined in the research protocol, peer-reviewed articles were only considered to ensure quality, excluding research book chapters, conference papers, book reviews, proceeding papers, editorial material, and books. The research tried to expand the search scope by selecting keywords that we consider adequate for the simultaneous analysis of female entrepreneurship, entrepreneurial intentions, entrepreneurial performance, and entrepreneurial outcomes topics. In this sense, the study may have neglected significant publications by only examining combined themes instead of each theme individually.

ACKNOWLEDGEMENT

This work is funded by National Funds through the FCT - Foundation for Science and Technology, I.P., within the scope of the project Ref. UIDB/05583/2020. Furthermore, we would like to thank the Research Centre in Digital Services (CISeD) and the Instituto Politécnico de Viseu for their support.

REFERENCES

Agarwal, S., & Lenka, U. (2015). Study on work-life balance of women entrepreneurs – review and research agenda. *Industrial and Commercial Training*, *47*(7), 356–362. doi:10.1108/ICT-01-2015-0006

Akter, M., Rahman, M., & Radicic, D. (2022). Gender-Aware Framework in International Entrepreneurship: How Far Developed?—A Systematic Literature Review. *Sustainability (Switzerland)*, *14*(22), 15326. doi:10.3390u142215326

Ali, J., Jabeen, Z., & Burhan, M. (2023). Measuring factors influencing entrepreneurial intention across gender in India: Evidence from Global Entrepreneurship Monitor (GEM) Database. *Journal of Research in Marketing and Entrepreneurship*, *25*(1), 63–82. doi:10.1108/JRME-08-2021-0105

Ali, J., Shabir, S., & Shaikh, A. (2021). Exploring antecedents of entrepreneurial intentions among females in an emerging economy. *International Journal of Social Economics, 48(7), 1044-1059.*, *48*(7), 1044–1059.

Alonso-Galicia, P. E., Fernández-Pérez, V., Rodríguez-Ariza, L., & del Mar Fuentes-Fuentes, M. (2015). Entrepreneurial cognitions in academia: Exploring gender differences. *Journal of Managerial Psychology*, *30*(6), 630–644. doi:10.1108/JMP-08-2013-0262

Baranik, L. E., Gorman, B., & Wales, W. J. (2018). What Makes Muslim Women Entrepreneurs Successful? A Field Study Examining Religiosity and Social Capital in Tunisia. *Sex Roles*, *78*(3–4), 208–219. doi:10.100711199-017-0790-7

Batjargal, B., Webb, J. W., Tsui, A., Arregle, J. L., Hitt, M. A., & Miller, T. (2019). The moderating influence of national culture on female and male entrepreneurs' social network size and new venture growth. *Cross Cultural & Strategic Management*, *26*(4), 490–521. doi:10.1108/CCSM-04-2018-0057

Bhatti, M. A., Al Doghan, M. A., Saat, S. A. M., Juhari, A. S., & Alshagawi, M. (2021). Entrepreneurial intentions among women: Does entrepreneurial training and education matters? (Pre- and post-evaluation of psychological attributes and its effects on entrepreneurial intention). *Journal of Small Business and Enterprise Development*, *28*(2), 167–184. doi:10.1108/JSBED-09-2019-0305

Brahem, M., & Boussema, S. (2022). Social media entrepreneurship as an opportunity for women: The case of Facebook-commerce. *International Journal of Entrepreneurship and Innovation*. doi:10.1177/14657503211066010

Brixiová, Z., Kangoye, T., & Said, M. (2020). Training, human capital, and gender gaps in entrepreneurial performance. In Economic Modelling, 85.. doi:10.1016/j.econmod.2019.11.006

Brixiová, Z., Kangoye, T., & Tregenna, F. (2020). Enterprising Women in Southern Africa: When Does Land Ownership Matter? *Journal of Family and Economic Issues*, *41*(1), 37–51. doi:10.100710834-020-09663-2

Burke, A. E., FitzRoy, F. R., & Nolan, M. A. (2002). Self-employment wealth and job creation: The roles of gender, non-pecuniary motivation and entrepreneurial ability. *Small Business Economics*, *19*(3), 255–270. doi:10.1023/A:1019698607772

Cardella, G. M., Hernández-Sánchez, B. R., & Sánchez-García, J. C. (2020). Women Entrepreneurship: A Systematic Review to Outline the Boundaries of Scientific Literature. *Frontiers in Psychology*, *11*(July), 1–18. doi:10.3389/fpsyg.2020.01557 PMID:32765357

Castelló-Sirvent, F., & Pinazo-Dallenbach, P. (2021). Corruption shock in Mexico: FsQCA analysis of entrepreneurial intention in university students. *Mathematics*, *9*(14), 1702. doi:10.3390/math9141702

Ćatić-Kajtazović, E., Glavaš, J., & Kljajić-Dervić, M. (2022). The effects of creativity supported at the university on entrepreneurial behavior. *Ekonomski Vjesnik*, *35*(1), 31–44. doi:10.51680/ev.35.1.3

Chaudhuri, S., Agrawal, A. K., Chatterjee, S., & Hussain, Z. (2022). Examining the role of gender on family business entrepreneurial intention: influence of government support and technology usage. *Journal of Family Business Management*.

Chipfunde, D., Yahaya, S. N., & Othman, N. A. (2021). The determinants influencing the performance of women entrepreneurs in malaysia: A conceptual framework. *Estudios de Economía Aplicada*, *39*(4). doi:10.25115/eea.v39i4.4577

Cobo, M. J., López-Herrera, A. G., Herrera-Viedma, E., & Herrera, F. (2011). Science Mapping Software Tools: Review, Analysis, and Cooperative Study Among Tools. *Journal of the American Society for Information Science and Technology*, *62*(7), 1382–1402. doi:10.1002/asi.21525

Cooper, A. C., & Artz, K. W. (1995). Determinants of satisfaction for entrepreneurs. *Journal of Business Venturing*, *10*(6), 439–457. doi:10.1016/0883-9026(95)00083-K

Dawson, C., & Henley, A. (2015). Gender, risk, and venture creation intentions. *Journal of Small Business Management*, *53*(2), 501–515. doi:10.1111/jsbm.12080

Dutta, N., & Mallick, S. (2018). Enabling Women Entrepreneurs: Exploring Factors That Mitigate the Negative Impact of Fertility Rates on Female Entrepreneurship. *Kyklos*, *71*(3), 402–432. doi:10.1111/kykl.12175

Echchabi, A., Omar, M. M. S., & Ayedh, A. M. (2020). Entrepreneurial intention among female university students in Oman. *Journal for International Business and Entrepreneurship Development*, *12*(4), 280–297. doi:10.1504/JIBED.2020.110251

Entrialgo, M., & Iglesias, V. (2018). Are the Intentions to Entrepreneurship of Men and Women Shaped Differently? the Impact of Entrepreneurial Role-Model Exposure and Entrepreneurship Education. *Entrepreneurship Research Journal*, *8*(1). doi:10.1515/erj-2017-0013

Faiza, S., Saeed, L., & Muhammad, A. (2022). Institutions and Women Entrepreneurship: The Mediating Role of Women Entrepreneurial Self Efficacy and Ethical Decision Making. *Journal of Asian Finance*, *9*(6), 33–0044. doi:10.13106/jafeb.2022.vol9.no6.033

Fernandes, C., Ferreira, J. J., Veiga, P. M., Kraus, S., & Dabić, M. (2022). Digital entrepreneurship platforms: Mapping the field and looking towards a holistic approach. *Technology in Society*, *70*(February), 101979. doi:10.1016/j.techsoc.2022.101979

Ferreira, J., Fernandes, C., & Ratten, V. (2019). The effects of technology transfers and institutional factors on economic growth: Evidence from Europe and Oceania. *The Journal of Technology Transfer*, *44*(5), 1505–1528. doi:10.100710961-019-09730-3

Gasparyan, A. Y., Ayvazyan, L., & Kitas, G. D. (2013). Multidisciplinary bibliographic databases. *Journal of Korean Medical Science*, *28*(9), 1270–1275. doi:10.3346/jkms.2013.28.9.1270 PMID:24015029

Gomes, S., Santos, T., Sousa, M., Oliveira, J. C., Oliveira, M., & Lopes, J. M. (2022). Entrepreneurial intention among women: A case study in the Portuguese academy. *Strategic Change*, *31*(2), 197–209. doi:10.1002/jsc.2489

Hallak, R., Assaker, G., & Lee, C. (2015). Tourism Entrepreneurship Performance: The Effects of Place Identity, Self-Efficacy, and Gender. *Journal of Travel Research*, *54*(1), 36–51. doi:10.1177/0047287513513170

Hansen, H., & Rand, J. (2014). The Myth of Female Credit Discrimination in African Manufacturing. *The Journal of Development Studies*, *50*(1), 81–96. doi:10.1080/00220388.2013.849337

Huang, Y., Li, P., Wang, J., & Li, K. (2022). Innovativeness and entrepreneurial performance of female entrepreneurs. *Journal of Innovation and Knowledge*, *7*(4), 100257. doi:10.1016/j.jik.2022.100257

Isa, F. M., Jaganathan, M., Ahmdon, M. A. S., & Ibrahim, H. M. (2019). Malaysian Women Entrepreneurs: Some Emerging Issues and Challenges of Entering Global Market. *International Journal of Academic Research in Business & Social Sciences*, *8*(12). doi:10.6007/IJARBSS/v8-i12/5261

Jha, P., & Alam, M. M. (2022). Antecedents of women entrepreneurs' performance: An empirical perspective. *Management Decision*, *60*(1), 86–122. doi:10.1108/MD-07-2020-0849

Jha, P., Makkad, M., & Mittal, S. (2018). Performance-oriented factors for women entrepreneurs–a scale development perspective. *Journal of Entrepreneurship in Emerging Economies, 10*(329–360), 148–167.

Kessler, M. M. (1963). Bibliographic coupling between scientific papers. *American Documentation*, *14*(1), 10–25. doi:10.1002/asi.5090140103

Kong, H., & Kim, H. (2022). Does National Gender Equality Matter? Gender Difference in the Relationship between Entrepreneurial Human Capital and Entrepreneurial Intention. *Sustainability (Switzerland)*, *14*(2), 928. Advance online publication. doi:10.3390u14020928

Kruse, P., Wach, D., Costa, S., & Moriano, J. A. (2019). Values Matter, Don't They?–Combining Theory of Planned Behavior and Personal Values as Predictors of Social Entrepreneurial Intention. *Journal of Social Entrepreneurship*, *10*(1), 55–83. doi:10.1080/19420676.2018.1541003

Kurczewska, A., & Białek, J. (2014). Is the interplay between self-efficacy and entrepreneurial intention gender-dependent? *Argumenta Oeconomica, 33*(2), 23–38. doi:10.15611/aoe.2014.2.02

Llados-Masllorens, J., & Ruiz-Dotras, E. (2022). Are women's entrepreneurial intentions and motivations influenced by financial skills? *International Journal of Gender and Entrepreneurship*, *14*(1), 69–94. doi:10.1108/IJGE-01-2021-0017

Marchiori, D., & Franco, M. (2020). Knowledge transfer in the context of inter-organizational networks: Foundations and intellectual structures. *Journal of Innovation and Knowledge*, *5*(2), 130–139. doi:10.1016/j.jik.2019.02.001

Martini, U., Malacarne, K., Pederzolli Giovanazzi, S., & Buffa, F. (2020). Sustainable tourism development in rural and marginal areas and opportunities for female entrepreneurship: Lessons from an exploratory study. *Worldwide Hospitality and Tourism Themes*, *12*(4), 421–430. doi:10.1108/WHATT-05-2020-0023

Meeralam, E. A., & Adeinat, I. (2022). Understanding the role of universities in fostering female entrepreneurship in the emerging ecosystem. *Gender in Management*, *37*(3), 388–404. doi:10.1108/GM-02-2021-0041

Milanov, H., Justo, R., & Bradley, S. W. (2015). Making the most of group relationships: The role of gender and boundary effects in microcredit groups. *Journal of Business Venturing*, *30*(6), 822–838. doi:10.1016/j.jbusvent.2015.04.001

Miranda, F. J., Sergio, A. C., & Jesús, R. (2017). Academic Entrepreneurial Intention. *International Journal of Gender and Entrepreneurship*, *9*(1), 66–86. doi:10.1108/IJGE-10-2016-0037

Murphy, P. J., Ferreira, J. J., Fernandes, C. I., & do Paço, A. (2021). Blended value and female entrepreneurial performance: Social and economic aspects of education and technology transfer. *The International Entrepreneurship and Management Journal*, *17*(2), 759–777. doi:10.100711365-019-00620-6

O'Connor, D. O., & Voos, H. (1981). Empirical laws, theory construction and bibliometrics. *Library Trends*, *30*(1), 9–20.

Oppedal Berge, L. I., & Garcia Pires, A. J. (2020). Gender, formality, and entrepreneurial success. *Small Business Economics*, *55*(4), 881–900. doi:10.100711187-019-00163-8

Palalic, R., Ramadani, V., & Dana, L. P. (2017). Entrepreneurship in Bosnia and Herzegovina: Focus on gender. *European Business Review*, *29*(4), 476–496. doi:10.1108/EBR-05-2016-0071

Pelegrini, G. C., & Moraes, G. H. S. M. D. (2022). Does gender matter? A university ecosystem, self-efficacy and entrepreneurial intention analysis in Brazilian universities. *Gender in Management*, *37*(2), 271–286. doi:10.1108/GM-01-2021-0007

Perez-Quintana, A., Hormiga, E., Martori, J. C., & Madariaga, R. (2017). The influence of sex and gender-role orientation in the decision to become an entrepreneur. *International Journal of Gender and Entrepreneurship*, *9*(1), 8–30. doi:10.1108/IJGE-12-2015-0047

Qader, A. A., Zhang, J., Ashraf, S. F., Syed, N., Omhand, K., & Nazir, M. (2022). Capabilities and Opportunities: Linking Knowledge Management Practices of Textile-Based SMEs on Sustainable Entrepreneurship and Organizational Performance in China. *Sustainability (Switzerland)*, *14*(4), 2219. doi:10.3390u14042219

Qazi, Z., Qazi, W., Raza, S. A., & Yousufi, S. Q. (2022). Investigating Women's Entrepreneurial Intention: The Moderating Role of Family Support. *ASR: CMU Journal of Social Sciences and Humanities*, *9*(1). Advance online publication. doi:10.12982/CMUJASR.2022.003

Raevskaya, A. A., Anastasia, A., & Tatarko, A. N. (2022). What makes a family work: Current problems of family psychology and psychotherapy. *Psychology in Russia-State of the Art*, *15*(3), 3–20. doi:10.11621/pir.2022.0301 PMID:36699141

Sánchez-Algarra, P., & Anguera, M. T. (2013). Qualitative/quantitative integration in the inductive observational study of interactive behaviour: Impact of recording and coding among predominating perspectives. *Quality & Quantity*, *47*(2), 1237–1257. doi:10.100711135-012-9764-6

Santos, G., Marques, C. S., & Ferreira, J. (2021). The influence of embeddedness on entrepreneurship, innovation and strategy: A gender perspective in the agri-food sector. *Sustainability (Switzerland)*, *13*(16), 9384. doi:10.3390u13169384

Schmidt, S., Bohnenberger, M. C., Nodari, C. H., & Da Silva, M. D. J. S. (2022). Gender, entrepreneurial behaviour and firm performance of Brazilian students: Integrating economic and behavioral perspectives. *Heliyon*, *8*(1), e08750. doi:10.1016/j.heliyon.2022.e08750 PMID:35059525

Schumpeter, J. (1942). *Capitalism, socialism and democracy*. Harper & Row.

Shahin, M., Ilic, O., Gonsalvez, C., & Whittle, J. (2021). The impact of a STEM-based entrepreneurship program on the entrepreneurial intention of secondary school female students. *The International Entrepreneurship and Management Journal*, *17*(4), 1867–1898. doi:10.100711365-020-00713-7

Shaw, K. L. (2006). Re-creating identity in exile: Hybridity and gender in the works of Assia Djebar, Leïla Sebbar, and Malika Mokeddem. T. U. of Alabama, Ed..

Sidratulmunthah, H., Hussain, S., & Imran Malik, M. (2018). Towards nurturing the entrepreneurial intentions of neglected female business students of Pakistan through proactive personality, self-efficacy and university support factors. *Asia Pacific Journal of Innovation and Entrepreneurship, 12*(3), 363–378. doi:10.1108/APJIE-03-2018-0015

Sweida, G. L., Sherman, C. L., Duranso, C. M. W., & Berkley, R. A. (2022). Lawns And Lemonade: Exploring The Relationship Between Gendered Childpreneur Activities, Adult Entrepreneurial Intentions And Industry Preference. *Journal of Developmental Entrepreneurship, 27*(02), 2250010. doi:10.1142/S1084946722500108

Thébaud, S. (2015). Business as Plan B: Institutional Foundations of Gender Inequality in Entrepreneurship across 24 Industrialized Countries. *Administrative Science Quarterly, 60*(4), 671–711. doi:10.1177/0001839215591627

Tranfield, D., Denyer, D., & Smart, P. (2003). Towards a Methodology for Developing Evidence-Informed Management Knowledge by Means of Systematic Review* Introduction: The need for an evidence-informed approach. *British Journal of Management, 14*(3), 207–222. doi:10.1111/1467-8551.00375

van Eck, N. J., & Waltman, L. (2010). Software survey: VOSviewer, a computer program for bibliometric mapping. *Scientometrics, 84*(2), 523–538. doi:10.100711192-009-0146-3 PMID:20585380

Van Emmerik, H., Euwema, M. C., & Wendt, H. (2008). Leadership behaviors around the world: The relative importance of gender versus cultural background. *International Journal of Cross Cultural Management, 8*(3), 297–315. doi:10.1177/1470595808096671

Vodă, A. I., Haller, A. P., Anichiti, A., & Butnaru, G. I. (2020). Testing entrepreneurial intention determinants in post-transition economies. *Sustainability (Switzerland), 12*(24), 1–28. doi:10.3390u122410370

Yap, C. S., Keling, W., & Ho, P. L. (2022). Determinants of entrepreneurial performance of rural indigenous women entrepreneurs in Sarawak, Malaysia. *Gender in Management: An International Journal.*.

Yoopetch, C. (2021). Women empowerment, attitude toward risk-taking and entrepreneurial intention in the hospitality industry. *International Journal of Culture, Tourism and Hospitality Research, 15*(1), 59–76. doi:10.1108/IJCTHR-01-2020-0016

Zhang, J., & Zhou, N. (2021). The Family's Push and Pull on Female Entrepreneurship: Evidence in China. *Emerging Markets Finance & Trade, 57*(5), 1312–1332. doi:10.1080/1540496X.2019.1697671

Chapter 3
Females in Social Entrepreneurship:
What We Know and What We Need to Know

Catarina Fernandes
Instituto Politécnico de Bragança, Portugal & Centro de Economia e Finanças, Universidade do Porto, Portugal

Rui Alexandre R. Pires
Instituto Politécnico de Bragança, Portugal

ABSTRACT

Social entrepreneurship (SE), which aims to solve social problems of deprived groups, has become a popular area of research and practice. The recent investigation on SE has been characterized by a greater focus on gender differences, emphasizing that the role and characteristics of females are more suitable for social entrepreneurial initiatives. This chapter investigates the predominant themes on females in SE and identifies further research opportunities. On the one hand, the main macro (e.g., sociocultural values) and micro (e.g., personality traits) levels determinants are examined. On the other hand, the macro (e.g., social change) and micro (e.g., women economic empowerment) levels outcomes of females in SE are analyzed. Furthermore, directions for future research are suggested which will enable future authors to focus their studies more effectively.

INTRODUCTION

Over the last years, social entrepreneurship (SE) has attracted increased interest from researchers of different scientific areas (e.g., entrepreneurship, sociology, anthropology, psychology, and politics Dacin et al., 2011; Hidalgo et al., 2021; Hota et al., 2020), public entities, and media. This is evidenced by a huge increase in the number of publications on SE in a multiplicity of journals (Hota et al., 2020).

In general, SE relates to the identification, assessment, exploitation, and exploration of opportunities that aim to solve social problems and, therefore, generate social value and societal change (Certo

DOI: 10.4018/978-1-6684-7669-7.ch003

& Miller, 2008; Ibáñez, 2022; Waqar et al., 2020). The most relevant social problems include, but are not limited, to persistent poverty, social exclusions, imbalanced status of women, inadequate education opportunities, and climate changes (Latif & Ali, 2021; Tan et al., 2020; Waqar et al., 2020). In this way, the mission of the social entrepreneur is to create and maintain social value by providing innovative solutions to social problems and to generate a social transformation (Bernardino et al., 2018; Dacin et al., 2011; Hidalgo et al., 2021). For social entrepreneurs wealth is only a means to a particular end (Hidalgo et al., 2021). On the contrary, for commercial entrepreneurs wealth creation is a way of measuring value generation (Hidalgo et al., 2021).

SE is embedded in a complex and multidimensional setting that comprises gender, which, in turn, influences values, beliefs, and actions "indirectly by shaping actors' perceptions of their interests and directly by constraining choice" (Risman, 2004, p. 432). Therefore, research on SE has attempted to understand gender differences, stressing that the role and features of females are more suitable for social entrepreneurial activity (e.g., Dixit et al., 2022; Gupta et al., 2019; Hechavarría & Brieger, 2022; Nicolás & Rubio, 2016; Tripathy et al., 2022) due to their innate characteristics as empathy, compassion, and care (Dickel & Eckardt, 2021; Rosca et al., 2020). In fact, social companies seem to be a place more adjusted to the women´s roles and personal traits than commercial companies (e.g., Nicolás & Rubio, 2016), since commercial entrepreneurship (CE) is usually related to masculine characteristics, such as aggressiveness, competitiveness, and independence (Gupta et al., 2019).

SE is widely recognized for its capability to promote, among others, social inclusion and women empowerment (e.g., Datta & Gailey, 2012; Dixit et al., 2022; Gramm et al., 2020).

Although existing literature has been investigating the female's role in SE, to the best of the authors´ knowledge, there is no literature review that specifically focuses on this topic. The main purpose of this chapter is to analyze the state of the art and future developments of females in social entrepreneurship. In other words, this chapter aims to examine and synthesize the predominant themes and identify further research opportunities on this topic. To achieve these goals the well-established literature review approach will be used (e.g., Grant & Booth, 2009).

This chapter makes significant contributions. First, by presenting an assessment of the research on females in SE, the chapter contributes to a complete and comprehensive understanding of the knowledge on the topic. Second, the chapter extends the understanding of the linkage between individual's features, in particular gender, and social entrepreneurial activity. Finally, the chapter proposes potential directions for further research.

The chapter is structured in six sections. The first section presents the introduction. The second section discusses the concept of social entrepreneurship, highlighting the main differences from CE. The third section explores the determinants, facilitators, and barriers, to females in SE, in particular contextual and individual factors. The fourth section explores the outcomes of females in SE, at macro and micro levels (e.g., economic development, poverty mitigation, and women empowerment). The fifth section provides some opportunities for future research. Finally, the sixth section offers the main conclusions and implications.

SOCIAL ENTREPRENEURSHIP: AN OVERVIEW

Concept of Social Entrepreneurship: An Analysis

In light of the multiple scientific areas that study SE, it makes sense that various definitions coexist. Accordingly, there is no consensus on a specific definition that is considered "the one" (Alegre et al., 2017; Bacq & Janssen, 2011; Certo & Miller, 2008).

Definitions of SE range from narrow to wide scope (Austin et al., 2006) and focus on four key pillars: 1) individual characteristics of social entrepreneurs, 2) operating sector of social entrepreneurs, 3) the processes and resources used by social entrepreneurs, and 4) the main mission and outcomes related to the social entrepreneur (Austin et al., 2006; Dacin et al., 2010; Ibáñez, 2022; Lasprogata & Cotten, 2003; Mair & Martí, 2006; Tiwari et al., 2017; Toma, 2022; Weerawardena & Sullivan Mort, 2006).

First, some definitions tend to emphasize qualities and behaviors of social entrepreneurs. SE "strives to achieve social value creation and this requires the display of innovativeness, proactiveness and risk management behavior. This behavior is constrained by the desire to achieve the social mission and to maintain the sustainability of the existing organization" (Weerawardena & Sullivan Mort, 2006, p. 32). Social entrepreneurs combine "activism with professional skills, visionary insights with pragmatism, and ethical fibre with tactical thrust" (Catford, 1998, p. 96). Also, the literature highlights other characteristics as altruism, agreeableness, and compassionate love for humanity (Kedmenec et al., 2015; Luc, 2022; Samuelsson & Witell, 2022).

Second, while for some researchers SE relates to nonprofit organizations (Lasprogata & Cotten, 2003), others view SE as innovative and social value creating activity irrespective of whether commercial activities are involved or not (Austin et al., 2006). In this sense, SE can be defined "on a continuous axis between social missions and commercial benefits. It is not clearly understood how much social entrepreneurship is for profit and how much is for the collective good" (Toma, 2022, p. 62).

Third, studies also define SE as process in which resources are combined in new ways to create social value (Lumpkin et al., 2013; Mair & Martí, 2006; Tiwari et al., 2017). In other words, SE "is the process of identifying, evaluating and exploiting opportunities aiming at social value creation by means of commercial, market-based activities and of the use of a wide range of resources" (Bacq & Janssen, 2011, p. 388) obtained "by attracting donations or through commercial strategies that reinvest profit in social action" (Ibáñez, 2022, p. 14).

Fourth, in line with the surveyed literature, the differentiating characteristic of SE is that the primary goal is a social mission, aiming to benefit society (Bacq & Janssen, 2011; Lasprogata & Cotten, 2003; Waqar et al., 2020) through the creation and improvement of social wealth (Mair & Martí, 2006; Zahra et al., 2009). SE is an innovative solution to solve the social demands of society.

In general, in accordance with the exposed above, SE differs from commercial (traditional) entrepreneurship "insofar as it emphasizes social outcomes ahead of economic returns" (Ayob, 2018, p. 1).

Differences Between Social Entrepreneurship and Commercial Entrepreneurship

SE displays several distinct features from CE. Rather than profit versus nonprofit, the majority of authors agree that the primary difference between SE and CE is related to the priority given to social wealth creation versus economic wealth creation (Åmo, 2014; Mair & Martí, 2006; Rahman et al., 2019) that is, the mission of each of them. In general, SE diverges from CE in that it focuses on social outcomes ahead of economic outcomes. In SE, social value creation is the main goal, while economic value creation, in the form of returns, is a means of ensuring the sustainability of the entrepreneurial activity.

SE lies in the restricted ability to capture economic value (Mair & Martí, 2006), given that the "customers", usually deprived people, frequently are unable to pay even a small amount of the price. Accordingly, social entrepreneurs face more restrictions regarding financial resource mobilization (Riedo et al., 2019). They do not have the capacity to attract venture capital as commercial entrepreneurs because often they are unable to offer an appealing return (Austin et al., 2006; Bacq et al., 2013). Social entrepreneurs are more focussed on employing available resources for social benefits rather than for economic and financial benefits. That is, in SE resources are used to address social problems or provide public goods due to a market failure. Thus, the mix of funding sources of SE is dominated by other sources than income from the sales. Usually social entrepreneurs depend on sponsoring or other philanthropic tools to finance their businesses (Riedo et al., 2019). Additionally, human resources mobilization is challenging as it is difficult to pecuniary reward staff as competitively as in commercial markets (Austin et al., 2006) and consequently, the ability to attract human resources depends on how much they value nonpecuniary compensations. The purpose of SE also creates challenges for measuring performance comparatively to CE which relies on objective and quantifiable measures such as market share and return on equity (Austin et al., 2006).

When distinguishing SE from CE research also points out the personal characteristics or personality traits of social entrepreneurs relatively to commercial entrepreneurs. In fact, certain individual features, innate or acquired, are likely to better fit within the social entrepreneurial context and thus exert influence on social entrepreneurial intentions and behaviors. A concept commonly used to describe social entrepreneurs is prosocial personality and dimensions as altruism, empathic concern, compassion, and personal distress highlighted (Riedo et al., 2019; Rosca et al., 2020; Samuelsson & Witell, 2022). Also, the existing literature shows that social entrepreneurs tend to be more overconfident and prone to commitment than commercial entrepreneurs (Hietschold & Voegtlin, 2022).

DETERMINANTS OF FEMALES IN SOCIAL ENTREPRENEURSIP

Determinants of females in SE include both contextual or macro level factors, which refer to environmental elements (e.g., culture and public policies) and individual or personal level factors, related to innate and acquired characteristics (i.e., personality traits, entrepreneurs' skills, and family background).

Contextual Determinants

Sociocultural norms, values, and stereotypes about the role of men and women (e.g., childcare responsibilities and dedication to family) prescribe proper or acceptable behaviors, including entrepreneurial involvement of women, as they shape opinions, feelings, and reactions (Anggadwita et al., 2021; Griffiths et al., 2013; Hechavarría et al., 2017; Hechavarría & Brieger, 2022; Noguera et al., 2013). Sociocultural context significantly influences the gender role patterns, namely the degree of participation of women in the work force and what type of work and career opportunities are permissible for them, and thus plays a critical role in women's entrepreneurship. Female entrepreneurs are more likely to be social entrepreneurs because SE involves empathy, compassion, and helpfulness, and these characteristics stereotypically tend to be associated with feminine characteristics in many societies (Gupta et al., 2019; Hechavarría et al., 2017; Nicolás & Rubio, 2016). "Cultural practices affect gendered patterns of social action across societies. Social action itself is gendered because it follows a culturally defined division of labor between the sexes" (Hechavarría & Brieger, 2022, p. 1133). In this way, the relationship between entrepreneur's gender and SE depends on the society's cultural patterns and gender stereotypes (i.e., roles and responsibilities), which enable or constraint the individual's ability to act. Traditionally, gender roles limit females, but not males, in exploring their capabilities as entrepreneurs (Kantor, 2002). For instance, in a society where female role is closely related to family commitments, childcare responsibilities, and household tasks, entrepreneurial activity is viewed as less appropriate for women (Noguera et al., 2013).

Public policies related to pro-work family policies, educational, and training programs as well as financial support programs and networks, also clearly impact on female SE (Llados-Masllorens & Ruiz-Dotras, 2022; Muravyev et al., 2009; Terjesen et al., 2016; Voronkova et al., 2019). The state policies to encourage the entrance of women in the labor market and their professional activity, as well as the creation of conditions for combining career with family duties, such as the provision of child care services and significant family leave, encourage female involvement in entrepreneurial activity (Terjesen et al., 2016). At the same time, building female entrepreneurship motivations, intentions, capacities and, thus, participation includes offering education and training programs, in particular related to SE (e.g., know the characteristics and specificities of SE, identify and evaluate social opportunities and develop the ability to communicate and interact with representatives of the community) (Terjesen et al., 2016; Voronkova et al., 2019), as well as financial education and literacy (Llados-Masllorens & Ruiz-Dotras, 2022). Especially in developing countries, due to the disadvantages and discrimination in education and the labor market, females usually do not have the same entrepreneurial opportunities as males (Minniti & Naude, 2010). Therefore, a set of public policies relates to human capital in terms of providing females with higher levels of education and training (e.g., entrepreneurship in general and in SE in particular). Also, although the gender-based differences in access to financing seem to depend on the level of a country's development[1], discrimination against women entrepreneurs exists, as they face more severe financial constraints than men entrepreneurs (Marlow & Patton, 2005; Muravyev et al., 2009), such as lack of access to basic banking services. Banks, the most important source of external finance, invest less money in female entrepreneurs, more socially oriented, than male entrepreneurs even in similar conditions (Yang et al., 2020), requiring a larger amount of collateral and consequently forcing women to primarily rely on their personal savings and loans from family and friends. In this context, the emergence of new sources of funding such as crowdfunding and social impact accelerator, disrupting traditional forms of financing, play an important role in supporting entrepreneurs in the social sector, primarily female entrepreneurs who are more likely to pursue social value creation. Governments must attempt to positively influence the supply of funds, creating and managing schemes which financially support women entrepreneurs (Marlow & Patton, 2005). As they face barriers related to their gender when seeking appropriate source of funding, dedicated public policies, and support initiatives are absolutely vital. Social entrepreneurial activities, in particular in developing countries, frequently result from programs launched to improve women's personal wellbeing and economic status and, consequently, to challenge gender inequalities, as is the case of microfinance and microcredit (Chant, 2014). Public efforts can also be directed toward increasing social capital in terms of easing access to entrepreneurial mentors, networks, and exposure (Terjesen et al., 2016). Such efforts improve, among others, the availability of information, cooperation with business partners, and female confidence (Muravyev et al., 2009; Terjesen et al., 2016).

Finally, national legislation and regulatory system that provides equal treatment to women and men has helped women to participate in the social entrepreneurial activity (Kimbu & Ngoasong, 2016). Social entrepreneurs succeed in strong institutional settings in which SE is improved with supportive regulation (Terjesen et al., 2016) and therefore, the regulatory environment markedly impacts on the feasibility and desirability of SE (Gupta et al., 2020). It is argued that state action to enact antidiscrimination legislation and equal pay regulation will weaken the constraints that prevent women from engaging in the socioeconomic activity (Cockburn, 1991).

Individual Determinants

Although it is unlikely that a complete and unique set of characteristics applies to all types of social entrepreneurial activity across all contexts (Dacin et al., 2010), the literature has been presenting several characteristics, innate and acquired, usually associated with social entrepreneurs, considering gender differences (e.g., Bernardino et al., 2018; Nga & Shamuganathan, 2010; Ryzin et al., 2009). On the one hand, personality traits influence the motivations, intentions, and the manner in which the individual acts and, consequently, it could be expected that social entrepreneurs usually have certain distinctive personality characteristics (Nga & Shamuganathan, 2010). On the other hand, the personality characteristics that often social entrepreneurs possess are gender related. Personality traits matter when analyzing gender disparities in SE and, thus, help to explain the gender bias observed (Bernardino et al., 2018).

Social entrepreneurs have a deep understanding of social problems, trying to create social value in an environment with various stakeholders, through continuous engagement in social projects/organizations (Bernardino et al., 2018; Hidalgo et al., 2021; Nga & Shamuganathan, 2010). Agreeableness, empathy, emotion, compassion, awareness of social injustice, and inequality which, among others, were found to be important in explaining individuals' involvement in SE, are more predominant in females (Bernardino et al., 2018; Muntean & Ozkazanc-Pan, 2016; Nga & Shamuganathan, 2010; Rosca et al., 2020). SE "is fueled by the desire to help others, which, in turn, is attributed to an individual's empathy, sympathy, and compassion; these behavioral traits are commonly accepted as being more feminine than masculine" (Yamini et al., 2022, p. 3). Accordingly, due to these feminine traits, women are a better fit for leading social enterprises. The success of women in SE, when compared with their status in mainstream entrepreneurship, may amplify the gendered dimensions of the entrepreneurship field (Muntean & Ozkazanc-Pan, 2016).

Personal characteristics are partly developed by innate nurturing, socialization, and education meaning that acquired characteristics, which may also be transformed over time, also exert influence on the women's engagement with SE such as life-long learning (tacit and explicit knowledge), the ability to easily communicate and building social relationships through relational competences and family background (Meutia & Ismail, 2012; Nga & Shamuganathan, 2010).

OUTCOMES OF FEMALES IN SOCIAL ENTREPRENEURSHIP

SE has been identified as a means for women empowerment (Datta & Gailey, 2012; Dixit et al., 2023; Sharma & Kumar, 2021), for boosting gender equality, specifically in developing and male-dominated countries (Kumar, 2013), and for economic growth and social change (Haugh & Talwar, 2016; Pareja-Cano et al., 2020). In other words, SE in general and females in SE in particular have relevant micro and macro level outcomes as is the case of women empowerment and social change, respectively. These outcomes are addressed in the following subsections.

Macro Level Outcomes

The initiatives of SE focus on finding durable solutions to social problems as illiteracy, unemployment, women and girl abuse, gender inequality, and poverty and, therefore, on creating social value (e.g., Tan et al., 2020; Waqar et al., 2020). Through the provision of unique and innovative solutions to social problems, SE promotes social change, economic growth, and sustainable development (e.g., Agrawal et al., 2021; Connor & Bent-Goodley, 2016; Haugh & Talwar, 2016; Nicolás & Rubio, 2016; Pareja-Cano et al., 2020; Wang, 2022), which represent the main macro level outcomes of SE addressed in the literature.

Most studies on SE, and particularly on females in SE, indicate social entrepreneurial activities as a major catalyst of social change and transformation. These studies report how social entrepreneurial efforts promote human capital development, poverty alleviation, gender equality, reduce discrimination, and empower women, among others (e.g., Connor & Bent-Goodley, 2016; Haugh & Talwar, 2016). In specific, SE contributes to social change by changing (i) attitudes towards women and paid work, (ii) power relations within the family unit, (iii) attitudes towards gender discrimination, and (iv) the role of men in the family unit (Haugh & Talwar, 2016). Moreover, women social entrepreneurs successful contribute to expand educational opportunities for girls and women, to empower vulnerable groups, and to evolve in business to meet change and economic growth (Connor & Bent-Goodley, 2016). In this way, women improve, not only their own lives and the life of their families and communities at the present, but also in the future. In other words, through SE women promote a positive and sustainable social change (Borquist & Bruin, 2019; Grimes et al., 2018; Pareja-Cano et al., 2020).

The literature is also consensual on the importance of entrepreneurial activities, including female social entrepreneurial activities, to economic growth and development (Terjesen et al., 2016). Due to their involvement in social entrepreneurship, women can improve their social and economic wellbeing and, also, enhance the social and economic wellbeing of the society through job creation and innovative products, processes, and services (Tripathy et al., 2022). In some cases, despite the situation of poverty, the involvement of women in social businesses have not only sustained the community but also enabled the economic improvement of this community (Connor & Bent-Goodley, 2016). As such, women in general, and specifically women social entrepreneurs, have an essential role in the economic advancement and prosperity of the nations, mainly in developing nations (Dixit et al., 2023). When social entrepreneurs develop innovative and durable solutions to mitigate social problems, they help to accelerate sustainable economic growth which leads to a higher rate of employment and better living standards (Wang, 2022).

Social entrepreneurial strategies lead, not only to social value creation, but also to economic value creation (Agrawal et al., 2021). Contributing to social transformation and economic growth, SE promotes sustainable development and allows to achieve sustainable development goals (SDGs) (Agrawal et al., 2021; Perekrestova, 2022). In fact, "social entrepreneurs can play an important role in achieving SDGs because of their ability to tackle problems that others neglect or cannot solve as effectively" (Perekrestova, 2022, p. 5). For instance, when social entrepreneurs encourage and convince the families of women that live in marginalized rural areas of patriarchal countries to engage in economic activities, an improvement of their social and standing status and their economic situation occurs (Agrawal et al., 2021; Haugh & Talwar, 2016; Perekrestova, 2022). This enhances gender equality and, therefore, contributes to achieve SDG 5 "Gender equality". In addition, providing sources of income specifically for women, social businesses also contribute to achieve another SDGs such as SDG 1 "No poverty" and SDG 8 "Decent work and economic growth".

Micro Level Outcomes

Women empowerment is one of the main micro level outcomes of SE pointed out in the previous literature on females in SE (e.g., Agrawal et al., 2021; Datta & Gailey, 2012; Dixit et al., 2022; Pareja-Cano et al., 2020; Sharma & Kumar, 2021). It can be achieved by the creation of equal opportunities in education, job, and society and SE may have a critical role in the creation of these opportunities (e.g., Datta & Gailey, 2012). In fact, SE develops efforts to remove gender inequalities in the society, encouraging and assisting females to be educated and providing them equal opportunities in the labor market through the creation of employment for women (Agrawal et al., 2021; Dixit et al., 2023).

In general terms, empowerment aims to remove social, political, or legal constrains that may be working against a deprived group as is the case of women, mainly both in developing and male-dominated countries and in patriarchal societies such as India and some Latin American Countries (e.g., Agrawal et al., 2021; Ciruela-Lorenzo et al., 2020; Datta & Gailey, 2012; Sharma & Kumar, 2021). Thus, empowerment can be defined as "the expansion in people's ability to make strategic life choices in a context where this ability was previously denied to them" (Kabeer, 1999, p. 437). In this way, women empowerment enables "women to take decisions in life and to deal with the existing hurdles in society to pursue freedom, follow their dreams and accomplish them" (Dixit et al., 2023, p. 2). That is, the key factor of women empowerment is their ability to make strategic choices for their own life. This is a reality when women have autonomy and freedom to make decisions for themselves (Ciruela-Lorenzo et al., 2020).

Women empowerment encompasses both economic and personal empowerment. On the one hand, economic empowerment is achieved through a self-sustained mode of financial independence (Dixit et al., 2023), which can occur through women's engagement in remunerative activity via wage employment and self-employment/own business. Many times, SE is the best/only source of income to women (e.g., Mishra et al., 2020; Perekrestova, 2022). Women's financial independence directly contributes to gender equality, poverty mitigation, and inclusive economic growth (Ciruela-Lorenzo et al., 2020). On the other hand, personal empowerment refers to an increase in self-sufficiency, self-confidence, autonomy, and development of inner strength (Sharma & Kumar, 2021).

Literature on females in SE reports several examples of women empowerment through SE. Women engaged with social businesses achieve financial independence and personal empowerment, which can be reverted whether these businesses are stopped (Agrawal et al., 2021; Sharma & Kumar, 2021). Social enterprises provide successful platforms for women empowerment (economic empowerment through financial independence and personal empowerment by gaining confidence and self-respect), and gender equality given their inclusive and sustainable approach to solve issues (Agrawal et al., 2021; Perekrestova, 2022). When women generate additional income the attitude of men in a predominantly patriarchal household change. Thus, SE empowers women and changes their socio-economic status.

When women become economically and personally empowered, they encourage other women to become like them, which starts a never-ending strong chain of empowered women and contributes to a profound social change. In addition, empower women makes them independent and major contributors to the economy (Dixit et al., 2023). That is, empowered women through their work and income, not only improve their financial and social status, but also are able to contribute towards the socioeconomic development of their community and country (Agrawal et al., 2021; Ciruela-Lorenzo et al., 2020). In this way, women empowerment has an intervening effect on the relationship between SE, social change, and economic development.

OPPORTUNITIES FOR FUTURE RESEARCH

The literature review shows some gaps and, thus, offers some potential opportunities for future research.

First, the advances of digital technologies enormously impact on the entrepreneurial process. They are not only increasing entrepreneurial opportunities, but also creating new challenges (Fernandes et al., 2022; Zhai et al., 2023). However, research on entrepreneurial activities allowed by digital technologies is fragmented, dispersed, and delayed (Zhai et al., 2023) and so also is the research on how such technologies enable female entrepreneurial action given their level of digital (il)literacy, especially in rural areas of developing countries. The "digital" offers substantial potential for previously deprived or marginalized groups, which may promote gender equality and women empowerment (e.g., economic stability) (Dhanamalar et al., 2020; Zhai et al., 2023). Nevertheless, how traditionally disadvantaged segments of the population, such as women, take advantage of the digital environment, given the level of digital knowledge required and the broad range of difficulties women often still face in accessing and using digital technologies (digital (il)literacy), remains underdeveloped. Further research should examine how the level of digital (il)literacy affects females in SE, and their ability to be empowered, so that they grow stronger economic and personally.

Second, the existing literature recognizes that female entrepreneurship is rich in nuances and particularities (Cardella et al., 2020). Women entrepreneurs are a heterogeneous group whose specificities, in particular religion and political ideology, shape prosocial values and motivations, and promote or inhibit the "spirit" of social entrepreneur. Religious context may promote restrictive gender norms which relegate women to domestic roles, excluding them from decision making or, on the contrary, may encourage an active role for women in the society. In this sense, entrepreneurship can play a "liberating" role for women. Moreover, religious beliefs and how faith is lived/practiced, and its connection to social and moral values, define how social problems are addressed and, consequently, the way how entrepreneurial activity manifests itself and is carried out. However, the influence of religion/faith on how female express SE remains underdeveloped, which represents an opportunity for future research. Also, the existing literature on SE does not question the political dimension (Jarrodi et al., 2019). While one's personal motivation to engage in social entrepreneurship can be supported by different political ideologies, defined as "a coherent and interrelated set of moral and political attitudes and values about the proper goals of society which consists of cognitive, affective and motivational components" (Jarrodi et al., 2019, p. 584), how such ideologies may encourage or shape female social entrepreneurial motivations, have yet to be analyzed. Although political ideology is a powerful motivational force due to its ability to encourage human beings of "committing atrocities (as well as acts of generosity and courage) and sacrificing even their own lives for the sake of abstract belief systems" (Jost & Amodio, 2012, p. 36) it is widely neglected in entrepreneurship research. Religious and political ideologies shape individuals' values and beliefs and serve existential and relational needs (e.g., security, and solidarity), helping to explain people's behavior and action that is, why individuals do what they do (Jost & Amodio, 2012).

Third, factors linked to the success of social entrepreneurial activity and cases of SE recognized as successful, have been broadly analyzed by the existing research. On the contrary, studies related to failure (or even voluntary exit) in SE, one of the most important events in an entrepreneurial journey, are very limited. While there is no consensus on a definition of failure in SE and how to measure it, with authors pointing out that failure should be measured not only in financial terms but also in social terms (more difficult to measure due to its ambiguous nature) (Smollan & Singh, 2021), future research should (make efforts) to investigate the failure in female social enterprises in multiple dimensions: 1) mechanisms to mitigate the probability of its occurrence (e.g., strategic partnerships and alliances), 2) macro-level (country/region) and micro-level (individual) impact and responses to it (permanent exit from entrepreneurial activity or entrepreneurial reentry subsequent to business failure, starting another social enterprise?), and 3) how contextual and individual factors influence women's responses to the failure of their social enterprises (e.g., stigma of negative social judgments).

CONCLUSION AND IMPLICATIONS

Over the past decades SE has received increased attention from academic researchers, public entities, and media. Although there is no consensus on a single definition of SE, the authors agree that the main drive for SE is to create social impact by providing solutions to social problems. The distinguishing characteristic of SE is that the main purpose of their organizations is to achieve a social mission, intending to benefit disadvantaged and traditionally excluded groups.

SE is embedded in a multi-faceted context that incorporate gender, which prompted research to focus on gender in SE, in particular women's role as social entrepreneur. On the one hand, a comprehensive review of the determinants of females in SE is presented: contextual or macro level determinants with almost the same impact on all women in a given territorial space (e.g., sociocultural norms), and individual or micro level, unique to each woman (e.g., personality characteristics). On the other hand, an analysis of the outcomes at both macro (e.g., social transformation) and micro (e.g., (e.g., women economic empowerment) levels is provided.

This chapter has several theoretical and practical implications. From the theoretical point of view, the knowledge of females in SE provided by this chapter is expected to encourage new researchers to involve in this interesting and emerging field. Additionally, it allows scholars, not only to position their current studies, but also to find new directions for future research. From the practical point of view, this chapter offers significant knowledge for policymakers, governments, and public authorities as it offers a detailed picture of SE that can be incorporated in the definition of their policies, thereby making their implementation more effective. For instance, policies to support female social entrepreneurs must incorporate the provision of childcare services and substantial family leave, entrepreneurial education and training, and finance programs.

REFERENCES

Agrawal, A., Gandhi, P., & Khare, P. (2021). Women empowerment through entrepreneurship: Case study of a social entrepreneurial intervention in rural India. *The International Journal of Organizational Analysis*. doi:10.1108/IJOA-03-2021-2659

Alegre, I., Kislenko, S., & Berbegal-Mirabent, J. (2017). Organized chaos: Mapping the definitions of social entrepreneurship. *Journal of Social Entrepreneurship*, *8*(2), 248–264. doi:10.1080/19420676.2017.1371631

Åmo, B. W. (2014). Antecedents, prevalence and manifestations of social entrepreneurship. *International Journal of Entrepreneurial Venturing*, *6*(2), 162–178. doi:10.1504/IJEV.2014.062750

Anggadwita, G., Ramadani, V., Permatasari, A., & Alamanda, D. T. (2021). Key determinants of women's entrepreneurial intentions in encouraging social empowerment. *Service Business*, *15*(2), 309–334. doi:10.100711628-021-00444-x

Austin, J., Stevenson, H., & Wei–Skillern, J. (2006). Social and commercial entrepreneurship: Same, different, or both? *Entrepreneurship Theory and Practice*, *30*(1), 1–22. doi:10.1111/j.1540-6520.2006.00107.x

Ayob, A. H. (2018). Diversity, trust and social entrepreneurship. *Journal of Social Entrepreneurship*, *9*(1), 1–12. doi:10.1080/19420676.2017.1399433

Bacq, S., Hartog, C., & Hoogendoorn, B. (2013). A quantitative comparison of social and commercial entrepreneurship: Toward a more nuanced understanding of social entrepreneurship organizations in context. *Journal of Social Entrepreneurship*, *4*(1), 40–68. doi:10.1080/19420676.2012.758653

Bacq, S., & Janssen, F. (2011). The multiple faces of social entrepreneurship: A review of definitional issues based on geographical and thematic criteria. *Entrepreneurship and Regional Development*, *23*(5–6), 373–403. doi:10.1080/08985626.2011.577242

Bernardino, S., Santos, J. F., & Ribeiro, J. C. (2018). Social entrepreneur and gender: What's personality got to do with it? *International Journal of Gender and Entrepreneurship*, *10*(1), 61–82. doi:10.1108/IJGE-07-2017-0040

Borquist, B. R., & de Bruin, A. (2019). Values and women-led social entrepreneurship. *International Journal of Gender and Entrepreneurship*, *11*(2), 146–165. doi:10.1108/IJGE-08-2018-0093

Cardella, G. M., Hernández-Sánchez, B. R., & Sánchez-García, J. C. (2020). Women entrepreneurship: A systematic review to outline the boundaries of scientific literature. *Frontiers in Psychology*, *11*, 1557. doi:10.3389/fpsyg.2020.01557 PMID:32765357

Catford, J. (1998). Social entrepreneurs are vital for health promotion - But they need supportive environments too. *Health Promotion International*, *13*(2), 95–97. doi:10.1093/heapro/13.2.95

Certo, T., & Miller, T. L. (2008). Social entrepreneurship: Key issues and concepts. *Business Horizons*, *51*(4), 267–271. doi:10.1016/j.bushor.2008.02.009

Chant, S. (2014). Exploring the "feminisation of poverty" in relation to women's work and home-based enterprise in slums of the Global South. *International Journal of Gender and Entrepreneurship*, *6*(3), 296–316. doi:10.1108/IJGE-09-2012-0035

Ciruela-Lorenzo, A. M., González-Sánchez, A., & Plaza-Angulo, J. J. (2020). An exploratory study on social entrepreneurship, empowerment and peace process. The case of Colombian women victims of the armed conflict. *Sustainability*, *12*(24), 10425. doi:10.3390u122410425

Cockburn, C. (1991). *In the way of women: Men's resistance to sex equality in organizations*. Macmillan Education, Ltd. doi:10.1007/978-1-349-21571-3

Connor, R. F., & Bent-Goodley, T. B. (2016). Zanzibari social entrepreneurs and poverty alleviation strategies: Understanding efforts to build local community sustainability. *Journal of Community Practice*, *24*(3), 302–318. doi:10.1080/10705422.2016.1201784

Dacin, M. T., Dacin, P. A., & Tracey, P. (2011). Social entrepreneurship: A critique and future directions. *Organization Science*, *22*(5), 1203–1213. doi:10.1287/orsc.1100.0620

Dacin, P. A., Dacin, M. T., & Matear, M. (2010). Social entrepreneurship: Why we don't need a new theory and how we move forward from here. *The Academy of Management Perspectives*, *24*(3), 37–57. doi:10.5465/AMP.2010.52842950

Datta, P. B., & Gailey, R. (2012). Empowering women through social entrepreneurship: Case study of a women's cooperative in India. *Entrepreneurship Theory and Practice*, *36*(3), 569–587. doi:10.1111/j.1540-6520.2012.00505.x

Dhanamalar, M., Preethi, S., & Yuvashree, S. (2020). Impact of digitization on women's empowerment: A study of rural and urban regions in India. *Journal of International Women's Studies*, *21*(5), 107–112.

Dickel, P., & Eckardt, G. (2021). Who wants to be a social entrepreneur? The role of gender and sustainability orientation. *Journal of Small Business Management*, *59*(1), 196–218. doi:10.1080/00472778.2019.1704489

Dixit, A. R., Malik, N., Seth, M., & Sethi, D. (2023). The role of social entrepreneurial leadership and benchmarking in women empowerment. *Benchmarking*, *30*(1), 180–195. doi:10.1108/BIJ-08-2021-0493

Fernandes, C., Ferreira, J., Veiga, P. M., Kraus, S., & Dabić, M. (2022). Digital entrepreneurship platforms: Mapping the field and looking towards a holistic approach. *Technology in Society*, *70*, 101979. doi:10.1016/j.techsoc.2022.101979

Gramm, V., Torre, C. D., & Membretti, A. (2020). Farms in progress-providing childcare services as a means of empowering women farmers in South Tyrol, Italy. *Sustainability*, *12*(2), 467. doi:10.3390u12020467

Grant, M. J., & Booth, A. (2009). A typology of reviews: An analysis of 14 review types and associated methodologies. *Health Information and Libraries Journal*, *26*(2), 91–108. doi:10.1111/j.1471-1842.2009.00848.x PMID:19490148

Griffiths, M. D., Gundry, L. K., & Kickul, J. R. (2013). The socio-political, economic, and cultural determinants of social entrepreneurship activity An empirical examination. *Journal of Small Business and Enterprise Development*, *20*(2), 1462–6004. doi:10.1108/14626001311326761

Grimes, M. G., Gehman, J., & Cao, K. (2018). Positively deviant: Identity work through B Corporation certification. *Journal of Business Venturing*, *33*(2), 130–148. doi:10.1016/j.jbusvent.2017.12.001

Gupta, P., Chauhan, S., Paul, J., & Jaiswal, M. P. (2020). Social entrepreneurship research: A review and future research agenda. *Journal of Business Research*, *113*, 209–229. doi:10.1016/j.jbusres.2020.03.032

Gupta, V. K., Wieland, A. M., & Turban, D. B. (2019). Gender characterizations in entrepreneurship: A multi-level investigation of sex-role stereotypes about high-growth, commercial, and social entrepreneurs. *Journal of Small Business Management*, *57*(1), 131–153. doi:10.1111/jsbm.12495

Haugh, H. M., & Talwar, A. (2016). Linking social entrepreneurship and social change: The mediating role of empowerment. *Journal of Business Ethics*, *133*(4), 643–658. doi:10.100710551-014-2449-4

Hechavarría, D. M., & Brieger, S. A. (2022). Practice rather than preach: Cultural practices and female social entrepreneurship. *Small Business Economics*, *58*(2), 1131–1151. doi:10.100711187-020-00437-6

Hechavarría, D. M., Terjesen, S. A., Ingram, A. E., Renko, M., Justo, R., & Elam, A. (2017). Taking care of business: The impact of culture and gender on entrepreneurs' blended value creation goals. *Small Business Economics*, *48*(1), 225–257. doi:10.100711187-016-9747-4

Hidalgo, G., Monticelli, J. M., & Bortolaso, I. V. (2021). Social capital as a driver of social entrepreneurship. *Journal of Social Entrepreneurship*, 1–24. doi:10.1080/19420676.2021.1951819

Hietschold, N., & Voegtlin, C. (2022). Blinded by a social cause? Differences in cognitive Biases between social and commercial entrepreneurs. *Journal of Social Entrepreneurship*, *13*(3), 431–452. doi: 10.1080/19420676.2021.1880466

Hota, P. K., Subramanian, B., & Narayanamurthy, G. (2020). Mapping the intellectual structure of social entrepreneurship research: A citation/co-citation analysis. *Journal of Business Ethics*, *166*(1), 89–114. doi:10.100710551-019-04129-4

Ibáñez, M. J. (2022). Social entrepreneurship review: A gap in the Latin American context. *Management Research*, *20*(1), 6–24. doi:10.1108/MRJIAM-09-2021-1232

Jarrodi, H., Byrne, J., & Bureau, S. (2019). A political ideology lens on social entrepreneurship motivations. *Entrepreneurship and Regional Development*, *31*(7–8), 583–604. doi:10.1080/08985626.2019.1596353

Jost, J. T., & Amodio, D. M. (2012). Political ideology as motivated social cognition: Behavioral and neuroscientific evidence. *Motivation and Emotion*, *36*(1), 55–64. doi:10.100711031-011-9260-7

Kabeer, N. (1999). Resources, agency, achievements: Reflections on the measurement of women's empowerment. *Development and Change*, *30*(3), 435–464. doi:10.1111/1467-7660.00125

Kantor, P. (2002). Gender, microenterprise success and cultural context: The case of South Asia. *Entrepreneurship Theory and Practice*, *26*(4), 131–143. doi:10.1177/104225870202600408

Kedmenec, I., Rebernik, M., & Perić, J. (2015). The impact of individual characteristics on intentions to pursue social entrepreneurship. *Ekonomski Pregled*, *66*(2), 119–137. https://www.researchgate.net/publication/279494290

Kimbu, A. N., & Ngoasong, M. Z. (2016). Women as vectors of social entrepreneurship. *Annals of Tourism Research*, *60*, 63–79. doi:10.1016/j.annals.2016.06.002

Kumar, A. (2013). Women entrepreneurs in a masculine society: Inclusive strategy for sustainable outcomes. *The International Journal of Organizational Analysis*, *21*(3), 373–384. doi:10.1108/IJOA-01-2013-0636

Lasprogata, G. A., & Cotten, M. N. (2003). Contemplating "enterprise": The business and legal challenges of social entrepreneurship. *American Business Law Journal*, *41*(1), 67–114. doi:10.1111/j.1744-1714.2003.tb00002.x

Latif, M., & Ali, S. (2021). Managerial ties as determinant of social entrepreneurial intentions: Does gender make a difference? *Journal of Public Affairs*, *21*(2), e2183. doi:10.1002/pa.2183

Llados-Masllorens, J., & Ruiz-Dotras, E. (2022). Are women's entrepreneurial intentions and motivations influenced by financial skills? *International Journal of Gender and Entrepreneurship*, *14*(1), 69–94. doi:10.1108/IJGE-01-2021-0017

Luc, P. T. (2022). The relationships between Big-Five personality traits and social entrepreneurship intention. *Cogent Business & Management*, *9*(1), 2137950. doi:10.1080/23311975.2022.2137950

Lumpkin, G. T., Moss, T. W., Gras, D. M., Kato, S., & Amezcua, A. S. (2013). Entrepreneurial processes in social contexts: How are they different, if at all? *Small Business Economics*, *40*(3), 761–783. doi:10.100711187-011-9399-3

Mair, J., & Martí, I. (2006). Social entrepreneurship research: A source of explanation, prediction, and delight. *Journal of World Business*, *41*(1), 36–44. doi:10.1016/j.jwb.2005.09.002

Marlow, S., & Patton, D. (2005). All credit to men? Entrepreneurship, finance, and gender. *Entrepreneurship Theory and Practice*, *29*(6), 717–735. doi:10.1111/j.1540-6520.2005.00105.x

Meutia, & Ismail, T. (2012). The development of entrepreneurial social competence and business network to improve competitive advantage and business performance of small medium sized enterprises: A case study of batik industry in Indonesia. *Procedia - Social and Behavioral Sciences*, *65*, 46–51. doi:10.1016/j.sbspro.2012.11.089

Minniti, M., & Naude, W. (2010). What do we know about the patterns and determinants of female entrepreneurship across countries? *European Journal of Development Research*, *22*(3), 277–293. doi:10.1057/ejdr.2010.17

Mishra, O., Sharma, R., & Agrawal, B. (2020). Facilitating women prosperity with higher purpose at Vyomini. *South Asian Journal of Business and Management Cases*, *9*(2), 198–207. doi:10.1177/2277977920905820

Muntean, S. C., & Ozkazanc-Pan, B. (2016). Feminist perspectives on social entrepreneurship: Critique and new directions. *International Journal of Gender and Entrepreneurship*, *8*(3), 221–241. doi:10.1108/IJGE-10-2014-0034

Muravyev, A., Talavera, O., & Schäfer, D. (2009). Entrepreneurs' gender and financial constraints: Evidence from international data. *Journal of Comparative Economics*, *37*(2), 270–286. doi:10.1016/j.jce.2008.12.001

Nga, J. K. H., & Shamuganathan, G. (2010). The influence of personality traits and demographic factors on social entrepreneurship start up intentions. *Journal of Business Ethics*, *95*(2), 259–282. doi:10.100710551-009-0358-8

Nicolás, C., & Rubio, A. (2016). Social enterprise: Gender gap and economic development. *European Journal of Management and Business Economics*, *25*(2), 56–62. doi:10.1016/j.redeen.2015.11.001

Noguera, M., Alvarez, C., Ribeiro, D., & Urbano, D. (2013). Sociocultural factors and female entrepreneurship in the innovative service sector in Catalonia: A qualitative analysis. In J. J. M. Ferreira, M. Raposo, R. Rutten, & A. Varga (Eds.), *Cooperation, Clusters, and Knowledge Transfer, Advances in Spatial Science* (Vol. 79, pp. 141–162). Springer Berlin., doi:10.1007/978-3-642-33194-7_8

Pareja-Cano, B., Valor, C., & Benito, A. (2020). How social enterprises nurture empowerment: A grounded theoretical model of social change. *Journal of Social Entrepreneurship*, 1–21. doi:10.1080/19420676.2020.1821753

Perekrestova, V. (2022). Normative coherence through social entrepreneurship: Fostering women's empowerment in Myanmar. *Development Policy Review*, *40*(S1), e12627. doi:10.1111/dpr.12627

Rahman, R. S. A. R. A., Kutty, F. M., & Othman, N. (2019). Gender and family background as antecedents on the social entrepreneurial strategic domain of university students. *International Journal of Innovation. Creativity and Change*, *7*(6), 336–346.

Riedo, V., Kraiczy, N. D., & Hack, A. (2019). Applying person-environment fit theory to identify personality differences between prospective social and commercial entrepreneurs: An explorative study. *Journal of Small Business Management*, *57*(3), 989–1007. doi:10.1111/jsbm.12377

Risman, B. J. (2004). Gender as a social structure: Theory wrestling with activism. *Gender & Society*, *18*(4), 429–450. doi:10.1177/0891243204265349

Rosca, E., Agarwal, N., & Brem, A. (2020). Women entrepreneurs as agents of change: A comparative analysis of social entrepreneurship processes in emerging markets. *Technological Forecasting and Social Change*, *157*, 120067. doi:10.1016/j.techfore.2020.120067

Ryzin, G. G., Grossman, S., DiPadova-Stocks, L., & Bergrud, E. (2009). Portrait of the social entrepreneur: Statistical evidence from a US panel. *Voluntas*, *20*(2), 129–140. doi:10.100711266-009-9081-4

Samuelsson, P., & Witell, L. (2022). Social entrepreneurs in service: Motivations and types. *Journal of Services Marketing*, *36*(9), 27–40. doi:10.1108/JSM-08-2017-0274

Sharma, S., & Kumar, A. (2021). Can social enterprises create holistic women empowerment? *Journal of Women's Entrepreneurship and Education*, *2021*(3–4), 96–112. doi:10.28934/JWEE21.34.PP96-112

Smollan, R., & Singh, S. (2021). How social entrepreneurs respond to enterprise failure. *Journal of Social Entrepreneurship*, *0*(0), 1–25. doi:10.1080/19420676.2021.1890189

Tan, L. P., Le, A. N. H., & Xuan, L. P. (2020). A systematic literature review on social entrepreneurial intention. *Journal of Social Entrepreneurship*, *11*(3), 241–256. doi:10.1080/19420676.2019.1640770

Terjesen, S., Bosma, N., & Stam, E. (2016). Advancing public policy for high-growth, female, and social entrepreneurs. *Public Administration Review*, *76*(2), 230–239. doi:10.1111/puar.12472

Tiwari, P., Bhat, A. K., & Tikoria, J. (2017). An empirical analysis of the factors affecting social entrepreneurial intentions. *Journal of Global Entrepreneurship Research*, *7*(1), 1–25. doi:10.118640497-017-0067-1

Toma, G. A. (2022). Social entrepreneurship: A conceptual taxonomy. *Journal of Community Positive Practices, 22*(1), 60–76. doi:10.35782/JCPP.2022.1.04

Tripathy, K. K., Paliwal, M., & Singh, A. (2022). Women's social entrepreneurship and livelihood innovation: An exploratory study from India. *Service Business, 16*(4), 863–881. doi:10.100711628-022-00493-w

Voronkova, O., Nikishkin, V., Frolova, I., Matveeva, E., Murzagalina, G., & Kalykova, E. (2019). Importance of the process of teaching the basics of social entrepreneurship for the sustainable development of society. *Entrepreneurship and Sustainability Issues, 7*(2), 1048–1058. doi:10.9770/jesi.2019.7.2(18)

Wang, W. (2022). Toward economic growth and value creation through social entrepreneurship: Modelling the mediating role of innovation. *Frontiers in Psychology, 13*, 914700. doi:10.3389/fpsyg.2022.914700 PMID:35783796

Waqar, A., Jamil, M., Firdause, A., & Fadzil, M. (2020). Comprehensive review of social entrepreneurship: Developing the conceptual framework for describing the phenomenon of social new venture creation. *International Journal of Scientific & Technology Research, 9*(4), 1987–1995.

Weerawardena, J., & Sullivan Mort, G. (2006). Investigating social entrepreneurship: A multidimensional model. *Journal of World Business, 41*(1), 21–35. doi:10.1016/j.jwb.2005.09.001

Yamini, R., Soloveva, D., & Peng, X. (2022). What inspires social entrepreneurship? The role of prosocial motivation, intrinsic motivation, and gender in forming social entrepreneurial intention. *Entrepreneurship Research Journal, 12*(2), 71–105. doi:10.1515/erj-2019-0129

Yang, S., Kher, R., & Newbert, S. L. (2020). What signals matter for social startups? It depends: The influence of gender role congruity on social impact accelerator selection decisions. *Journal of Business Venturing, 35*(2), 105932. doi:10.1016/j.jbusvent.2019.03.001

Zahra, S. A., Gedajlovic, E., Neubaum, D. O., & Shulman, J. M. (2009). A typology of social entrepreneurs: Motives, search processes and ethical challenges. *Journal of Business Venturing, 24*(5), 519–532. doi:10.1016/j.jbusvent.2008.04.007

Zhai, Y., Yang, K., Chen, L., Lin, H., Yu, M., & Jin, R. (2023). Digital entrepreneurship: Global maps and trends of research. *Journal of Business and Industrial Marketing, 38*(3), 637–655. doi:10.1108/JBIM-05-2021-0244

ENDNOTE

1 "The likelihood of female entrepreneurs receiving a bank loan is higher in more financially developed countries while the size of required collateral is lower" (Muravyev et al., 2009, p. 283).

Chapter 4
What Drives the Levels of Digital Entrepreneurial Competencies of University Students?
A Research Roadmap and Preliminary Results

Vladimir M. Simović
Australian University, West Mishref, Kuwait

Ivana S. Domazet
Institute of Economic Sciences, Belgrade, Serbia

ABSTRACT

The purpose of this chapter is to provide a methodological framework for assessing digital entrepreneurial competencies (DEC) of university students and to point out the importance of different socio-demographic, institutional, and contextual factors as drivers of DEC levels. The chapter provides a roadmap for measuring DEC levels of university students along with the detailed corresponding methodology. The preliminary results of the pilot study targeting the first competence area of the corresponding DEC framework (EmDigital) and conducted simultaneously in Kuwait and Serbia are also presented in this chapter, demonstrating the perceived DEC levels and exact DEC levels of university students in two countries. Those results indicate that different factors drive the DEC levels of university students. This is the first research of this kind in academic literature.

INTRODUCTION

Following the strategic documents of the European Union (European Commission, n.d.), creativity, entrepreneurship, learning-to-learn, digital competence and other 21st century skills and competences are emerging as more and more important for innovation, growth, and participation in a digital society

DOI: 10.4018/978-1-6684-7669-7.ch004

and economy (EU Science Hub - European Commission, 2020). The digital competences represent one of eight key competences for lifelong learning as proposed by Reference Framework for lifelong learning (The European Parliament, 2006). The digital competences refer to the confident and critical usage of the full range of the digital technologies for communication, information and basic problem solving in all aspects of life.

Digital entrepreneurial competences (DEC) are a specific variation of general digital competences and entrepreneurial competences. DEC are recognized as critical for the success of digital entrepreneurship by the World Development Report 2016 (Van Welsum, 2016). Digital entrepreneurship is broadly defined as creating new ventures and transforming existing businesses by developing novel digital technologies and/or novel usage of such technologies, (European Commission, 2015). Ngoasong (2017) defines DEC as a set of knowledge and skills required to search and acquire new information, to identify and pursue entrepreneurial opportunities and to innovate. The interest in DEC is driven by the rising importance of digital entrepreneurship which has been viewed as a critical pillar for economic growth, job creation and innovation by many countries including the Member States of the European Union (Zhao & Collier, 2016). Van Welsum, (2016) suggests that critical DEC includes communication skills, the ability to identify new technology enabled business opportunities and the ability to exploit data in regards to big data emergence. One way to acquire the DEC is through formal education (Fayolle & Gailly, 2013) The implementation of the entrepreneurship education in schools, colleges and universities is one of the strategic interventions proposed by European Union's Entrepreneurship 2020 Action Plan. (European Commission, 2020) The students' entrepreneurship is considered as one of the driving forces of the overall social welfare (Scuotto & Morellato, 2013).

The key challenge in regards to DEC is to identify and bridge the gap between the competences the students acquire through the system of formal education and the competences needed in real-life situations. To do so, it is necessary to develop mechanisms for measuring the actual level of DEC the university students acquire during the course of their formal university education. Around 83,33% of higher education institutions (HEI) in Kuwait (both state-owned and private) offer entrepreneurial courses in their curriculums alongside IT (digital) courses. In Serbia this percentage is around 33,47%. According to the UNESCO report (UNESCO, 2021) the total number of students in Kuwait in tertiary education (aged between 18 and 22) is around 213.000 in 2019. Given the fact that the average duration of university education is 4 years, it can be estimated that in one year the number of graduates in Kuwait would be around 53.000. Out of that number, around 83,33% (44,000) of students will be in possession of some level of DEC on their graduation. The data of the Statistical Office of the Republic of Serbia (Republican Bureau of Statistic, 2020) shows that in 2018 the number of HEI graduates in Serbia was around 42.500. It can be estimated that out of that number around 14.000 graduates leave the HEI in Serbia each year in possession of some level of DEC. Based on above estimations it can be assumed that by 2030 the number of these graduates in Kuwait and Serbia would be around 440.000 for Kuwait and around 140.000 for Serbia respectively. No one knows and no one ever tried to measure the level of their DEC and their readiness for the labor market. Simovic & Domazet (2021) propose the creation of the DEC framework and corresponding methodology which can be used for the purpose of measuring the level of DEC the students acquire during their formal university education.

This chapter is providing a roadmap for assessing the DEC levels of university students and the methodology to align with the proposed roadmap, as well as some preliminary results regarding perceived and actual DEC levels of university students in two countries - Kuwait and Serbia.

LITERATURE REVIEW

We live in an extremely interconnected world. Dramatically, the globe has changed throughout time while the most significant changes are brought about by technical advancements, particularly digital technology (Cavallo et al. 2019; Steininger, 2019; Fachrunnisa et al., 2020). The current situation is consistent with the fourth industrial revolution, which has ushered in a new trend - the digital transformation (Ivanovic et al. 2021; Fachrunnisa et al. 2020; Vial, 2019; Domazet 2018). The technology expansion created conditions for the expansion of digital entrepreneurship.

The term digital entrepreneur is characterized as tending to take chances and exhibiting high degrees of independence, self-efficacy, and control (Colombo & Delmastro, 2001; Sebora et al., 2009). Entrepreneurs can develop novel company models that may upend well-established patterns of value creation thanks to the flexibility of digital entrepreneurship processes (Simovic et al. 2022; Henfridsson & Yoo, 2014; Nambisan, 2017; Valacich & Schneider, 2018). However, because of this fluidity, digital entrepreneurs must also construct and develop their business models in an unpredictable and uncertain environment where they must continuously evaluate their model considering developing opportunities and constantly altering threats (Pavlovic et al. 2019; Ojala, 2016).

Complementary to this, Digital entrepreneurship refers to a variety of new opportunities and business models made possible by the widespread use of digital technology and internet infrastructure (Davidson & Vaast, 2010; Martinez Dy et al., 2018; Nambisan, 2017). The concept of digital entrepreneurship goes beyond traditional ideas of entrepreneurship in that it involves a group of players that is continually changing and extremely diversified (Autio et al., 2018). Studies on digital entrepreneurship have identified technology as a transformative force. Due to the ability of digital artifacts to facilitate the decoupling, disintermediation, and generativity of practices, they have become a powerful transformative (Li et al., 2018) and disruptive (Bharadwaj et al., 2013) force in a variety of businesses (Autio et al., 2018; Yoo et al., 2010).

According to several academics, there needs to be more agreement or clarity regarding the goals, characteristics, and limitations of digital entrepreneurship (Davidsson & Gordon, 2009). Subsequently, Dimov (2016) asserts that research and practice sometimes differ. Considering the growing number of research released each year, the body of knowledge on digital entrepreneurship has multiplied significantly. However, there have been few attempts to thoroughly review the prior research on digital entrepreneurship. Consequently, only five systematic evaluations of prior literature on digital entrepreneurship have been found (Steininger, 2019; Zaheer et al., 2019; Secundo et al., 2020; Kimjeon & Davidsson, 2022; Da Fonseca & Campos, 2021).

For instance, the literature on the various functions that information technology can perform to help company operations and value development has been organized by Steininger (2019). Through a literature survey, Zaheer et al. (2019) aimed to determine how traditional perceptions of business processes are changing in the digital age. Additionally, Secundo et al. (2020) systematic 's review focused on the methods used in academic digital entrepreneurship. Concerning the impact of environmental issues and challenges with climate change mitigation on the usage of various technologies in entrepreneurial activities, this has been systematized by Kimjeon & Davidsson (2022). Finally, Da Fonseca & Campos (2021) conducted a thorough review to examine how consumers and digital entrepreneurship interact.

The rapid development of digital technologies has sparked a strong interest among academics in using them for educational purposes, not only in formal settings (Farrokhnia et al., 2019; Hassanzadeh et al., 2016; Heidari et al., 2020; Noroozi et al., 2016, 2018; Seo et al., 2021; Winkler et al., 2021), but also informally, outside the normal classroom settings.

Digital entrepreneurial competences (DEC) represent a specific combination of general digital and entrepreneurial competences (Simovic and Domazet, 2021) and a relatively new area of interest of the academic community, imposed by fast growth of digital entrepreneurship in the world, especially during and after Covid-19 pandemic (Ahrens, 2021). Understanding DEC requires understanding general digital and entrepreneurial competences. One of the eight fundamental competencies is digital competence, which refers to the confident and critical application of a wide range of digital technologies for information, communication, and basic problem-solving in many aspects of life. In the same vein, the European Commission (2006, 2018) defines digital competence as one of the nine key competences that enable citizens to participate actively in society, stating that "digital competence means the safe, critical and responsible use of, and the commitment to, digital technologies for learning, working and for participation in society".

Entrepreneurship is a natural phenomenon in business that has been linked in its broader sense to the progress of any society. Throughout history, this term has always been related to innovation (Prendes-Espinosa, et al, 2021). Understanding the meaning of entrepreneurship is necessary to understand its impact on the development of economies and communities in different ways.

According to Barot (2015) entrepreneurship is defined as "practice begins with action and creation of new organization". Entrepreneurship can also be regarded as "the ability to turn ideas into action through creativity, innovation and risk-taking by planning projects to achieve certain objectives" (European Commission, 2006, P.8)

One of the key questions regarding DEC is whether it is possible to measure the levels of DEC university students acquire during their university education. This chapter provides empirical evidence on the levels of DEC of university students in two countries - Kuwait and Serbia. The research was based on the use of self-assessment and knowledge and ability questions as in the Kluser and Priego (2018). It reveals the data on the association of the DEC levels and different socio-demographic factors of the university students as their drivers.

THE DEC CHALLENGE AND RESEARCH ROADMAP

As stated earlier, university students graduate and enter the labor market in possession of some levels of DEC acquired during university education. The challenge lies in the fact that no one ever tried to develop the methodology and measure the exact levels of DEC students possess at the time they enter labor market, after graduation.

Following the stated challenge, the main objective of this chapter is to provide a roadmap that will help to determine whether the system of formal IT and entrepreneurial education on the university level in Kuwait and Serbia provides the necessary DEC to students which would enable them to start own digital entrepreneurial projects and be a part of startup teams.

To achieve the main objective, the roadmap was specified as follows:

1. Mapping the existing knowledge regarding digital and entrepreneurial competences, by analyzing available competence frameworks, as a basis for the formulation of DEC framework. This step focuses on the analysis of the European digital and entrepreneurial competence frameworks, but

the relevant frameworks from other parts of the world will also be taken into consideration. The following frameworks will be addressed. Digital Competence Framework for citizens - DigComp (Vuorikari et al., 2016) which recognizes 21 digital competences which may be considered critically important in terms of participation in society and economy. e-Competence Framework which provides a reference of 40 digital competences at five proficiency levels which describe the competences, skills and knowledge requirements of the ICT professionals in ICT business (Council of European Professional Informatics Societies, n.d). This framework is relevant for this project because it focuses on workplace digital competences. Besides digital competences related frameworks in Europe, there are other similar initiatives in other parts of the world. During 2019 in Canada a Digital Competence Framework was developed. This framework breaks down digital competence into 12 dimensions (Québec, Ministère de l'Éducation et de l'Enseignement supérieur, 2019). Entrepreneurial skills are also considered as one of the key 8 competences following Reference Framework for lifelong learning, besides digital competences (The European Parliament and of the Council, 2006). To improve entrepreneurial capacity of European citizens and organizations Joint Research Centre (JRC) of the European Commission on behalf of the Directorate General for Employment, Social Affairs and Inclusion (DG EMPL) has created the Entrepreneurship Competence Framework also known as EntreComp (Bacigalupo et al., 2016). Each of the 3 competence areas defined by EntreComp is broken into 5 specific competences making a framework of 15 specific entrepreneurial competences (European Commission, n.d).

2. Formulating the DEC framework. The most ambitious step in this roadmap is to develop a new framework for DEC. To do so, a research team will:
    a. use the existing digital and entrepreneurial competence frameworks,
    b. conduct the analysis of the contemporary academic literature on this subject,
    c. use its own experience in this field and periodical consultations with all interested stakeholders (policymakers in education and science; academic institutions; students' organizations; scientific research organizations; industry (companies).

The only way to measure DEC is to develop a relevant framework as a set of fundamental competence areas.

3. Developing an assessment methodology upon the associated DEC framework The DEC framework will be used to develop a methodology for measuring DEC the students acquire during their formal education at HEI in Kuwait and Serbia. The methodology will later be used for development of an online DEC assessment tool. Similar attempts were made in other countries in regard to general digital competences. In the EU, based on the DigComp framework and corresponding methodology, an online digital competence assessment tool called The Digital Competence Wheel was created (Skov, 2016). The purpose of this tool is to provide an overview of which digital competences exist and how to improve the most relevant digital skills (Martinc, 2018). e-Competence Framework was deployed in Estonia to help build a common language between employers and universities for curriculum development (European Commission, n.d). This framework also has its manifestation in the form of an online tool called e-CF Profiling tool which is used to identify skill gaps between a user-generated profile and one of the 23 ICT professional profiles built in the system (European Commission, n.d).

4. Assessing the level of DEC of the students in Kuwait and Serbia using an online tool created for this purpose The DEC framework and associated methodology will be used to create an online tool which will be used for assessing the DEC of the students who are attending the undergraduate and graduate programs in HEI that offer IT and entrepreneurial education in their curriculum. The online assessment tool will be developed using the best practice of other online competences assessment tools (the Digital Competence Wheel, e-CF Profiling, etc). The subcontractors will be hired to develop the tool based on precise specifications. The tool will collect the data on students' DEC which will be processed to draw valuable conclusions later.
5. Conducting a gap analysis of DEC of the students in Kuwait and Serbia the purpose of gap analysis is to determine whether the system of formal IT and entrepreneurial education on the university level in Kuwait and Serbia provides the necessary DEC to students which would enable them to start their digital entrepreneurial projects and be a part of startup teams. The gap analysis will cover 2 aspects of DEC of the students in Kuwait and Serbia:
    a. The perceived level of DEC by the students using the self-assessment method.
    b. The actual level of DEC is measured using real-life scenarios and assignments.

The assessment of DEC of the students in Kuwait and Serbia will cover both dimensions using self-assessment and real-life assignments integrated in the associated online assessment tool. The DEC assessment of the students in Kuwait and Serbia will provide valuable data which will be further processed using qualitative and quantitative methods to provide a realistic assessment of the efficiency of the system of formal education in both countries in the area of DEC and policy recommendations for improvements. The analysis will also cover the association of DEC and different external factors (gender, age, education of parents, state/private university, educational profile, the age of the professor, etc.) to determine whether some factors have a greater impact on the level of students DEC than the others.

THE METHODOLOGY TO ALIGN WITH THE ROADMAP

The research methodology is based on the use of the mixed-methods approach. In the initial phase a comprehensive review of the academic and gray literature as well as an in-depth analysis of case studies should be conducted to identify all necessary methodological data which will be used in combination with Digital Competence Framework, e-Competence Framework and Entrepreneurship Competence Framework for the development of a draft proposal of the DEC assessment methodology.

In the second phase of the research, a draft proposal needs to be validated, using a smaller sample of students in Kuwait and Serbia to identify possible bottlenecks before officially being used for assessing the DEC of the students in both countries. The validation of DEC methodology will be based on the experiment. As per (Litt, 2013), experiments provide the most precise and reliable measure of the level of an individual's competences. The following specifications of this experimental study apply:

λ Target group: University students, (Final year and Master)
λ Target area: Kuwait and Serbia
λ Sampling: Probability Sampling
λ Data Collection: IT Lab Experiment
λ Experiment length: 60-75 min

λ Sample size: 40 respondents from 2 countries (Kuwait and Serbia).

The experiment should represent small-scale in-person testing of the methodology which will be used for larger-scale testing using an online assessment tool, at a later stage. The experiment should integrate two assessment mechanisms: self-assessment tools and real-life scenarios in the form of practical assignments as in the case of Van Deursen and Van Dijk (2009). Self-assessment tools should evaluate the DEC of the students using four estimation levels as proposed by Kuzminska et al. (2019): foundation, intermediate, advanced, and highly specialized. Four-point Likert scale should be used for this purpose as in the case of Lopez-Meneses et al. (2020). Real-life scenarios should be based on practical assignments designed to measure specific types of DEC: digital literacy, communication, and collaboration, problem-solving, data security, business plan development, risk management, financial literacy, business opportunities identification, etc.

In the third phase of the research, after a revision following experimental results conducted on a smaller sample of students, a final version of the DEC assessment methodology should be used to develop an online tool to assess the level of DEC students in Kuwait and Serbia.

The fourth research phase should include a larger sample of respondents to gather more data on DEC of the students in Kuwait and Serbia. The following specifications of this survey apply:

λ Target group: University students, (Final year and Master)
λ Target area: Kuwait and Serbia
λ Sampling: Non-probability Sampling
λ Data Collection: Online survey
λ Survey length: 45 - 60 min
λ Sample size: 1.000 respondents from 2 countries (Kuwait and Serbia).

The students should be given access to an online assessment tool and the assessment of their DEC should be conducted using the same concept of self-assessment tools and real-life scenarios as in the previous stage. Students' participation in this survey should be ensured using pre-arranged visits to HEI from a sample, during which the members of the project team will present the project and DEC assessment tool. The events will be organized in IT classrooms of the participating HEI and the students who attend those events will be instantly involved in a survey using the DEC assessment tool. Other students should receive the relevant project information (including video tutorial for the use of DEC assessment tool) and link to online tools via email, through the academic service of their universities.

In the final phase of the research, the data regarding students' DEC assessment should be processed. A combination of qualitative and quantitative methods should be used to process the data and make valid conclusions and recommendations. The analysis of the data collected using an online DEC assessment tool should be conducted using two sets of statistical methods. At the first stage, the methods of multivariate analysis should be used to determine associations between the core DEC and relevant predictors and control variables, such as main socio-demographic variables (gender; age; education of parents, etc.), contextual variables (region; year of study; private/state university, etc.), characteristics of courses (educational profile: economy, management, organization, engineering, science; characteristics of teaching staff: gender, age of professor, etc.). The data should be collected in a cross-sectional framework due to final-year students will be targeted and the survey is anonymous. The point of applying the appropriate statistical technique is to assess the efficacy of the educational program in providing students with

DEC that will help build the comparative advantages and would increase employment chances of young graduates on the one hand or would be persuasive in choosing the entrepreneurial career on the other.

In that respect, at least several types (groups) of DEC should be recognized: starting with the basic (core) one which will be followed with more advanced competences. Using the framework of structural equation modeling (SEM), both the confirmatory factor analysis and the explanatory factor analysis should be conducted to validate the applied measurement scales and confirm the exact number of factors (Anderson & Gerbing, 1988). The set of variables that should be included in the analysis includes different measurement scales. The self-assessment of the competences will be ranked on a four-point Likert scale like in Kuzminska et al. (2019), while other control variables will include the nominal scale of evaluation (personal data) or categorical scale (binomial or multinomial) for characteristics of educational programs, gender, region and alike.

In the following step, the principal component analysis (PCA) could be used to extract the factors (Kovačić, 1994). In statistical software that will be used for data analysis, for example, the Kaiser-Guttman rule could be applied to select the exact number of factors with eigenvalues greater than one. Goodness-of-fit indices should be undertaken for testing the specified measurement model. After acceptable empirical test values, the variables for further analysis should be calculated as unweighted arithmetic means of respective item scores.

In the second step the linear probability and multiple response regression models should be employed. The dependent variables should be constructed using grades associated with each competence or if the data are grouped with the group of competences (DEC; core / more advanced). Predictor variables should be chosen from a pool representing students' personal characteristics, contextual variables, and characteristics of courses. Appropriate goodness-of-fit statistics should be conducted to test for adequacy of constructed models. These models should be estimated so that the more reliable predictors of the current state of student competences could be evaluated. Not only single predictors should be examined, but also the interaction terms should be constructed (using, for example, gender of students of teachers in interaction with the other predictors) that will moderate the effects of single factors and help to understand better what causes the current level of student self-assessment of competences. Also, potential gaps between the theoretical knowledge (students' self-assessment based on the survey questionnaire) and the practical one should be estimated.

Using the same set of predictors, the difference in the level of competences should be tested by using a battery of statistical tests (for example, Chi-square or Student t-test). Also, a Chow-test could be applied for testing structural differences in the estimates of parameters (Chow, 1960). Furthermore, to provide policy-oriented recommendations it would be useful to see whether there are differences among the supply of the educational programs that offer courses for the advancement of DEC as well as are those differences associated with the ownership status of HEI or educational profile of the studies. The transdisciplinary of this research lies in the fact that it combines the elements of IT (digital competences) with entrepreneurship (entrepreneurial competences) and general education (general competences).

PRELIMINARY FINDINGS

The methodology specified in the previous section of this chapter was used to obtain some preliminary results regarding DEC levels of university students. The DEC framework needed for the development of the relevant DEC methodology and corresponding assessment tool was not developed from the scratch because, due to the rising interest of the research community in digital entrepreneurship and relevant competences, in early 2021 a team of Spanish scientists (Prendes-Espinosa et al.2021) published an article in which they have developed a DEC framework they have called EmDigital. The framework was based on digital competence framework DigComp and the entrepreneurship competence framework EntreComp. EmDigital framework is broken into 4 competence areas and 15 specific competences as shown in Table 1.

Based on the EmDigital framework the assessment tool was developed to identify the levels of DEC perceptions on one side, as well as actual DEC levels of the university students in Kuwait and Serbia, on the other side. The questionnaire had 12 questions for DEC levels of self-assessment and 12 questions for knowledge and ability assessment.

Table 1. Competence areas and specific competences of EmDigital

Competence area	Specific Competence
Identification of opportunities	Search of and analysis of information Creativity and innovation Prospecting
Action planning	Success orientation Leadership Planning and management of digital identity
Initiative and collaboration	Initiative Communication and collaboration Creation of digital value Responsibility and commitment
Management and safety	Learning from experience Problem solving Planning and organization Techno-ethical approach Motivation and perseverance

Source: Prendes-Espinosa et al. 2021

The research was conducted between June 2021 and January 2022 on a sample of 1490 students in both countries. Since the ultimate goal of this research is the development of online DEC assessment tool for the entire EmDigital framework, in this phase, a pilot study was conducted for the first EmDigital competence area - Identification of opportunities.

Table 2. Student's perceptions of the DEC levels for the first competence area of EmDigital (SEQ1-SEQ6)

Questions		SEQ1	SEQ2	SEQ3	SEQ4	SEQ5	SEQ6
Mean		3.23	3.32	2.97	2.83	2.74	2.86
		(0.018)	(0.017)	(0.021)	(0.023)	(0.025)	(0.024)
95% Confidence Interval for Mean	Lower Bound	3.19	3.29	2.93	2.79	2.69	2.81
	Upper Bound	3.26	3.35	3.01	2.88	2.79	2.91
Std. Deviation		0.68	0.64	0.81	0.89	0.95	0.94
Skewness		-0.70	-0.56	-0.61	-0.36	-0.30	-0.30
		(0.063)	(0.063)	(0.063)	(0.063)	(0.063)	(0.063)
Kurtosis		0.84	0.11	0.05	-0.60	-0.83	-0.93
		(0.127)	(0.127)	(0.127)	(0.127)	(0.127)	(0.127)

Source: Authors

The results of the student's perceptions (self-assessment) for the first competence area of EmDigital (Identification of opportunities) are presented in Table 2 and Table 3.

Table 3. Student's perceptions of the DEC levels for the first competence area of EmDigital (SEQ7-SEQ12)

		SEQ7	SEQ8	SEQ9	SEQ10	SEQ11	SEQ12
Mean		3.07	2.96	2.97	3.14	2.72	2.99
		(0.022)	(0.022)	(0.022)	(0.021)	(0.023)	(0.021)
95% Confidence Interval for Mean	Lower Bound	3.03	2.92	2.92	3.10	2.67	2.95
	Upper Bound	3.12	3.00	3.01	3.18	2.76	3.03
Std. Deviation		0.86	0.85	0.84	0.81	0.88	0.82
Skewness		-0.59	-0.58	-0.48	-0.64	-0.18	-0.58
		(0.063)	(0.063)	(0.063)	(0.063)	(0.063)	(0.063)
Kurtosis		-0.45	-0.19	-0.36	-0.24	-0.71	-0.05
		(0.127)	(0.127)	(0.127)	(0.127)	(0.127)	(0.127)

Source: Authors

The results indicate that university students perceive the highest levels of DEC under the sub-competence area Search for and analysis of information (SEQ1 and SEQ2). The differences in the values of perceived DEC for the first competence area Identification of opportunities indicate that different socio-demographic, institutional and contextual factors have an impact on the university student's perception of the acquired DEC. Those factors will drive the perception of DEC of university students.

The data in Table 4 show the exact levels of university students DEC under the first competence area of EmDigital - Identification of opportunities. As explained earlier, a set of 12 knowledge and ability questions for developed for this purpose.

Table 4. Levels of university students DEC under the first competence area of EmDigital- Identification of opportunities

Question	Answer	Full Sample	Question	Answer	Full Sample
EQ1	FALSE	70.5	EQ7	FALSE	70.5
	TRUE	29.5		TRUE	29.5
EQ2	FALSE	59.1	EQ8	FALSE	51.7
	TRUE	40.9		TRUE	48.3
EQ3	FALSE	71.1	EQ9	FALSE	70.5
	TRUE	28.9		TRUE	29.5
EQ4	FALSE	50.3	EQ10	FALSE	49.7
	TRUE	49.7		TRUE	50.3
EQ5	FALSE	55.0	EQ11	FALSE	91.9
	TRUE	45.0		TRUE	8.1
EQ6	FALSE	85.9	EQ12	FALSE	60.4
	TRUE	14.1		TRUE	39.6
Mean	FALSE		65.5		
	TRUE		34.5		
St. deviation	FALSE		13.7		
	TRUE		13.7		
MIN	FALSE		49.7		
	TRUE		8.1		
MAX	FALSE		91.9		
	TRUE		50.3		
MAX/MIN	FALSE		1.85		
	TRUE		6.21		

Source: Authors

The results of the knowledge and ability assessment of the university students regarding levels of their DEC, presented in Table 4, indicate that on average, university students showed a low level of DEC for the first competence area of EmDigital. The students answered correctly every third knowledge and ability question. The fact that there are differences in the proportion of correct answers for different sub-competence areas indicates that different socio-demographic, institutional and contextual factors would also drive the university students' actual levels of DEC.

RECOMMENDATIONS AND FUTURE RESEARCH DIRECTIONS

The summary of the research roadmap and relevant methodology presented in this chapter represents a way for universities worldwide to measure the effectiveness of their educational efforts regarding DEC. A similar approach, with some methodological adjustments, can be used for any other competence area as well.

The preliminary results of DEC assessment presented in this chapter reveal the importance of different socio-demographic, institutional and contextual factors as drivers of university students' perception and actual levels of acquired DEC. Any future research should investigate in more detail the impact of various factors on the levels of students' perceptions regarding DEC and the levels of their actual knowledge and acquired levels of DEC. Understanding better the impact of various external factors on the perception and the actual levels of university students DEC creates the opportunity for the universities to adjust their syllabuses and learning objectives to individual students and their preferences and abilities. The more personalized approach to educating students leads to more competent students ready for the contemporary labor market.

CONCLUSION

The main purpose of this chapter was to provide a roadmap for assessing university students' DEC as one of the core competencies for the contemporary labor market.

Different competence frameworks (DigComp, e-Competence Framework, Digital Competence Framework, EntreComp) cover different aspects of general digital and entrepreneurial competences as addressed in the introductory and literature review parts of this chapter. This chapter systematized the current knowledge in the area of general digital and entrepreneurial competences and use the existing competence frameworks to provide a proposal for the new DEC framework.

Competence frameworks all have corresponding methodologies which are used for different kinds of assessments. In case of DigComp, the methodology which included 54 measurable aspects of digital competences that substantiate 16 competences under four main competence areas was developed based on this framework. No DEC methodology exists up to date. The existing digital competencies assessment methodologies are focused on digital competences in general and/or entrepreneurial competences. This chapter proposed a more specific approach and provided an advance in terms of developing a methodology focused on the DEC of university students. The corresponding DEC framework will serve as a basis for DEC methodology development.

Competence assessment tools based on relevant frameworks and methodologies are used in various research. This chapter showed no evidence on research focused on measuring the level of DEC the students acquire during their formal education. One of the main conclusions of this chapter is that an online DEC assessment tool which will be based on DEC framework and corresponding methodology should be developed to enable, for the first time, empirical assessment of university students' DEC and to provide the data on the levels of DEC the students acquire during their formal university education. Besides DEC tool development and university students' DEC assessment, this research should provide evidence on the association of different levels of DEC of university students and socio-demographic and contextual factors.

ACKNOWLEDGMENT

This chapter is supported by Australian University, Kuwait under internal seed grant No. IRC-2020/2021-SOB-MARKETING-PR11, by Kuwait Foundation for the Advancements of Sciences (KFAS) under grant No.CN21-18IQ-1382 and the Ministry of Education, Science and Technological Development of the Republic of Serbia.

REFERENCES

Ahrens, A., Bhati, P. P., Zascerinska, J., Zascerinskis, M., Aleksejeva, A., & Abjalkiene, I. (2021). Engineering Master Students' Views on Digital Entrepreneurship in a Host European Country. In *Environment. Technologies. Resources: Proceedings of the International Scientific and Practical Conference* (Vol. 2, pp. 225-231). Research Gate.

Anderson, J. C., & Gerbing, D. W. (1988). Structural equation modeling in practice: A review and recommended two-step approach. *Psychological Bulletin, 103*(3), 411–423. doi:10.1037/0033-2909.103.3.411

Autio, E., Nambisan, S., Thomas, L. D., & Wright, M. (2018). Digital affordances, spatial affordances, and the genesis of entrepreneurial ecosystems. *Strategic Entrepreneurship Journal, 12*(1), 72–95. doi:10.1002ej.1266

Bacigalupo, M., Kampylis, P., Punie, Y., & Van den Brande, G. (2016). *EntreComp: The Entrepreneurship Competence Framework*. Publication Office of the European Union. doi:10.2791/593884

Barot, H. (2015, January). Entrepreneurship - A Key to Success. *International Journal of Business and Management, 3*(1), 163–165.

Bharadwaj, A., Sawy, O. A. E., Pavlou, P. A., & Venkatraman, N. (2013). Digital business strategy: Toward a next generation of insights. *Management Information Systems Quarterly, 37*(2), 471–482. doi:10.25300/MISQ/2013/37:2.3

Cavallo, A., Ghezzi, A., Dell'Era, C., & Pellizzoni, E. (2019). Fostering digital entrepreneurship from startup to scaleup: The role of venture capital funds and angel groups. *Technological Forecasting and Social Change, 145*, 24–35. doi:10.1016/j.techfore.2019.04.022

Colombo, M. G., & Delmastro, M. (2001). Technology-based entrepreneurs: Does the internet make a difference? *Small Business Economics, 16*(3), 177–190. doi:10.1023/A:1011127205758

Council of European Professional Informatics Societies (CEPIS). (n.d.). *Terms of Reference for the Information Society Group*. CEPIS. https://cepis.org/app/uploads/2020/01/13.TermsofReferencefor InformationSocietyGroup1-1.pdf

Da Fonseca, A. L. A., & Campos, R. D. (2021). The cultural intertwining of consumption and entrepreneurship: A selective review of qualitative studies. *Journal of Business Research, 135*, 149–162. doi:10.1016/j.jbusres.2021.06.032

Davidson, E., & Vaast, E. (2010). Digital entrepreneurship and its socio-material enactment. In *43rd Hawaii International Conference on System Sciences* (pp. 1–10). IEEE.

Dimov, D. (2016). Toward a design science of entrepreneurship. In *Models of start-up thinking and action: Theoretical, empirical, and pedagogical approaches* (Vol. 18, pp. 1–31). Emerald Group Publishing Limited.

Domazet, I. (2018). Improving competitiveness and economic development through FDI. In *Developmental State and Millennium Development Goals: country experiences* (pp. 169–189). World Scientific Publishing Co. doi:10.1142/9789813235281_0008

Enterprises. (2023). A report of the Strategic Policy Forum on Digital Entrepreneurship. *Europea.* http://ec.europa.eu/DocsRoom/documents/9462/attachments/1/translations/en/renditions/native

EU Science Hub - European Commission. (2020). *Learning And Skills for The Digital Era.* EC. https://ec.europa.eu/jrc/en/research-topic/learning-and-skills

European Commission. (2020). *The Entrepreneurship 2020 Action Plan - Internal Market, Industry, Entrepreneurship and SMEs.* EC. https://ec.europa.eu/growth/smes/promoting-entrepreneurship/action-plan_en

European Commission. (2015). *Digital Transformation of European Industry and European Commission.* EC.

Fachrunnisa, O., Adhiatma, A., Lukman, N., & Ab Majid, M. N. (2020). Towards SMEs' digital transformation: The role of agile leadership and strategic flexibility. *Journal of Small Business Strategy, 30*(3), 65–85. https://libjournals.mtsu.edu/index.php/jsbs/article/view/1610

Farrokhnia, M., Pijeira-Díaz, H. J., Noroozi, O., & Hatami, J. (2019). Computer-supported collaborative concept mapping: The effects of different instructional designs on conceptual understanding and knowledge co-construction. *Computers & Education, 142*, 103640. doi:10.1016/j.compedu.2019.103640

Fayolle, A., & Gailly, B. (2013). The Impact of Entrepreneurship Education on Entrepreneurial Attitudes and Intention: Hysteresis and Persistence. *Journal of Small Business Management, 53*(1), 75–93. doi:10.1111/jsbm.12065

Hassanzadeh, M., Hatami, J., Latifi, S., Farrokhnia, M. R., & Saheb, T. (2016, September). Teaching science for understanding: The positive impact of simultaneous concept mapping and computer simulations. In *International Conference on Concept Mapping* (pp. 192-202). Springer, Cham.10.1007/978-3-319-45501-3_15

Heidari, E., Salimi, G., & Mehrvarz, M. (2020). The influence of online social networks and online social capital on constructing a new graduate students' professional identity. *Interactive Learning Environments*, 1–18. doi:10.1080/10494820.2020.1769682

Henfridsson, O., & Yoo, Y. (2014). The liminality of trajectory shifts in institutional entrepreneurship. *Organization Science, 25*(3), 932–950. doi:10.1287/orsc.2013.0883

Ivanovic, Dj., Simovic, V., Domazet, I., & Antonijević, M. (2021). Average Matching Levels for Two DigComp Competence Areas of the Female Entrepreneurs in Serbia. *Journal of Women's Entrepreneurship and Education., 3-4*, 42–60.

Kimjeon, J., & Davidsson, P. (2022). External enablers of entrepreneurship: A review and agenda for accumulation of strategically actionable knowledge. *Entrepreneurship Theory and Practice, 46*(3), 643–687. doi:10.1177/10422587211010673

Kluzer, S., & Pujol Priego, L. (2018). DigComp into Action - Get inspired, make it happen. S. In: Carretero, Y. Punie, R. Vuorikari, M. Cabrera, and O'Keefe, W. (Eds.). JRC Science for Policy Report, EUR 29115 EN. Publications Office of the European Union. doi:10.2760/112945

Kovačić, Z. (1994). *Multivarijaciona analiza*. Beograd: Ekonomski fakultet

Kuzminska, O., Mazorchuk, M., Morze, N., Pavlenko, V., & Prohorov, A. (2019). Study of Digital Competence of the Students and Teachers in Ukraine. *14th International Conference, ICTERI 2018*, Kyiv, Ukraine. 10.1007/978-3-030-13929-2_8

Li, L., Su, F., Zhang, W., & Mao, J. Y. (2018). Digital transformation by SME entrepreneurs: A capability perspective. *Information Systems Journal, 28*(6), 1129–1157. doi:10.1111/isj.12153

Litt, E. (2013). Measuring users' internet skills: A review of past assessments and a look toward the future. *New Media & Society, 15*(4), 612–630. doi:10.1177/1461444813475424

López-Meneses, E., Sirignano, F. M., Vázquez-Cano, E., & Ramírez-Hurtado, J. M. (2020). University students' digital competence in three areas of the DigCom 2.1 model: A comparative study at three European universities. *Australasian Journal of Educational Technology*, 69–88. doi:10.14742/ajet.5583

Martinc, M. (2018). *The Digital Competency Wheel*. LearnPatch. https://learnpatch.com/2018/12/the-digital-competencywheel/

Martinez Dy, A., Martin, L., & Marlow, S. (2018). Emancipation through digital entrepreneurship? A critical realist analysis. *Organization, 25*(5), 585–608. doi:10.1177/1350508418777891

Nambisan, S. (2017). Digital entrepreneurship: Toward a digital technology perspective of entrepreneurship. *Entrepreneurship Theory and Practice, 41*(6), 1029–1055. doi:10.1111/etap.12254

Ngoasong, M. Z. (2017). Digital entrepreneurship in a resource-scarce context: A focus on entrepreneurial digital competencies. *Journal of Small Business and Enterprise Development, 25*(3), 483–500. doi:10.1108/JSBED-01-2017-0014

Noroozi, O., Biemans, H., & Mulder, M. (2016). Relations between scripted online peer feedback processes and quality of the written argumentative essay. *The Internet and Higher Education, 31*, 20–31. doi:10.1016/j.iheduc.2016.05.002

Ojala, A. (2016). Business models and opportunity creation: How IT entrepreneurs create and develop business models under uncertainty. *Information Systems Journal, 26*(5), 451–476. doi:10.1111/isj.12078

Pavlović, D., Bjelica, D., & Domazet, I. (2019). What Characteristics in the Youth Labor Market of Serbia Are Likely to Result in Employment? *Stanovnistvo, 57*(2), 35–47. doi:10.2298/STNV190823006P

Prendes-Espinosa, P., Solano-Fernández, I. M., & García-Tudela, P. A. (2021). EmDigital to promote digital entrepreneurship: The relation with open innovation. *Journal of Open Innovation*, *7*(1), 63. doi:10.3390/joitmc7010063

Québec Ministère de l'Éducation et de l'Enseignement supérieur, (2019). *Digital Competency Framework*. Québec Ministère de l'Éducation et de l'Enseignement. http://www.education.gouv.qc.ca/fileadmin/site_web/documents /ministere/Cadre-reference-competence-num-AN.pdf

Republic Bureau of Statistics (2020). Sta*tistical Release. Statistics of social activities, Serbia, Number 166*. RBS.

Scuotto, V., & Morellato, M. (2013). Entrepreneurial Knowledge and Digital Competence: Journal of the Knowledge Economy, 4(3), 293-303. Springer. doi:10.100713132-013-0155-6

Sebora, T. C., Lee, S. M., & Sukasame, N. (2009). Critical success factors for e-commerce entrepreneurship: An empirical study of Thailand. *Small Business Economics*, *32*(3), 303–316. doi:10.100711187-007-9091-9

Secundo, G., Rippa, P., & Cerchione, R. (2020). Digital Academic Entrepreneurship: A structured literature review and avenue for a research agenda. *Technological Forecasting and Social Change*, *157*, 120118. doi:10.1016/j.techfore.2020.120118

Seo, K., Dodson, S., Harandi, N. M., Roberson, N., Fels, S., & Roll, I. (2021). Active learning with online video: The impact of learning context on engagement. *Computers & Education*, *165*, 104132. doi:10.1016/j.compedu.2021.104132

Simović, V., et al., (2022) Identification of Opportunities as the Component of Digital Entrepreneurial Competences of University Students: A pilot study in Kuwait and Serbia. In: *ICEEG 2022: 2022 6th International Conference on E-Commerce, E-Business and E-Government*. Association for Computing Machinery. 10.1145/3537693.3537724

Simović, V., & Domazet, I. (2021). An overview of the frameworks for measuring the digital competences of college students: A European perspective. In T. Neimann (ed.) Stagnancy Issues and Change Initiatives for Global Education in the Digital Age. IGI Global Publishing House. doi:10.4018/978-1-7998-4993-3.ch012

Skov, A. (2016). The Digital Competence Wheel. *Digital Competence*. https://digital-competence.eu/.

Steininger, D. M. (2019). Linking information systems and entrepreneurship: A review and agenda for IT-associated and digital entrepreneurship research. *Information Systems Journal*, *29*(2), 363–407. doi:10.1111/isj.12206

The European Parliament. (2006). Recommendation of the European Parliament and of the Council. EP. https://eur-lex.europa.eu/legal-content/EN/TXT/?uri=celex%3A 32006H0962.

UNESCO Sustainable Development Goals. (n/d). *Sustainable Goals.* UNESCO. http://uis.unesco.org/en/country/kw#slideoutmenu Accessed on November 23, 2022.

Valacich, J., & Schneider, C. (2018). *Information systems today: Managing in the digital world* (8th ed.). Pearson.

Van Deursen, A., & van Dijk, J. (2009). Improving digital skills for the use of online public information and services. *Government Information Quarterly*, *26*(2), 333–340. doi:10.1016/j.giq.2008.11.002

Van Welsum, D. (2016). *Enabling Digital Entrepreneurs.* World Bank Group. doi:10.1596/23646

Vial, G. (2021). Understanding digital transformation: A review and a research agenda. *Managing Digital Transformation*, 13-66. doi:10.1016/j.jsis.2019.01.003

Vuorikari, R., Punie, Y., Carretero Gomez S., & Van den Brande, G. (2016). *DigComp 2.0: The Digital Competence Framework for Citizens. Update Phase 1: The Conceptual Reference Model.* Luxembourg Publication Office of the European Union. doi:. doi:10.2791/11517

Winkler, R., Söllner, M., & Leimeister, J. M. (2021). Enhancing problem-solving skills with smart personal assistant technology. *Computers & Education*, *165*, 104148. doi:10.1016/j.compedu.2021.104148

Yoo, Y., Henfridsson, O., & Lyytinen, K. (2010). Research commentary—The new organizing logic of digital innovation: An agenda for information systems research. *Information Systems Research*, *21*(4), 724–735. doi:10.1287/isre.1100.0322

Zaheer, H., Breyer, Y., & Dumay, J. (2019). Digital entrepreneurship: An interdisciplinary structured literature review and research agenda. *Technological Forecasting and Social Change*, *148*, 119735. doi:10.1016/j.techfore.2019.119735

Zhao, F., & Collier, A. (2016). *Digital Entrepreneurship: Research and Practice.* In the 9th Annual Conference of the EuroMed Academy of Business, Warsaw, Poland.

ADDITIONAL READING

Allen, J. (2019). *Digital Entrepreneurship* (1st ed.). Routledge. doi:10.4324/9780429506567

Bartolomé, J., Garaizar, P., & Larrucea, X. (2022). A pragmatic approach for evaluating and accrediting digital competence of digital profiles: A case study of entrepreneurs and remote workers. *Technology, Knowledge, and Learning*, *27*(3), 843–878. doi:10.100710758-021-09516-3

Ferreras-Garcia, R., Sales-Zaguirre, J., & Serradell-López, E. (2021a). Developing entrepreneurial competencies in higher education: A structural model approach. *Education + Training*, *63*(5), 720–743. doi:10.1108/ET-09-2020-0257

Kruger, S., & Steyn, A. A. (2021). A conceptual model of entrepreneurial competencies needed to utilize technologies of Industry 4.0. *International Journal of Entrepreneurship and Innovation*, *22*(1), 56–67. doi:10.1177/1465750320927359

Nasiri, N., & Hamelin, N. (2018). Entrepreneurship driven by opportunity and necessity: Effects of educations, gender, and occupation in MENA. *Asian Journal of Business Research*, *8*(2), 57–71. doi:10.14707/ajbr.180049

KEY TERMS AND DEFINITIONS

Competence: A combination of knowledge, skills, and attitudes in various life situations.

Competence Assessment Tool: An online tool for self-assessment and knowledge and ability assessment of the relevant competence

Digital Competence: The confident and critical usage of digital technologies for communication, information and basic problem-solving in all aspects of life.

Digital Entrepreneurial Competence: A specific combination of knowledge, skills, and attitudes needed for starting a digital entrepreneurial project.

Entrepreneurial Competencies: A series of skills enabling an individual to enhance a concept, idea, or product, take risks, and demonstrate initiative and leadership in order to complete a project.

Knowledge: The 'set of know-what' (e.g., programming languages, design tools, etc.) and can be described by operational descriptions.

Skills: The 'ability to carry out managerial or technical tasks' – which are components of competences and specify some core abilities that form a competence.

Chapter 5
Women's Entrepreneurship as a Driver of Diversity Management in Italian Businesses

Fabio Greco
University Federico II of Naples, Italy

Francesco Carignani
University Federico II of Naples, Italy

Gesualda Iodice
University Federico II of Naples, Italy

Francesco Bifulco
University of Naples Federico II, Italy

ABSTRACT

Two phenomena are described in this chapter. The inclusion of women in executive and administrative positions is, on the one hand, a crucial problem in diversity management. On the other side, there are more and more successful female business owners. Therefore, the main research issue guiding this work is whether female entrepreneurs' success stories might encourage the hiring of more female managers in organizations. The authors apply a qualitative technique based on several case studies that have been used in prior research on entrepreneurs. Five case studies of successful female entrepreneurs were chosen in order to create study findings with management and theoretical implications.

INTRODUCTION

Women currently make up over half of the workforce, but their representation in decision-making and managerial roles remains limited. This is referred to in economic literature as the "glass ceiling" (Powell, 1999; Cotter et al., 2001; Adams, 2012). The metaphor alludes to all the hurdles created by economic, societal, and cultural issues, as well as prejudice, that prohibit women from advancing in their careers.

DOI: 10.4018/978-1-6684-7669-7.ch005

To overcome the glass ceiling, numerous European nations have passed legislation requiring quotas for the number of women on corporate boards. Some studies on diversity management focused on the gender issue, demonstrating how diversity management is a priority for companies, but how it is often insufficient if not accompanied by correct communication of what employees' perceptions of diversity management are, embracing a holistic perspective (Martins & Parsons, 2007), where entrepreneurial identity cannot be separated from social contexts such as macro-cultural, institutional, national, and international (Karatas, 2017). At the same time, researchers emphasize the need to see unique subjects as distinct identities (Gagnon et al., 2021).

In Italy, only 28% of managers are female. In the third quarter of 2020, Italy was fifth last in the ranking of Member States by percentage of female managers. Even at European level, female managers remain a minority, with only 3.3 million women against 6.2 million men, even though women represent almost half of all employed people in the EU (46%). Indeed, in Europe 36% of managers, 27% of board members, and 17% of senior executives are women (Eurostat, 2021).

In this chapter, two phenomena are discussed. On the one hand, a major issue in diversity management is the inclusion of women in executive and managerial jobs (Barak et al. 2015; Ozturk & Tatli, 2016; Francis et al. 2021). On the other hand, the number of successful female entrepreneurs is increasing (Reavley et al., 2008; Quader, 2012). So, the research question driving this work is: can the examples of female entrepreneurs influence the inclusion of a greater number of female managers in organisations? The authors adopt a qualitative methodology based on multiple case studies (Kantur & İşeri-Say, 2013; Yin, 2009; Omar, 2015) used in other studies on entrepreneurship. Five successful female entrepreneurship case studies were chosen to produce research findings that could be used to derive managerial and theoretical implications.

Figure 1. Managers in the EU
(Eurostat, 2020)

Diversity Management and Women Entrepreneurs

Studies on diversity management have developed since the 90s, in the US context, to analyze racial issues related to workers (Dye & Golnaraghi, 2015). Already at the end of the 90s, however, a different type of approach to diversity management was established, where integration was seen as a resource of added value to decision-making processes and can be particularly useful for interfacing in different markets from its own reference (Gilbert et al., 1999). Since the beginning of the 2000s, therefore, the differences between workers have been seen as something that can generate problems but which, if managed effectively, can bring added value to the company, which can be linked to innovative and creative processes, thus highlighting a close link between these two factors and diversity management (Lambert, 2016). Diversity among workers has therefore been interpreted by numerous recent studies as an important resource to be developed through certain strategies (Shen et al., 2009), and must be seen as a sustainable resource to be used in the market as a competitive advantage (Urbancová et al., 2020). However, to be used as such a resource, some studies show that correct internal communication regarding employees and how they are perceived is essential, thus suggesting the implementation of a holistic perspective (Martins & Parsons, 2007) where the identity of the company cannot ignore the context of the society in which it operates (Karatas, 2017). However, if there is no correct corporate organization at the base, there is a risk that the different skills linked to the differences brought by a diverse workforce are not transformed into resources, meaning they are wasted and diversity management becomes merely policies of inclusion (Roberson, 2006). However, it is important to not focus solely on the processes and policies of diversity management, but also on the entire regulatory and values-related dimensions, elements more closely linked to the cultural changes of a company (Pless & Maak, 2004).

Over the years, the importance of women to a company's entrepreneurial activities has been emphasized (Noguera et al., 2013), yet the position of entrepreneur is still firmly associated with men (Elam, 2019). Economic growth is fundamentally influenced by female entrepreneurship which generates income, employment, and wealth, while also diversifying the entrepreneurial landscape (Nissan et al., 2012). Indeed, the participation of women in entrepreneurial life has an extremely positive impact on a social level, thus leading to widespread well-being (Rouse et al., 2013). The literature has therefore been divided into a strand of topics related to territorial (Yadav & Unni, 2016), cultural (Folberg, 2016), and social factors such as religion (Anggadwita et al., 2015). Another line of studies has instead focused on topics more related to management, with works that have analyzed some female entrepreneurial experiences, outlining the skills and abilities that were found to be common (Manzanera-Román & Brändle, 2016). Stakeholder analyzes were carried out to understand how they influence female entrepreneurship, in particular how it is influenced by public policy, innovation, and development, especially creative (Nair, 2020) and how there are still many barriers for women in their entrepreneurial rise such as the difficulty in finding finance and, in many social contexts, family duties (Tur-Porcar et al., 2017). The problems faced by women entrepreneurs are of an individual nature, in relationships with other single subjects, but at the same time affect the community (Brush et al., 2009). In particular, there are three levels that concern the collective level and on which the studies have mainly focused: gender role expectations and identities, societal cultural dimensions, and the entrepreneurial environment (Bullough et al., 2022). At an educational level, it emerged that careers linked to management are still perceived as a masculine thing, meaning young women would limit their ambitions, feeling they do not have the skills and abilities. Entrepreneurship education can fill these gaps and reduce gender differences in entrepreneurship (Wilson et al., 2007). Recent studies on Covid-19 have shown how it has contributed to solidifying the figure of the female entrepreneur in a scenario where she plays a fundamental role in the dynamics of empowerment in the company in relation to the post-pandemic economic recovery (Kumari & Eguruze, 2022).

The Glass Ceiling in Italian Companies

Over the years, the literature has shown that there is a barrier for females to reach top positions in a company, with strong analyzes focusing on the perception of disparities in the treatment of women at the top of management (Ragins et al., 1998). Above all, it is the beliefs related to an individual's sex that creates a network of extremely binding expectations and interpersonal reactions that underlie what is defined as the "glass ceiling" (Ridgeway, 2001). But it is also interesting to note how the women who manage to reach the top, once they manage to hold high positions in company management, by carrying out the glass escalator, find themselves facing a phenomenon closely connected to the glass ceiling, i.e., the "glass cliff", i.e., being in extremely precarious positions and exposed to continuous risks compared to male counterparts (Ryan & Haslam, 2005). Further studies on the "glass cliff" have highlighted how companies in difficulty tend to choose female candidates for company leadership roles, in contrast to situations of normality where there is an absence of risks, when males are the preferred choice (Haslam & Ryan, 2008). These factors are consequently reflected in the characteristics of male and female subjects in the boardroom: women are more likely to make risky choices than men, who are more likely to make safer, more traditional choices, just as female directors are more benevolent and universally concerned, while men are more oriented towards power (Adams & Funk, 2012). This is probably also the result of a different conception of the path to advancing in the corporate structure, where for men, in general, the quality of performance is fundamental, while for women, the development of specific skills, which they feel they must achieve first to achieve a new role is fundamental (Hartman & Barber, 2020). Regarding the background of board directors, men often come with previous experience on boards with significant roles, while women often come with experience as directors of boards, but with smaller companies (Singh et al., 2018). It has been argued that to break the glass ceiling, women must aim at improving their level of education and actively participate in the company (Adams & Kirchmaier, 2016), meaning they need to demonstrate a higher level of skills than a man to reach the same managerial roles (Eagly & Carli, 2003).

However, other studies have shown how these two factors do not influence the achievement of a position on a board for a woman any more than it is influenced by religious, social, and government dynamics factors, where the most incisive factors are the sector in which the company operates, the geographical area, and the time factor, also showing that greater gender parity by no means guarantees more female directors on boards of directors (Tyrowicz et al., 2020). On this last point, however, other studies differ, arguing that the breaking of the glass ceiling is not given by a higher percentage of women on boards of directors with gender equality laws, but by the increase in the appointment of female figures as independent directors and in monitoring committees (Nekhili et al., 2020). An important factor for breaking the glass ceiling and for reducing the corporate gap between men and women is the presence of mentors or supervisors. Where there are mentors or supervisors, the ascent to top positions is easier for women than for men, and if the mentor or supervisor is a woman, it is easier still (Choi, 2019).

The glass ceiling has also been extensively analyzed in the literature on a geographical basis, with numerous works focusing on the different contexts in European countries (Bridges & Mann, 2019; Loukil et al., 2019; Sułkowski, 2019; Ginalski, 2021; Casado- Díaz et al., 2022), as well as those relating to the rest of the world (Bukstein & Gandelman, 2019; Patterson & Benuyenah, 2021; Zhu, 2022). The Italian context is characterized by the strong presence of SMEs and by the strong characterization of these companies through family-led management: these family SMEs are characterized as places where it is easier to go beyond glass ceilings (Songini & Gnan, 2014). In Italian society, the role of women has long been linked to the management of the house, thus binding them to responsibilities that can negatively affect career ambitions, above all in reaching managerial positions within companies (Scholarios & Taylor, 2011). According to various scholars, the gender gap is also a problem linked to the cultural fabric of society and not only to a mere disparity in the labor market (Baldarelli, 2016; Caporale, 2022;). According to a survey of Gi Group Holding who specialize in the search for and selection of middle and senior management profiles (2022), the demolition of the glass ceiling with the abundant presence of female management seems to be less important (22%) than the development of a broader corporate culture that focuses on welfare and wellbeing (46%). In 2019, according to the ManagerItalia Report on women, the number of women in managerial positions grew from 17.6% in the previous year, but still only represented 32.3% among the under 35s and 28% among the under 40s (Rapporto Donna ManagerItalia, 2021). The glass ceiling in the Italian context, however, is not only an issue within companies, but also involves other bodies and institutions, such as universities (Roberto et al., 2020). Certainly, the period between 2008 and 2015, with the approval of laws regulating gender quotas, marked an important step forward in the Italian context, with a strong increase in the number of women on corporate boards, but it is still necessary that these appointments are made in a genuine manner and not dictated by legal obligations or with the intention of reflecting a specific corporate image externally (Pastore & Tommaso, 2016). The period between 2012 and 2018, during which Italy experienced an important economic crisis, marked a new increase in the economic gap in terms of the compensation of members of top management based on gender, highlighting an increase in the glass ceiling phenomenon (Piazzalunga & Di Tommaso, 2019). Further contributions point out how the Italian context, despite the adoption of specific legal measures, needs more time than other countries for the effects to really have an impact on company management, beyond the legal obligations, given the conservative views on gender in Italian society (Maida & Weber, 2022).

Practical Evidence

This work fits into the conceptual framework outlined by the presence of women in managerial positions. This strand is closely related to the balances and imbalances that occur in response to the symmetries and asymmetries of knowledge and skills with respect to the inclusion and acceptance of gender diversity in the workplace.

As evidenced by the literary survey provided upstream of the survey, diversity management is an essential managerial tool for promoting competitiveness and creating a sustainable competitive advantage for businesses. The inclusion of gender equality in companies, in fact, is expressed in the creation of social and psychophysical welfare of workers involved in the process of creating business value, which is reflected in the external image transmitted by the company and in the values that the company communicates towards the clients and customers it targets and the sector in which it operates. Furthermore, gender balance in working environments is a fundamental prerequisite for resilient and inclusive democratic societies.

The present research explores the correlation between increases in successful cases of female entrepreneurship and the awareness of organizations that the inclusion of women in top management positions can generate a differential increase in the company's profitability levels, and in general can result in a position of solid and lasting competitive advantage over time.

To achieve this objective, it was chosen to explore, through a qualitative and longitudinal approach, the participation of women in senior management positions in the international labour market. In particular, an analysis has been carried out that traces and analyses the development of the situation in the period 2000-2021.

In order to have a holistic, up-to-date, and reliable picture of the phenomenon investigated, EIGE statistics were chosen. Specifically, the data extracted from the European Institute for Gender Equality concerned the participation of women in senior management positions of the largest listed companies of the European and non-European context. It should be noted that for the European countries, the data concern the 50 largest members of the main blue-chip index in the countries concerned. On the other hand, for non-European countries the data related to companies falling under the MSCI ACWI index.

Table 1. Female participation in senior management positions

TIME	2003	2004	2005	2006	2007	2008	2009	2010	2011	2012	2013	2014	2015	2016	2017	2018	2019	2020	2021
GEO (Labels)																			
Slovenia	22,9	19,0	18,9	19,3	15,4	18,4	10,0	9,8	14,2	16,7	21,6	19,9	21,5	24,8	22,6	23,9	24,6	22,9	19,4
Romania	21,4	17,2	12,8	13,0	17,6	12,0	11,7	21,3	10,4	11,9	7,8	11,0	11,8	10,1	11,0	11,0	12,6	12,8	17,5
Norway	20,9	22,4	28,8	34,5	34,2	42,9	41,6	38,9	41,3	43,7	42,0	37,6	38,8	42,6	42,1	40,2	40,2	40,4	41,5
Sweden	17,5	21,3	24,0	24,4	23,8	26,9	26,8	26,4	24,7	25,5	26,5	27,6	32,6	36,9	35,9	36,1	37,5	38,6	37,9
Latvia	16,8	9,9	19,3	20,8	17,4	15,8	17,1	23,5	26,6	28,2	29,6	31,7	30,4	28,5	28,8	29,0	31,7	25,8	22,2
United Kingdom	15,2	13,2	12,7	12,1	11,4	12,4	12,3	13,3	16,3	18,8	23,0	24,2	27,8	27,0	27,2	29,9	32,6	34,7	37,8
Estonia	14,7	13,5	12,7	13,1	10,1	8,4	6,4	7,0	6,7	7,8	7,3	7,1	9,1	8,8	7,4	8,0	9,4	8,3	9,1
Denmark	12,5	13,3	11,0	12,1	15,5	16,9	17,6	17,7	16,3	20,8	22,9	24,0	25,8	27,1	30,3	27,7	30,0	33,6	34,9
Finland	11,7	16,3	19,9	20,4	18,5	20,4	23,6	25,9	26,5	28,6	29,8	29,2	29,2	30,1	32,8	34,5	34,2	35,5	35,2
Bulgaria	31,4	18,3	18,7	17,1	14,5	11,8	17,2	11,2	15,2	11,6	16,7	17,6	19,6	15,3	17,1	14,5	18,5	12,9	21,7
Hungary	11,1	8,9	9,6	13,3	10,8	16,3	13,5	13,6	5,5	3,4	11,3	11,8	17,8	12,3	14,5	14,9	12,9	9,9	9,4
Germany (until 1990 former territory of the FRG)	9,8	11,7	12,2	13,2	11,3	13,3	12,9	12,6	15,2	17,9	21,5	24,8	26,1	29,5	31,9	33,8	35,6	36,3	36,0
European Union - 28 countries (2013-2020)	8,5	9,0	9,8	9,7	10,4	10,8	11,0	11,9	13,7	15,8	17,8	20,2	22,7	23,9	25,3	26,7	28,8		
European Union - 27 countries (from 2020)	9,2	8,8	9,6	9,8	10,3	10,6	10,9	11,8	13,4	15,4	17,5	19,8	22,2	23,6	25,1	26,4	28,4	29,5	30,6
Greece	7,8	7,3	7,1	3,8	11,2	5,7	5,1	6,2	6,3	7,9	8,4	8,9	9,8	9,1	11,3	9,1	10,3	11,0	19,6
Netherlands	7,6	4,9	6,9	8,4	13,9	14,5	15,0	14,9	17,8	21,5	25,1	24,9	25,5	27,5	29,5	30,7	34,2	36,4	38,1
Slovakia	7,6	8,4	11,1	9,7	23,5	18,0	18,2	21,6	14,6	13,8	24,0	18,2	12,7	12,5	15,1	24,1	29,1	31,4	27,7

Source: Istituto europeo per l'uguaglianza di genere EIGE

The longitudinal analysis carried out provides information about the presence of women in top management positions, which is more common in Northern European countries.

The country that stands out for its focus on female inclusion in top management roles is Iceland, which has gone from 4% in the early 2000s to over 40% of women in roles of social and economic prestige within their companies in about twenty years. In addition, the analysis highlights a symmetry of results between neighboring geographical areas, whose historical and cultural dialogue is reflected in the sharing of methods and practices impacting on the quality of community life. The Scandinavian countries belonging to the northern European area note a female presence at the top of working environments that stands at 40%. In these countries, the principle of gender equality is not foreign to the culture of the European Union and is not an external issue. On the contrary, this principle is inherent in the culture of the Nordic countries and guides their paths not only in civil but also political issues, creating welfare systems that are widely evolved and comparable to benchmarks of international importance.

Using the model of the Nordic countries, other countries in Europe have in the last twenty years exceeded the 30% share of women in top management positions. This is the case in France, who increased female presence in top roles from 5.3% to 45.3%, the best result in the Central European area. Similarly, Germany increased from 9.8% at the beginning of 2000 to 36%, thus quadrupling the initial value in less than twenty years.

The results relating to Italy are close to the level of northern European quotas, showing a presence of women in top management positions in the year 2021 equal to 38.8%, compared to 1.9% in 2003. In the evolution of the Italian entrepreneurial culture, 2012 marks an important acceleration of this phenomenon, which sees, in just one decade, the number of women in top manager positions quadruple. The opposite view clearly shows that in Europe men generally occupy higher positions than women. In none of the Member States has a female presence in managerial positions exceeded 50%. This is obviously linked to the pay asymmetries between men and women. The pay gap is a gap whose closure is prevented by numerous factors, including social and cultural stereotypes, legal factors, economic factors, and gender segregation in employment. According to the most recent ISTAT data published by the National Institute of Statistics, the pay gap between women and men is present, on average, in all European countries and notes that the greatest difference in hourly pay is for managerial positions, with women paid 23% less than men, based on data to the year 2014.

This scenario, according to the survey conducted by the Equileap research team (the leading organization that measures gender equality in the corporate sector), qualifies Italy as one of the countries with the best results in the world in terms of gender equality in the workplace. The latest report, published in 2022, analysed the structures and superstructures of 3,895 listed companies, representing 102 million employees globally. According to data released by the institute, Italy holds this record together with France, Spain, the United Kingdom, and Sweden, as a result of the strict legislation on gender equality that these countries enacted and applied. On the other hand, there are countries like Japan, Hong Kong, and the United States where attention to gender equality does not seem to be a priority for governments.

Italy, in particular, owes its outcome to the 2021 Equality Bill, which is responsible for amending the current Equal Opportunities Code and promoting a fight against gender discrimination, including mandatory reporting of the gender pay gap. In October 2021, the law on pay inequality between men and women was approved and several initiatives included in the National Recovery and Resilience Plan (PNRR) support women in the world of work, encouraging the employment of women and offering incentives for companies with women in charge (orriere.it). Of the sixty-two Italian companies listed on the stock exchange that were analyzed in the Gender Equality Global Report & Ranking (2022 edition), five companies figure in the world's top one hundred companies that promote gender equality in the workplace. The report paints a picture of companies that are increasingly investing in the fight against gender inequality that has characterized and still characterizes most working environments but on which the Italian government is also working to change this trend.

Below is an overview of the Italian companies present in the top one hundred companies with the best score on gender equality in the workplace. For each company mentioned, the ranking assigned by the Equileap research, as well as a summary of the efforts they have made so far in reference to the subject of research, are highlighted.

Table 2. Gender equality and diversity management in various firms

Firm	Gender Equality Score	Industry	Diversity management focal point
Enel	68%	Utilities	*Gender Equality* Equal pay, equal leadership, and equal opportunities
Hera	66%	Utilities	*Female Empowerment* Equal access to development and professional growth
Eni	63%	Energy	*Gender Pay Gap* Access to professional opportunities and career paths
Poste Italiane	63%	Financials	*Gender Equality* Equal pay and work-life balance
UniCredit	63%	Financials	*Social inclusion and sustainability* Equal access to career development and professional growth, zeroing of gender gaps and reduction of diversity

Source: Authors elaboration

The first Italian company to figure within the top one hundred world positions for commitment and attention to gender equality in the workplace is **Enel**, which is placed 17th out of about four thousand companies, with a gender equality ranking of 68%. The position in the global top 100 obtained by the company, for the third consecutive year, identifies Enel as the highest performing Italian company in terms of gender equality. In line with recent policies implemented by government, reflecting adherence to the Equal by 30 campaign in which public and private sector organisations commit to work for equal pay, equal leadership and equal opportunities for women in the clean energy sector by 2030, the strength of the company's strategy lies in the awareness that the sustainable business model lies in promoting the involvement of all internal resources in the organization and in innovation driven by the interrelation of knowledge and skills that are heterogeneous with each other. Moreover, the company's focus on increasing representation and empowering women "is creating new opportunities and bringing out the wide diversity of talents that coexist in our Group", according to Guido Stratta, Director of People and Organization at Enel (enel.com).

In the global ranking on gender equality drawn up by Equileap, in reference to the first one hundred companies that are distinguished by commitment to the definition and implementation of policies on gender equality in the corporate sphere, the second Italian company to appear is **Hera**, with a score of 66%. The multiutility made its entry into the world ranking for the first time in the year 2020. This outcome is intrinsically related to the growing focus of the company on equal access to development and female professional growth. This need is concretely implemented at the action level in the definition of meritocratic systems whose architecture is based on compensation tools and benefits focused on performance, complexity of role, and comparison with the market, beyond gender or generation, and career paths (gruppohera.it). The attention to diversity management is, for Hera, a central theme in the choices of investors and the financial community in general. Therefore, the company is constantly striving to raise its standards to achieve levels of excellence and, consequently, a sustainable competitive advantage.

According to the same rankings, the Italian company **Eni** has a score of 63%. In order to achieve this, Eni has launched an integrated approach based on the implementation of actions focused on remuneration policies and broader initiatives aimed at extending women's access to professional opportunities and career paths. In particular, since 2011, Eni has promoted an annual monitoring of its gender pay gap and identifies any actions to be corrected in order to reach ever better levels. The data collected from the annual surveys are publicly available on the company's official website. The initiatives undertaken by the ENI group fit into the framework of programs intended to "develop a widespread culture of inclusion starting from the strengthening of awareness of unconscious prejudices (unconscious bias) and the overcoming of gender stereotypes, elements that constitute a further pillar of our strategy on gender pay gap" (eni.com).

The same ranking is also shared by the Italian company **Poste Italiane,** the first employer in the country, which is present in the ranking due to the achievements obtained in reference to the gender pay gap in each pay bracket. This outcome is part of the strategic trajectories outlined by the National Recovery and Resilience Plan and, in general, is guided by the achievement of the United Nations Sustainable Development Goals (SDGs). As explained by Giuseppe Lasco, Co-director General of Poste Italiane: "This goal confirms the goodness of the path taken to ensure gender equality in all its manifestations, ensuring equal pay and work-life balance, overcoming every stereotype as clearly outlined in the Policy Diversity and Inclusion" (myposte.poste.it)

UniCredit has a gender equality ranking of 63%. This company has chosen to direct its action towards innovative solutions to gender equality and sustainability with the aim of expanding the offer of investment solutions for customers and innovate its governance systems, aligning them with current and prospective customer needs to achieve strong returns. This outcome comes from the awareness of top management of the role played by the inclusion of women in the workplace, the eradication of gender gaps, and increasing diversity. In particular, the UniCredit group interprets diversity as a "social value that can also offer a positive economic return for companies that know how to value and carry on with determination and consistency. Managing the assets of our customers cannot be separated from a selection of sustainable investments that help create a better society for future generations", says Mirko Bianchi, CEO of Group Wealth Management & Private Banking at UniCredit (unicreditgrou.eu).

In order to respond to the research question and interpret possible correlations in the Italian scenario between the inclusion of women within organizations in top management positions and the increase in the success of female entrepreneurship, the authors have chosen to follow the introductory overview on the European scenario using a multiple-type exploratory logic case study of five female entrepreneurs who have projected their name and the company they represent on the national and international scene.

The authors select the following successful female entrepreneurs:

1. Chiara Ferragni
2. Chiara Mastromonaco
3. Silvia Wang
4. Miuccia Prada
5. Clio Zammatteo

Chiara Ferragni

As can be read in the biography on the website that launched her career and made her one of the most appreciated icons in the world, Chiara Ferragni is CEO and founder of TBS Crew srl and Chiara Ferragni Brand and, since 2021, is a member of the board of directors of Tod's Group. Her career in the digital world began in the year 2009, when she launched her personal space in the digital environment, the blog TheBlondeSalad.com, which focused on content dedicated to the world of fashion and lifestyle and soon transformed into a Talent and Marketing Agency. Four years after the launch of her first company, the entrepreneur Chiara Ferragni registered and created her brand Chiara Ferragni Collection, initially dedicated to footwear, which then evolved into a total look. The success of these two initiatives is such that in 2015 The Blonde Salad and Chiara Ferragni Collection became a case study for Harvard Business School, while their creator entered the Forbes 30 Under 30 list. The interests of Chiara Ferragni also include issues outside working areas, for which her talent has garnered wide acclaim. Among the activities that Ferragni devotes attention to, the commitment to social and civic causes stands out.

Chiara Mastromonaco has an interdisciplinary professional background summed up by three keywords: sustainability, fashion, and food.

Her career, built in the world of fashion, underwent a turning point in 2012 when she applied her knowledge and skills to the food sector, working for the family winery. Her interests were attracted by the dynamics triggered by the changes that the Italian food industry was facing in those years, specifically the growing market need characterized by "luxury-set mind".

After four years, Chiara Mastromonaco co-founded with Diego Pelle, a Roman restaurateur, the company Direttoo, "the first digital platform where restaurateurs can quickly buy everything they need and analyze their business correctly".

The main goal of the platform lies in the optimization of the ordering and sales process through an innovative contribution to the value chain of food and beverage companies.

Silvia Wang's personal and professional history is guided by the awareness that the future would provide Wang with the opportunity to create value for herself and for others through entrepreneurship.

Silvia Wang earned her degree at Bocconi University in Milan but started her career outside Italy as a Marketing Manager in Southeast Asia. It is here that she sharpened her knowledge and skills at start-ups that have revolutionized the e-commerce fashion landscape. Three years after moving, in 2015, Silvia Wang returned to Italy and co-founded with her husband, Marco Oglienco, ProntoPro, the platform that connects professionals with those who need their services. The startup is part of a market characterized by a substantial vacuum due to the absence of large foreign competitors. This feature, together with the founders' marketing and management skills, made the startup the number 1 service marketplace in Italy.

In 2018, the ProntoPro platform reached over 1 million users, including over 300,000 professionals. ProntoPro, moreover, has received €10+ million investments, has grown to have more than 100 employees, and has expanded to 5 other countries.

Miuccia Prada

The biographical portrait of the fashion designer Miuccia Prada paints the picture of a professional who has built her career and spread her name around the world on the triad of creativity, boldness, and determination. Her entry into the world of fashion, after graduating in Political Science from the University of Milan, follows in the footsteps of her grandfather, Mario Prada, founder of the luxury company. The turning point in her professional career occurred when she met Patrizio Bertelli, a Tuscan entrepreneur who in the 70s became a partner of the company and who together with Miuccia Prada is considered the creator of the development and expansion of Prada towards new production sectors and foreign markets. It is thanks to their leadership that the Prada Group, to date, is considered among the world leaders in the luxury fashion industry. This success stems from an innovative approach not only in the design and creation of high quality and creative items of clothing and accessories, but also the value created by the company Prada. The success of the company and the entrepreneur who is driving it is determined by their subversive attitude, countertrends, and innovative creations brought to the catwalk by Miuccia Prada and the value asset that the latter has communicated and communicates today through the company. In 2018, her name was added to the Forbers list of the richest billionaires in the world, with estimated assets of $3.2 billion, an expression of Made in Italy at the top of international fashion.

Clio Zammatteo

The personal and professional history of Clio Zammatteo intertwines an international background that the entrepreneur has assimilated from her personal experiences with her passion for cosmetics and the world of make-up. Her career began as a youtuber in 2008, the year in which Clio Zammatteo opened her first channel in digital environments in which she gave make-up advice addressing a large and undifferentiated audience. Its popularity is such as to make it the protagonist of a television show, just four years after the launch of the YouTube channel. The presenter communicates through TV channels what she has refined and perfected on digital screens, leaving her image and message unchanged, and consequently the asset value of which it is an expression. Her talent turned into real and tangible creation of value when she launched, in 2017, her first line of cosmetics and opened, in the same year, her first store, in Italy, where she returned after twelve years in America, to expand their company and devote themselves to the diversification of their revenue, such as the design and dissemination of the docu-reality series in which she is the protagonist with her family.

The above overview of the rise of entrepreneurial women presents, from a managerial point of view, features that are repeated and that, according to the authors, can be considered essential for those who choose to do entrepreneurship, despite the number of case studies analyzed being quantitatively small. All the women whose entrepreneurial histories have been analysed have, in particular, clear correlations with each other.

The first common factor in the cases reported relates to the personal and educational sphere of successful entrepreneurs. In particular, this point suggests that all female entrepreneurs have an international background, with significant experience of training or working abroad and that multicultural work experiences are crucial. These experiences have proved, over the course of their careers, fundamental for the creation of networks and the international projection of the companies they have represented and have raised by themselves.

Secondly, all the women analyzed created value based on a value asset that is distinguished by the heterogeneity of the elements that compose it. The links between knowledge, passions, and experiences have constituted the base from which to create and to distribute concrete value.

Moreover, one major measure of the success that these women entrepreneurs have achieved has been determined by the tool with which they have expressed their talent and conveyed their content: the digital environment. This tool, taking the form of a YouTube channel, a blog, or a digital platform, has significantly raised their ability to spread their message and, as a result, increased the range of job opportunities which these creators have had access to during their career.

CONCLUSION

Through the review of the reference literature, it was verified that the issue of gender inclusion falls within the field of studies on diversity management (Manzanera-Román & Brändle, 2016). The barriers that together with the "glass ceiling" prevent organizations from adopting an approach based on diversity (including gender) have been identified in the contributions examined (Nair, 2020). Results of successful business case studies by female entrepreneurs have been reported. These results are useful because they are successful entrepreneurial cases that have become viral in the press, media, and social networks. This indicates that the national business ecosystem cannot fail to have grasped this type of information and market trend. A high performing female leadership appears evident in these cases and emerged without too much investigative effort. The stories and information available focus precisely on the ability of these women to conceive and develop effective and efficient business models. According to the professional reports consulted, 16% of the managers interviewed believe that the goal of gender equality in managerial roles is unattainable and only 35% of the managers interviewed declare that their company has a plan for gender equality. At the same time, it is possible to note that among the executives of Italian companies there is a growing awareness that a company with balanced leadership from the point of view of gender performs better. The two trends that the authors have compared confirm the spread of this awareness. The increase in cases of successful female entrepreneurship and the increase in attention to gender equity by large Italian companies are two phenomena that have both occurred in the last ten years. The managers of large companies have witnessed the rise of new companies led and founded by female entrepreneurs by adopting some of their management practices. This coincidence of trends suggests that gender equity is no longer considered as a maneuver to increase the system of good corporate values but above all a feature to create greater organizational diversity and to consider the latter as a lever for improved corporate performance.

REFERENCES

Adams, R. B., & Funk, P. (2012). Beyond the glass ceiling: Does gender matter? *Management Science, 58*(2), 219–235. doi:10.1287/mnsc.1110.1452

Adams, R. B., & Kirchmaier, T. (2016). Women on boards in finance and STEM industries. *The American Economic Review, 106*(5), 277–281. doi:10.1257/aer.p20161034

Anggadwita, G., Mulyaningsih, H. D., Ramadani, V., & Arwiyah, M. Y. (2015). Women entrepreneurship in Islamic perspective: A driver for social change. *International Journal of Business and Globalisation, 15*(3), 389–404. doi:10.1504/IJBG.2015.071914

Baldarelli, M. G., Del Baldo, M., & Vignini, S. (2016). *Pink accounting in Italy: Cultural perspectives over discrimination and/or lack of interest.* Meditari Accountancy Research.

Bridges, S., & Mann, S. (2019). Sexual orientation, legal partnerships and wages in Britain. *Work, Employment and Society, 33*(6), 1020–1038. doi:10.1177/0950017019873265

Brush, C. G., De Bruin, A., & Welter, F. (2009). A gender-aware framework for women's entrepreneurship. *International Journal of Gender and Entrepreneurship, 1*(1), 8–24. doi:10.1108/17566260910942318

Bukstein, D., & Gandelman, N. (2019). Glass ceilings in research: Evidence from a national program in Uruguay. *Research Policy, 48*(6), 1550–1563. doi:10.1016/j.respol.2019.03.007

Bullough, A., Guelich, U., Manolova, T. S., & Schjoedt, L. (2022). Women's entrepreneurship and culture: Gender role expectations and identities, societal culture, and the entrepreneurial environment. *Small Business Economics, 58*(2), 985–996. doi:10.100711187-020-00429-6

Caporale, C. (2022). Soffitto di cristallo. In *Italia a che punto siamo?* Business Community.

Casado-Díaz, J. M., Driha, O., & Simón, H. (2022). The gender wage gap in hospitality: New evidence from Spain. *Cornell Hospitality Quarterly, 63*(3), 399–417. doi:10.1177/1938965520971273

Choi, S. (2019). Breaking through the glass ceiling: Social capital matters for women's career success? *International Public Management Journal, 22*(2), 295–320. doi:10.1080/10967494.2018.1425225

Dye, K., & Golnaraghi, G. (2015). Organizational benefits through diversity management. The Oxford Handbook of Diversity in Organizations, 255.

Eagly, A. H., & Carli, L. L. (2003). The female leadership advantage: An evaluation of the evidence. *The Leadership Quarterly, 14*(6), 807–834. doi:10.1016/j.leaqua.2003.09.004

Elam, A. B., Brush, C. G., Greene, P. G., Baumer, B., Dean, M., & Heavlow, R. (2019). *Global Entrepreneurship Monitor 2018/2019 Women's Entrepreneurship Report.* Babson College: Smith College and the Global Entrepreneurship Research Association.

Folberg A.M. (2016). *Preferences for organizations that emphasize interpersonal relationships or entrepreneurship among Arab-and Jewish-Israeli women: The roles of culture, goal orientation, and traditionalism*. University of North Carolina.

Gagnon, S., Augustin, T., & Cuckier, W. (2021). Interplay for change in equality, diversity and inclusion studies. *Human Relations*, 00187267211002239.

Gilbert, J. A., Stead, B. A., & Ivancevich, J. M. (1999). Diversity management: A new organizational paradigm. *Journal of Business Ethics*, *21*(1), 61–76. doi:10.1023/A:1005907602028

Ginalski, S. (2021). Who runs the firm? A long-term analysis of gender inequality on Swiss corporate boards. *Enterprise and Society*, *22*(1), 183–211. doi:10.1017/eso.2019.64

Hartman, R. L., & Barber, E. G. (2020). Women in the workforce: The effect of gender on occupational self-efficacy, work engagement and career aspirations. *Gender in Management*, *35*(1), 92–118. doi:10.1108/GM-04-2019-0062

Haslam, S. A., & Ryan, M. K. (2008). The road to the glass cliff: Differences in the perceived suitability of men and women for leadership positions in succeeding and failing organizations. *The Leadership Quarterly*, *19*(5), 530–546. doi:10.1016/j.leaqua.2008.07.011

Karatas, M. (2017). Diversity Dimensions of Entrepreneurship: Addressing Multiple Strands of Diversity in Entrepreneurship Research. In *Management and Diversity*. Emerald Publishing Limited. doi:10.1108/S2051-233320160000004011

Kumari, G., & Eguruze, E. S. (2022). Positive deviance traits and social entrepreneurship for women empowerment amid COVID-19. *IIM Kozhikode Society & Management Review*, *11*(1), 109–125. doi:10.1177/22779752211030697

Lambert, J. (2016). Cultural diversity as a mechanism for innovation: Workplace diversity and the absorptive capacity framework.

Loukil, N., Yousfi, O., & Yerbanga, R. W. K. (2019). Does gender diversity on boards reduce information asymmetry problems? Empirical evidence from the French market. *Journal of Family Business Management*.

Maida, A., & Weber, A. (2022). Female leadership and gender gap within firms: Evidence from an Italian board reform. *Industrial & Labor Relations Review*, *75*(2), 488–515. doi:10.1177/0019793920961995

Manzanera-Román S., Brändle G. (2016). Abilities and skills as factors explaining the differences in women entrepreneurship. *Suma de negocios*, *7*(15), 38-46.

Martins, L. L., & Parsons, C. K. (2007). Effects of gender diversity management on perceptions of organizational attractiveness: The role of individual differences in attitudes and beliefs. *The Journal of Applied Psychology*, *92*(3), 865–875. doi:10.1037/0021-9010.92.3.865 PMID:17484566

Nair, S. R. (2020). The link between women entrepreneurship, innovation and stakeholder engagement: A review. *Journal of Business Research*, *119*, 283–290. doi:10.1016/j.jbusres.2019.06.038

Nekhili, M., Gull, A. A., Chtioui, T., & Radhouane, I. (2020). Gender-diverse boards and audit fees: What difference does gender quota legislation make? *Journal of Business Finance & Accounting*, *47*(1-2), 52–99. doi:10.1111/jbfa.12409

Nissan, E., Carrasco, I., & Castaño, M. S. (2012). Women entrepreneurship, innovation, and internationalization. In *Women's entrepreneurship and economics* (pp. 125–142). Springer. doi:10.1007/978-1-4614-1293-9_9

Noguera, M., Álvarez, C., & Urbano, D. (2013). Socio-cultural factors and female entrepreneurship. *The International Entrepreneurship and Management Journal*, *9*(9), 183–198. doi:10.100711365-013-0251-x

Omar, S. S. (2015). The entrepreneurial network of Muslim women entrepreneurs: The study of multiple-cases of small businesses in the southern region of Malaysia. *International Journal of Economics and Financial Issues*, *5*(1), 106–115.

Ozturk, M. B., & Tatli, A. (2016). Gender identity inclusion in the workplace: Broadening diversity management research and practice through the case of transgender employees in the UK. *International Journal of Human Resource Management*, *27*(8), 781–802. doi:10.1080/09585192.2015.1042902

Pastore, P., & Tommaso, S. (2016). Women on corporate boards. The case of 'gender quotas' in Italy. *Corporate Ownership and Control*, *13*(4), 132–155. doi:10.22495/cocv13i4p13

Patterson, L., & Benuyenah, V. (2021). The real losers during times of economic crisis: Evidence of the Korean gender pay gap. *International Journal of Manpower*, *42*(7), 1238–1256. doi:10.1108/IJM-02-2020-0045

Piazzalunga, D., & Di Tommaso, M. L. (2019). The increase of the gender wage gap in Italy during the 2008-2012 economic crisis. *The Journal of Economic Inequality*, *17*(2), 171–193. doi:10.100710888-018-9396-8

Pless, N., & Maak, T. (2004). Building an inclusive diversity culture: Principles, processes and practice. *Journal of Business Ethics*, *54*(2), 129–147. doi:10.100710551-004-9465-8

Quader, M. S. (2012). A characteristic model of successful women entrepreneurs in the UK. *Journal of Services Research*, *12n*, 1.

Ragins, B. R., Townsend, B., & Mattis, M. (1998). Gender gap in the executive suite: CEOs and female executives report on breaking the glass ceiling. *The Academy of Management Perspectives*, *12*(1), 28–42. doi:10.5465/ame.1998.254976

Manager Italia. (2021). Rapporto Donnna. *Manager Italia*. https://www.manageritalia.it/resources/manageritalia-rapporto-donne-manager-2020-marzo-2021.pdf

Ridgeway, C. L. (2001). Gender, status, and leadership. *The Journal of Social Issues*, *57*(4), 637–655. doi:10.1111/0022-4537.00233

Roberson, Q. M. (2006). Disentangling the meanings of diversity and inclusion in organizations. *Group & Organization Management*, *31*(2), 212–236. doi:10.1177/1059601104273064

Roberto, F., Rey, A., Maglio, R., & Agliata, F. (2020). The academic "glass-ceiling": Investigating the increase of female academicians in Italy. *The International Journal of Organizational Analysis*, *28*(5), 1031–1054. doi:10.1108/IJOA-06-2019-1779

Rouse, J., Treanor, L., & Fleck, E. (2013). The gendering of entrepreneurship: Theoretical and empirical insights. *International Journal of Entrepreneurial Behaviour & Research*, *19*(5), 452–459. doi:10.1108/IJEBR-06-2013-0083

Ryan, M. K., & Haslam, S. A. (2005). The glass cliff: Evidence that women are over-represented in precarious leadership positions. *British Journal of Management*, *16*(2), 81–90. doi:10.1111/j.1467-8551.2005.00433.x

Scholarios, D., & Taylor, P. (2011). Beneath the glass ceiling: Explaining gendered role segmentation in call centres. *Human Relations*, *64*(10), 1291–1319. doi:10.1177/0018726711416265

Shen, J., Chanda, A., D'netto, B., & Monga, M. (2009). Managing diversity through human resource management: An international perspective and conceptual framework. *International Journal of Human Resource Management*, *20*(2), 235–251. doi:10.1080/09585190802670516

Singh, V., Terjesen, S., & Vinnicombe, S. (2008). Newly appointed directors in the boardroom: How do women and men differ? *European Management Journal*, *26*(1), 48–58. doi:10.1016/j.emj.2007.10.002

Songini, L., & Gnan, L. (2014). The glass ceiling in SMEs and its impact on firm managerialisation: A comparison between family and non-family SMEs.

Sułkowski, Ł., Bogacz-Wojtanowska, E., Wrona, S., Jędrzejczyk-Kozioł, A., Góral, E., & Mormul, K. (2019). Unsustainable power distribution? women leaders in Polish academia. *Economia e Sociologia*, *12*(3), 162–180. doi:10.14254/2071-789X.2019/12-3/11

Tur-Porcar, A., Mas-Tur, A., & Belso, J. A. (2017). Barriers to women entrepreneurship. Different methods, different results? *Quality & Quantity*, *51*(5), 2019–2034. doi:10.100711135-016-0343-0

Tyrowicz, J., Terjesen, S., & Mazurek, J. (2020). All on board? New evidence on board gender diversity from a large panel of European firms. *European Management Journal*, *38*(4), 634–645. doi:10.1016/j.emj.2020.01.001

Urbancová, H., Hudáková, M., & Fajčíková, A. (2020). Diversity management as a tool of sustainability of competitive advantage. *Sustainability*, *12*(12), 5020. doi:10.3390u12125020

Wilson, F., Kickul, J., & Marlino, D. (2007). Gender, entrepreneurial self–efficacy, and entrepreneurial career intentions: Implications for entrepreneurship education. *Entrepreneurship Theory and Practice*, *31*(3), 387–406. doi:10.1111/j.1540-6520.2007.00179.x

Yadav, V., & Unni, J. (2016). Women entrepreneurship: Research review and future directions. *Journal of Global Entrepreneurship Research*, *6*(1), 1–18. doi:10.118640497-016-0055-x

Zhu, X., Cooke, F. L., Chen, L., & Sun, C. (2022). How inclusive is workplace gender equality research in the Chinese context? Taking stock and looking ahead. *International Journal of Human Resource Management*, *33*(1), 99–141. doi:10.1080/09585192.2021.1988680

Chapter 6
Female Entrepreneurship:
Challenges Faced in a Global Perspective

Teresa Jacob
CHRIST University (Deemed), India

Vismaya Rachel Thomas
CHRIST University (Deemed), India

Ginu George
CHRIST University (Deemed), India

ABSTRACT

Women being employees is a very appreciative aspect. But women being employers is a bold and massive decision that they make, considering their busy life schedule, which traditionally includes looking after their families and themselves. This book chapter aims to identify the diverse challenges female entrepreneurs face, which could be in the context of society, structure, or finance. Identifying and vocalizing these challenges faced by these emerging entrepreneurs is inadequate, but tackling them is equally called for. This study provides a framework and scope for further research to look into more opportunities and measures to tackle these roadblocks. Last but not least, this book chapter anticipates inspiring all women and driving them to explore the essence of entrepreneurship.

INTRODUCTION TO ENTREPRENEURSHIP

Entrepreneurship, in itself, is a trending and broad path taken. However, it is often observed that the ventures started by entrepreneurs are growing and flourishing. It begins with the germination of ideas, eventually developing and bringing them into existence. The success of this idea in innovation depends on how good the identified opportunity is (Girotra et al., 2010). A clear definition in one of the studies is, "Entrepreneurship is the process of doing something new and something different to create wealth for the individual and add value to society." (Kao, 1993)

DOI: 10.4018/978-1-6684-7669-7.ch006

Some primary attributes that an entrepreneur must possess are savviness, prudence, self-motivation, optimism, innovation, and so forth. These attributes together build up the quality of an entrepreneur. Thaddeus (2012), in his study, stated that the quality of the entrepreneurs in various nations accounts for a considerable portion of the disparity in their rates of economic growth. He also stated that entrepreneurs are critical agents of the growth of innovation and technical progress, which leads to increased production, exports, Gross Domestic Product (GDP) rates, etc. The concept of entrepreneurship is conventionally related to the idea of self-employment, and hence to bolster entrepreneurship, it is essential to raise the rates of self-employment (Bogenhold, 2004). In order to do this, it is essential to recognize the challenges, eliminate them and provide skill sets and training (Nawaser et al., 2011). Hence an entrepreneur must be ready to break new paths, dig in and gain in-depth knowledge about the idea, take risks, have a well-structured business plan, manage, and control their financial and other resources, and moreover, have the determination to pursue the idea and take good advantage of the opportunity in hand.

INTRODUCTION TO FEMALE ENTREPRENEURSHIP

A Female entrepreneur is a woman who is ingenious, looks out for opportunities, has a noble level of determination and commercial acumen, and, most of all, is a noteworthy risk taker (Vinze, 1987). Nonetheless, a study by Kepler & Shane found differences in male and female entrepreneurs based on their effort and performance (2007). Even though half of the ventures that were started in the year 2021 were established by women, according to global statistics, only one-third of the businesses in the world are owned and established by them (*Women Entrepreneurship Is Soaring in the US, a New Survey Finds*, 2022).

Starting a business from scratch, in general, is a strenuous process, but as a woman, it requires extra exertion in this male-dominated society. The benchmark used by most individuals to measure the performance of female entrepreneurs is the accomplishments or achievements of businessmen. This measurement tactic needs to change. Back in the day, women didn't have a right over ancestral property or the bare minimum of having a bank account of their own (Pareek & Bagrecha, 2018). According to Birley (1987), in the 1980s, women were more than content with the money they earned from self-employment at a small-scale level or even as regular employees. But lately, women tend to leave their existing workplace due to the frustration of encountering a glass ceiling and low growth rate in the workplace. The author indicates that corporate downsizing contributes to this phenomenon (Buttner, 1993).

Undeniably, there is an escalation in the role of women in entrepreneurship in contrast to the past few decades. Studies show that in the last 20 years women entrepreneurship has increased by 114% (Mrkonjić, 2022). But this factor repeatedly seems insignificant compared to the male entrepreneurs at a colossal level. It is far-reaching to channel the full potential of a valuable resource - women, in terms of entrepreneurship, as they can contribute to more remarkable economic development and social reform, which is a pressing priority. Female Entrepreneurship can be used as an efficacious tool in enhancing the standard of life and for women to be self-reliant in society. In this monolithic society, female entrepreneurs must possess qualities such as integrity, humility, willingness to learn, resilience and persistence, intuition, adaptability, communication skills, empathy, and above all, a robust support system (Ilgaz, 2022). Female entrepreneurs are considered to have a different approach to managing their enterprise when compared to male entrepreneurs. They tend to prioritize relationships with their stakeholders and possess better managerial ability when it comes to risk-bearing, operations planning, and resource planning. They also seemed to be more concerned with their work quality than male entrepreneurs (Krueger, 2000). Moreover, society has started to consider women entrepreneurs' work more skillful and efficient if they can balance both their business and their household (Alam et al., 2011).

Determining the factors and motives that drive female entrepreneurs to start their own enterprises is crucial. A few of the factors that motivate women to step into the realm of entrepreneurship can be categorized into three: (1) Cognitive, which includes self-challenge, flexibility in work, etc., (2) Regulatory, where extraordinary opportunities, perceptions of the society, and economic conditions play a significant role, and finally (3) Normative, which includes family and other networks, role modeling, and financial independence (Bui et al., 2018). A qualitative comparative analysis showed that when women's motive is to attain an excellent work-life balance, their chances of succeeding are less likely. When their motive is to take risks, their chances of succeeding are more. (Rey-Martí et al., 2015). Another research showed that both male and female entrepreneurs create their enterprises to attain the goal of autonomy, self-satisfaction, achievements, and other non-financial motives. However financial motives are not entirely out of their priority list (Cromie, 1987).

Hence, women have risen out of pure anonymity to become beacons of light to the world by breaking stereotypes that society has been building on for many years. This book chapter will be throwing light on various aspects of female entrepreneurship, including the global challenges and their presence across various industries.

NEED FOR FEMALE ENTREPRENEURS

The need of the hour is for developing countries to progress toward becoming developed ones, and this can only be done by the flourishing of entrepreneurship. In the past, the entrepreneurial sector may have been male dominated, but with women being almost half the world's population, not utilizing this versatile capability would connote failure. The matter of gender equality in entrepreneurship no longer remains a social issue to provide equal chances to women but also extends to the impact it has on economic development. This acceleration of economic growth can be done by giving budding women entrepreneurs identical access and a chance to enhance their skills (Sarfaraz et al., 2014). It is high time to break the social norms and conservative beliefs that a woman's duty is limited to her household affairs. This new generation of women is shattering these societal convictions by proving their tenacity and caliber, time after time, even during hardships (Amrita et al., 2018). Due to more awareness regarding the need for education and when the world moves towards industrialization, female participation in entrepreneurship also rose considerably (Pareek & Bagrecha, 2018).

Based on the McKinsey Global Institute report, there is an impact of female entrepreneurship on the global economy if nurtured the right way. It reveals that if women are given the same opportunities as men, it could add up to $12 trillion to the GDP of the global economy by the year 2025 (Woetzel et al., 2015). Women being business leaders have the power to pave the way toward rapid economic growth by furnishing a solution to poverty alleviation. This, in turn, would uplift the quality of life, specifically regarding their children's education and health (Welsh et al., 2016). Acs et al., (2011), in their study, have termed the involvement of women in business as a vehicle to construct employment opportunities' and have agreed that it is the fundamental driver for the economic development. Kamberidou (2013) mentions in her study that female entrepreneurship is not just about creating jobs for themselves but also creating jobs for others. Waseem (2018) also acknowledges that female entrepreneurship eradicates poverty by generating a bulk of employment opportunities and boosts innovation and competition in the market. The author, Fazalbhoy (2014), appreciates women entrepreneurs for their growing contribution and involvement in the technology for business, increased investments, and causing a revolutionary motivation for other young women. This study also briefly discusses how they cater to various organizational and business problems by providing management solutions.

Women entrepreneurs bring new perspectives to the table with diversification in products and processes, resulting in an elevated standard of entrepreneurship (Verheul et al., 2006). Female entrepreneurs are said to perceive things differently than men and carry different skills and approaches to business. The fear of failure does exist to a large extent, but once they surpass that, they are asserted as ambitious and open to challenges. They are supposedly better listeners and great at multitasking and creativity. As a leader, they are described to be correlative and egalitarian managers (Kamberidou, 2020). In their study, Woolley and Malone (2011) also found that women take criticism and constructive feedback well and have open minds that keep people engaged in conversations better. This shows that women entrepreneurs can better accustom their services and products to their customers' needs which is a very needed skill in business.

Aside from pushing economic growth, female entrepreneurs would result in women feeling empowered and that their opinions and decisions are valued. This opens a new horizon of opportunities and a platform to prove that they are not bound to their households. These self-sustaining women would be recognized for their work as they acquire the skill to work well in a team while connecting to many businesspeople. This would lead to women believing in their abilities, and this heightened self-esteem would encourage them to take risks.

NECESSITY VS OPPORTUNITY ENTREPRENEURSHIP

An important factor that drives anyone, irrespective of gender, into entrepreneurship is the motivation or intention behind it. It is necessary to understand what exactly these intentions are to be able to prompt female entrepreneurs into entering the business world. Generally, the motivation behind what makes an entrepreneur engaged in business could either be necessity-based or opportunity based.

When people have no alternative but to venture as an entrepreneur to get away from job scarcity and assist their household is called necessity entrepreneurship. In this scenario, the entrepreneur has no choice but to start a business. This could be with an intention to make a living to ensure that there is food on the table, a roof over their head, and clothes to protect them. This situation is forced onto them to secure their future and to avoid anything adverse happening to them or their family.

On the contrary, people who become entrepreneurs by looking for an opportunity to make a difference or to achieve self-esteem and status in society are called opportunity entrepreneurs. Here, the entrepreneur starts a business with the desire to make a difference or to recognize a prospective business activity and pursue it. Necessity is a 'Push' with no choice left, whereas opportunity is a 'Pull' when the choice is voluntary (Dawson & Henley, 2012). Necessity-based is more of a compulsion to avoid a bad situation, whereas opportunity-based is more like an urge to do something to obtain self-satisfaction.

It is well documented in the Global Entrepreneurship Monitor (GEM) Report 2020-21 that, in most countries, women emerge as necessity entrepreneurs due to the need to escape unemployment. This study is also significant as it shows that Entrepreneurship originating from opportunity is more beneficial and contributes more to the economy (Calderon et al., 2014). Z. Acs (2006) also confirms the same and puts forward that opportunity entrepreneurs are positively associated with the GDP per capita. The paper also recommends taking the ratio between opportunity and necessity entrepreneurs as an indicator of economic progression.

From the World Development Report 2012, there is evidence implying that women are more inclined to become necessity entrepreneurs in developing countries. In contrast, they tend to become opportunity entrepreneurs in developed countries (Cavada et al., 2018). According to a study conducted by the World Bank (2012), it is well corroborated that developed countries tend to bring out women entrepreneurs based on their opportunities. They yearn to do something for themselves or society. It is also discussed that in developing countries, most women entrepreneurs are more likely to be born out of necessity. This is because they find self-employment more feasible and practical to provide for their family. Due to the high unemployment rates, more people are forced to enter entrepreneurship from developing countries. Moreover, people tend to turn to entrepreneurship due to the readily available capital like bank loans or other funds. (Dawson & Henley, 2012).

The government or policymakers must take cognizance of this, as this would aid them in drafting policies or programs to target these entrepreneurs specifically. We can see the direct link between the type of motivation for entrepreneurship and if the country is in the development phase or has reached the developed stage. Hence, the understanding of the differences between these entrepreneurs is relevant in today's context.

ROLE OF FEMALE ENTREPRENEURSHIP ACROSS INDUSTRIES

Historically researchers were satisfied by the assumption that the success of entrepreneurial ventures depends on the characteristics of the entrepreneur. Later, new claims were made, saying that success not just depends on the characteristics but also on the industry they choose to step into and the strategies they adopt (Sandberg & Hofer, 1987). In their research, one of the findings was that the industry structure has more impact on the venture's performance but when these three variables function together, it roots in the entrepreneur's success.

Various studies show that the industries women choose to venture into as an entrepreneur differs from what men generally choose. Women also tend to enter industries that are stereotypically dominated by men, increasingly melting the gender-specific norms and ideas of these sectors and industries (Debroux, 2016). This chapter will look into a few types of industries and analyze their role in each one of them. The following industries are chosen on the basis of the availability of literature and applicability of the same with regards to the subject matter.

Service Industry

The Service industry has been flourishing since the 1980s. Over 20 years, this industry has been providing employment opportunities more than any other industry (Dobón & Soriano, 2008). The categories of the service industry that entrepreneurship has associated with are healthcare services, personal services, accounting services, business, legal services, recreation services, and more (Rodie & Martin, 2001). The presence of female entrepreneurs in the service industry is generally more than in any other industry. In the UK, as of the early 2000s, almost 50% of female entrepreneurs managed their businesses in this industry (Shahedul, 2012). The Chinese statistics say that for decades, their economy focused largely on manufacturing and agriculture but recently, this trend has been changing. Female entrepreneurs in China, almost 45%, are being forced into service-business sectors due to the reformation of state-owned enterprises and industrial restructuring (Deng et al., 2011). Hence, it can be inferred that the presence of female entrepreneurs is most in number when it comes to the service industry as more doors are open to them due to the shift from a labor-driven economy to a knowledge-driven one.

Fashion Industry

The study on the entrepreneurial activities in the fashion industry are an area that scholars and researchers haven't dived deeply into. But according to Henry (2009), women are more pertinent to creative work and its related industries, and it also has the scope of employment and new business opportunities. It is said that women dominate fashion schools and firms and own most of the independent fashion brands in the world (Brydges & Hracs, 2019). Careers in the fashion industry are possible lately because of the higher education programs that are prevalent these days all around the globe. This education is also said to anchor more on hard skills and does not seem to encourage being progressive or dynamic (Fernandes et al., 2020). Not just establishing businesses in the fashion industry but building it on an international level influence and inspires other women and is considered a root cause for their improvement and development opportunities (Bello, 2019).

Construction Industry

The construction industry is stereotypically male-dominated, and there are fewer chances of seeing female entrepreneurs in this field. It was revealed in a study conducted in Malaysia that the women involved in the construction industry tend to have traits that are masculine (Jaafar et al., 2014). When it comes to the strategies that female entrepreneurs use to sustain themselves in this field are mainly from the defender category, where they tend to concentrate on taking up fewer projects but finishing them with the finest quality and reasonable prices. The other strategies that they use are from the analyzer and prospector categories. The analyzer category, as the name suggests, does not jump to conclusions but analyzes every situation and makes decisions prudently.

On the other hand, prospector categories tend to become first in the market by providing new products and services (Olson & Currie, 1992). Challenges female entrepreneurs face in the construction industry include winning projects, managing more than one project at a time, location of the projects, procurement of working capital, society doubting their capability to manage a construction project, etc. (Sospeter, 2012). Therefore women's propensity to venture into the construction field seems less likely, but not very rare too.

Technology Industry

The participation rate of women in the early years in different capital-generating activities was extremely low, be it in the area of science, mathematics, engineering, etc., which paved the way for the extensive study on female entrepreneurship in these fields and technology is one of them (Siles, 2011). But there is evidence from studies conducted in the early 2000s that women have started to enter web-based ventures for numerous reasons like more female venture capitalists, Initial Public Offers (IPOs) set up by female entrepreneurs, etc. (Forson & Özbilgin, 2003). Considering the woman entrepreneur's age, it is probable that there are chances for them to be older than their male counterparts while stepping into the technology industry because they either wait for their children to reach a certain age, or it could be the time that they take to complete their education and to gain experience by working in organizations in a chosen field. It was also observed that when the parents of these women are highly educated, they tend to encourage their daughters to step into non-traditional areas of business which also includes highly technological industries and sectors. On the other hand, most women, when it comes to education, tend to take up non-technical areas as their field of specialization (Aylward, 2007).

Numerous studies show that the presence of female entrepreneurs is more in number in Small and Medium-sized Enterprises (SMEs) because of the ease of entry and exit and various other challenges. The next top presence was found in the fashion industry, where most of the world's top brands are managed by female entrepreneurs. They are hesitant to enter the construction and technology industries due to the stereotypical views of men dominating these industries. They are also said to have masculine traits once they opt for such industries.

CHALLENGES FACED BY FEMALE ENTREPRENEURS: GLOBAL PERSPECTIVE

Women continue to thrive through various hurdles, from their perception of themselves to how world reacts to certain situations. Female entrepreneurs tend to stay indoors due to the lack of confidence and the fear of being swallowed up by the big sharks. The pandemic is one of the greatest challenges encountered by all entrepreneurs that profoundly impacted the businesses that women were slowly building up in this difficult society. According to the World Bank Group (2022), the pandemic has forced about 70 million people into a very high poverty. According to the GEM Report 2021, the odds of women shutting down their businesses were higher by 20% than their male counterparts. The pandemic cut the women's foothold in business who just began to understand and capture the market.

These hurdles need to be identified, addressed, and put to a halt in perpetuity. Several studies have been conducted worldwide about female entrepreneurship, portraying its vitality, roles played by women, challenges faced, and so on. Most of them focus on one region or area of study. This study will concentrate on the challenges specific to various areas or countries from a global perspective.

Asia

Asia has been successful in producing a high number of women entrepreneurs. This could be due to the highly populous continent, with 60% of the world's population in Asia. This high population would result in many families being affected by unemployment and poverty, forcing people to turn to entrepreneurship as a means to escape. In the Indian context, it is found that women-led businesses employ around 22-27 million people. This shows the extent to which women have impacted people's employment opportunities. This study also shows that when women play a big role, the national economy could rise by USD 770 Bn (Wiriya, 2022). Women entrepreneurs played a vital role in Malaysia's economic development as the government recognized the importance that must be given to them. They put efforts into developing strong and victorious businesswomen (Ndubisi & Kahraman, 2005). Asian female entrepreneurs are said to be motivated by both the pull and the push factors. There are necessity-based entrepreneurs who are motivated by factors such as the financial stability of their families and the gender inequality they face at the workplace. The women motivated by opportunity-based factors that pull them towards entrepreneurship would be the desire for career advancement and the need for independence (Tan, 2007; Zgheib, 2018). But still, there are factors that demotivate women with great business ideas, even before they set a foot forward.

In South Asian countries, one of the biggest challenges that women entrepreneurs face is limited access to technology, inability to finance their ideas, insufficient marketing knowledge to penetrate the market, and lack of basic education that is vital for efficient management (Shah & Saurabh, 2015). Pakistan is particularly Islamic, and people are influenced by patriarchal and conservative beliefs that women are subordinate to men. So, when a woman becomes the breadwinner, it is perceived as something new and unusual to which not many would be open. This is the primary challenge that female entrepreneurs face in this country. Due to these traditional beliefs, a woman's education is considered unnecessary. Other factors that hinder females from taking up positions for career enhancement are religious extremism, lack of resources, and limited availability of finance. This study showed that the aspiration to make a better place for women and the degree of independence inspires women to become entrepreneurs (Yunis et al., 2018). In their paper, Umar et al. (2022) mentioned that a few barriers hindering Pakistani women from reaching their full potential were restricted financial, family, government, and political support. Even in India, with its high population, the rate of female entrepreneurs still isn't a significant figure. Pareek and Bagrecha's (2018b) study revolves around the socio-personal challenges women face in the country. The paper talks about impediments such as patriarchal social order, lack of education and technological knowledge, and restrictive family ideologies that believe women are supposed to get married and look after their families. The foremost constraint women entrepreneurs face in Bangladesh is the lack of capital. The alternative of borrowing funds is not feasible as the interest rates are high and the installment period is low, due to which these women struggle to generate money and keep it in business. The absence of required educational qualifications hinders women while making sound managerial decisions. Social constraints also add to this, as women are expected to get married after attaining a certain age after which running a business is not encouraged by families (Rahmatullah & Zaman, 2014). Women usually tend to start businesses only when they have full support from their families. Alam et al. (2011), in their study of female entrepreneurs in Malaysia, stated family support makes a difference in the decision of women or not to pursue entrepreneurship. He mentions that socially constructed beliefs inhibit women from reaching their full potential. Apart from similar constraints like meager funds, women in Korea experience fear of failure and have doubts if they can maintain a work-life balance (Cho et al., 2020). There is evidence that corresponds to similar constraints regarding finance availability in Vietnam, that women made cautious investments by not taking loans at an early stage but instead utilizing their savings. This led to instability in staffing human resources, which was not favorable in the longer run. Some women also felt that complex legal structure curbed their chances of being entrepreneurs due to inaccessible government information and high taxation rates.

In Asian countries, it can be observed that the strict patriarchal system of society is the biggest hindrance to potential businesswomen. Even if they decide that this societal order will not shatter their passion for entrepreneurship, they still find difficulty in obtaining finance to fund their idea. Once they obtain the capital for it, due to the low educational level among women, they are not accustomed to the business ways and hence inability to make rational and quick decisions.

Middle East

The middle east has a population of around 6 percent of the world population and is still rapidly growing. The region's labor force growth rate is, in fact, higher than its population growth rate (*Growth and Stability in the Middle East and North Africa -- Economic Overview*, n.d.). A rise in the level of women participating in different businesses could lead to an escalation of USD 2.7 trillion in the Arab economy by 2025 (*How Women Are Transforming the Arab World's Start-up Scene*, 2020).

The middle east is said to be a very religious-driven region, Islam being the most prominent one. They consider their culture very rich and are not flexible. Only children from privileged families have better chances of starting businesses and becoming industry leaders (Pistrui & Sreih, 2010). They also hinted at the rise in change but at a very low rate. Education has been associated with entrepreneurship in the country of Saudi Arabia. More than 50 percent of female entrepreneurs have at least a post-secondary education. One of the main challenges that female entrepreneurs face is the perplexity of choosing which area to venture into and to be on the safer side, they tend to choose the ones which have the least barriers to entry (Danish & Smith, 2012). Research done in Jordan finds out that it is not always the religion that is a limitation. It is the social stereotypes and other traditions that create barriers to their entry into the field of entrepreneurship. Even though the women there are encouraged to be educated, they are pushed to marriage and start a family (Mehtap et al., 2016). In Turkey, women are said to be legally discriminated against, and there is a paucity of political and economic power and a lack of knowledge about their basic rights and skills (Welsh et al., 2016). A study conducted on Iranian women suggested that they have the potential to become a barrier to entrepreneurship by being satisfied with the growth that they have at present. They also stop themselves from making connections and expanding their network, which men seem to do effortlessly (Arasti et al., 2012). Lerner et al., (1997) stated that the rate of self-employment of women in Israel was less than that of men, which can be due to the effects of networks they make. Single or multiple networks for guidance in the business had a positive relationship with their profitability. Lebanese women face cultural and religious barriers, as Arab women are not supposed to be part of any business transactions, as a result, many tend to avoid indulging in entrepreneurship (Zgheib, 2018).

In short, the challenges women in middle eastern countries face are mainly cultural and religious barriers, gender discrimination and social stereotypes, and lack of network and guidance. Financial constraints are also prevalent in this region as the women do not have any savings apart from those hailing from royal or privileged families.

Africa

After Asia, statistics prove that Africa comes second in size and population. Most of the population in this continent are self-sufficient and are engaged in various agricultural activities which provide for their necessities alone. Hence, the standard of living and the revenue of the continent is low compared to others. But at the same time, due to the change in the political direction and democratic structures, certain countries of Africa have been seeing a difference in their economic growth (*Statistics and Data of All Countries in Africa*, n.d.). It is established that female entrepreneurs were the reason for around 250 to 300 billion US Dollars of economic growth in Africa in 2016. (*Africa: First Female Entrepreneurs in the High-tech Sector as New Role Models*, 2018)

The majority of the SMEs in the regions of Ghana and South Africa are found to be managed by women entrepreneurs. But the issue arises when these SMEs are home-based, i.e., managed from home itself, and do not come under official statistics. Hence, it is difficult for female entrepreneurs to access finance from different schemes, and thus, financial constraints arise. The administrative costs of these financial schemes are relatively higher than the benefits they provide. This discourages female entrepreneurs from approaching and availing such financial assistance (Abor & Quartey, 2010). When it comes to Sudan, women regard the moral support of their families as a key resource. It was also said that support from external sources was hindered and limited for various reasons, including national economic challenges, political instability, and the nation's hassle of establishing peace with others (Welsh et al., 2013). Isaga (2019) mentions that a large part of female entrepreneurs in Tanzania started their ventures with the primary motive of creating employment, i.e., enabling other women to participate and encourage what they want to pursue to supplement their income.

Meanwhile, in Kenya, women have limited constraints in starting up a micro-enterprise, but they face roadblocks when it comes to growing it into a medium-scale enterprise. Researchers found that this occurs due to the lack of training and skills. It is suggested that the government introduce support for basic training, mentoring, and financial assistance (Lock & Smith, 2016). This can help equip them with the necessary knowledge of how to make business plans, access funds from different financial institutions, and so on, which seems to be lacking in female entrepreneurs (Rudhumbu et al., 2020). They also mentioned that in Botswana, the government is said to have set up an opportune legal and regulatory market environment that women can exploit. Female entrepreneurs in Nigeria give credit for their success from their businesses to their families as they are said to encourage, mold, and influence their entrepreneurial activities (Halkias et al., 2011).

Therefore, it can be implied that female entrepreneurs face the major hurdles in Africa are lack of financial assistance, financial schemes, stagnant growth, lack of training and mentoring programs, nationwide economic crisis, and political instability. At the same time, there is evidence from different countries, such as Sudan and Nigeria, that the moral support from their families is one of the main reasons other challenges do not create adverse effects on their business. Sriram and Mersha (2010) stated that the active involvement of the government in the entrepreneurial activities of African countries has a positive impact on the same. The government's effort to promote entrepreneurship has increased compared to previous years. For an industrializing world, this implies having a diversified market, a strong business network and connections, and a more stable trading environment worldwide.

Europe

The European Union (EU) is the third largest economy, following the United States and China. It is predicted by the International Labour Organization (2018) that by the year 2050, if the gap between gender is eliminated, then it can increase the per capita of the EU from 3.2% to 5.5%. The European Commission is initiating an action plan to bridge the entrepreneurial and digital gap between genders. The European Institute of Innovation and Technology (EIT), a body of the EU, supports women who want to become entrepreneurs in agriculture and manufacturing (*Women Entrepreneurship & Leadership*, 2022). Despite all these efforts, the number of women emerging as entrepreneurs is still significantly low compared to the other region's numbers.

A study of female entrepreneurs in the West Midlands indicates that they generally encounter personal barriers such as duty towards their family. They are also ill-equipped with the essential skills to understand the market's workings (Lockyer & George, 2012).

Concerning the UK, women have shown that the fear of failure is a significant factor that affects the financial barrier. Due to this inadequate confidence, they often refuse to take the first step by seeking fewer funds and being risk averse. Most women believe they would not be provided a bank loan so they don't ask for one. In this paper, the authors also comment that the probability of women becoming entrepreneurs increases significantly when they have good terms with the bank manager or the access to funding is easier (Kwong et al., 2012). In Italy, women are less likely to know the laws that specifically apply to them to provide them a ground to start a business. Hence, training prospective women entrepreneurs are needed so that they are motivated to enter business and can take advantage of such laws (Bianchi et al., 2016). The laws in Spain for a very long time didn't allow women much freedom to start a business in industries of their choice. Despite their participation in business activities, women were never registered as owners nor compensated for it. They were also only allowed to enter the service sector in the field of business. These structural barriers demotivated women from setting foot or taking the lead in various business sectors (Galvez & Fernández, 2007).

We can see that the major obstacles that impede women from becoming entrepreneurs in the Europe are fear of failure, which further extends to the lack of finance, legal and structural constraints, and the shortfall of family and societal support. The government must ensure the policies are in place to nurture a woman's skills and that they are aware of such policies to be a successful entrepreneur.

North America

The World Bank report is proof that female entrepreneurs have a huge impact on economic development. It elucidates that female business owners' chip almost USD 3 trillion into the US economy. They are also responsible for the creation of about 23 million jobs. There was a dramatic increase in the number of startups found by female entrepreneurs when the pandemic hit the world. This showed the zeal of women to seize opportunities and was the reason behind almost 50% of the new businesses opened in 2021 (*Women Entrepreneurship Is Soaring in the US, a New Survey Finds*, 2022). Despite this, women still seem to come across trouble while starting a business.

A study in Canada and the United States (US) disclosed that most women earn less than their spouses, and hence it is expected of them to take up most of the family responsibilities. This leaves the women with little time to invest in business activities, discouraging them from pursuing their goals (Robichaud et al., 2014). Derived from a research paper based in Mexico, it can be inferred that there are cultural challenges like insufficient credibility and immense pressure put on women in society. It also highlights the structural difficulties, such as insufficient funding and programs encouraging women to pursue this way of life (Cavada et al., 2018).

North America is perceived to be a developed continent, and indeed the opportunities in this region are abundant. Female entrepreneurs have opened doors for employment to many and contributed to the nation's growth. Hence it is feasible to give these female entrepreneurs the platform they deserve.

Latin America

Latin America shows high rates of female entrepreneurs, which could be the result of the capital support they receive. In a study, it is revealed that there is a positive association between female entrepreneurs and economic growth. As a matter of fact, women's presence in the business field is the reason for 19% of Latin America's economic development (The Startup VC Team, 2020). This shows that more importance has to be placed on this aspect so that potential is not gone useless. Understanding what is stopping women from meeting their full capabilities in the business world is important.

According to Alecchi (2020), one vital factor that nips women from the bud of being entrepreneurs is the crime and violence against the female gender, which creates a physiological and psychological barrier to economic growth. It slows business productivity and creates a sense of fear in women. In Latin America and the Caribbean, female entrepreneurs are more inclined to be opportunity-driven rather than necessity-driven. Since in the past it has shown that opportunity-based entrepreneurs seem to contribute higher to economic growth, women entrepreneurs are no doubt a valuable resource to this region. But, the large businesses owned by women only constitute about 9% in Latin America and the Caribbean. One primary reason for this could be that women enter into businesses in the informal sector which does not aid much in expansion. This, in return, hampers the development and innovation of the economy. Another important aspect to the limited availability of finance, without which it is extremely difficult for women entrepreneurs to grow and expand (Allahar, 2015).

Latin America has shown great progress toward gender equality by reforming the legal framework (Alecchi, 2020). Women in Latin America now have more opportunities than they did back then. It is a positive indication that they are emerging as entrepreneurs born out of the opportunity. It is also one of the highest growths in the world, yet it cannot be compared with male entrepreneurs.

Australia

It is revealed in Billson's (2022) research that in the last ten years, in Australia, almost 66% of new businesses have been started by women entrepreneurs. Australia is proof of many famous women entrepreneurs that came up during the last few decades, which is a positive indication. It can be said that these women inspire the rest to commercialize their ideas and put them into action. But sadly, that is still not enough.

As Bennett and Dann (2000) claimed, even though women do not have the capital to start a business, they hesitate to approach the bank to fund their startup. Instead, they tend to use up their savings or borrow money from their family or friends. Even though this means that they do not have to deal with high amounts of debt, the capital invested in the business would be very little compared to men, which will limit most of the financial decisions they have to make.

It is reported that most women face complications in strategy planning and implementation, which could be the result of a limited practical understanding of business. This leads to women owners losing customers, which affects the profitability of the business (Saxon & Gillin, 2004).

There is a need to understand the various challenges female entrepreneurs face in Australia, but the limited research makes it hard. This provides a further scope of understanding the difficulties that women encounter in this region. **Table 1** shows a comprehensive view of the impact and challenges faced by female entrepreneurs from a global perspective.

Table 1. Comprehensive view of the impact and challenges of female entrepreneurship in a global perspective

REGIONS	IMPACT OF FEMALE ENTREPRENEURSHIP	CHALLENGES FACED BY FEMALE ENTREPRENEURSHIP
Asia	Employed around 22 - 27 million people.	❖ Limited access to capital and technology ❖ Lack of market knowledge and basic education ❖ Conservative and patriarchal beliefs ❖ Fear of failure
Middle East	Could lead to an escalation of USD 2.7 trillion in the economy by 2025.	❖ Perplexity of choosing an industry ❖ Social stereotyping and discrimination ❖ Lack of network and guidance ❖ Lack of capital
Africa	Contributed around USD 250 - 300 billion to the economic growth.	❖ Financial constraints ❖ Region's economic challenges and political instability ❖ Lack of training and skills
Europe	Can increase the per capita income from 3.2% to 5.5%.	❖ Personal commitments towards family ❖ Ill equipped with essential skills ❖ Fear of failure ❖ Financial barriers ❖ Legal and structural constraints
North America	Chipped in USD 3 trillion into the economy and created 23 million jobs.	❖ Family responsibilities ❖ Insufficient credibility ❖ Insufficient funding and programmes
Latin America	Reason for 19% of economic development.	❖ Physiological and psychological barriers ❖ Limited availability of finance
Australia	Established almost 66% of new businesses.	❖ Inadequate supply of capital ❖ Complications in strategy planning and implementation

SUGGESTIONS

Identifying and vocalizing the challenges faced by these emerging entrepreneurs worldwide is inadequate but tackling them is equally called for. This chapter aspires to suggest certain means to overcome such challenges faced by emerging female entrepreneurs.

The women who decide to venture into the business world require their family's moral support, particularly their partner's. The idea of shared responsibility should be brought forward in a society where it is not just the duty of women to take care of everything- household chores, children, and family as a whole, while they are self-employed. These factors should be no more a hindrance but a source of encouragement and edification for female entrepreneurs. When granting maternity leaves in organizations, policymakers can ensure that it shouldn't be restricted to pregnant women and their partners, irrespective of gender. The partners must be eligible for such leaves so that they can stay back at home and look after their children until they reach a certain age so that it doesn't restrict women from returning to their workplace. The need for gender equality must be introduced in the educational curriculums in every school so that the students from such a young age will know the importance of women in the workplace and the morality behind shared responsibility.

It's not just about the women who have families or spouses to support, but the policymakers should also focus on those women who are single-handedly raising their children. There must be policies that can provide relief to the household and childcare responsibilities so that they can redirect their attention to following their passion and handling the business.

One of the limitations that were found in the study was the inability to connect and create networks. Making new connections with other business and entrepreneurial enthusiasts is vital for female entrepreneurs to acquire knowledge regarding new trends and opportunities, better guidance, and attract more investors. This can also eliminate the financial constraints up to a limit. Women's financial literacy should be increased so that they are aware of the numerous schemes and loans available to them, where, how, and different rates at which it is being issued.

Another change that could be brought forward is the introduction of 'Women Economic Zones.' Just like the world has 'Special Economic Zones (SEZ), introducing something similar solely for women could encourage them to step forward and start their own businesses. The suggested perks that can be provided for them can range from tax concessions/exemptions and subsidies to duty-free imports and Foreign Direct Investments (FDI).

Creating awareness is another factor that must be looked into. Female entrepreneurs tend to lose motivation and become discouraged due to certain external elements, which must be avoided. Ways to motivate them and get them back on track can be through various ways. One of the easiest ways to do this is to make movies and biographies of successful entrepreneurs, and the challenges they overtook would impact a larger audience.

CONCLUSION

The barriers faced by women in becoming entrepreneurs could vary extensively. Despite being a highly capable stratum of society, conservative gender ideologies and restrictive beliefs hinder women from reaching their maximum potential. As an additive, women hesitate to take that step because of the fear of failure and lower self-confidence that they wouldn't be able to manage family life and business. Women face structural deficiencies regarding lack of education, legal discrimination, and scarce government support (Welsh et al., 2016). Finance, the backbone of any business venture, is also a meager resource. Apart from all the above, when the pandemic hit the world in 2020, it further harmed women entrepreneurs' growth.

This study has reflected female entrepreneurship's need, role, motives, and challenges. They are essential to the world, as female entrepreneurs, given a chance, would contribute to economic growth and become great influential personalities and leaders because of their ability to multitask and handle different situations best.

REFERENCES

Abor, J., & Quartey, P. (2010). Issues in SME development in Ghana and South Africa. *International Research Journal of Finance and Economics, 39*, https://www.eurojournals.com/finance.htm

Acs, Z. (2006). How Is Entrepreneurship Good for Economic Growth? *Innovations: Technology, Governance, Globalization, 1*(1), 97–107. doi:10.1162/itgg.2006.1.1.97

Acs, Z. J., Bardasi, E., Estrin, S., & Svejnar, J. (2011). Introduction to special issue of Small Business Economics on female entrepreneurship in developed and developing economies. *Small Business Economics, 37*(4), 393–396. doi:10.100711187-011-9372-1

Africa: First female entrepreneurs in the high-tech sector as new role models. (2018, September 28). Roland Berger. https://www.rolandberger.com/en/Insights/Publications/Africa-First-female-entrepreneurs-in-the-high-tech-sector-as-new-role-models.html

Alam, S. S., Jani, M. F. M., & Omar, N. A. (2011). An Empirical Study of Success Factors of Women Entrepreneurs in Southern Region in Malaysia. *International Journal of Economics and Finance*, *3*(2). doi:10.5539/ijef.v3n2p166

Alecchi, B. A. (2020). Toward Realizing the Potential of Latin America's Women Entrepreneurs: An Analysis of Barriers and Challenges. *Latin American Research Review*, *55*(3), 496–514. doi:10.25222/larr.108

Allahar, H. (2015). Female Entrepreneurship: The Experience of Latin America and the Caribbean. *European Academic Research*, *2*(10), 12739–12762. https://www.researchgate.net/publication/279191666_Female_Entrepreneurship_The_Experience_of_Latin_America_and_the_Caribbean#fullTextFileContent

Amrita, K., Garg, C. P., & Singh, S. (2018). Modelling the critical success factors of women entrepreneurship using fuzzy AHP framework. *Journal of Entrepreneurship in Emerging Economies*, *10*(1), 81–116. doi:10.1108/JEEE-03-2017-0017

Arasti, Z., Panahi, S. M. S., Zarei, B., & Rezaee, S. O. (2012). A Qualitative Study on Individual Factors Affecting Iranian Women Entrepreneurs' Growth Orientation. *International Business Research*, *5*(3). Advance online publication. doi:10.5539/ibr.v5n3p81

Aylward, E. (2007). *Traditional and Non-Traditional Female Entrepreneurs: An Exploration into what Influences their Selection of Industry Sector* [Masters Thesis, Waterford Institute of Technology].

Bello, H. S. (2019). Female Entrepreneurship in the African Fashion Industry: A Review of Its Determinants and Characteristics. *Palgrave Studies of Entrepreneurship in Africa*, 99–113. doi:10.1007/978-3-319-91265-3_5

Bennett, R., & Dann, S. (2000). The Changing Experience of Australian Female Entrepreneurs. *Gender, Work &Amp. Organization*, *7*(2), 75–83. doi:10.1111/1468-0432.00095

Bianchi, M., Parisi, V., & Salvatore, R. (2016). Female entrepreneurs: Motivations and constraints. An Italian regional study. *International Journal of Gender and Entrepreneurship*, *8*(3), 198–220. doi:10.1108/IJGE-08-2015-0029

Billson, B. (2022, March 14). *"Disappointing": Why it's easier for men to grow a business than women in Australia.* Kochie's Business Builders. https://www.kochiesbusinessbuilders.com.au/disappointing-why-its-easier-for-men-to-grow-a-business-than-women-in-australia/

Birley, S. (1987). Female entrepreneurs: Are they really any different? *Journal of Small Business Management, 27*(1), 32.

Bogenhold, D. (2004). Entrepreneurship: Multiple meanings and consequences. *International Journal of Entrepreneurship and Innovation Management, 4*(1), 3. doi:10.1504/IJEIM.2004.004496

Brydges, T., & Hracs, B. J. (2019). What motivates millennials? How intersectionality shapes the working lives of female entrepreneurs in Canada's fashion industry. *Gender, Place &Amp. Culture (Québec), 26*(4), 510–532. doi:10.1080/0966369X.2018.1552558

Bui, H. T., Kuan, A., & Chu, T. T. (2018). Female entrepreneurship in patriarchal society: Motivation and challenges. *Journal of Small Business &Amp. Entrepreneurship, 30*(4), 325–343. doi:10.1080/08276331.2018.1435841

Buttner, E. H. (1993). Female entrepreneurs: How far have they come? *Business Horizons, 36*(2), 59–65. doi:10.1016/S0007-6813(05)80039-4

Calderon, Iacovone, & Juarez. (2014). *Opportunity vs Necessity: Understanding the Heterogeneity of Female Micro-Entrepreneurs.* World Bank. https://www.worldbank.org/content/dam/Worldbank/Event/DEC/ABCDE/ABCDE-2015/378.%20Gabriela%20Calderon.pdf

Cavada, M. C., Bobek, V., Skoko, H., & Maček, A. (2018). Cultural Foundations of Female Entrepreneurship in Mexico: Challenges and Opportunities. *Naše Gospodarstvo/Our Economy, 64*(1), 28–40. doi:10.2478/ngoe-2018-0004

Cho, Y., Park, J., Han, S. J., Sung, M., & Park, C. (2020). Women entrepreneurs in South Korea: Motivations, challenges, and career success. *European Journal of Training and Development, 45*(2/3), 97–119. doi:10.1108/EJTD-03-2020-0039

Cromie, S. (1987). Motivations of aspiring male and female entrepreneurs. *Journal of Organizational Behavior, 8*(3), 251–261. doi:10.1002/job.4030080306

Danish, A. Y., & Smith, H. L. (2012). Female entrepreneurship in Saudi Arabia: Opportunities and challenges. *International Journal of Gender and Entrepreneurship, 4*(3), 216–235. doi:10.1108/17566261211264136

Dawson, C., & Henley, A. (2012). "Push" versus "pull" entrepreneurship: An ambiguous distinction? *International Journal of Entrepreneurial Behavior &Amp. Research, 18*(6), 697–719. doi:10.1108/13552551211268139

de Siles, L. E. (2011, May 6). *Female Entrepreneurship Theory: A Multidisciplinary Review of Resources.* SSRN. https://papers.ssrn.com/sol3/papers.cfm?abstract_id=1833385

Debroux, P. (2016). *Female Entrepreneurship in East and South-East Asia: Opportunities and Challenges (Chandos Asian Studies Series)* (1st ed.). Chandos Publishing.

Deng, S., Wang, X., & Alon, I. (2011). Framework for female entrepreneurship in China. *International Journal of Business and Emerging Markets, 3*(1), 3. doi:10.1504/IJBEM.2011.037682

Dobón, S. R., & Soriano, D. R. (2008). Exploring alternative approaches in service industries: The role of entrepreneurship. *Service Industries Journal, 28*(7), 877–882. doi:10.1080/02642060701846879

Fazalbhoy, S. (2014). Women Entrepreneurship as the Way for Economic Development. *Annual Research Journal of Symbiosis Centre for Management Studies, 2*(1), 117–127. https://www.scmspune.ac.in/chapter/pdf/Chapter%2010.pdf

Fernandes, C. E., Pereira, M., & Madeira, M. J. (2020). Fashion design entrepreneurship: A qualitative approach. In Textiles, Identity, and Innovation: In Touch (1st ed.). CRC Press. doi:10.1201/9780429286872-23

Forson, C., & Özbilgin, M. (2003). Dot-Com Women Entrepreneurs in the UK. *International Journal of Entrepreneurship and Innovation, 4*(1), 13–24. doi:10.5367/000000003101299366

Galvez, L., & Fernández, P. (2007). Female Entrepreneurship in Spain during the Nineteenth and Twentieth Centuries. *Business History Review, 81*(3), 495–515. doi:10.1017/S0007680500036692

Girotra, K., Terwiesch, C., & Ulrich, K. T. (2010). Idea Generation and the Quality of the Best Idea. *Management Science, 56*(4), 591–605. doi:10.1287/mnsc.1090.1144

Global Entrepreneurship Monitor Releases New Research Highlighting Women's Entrepreneurship Trends Across the Globe. (n.d.). GEM Global Entrepreneurship Monitor. https://www.gemconsortium.org/reports/womens-entrepreneurship

Growth and Stability in the Middle East and North Africa -- Economic Overview. (n.d.). IMF. https://www.imf.org/external/pubs/ft/mena/04econ.htm

Halkias, D., Nwajiuba, C., Harkiolakis, N., & Caracatsanis, S. M. (2011). Challenges facing women entrepreneurs in Nigeria. *Management Research Review, 34*(2), 221–235. doi:10.1108/01409171111102821

Henry, C. (2009). Women and the creative industries: Exploring the popular appeal. *Creative Industries Journal, 2*(2), 143–160. doi:10.1386/cij.2.2.143/1

How women are transforming the Arab world's start-up scene. (2020, February 7). World Economic Forum. https://www.weforum.org/agenda/2018/07/start-up-middle-east-arab-women-transforming-entrepreneurship/

Ilgaz, Z. (2022, June 23). 8 Qualities to Drive Your Success as a Female. *Entrepreneur.* https://www.entrepreneur.com/leadership/8-qualities-female-entrepreneurs-need-to-succeed/428136

International Labor Organization. (2018). *Women in Business and Management: Gaining Momentum in Eastern Europe and Central Asia.* International Labor Office. https://www.ilo.org/wcmsp5/groups/public/---ed_dialogue/---act_emp/documents/publication/wcms_624225.pdf

Isaga, N. (2019). Start-up motives and challenges facing female entrepreneurs in Tanzania. *International Journal of Gender and Entrepreneurship, 11*(2), 102–119. doi:10.1108/IJGE-02-2018-0010

Jaafar, M., Othman, R., & Jalali, A. (2014). Main Determinations of Female Entrepreneurs in the Construction Industry in Malaysia. *Project Management Journal, 45*(1), 76–86. doi:10.1002/pmj.21391

Kamberidou, I. (2013). Women entrepreneurs: 'we cannot have change unless we have men in the room.'. *Journal of Innovation and Entrepreneurship*, *2*(1), 6. doi:10.1186/2192-5372-2-6

Kamberidou, I. (2020). "Distinguished" women entrepreneurs in the digital economy and the multitasking whirlpool. *Journal of Innovation and Entrepreneurship*, *9*(1), 3. doi:10.118613731-020-0114-y

Kao, R. W. (1993). Defining Entrepreneurship: Past, Present and? *Creativity and Innovation Management*, *2*(1), 69–70. doi:10.1111/j.1467-8691.1993.tb00073.x

Kepler, E., & Shane, S. (2007). *Are Male and Female Entrepreneurs Really That Different*. Research Papers in Economics.

Krueger, D. (2000). Characteristics Of The Female Entrepreneur. *Journal of Business and Entrepreneurship, 12*(1), 87-0_12. https://christuniversity.knimbus.com/loginAndLaunch?docUrl=?url=https://www.proquest.com/scholarly-journals/characteristics-female-entrepreneur/docview/214235108/se-2

Kwong, C., Jones-Evans, D., & Thompson, P. (2012). Differences in perceptions of access to finance between potential male and female entrepreneurs. *International Journal of Entrepreneurial Behavior &Amp. Research*, *18*(1), 75–97. doi:10.1108/13552551211201385

Lerner, M., Brush, C., & Hisrich, R. (1997). Israeli women entrepreneurs: An examination of factors affecting performance. *Journal of Business Venturing*, *12*(4), 315–339. doi:10.1016/S0883-9026(96)00061-4

Lock, R., & Smith, H. L. (2016). The impact of female entrepreneurship on economic growth in Kenya. *International Journal of Gender and Entrepreneurship*, *8*(1), 90–96. doi:10.1108/IJGE-11-2015-0040

Lockyer, J., & George, S. (2012). What women want: Barriers to female entrepreneurship in the West Midlands. *International Journal of Gender and Entrepreneurship*, *4*(2), 179–195. doi:10.1108/17566261211234661

Mehtap, S., Caputo, A., & Pellegrini, M. M. (2016). Encouraging Female Entrepreneurship in Jordan: Environmental Factors, Obstacles and Challenges. *Entrepreneurship and Management in an Islamic Context*, 207–225. doi:10.1007/978-3-319-39679-8_13

Mrkonjić, E. (2022, July 7). *Women Entrepreneurs Statistics: Equality in 2022*. Writer's Block Live. https://writersblocklive.com/blog/women-entrepreneurs-statistics/

Nawaser, K., Khaksar, S. M. S., Shaksian, F., & Afshar Jahanshahi, A. (2011). Motivational and Legal Barriers of Entrepreneurship Development. *International Journal of Business and Management*, *6*(11). doi:10.5539/ijbm.v6n11p112

Ndubisi, N. O., & Kahraman, C. (2005). Malaysian women entrepreneurs: Understanding the ICT usage behaviors and drivers. *Journal of Enterprise Information Management*, *18*(6), 721–739. doi:10.1108/17410390510628418

Olson, S. F., & Currie, H. M. (1992). Female Entrepreneurs: Personal Value Systems and Business Strategies in a Male-Dominated Industry. *Journal of Small Business Management, 30*(1). https://www.proquest.com/docview/221006040/abstract/18AF1B10320A46E9PQ/1?accountid=38885

Pareek, P., & Bagrecha, C. (2018). An analysis of the financial challenges faced by women entrepreneurs. *International Journal of Scientific and Engineering Research, 9*(10), 2229–5518. https://www.researchgate.net/publication/362429718_An_analysis_of_the_financial_challenges_faced_by_women_entrepreneurs

Pareek, P., & Bagrecha, C. (2018b). Socio – Personal Challenges Faced by Indian Women Entrepreneur. *International Journal of Management Studies, V*(4(8)), 38. doi:10.18843/ijms/v5i4(8)/05

Pistrui, D., & Sreih, J. F. (2010). Islam, entrepreneurship and business values in the Middle East. *International Journal of Entrepreneurship and Innovation Management, 12*(1), 107. doi:10.1504/IJEIM.2010.033170

Rahmatullah, M., & Zaman, F. (2014). Female Entrepreneurship in Bangladesh: Constraints, Motivation and Success. *Bangladesh e-Journal of Sociology, 11*(2), 65–77. https://www.academia.edu/22377887/Motivational_factors_and_the_constraints_of_women_entrepreneurship_development_in_Bangladesh

Rey-Martí, A., Tur Porcar, A., & Mas-Tur, A. (2015). Linking female entrepreneurs' motivation to business survival. *Journal of Business Research, 68*(4), 810–814. doi:10.1016/j.jbusres.2014.11.033

Robichaud, Y., Cachon, J.-C., & McGraw, E. (2014). Why Are Female-Owned Businesses Smaller? An Empirical Study in Canada and the United States. *Journal of Management Policy and Practice, 16*(1). http://www.m.www.na-businesspress.com/JMPP/RobichaudY_Web16_1_.pdf

Rodie, A. R., & Martin, C. L. (2001). Competing in the service sector - The entrepreneurial challenge. *International Journal of Entrepreneurial Behavior &Amp. Research, 7*(1), 5–21. doi:10.1108/13552550110385718

Rudhumbu, N., du Plessis, E. E., & Maphosa, C. (2020). Challenges and opportunities for women entrepreneurs in Botswana: Revisiting the role of entrepreneurship education. *Journal of International Education in Business, 13*(2), 183–201. doi:10.1108/JIEB-12-2019-0058

Sandberg, W. R., & Hofer, C. W. (1987). Improving new venture performance: The role of strategy, industry structure, and the entrepreneur. *Journal of Business Venturing, 2*(1), 5–28. doi:10.1016/0883-9026(87)90016-4

Sarfaraz, L., Faghih, N., & Majd, A. (2014). The relationship between women entrepreneurship and gender equality. *Journal of Global Entrepreneurship Research, 2*(1), 6. doi:10.1186/2251-7316-2-6

Saxon, R., & Gillin, M. (2004). *Female entrepreneurship in Australia*. Swinburne University of Technology. https://researchbank.swinburne.edu.au/file/f6045220-08ee-4c62-9b1b-409764424687/1/PDF%20%28Published%20version%29.pdf

Shah, H., & Saurabh, P. (2015). Women Entrepreneurs in Developing Nations: Growth and Replication Strategies and Their Impact on Poverty Alleviation. *Technology Innovation Management Review*, *5*(8), 34–43. doi:10.22215/timreview/921

Shahedul, Q. M. (2012). A Characteristic Model of Successful Women Entrepreneurs in the UK. *Journal of Services Research*, *12*(1), 89–113. https://www.proquest.com/docview/1019285931?fromopenview=true&pq-origsite=gscholar

Sospeter, N. G. (2012). Challenges Facing Women Entrepreneurs in the Construction Industry in Tanzania. *Journal of Business and Economics*, *7*(11). Advance online publication. doi:10.15341/jbe(2155-7950)/11.07.2016/016

Sriram, V., & Mersha, T. (2010). Stimulating entrepreneurship in Africa. *World Journal of Entrepreneurship, Management and Sustainable Development*, *6*(4), 257–272. doi:10.1108/20425961201000020

Statistics and data of all countries in Africa. (n.d.). Worlddata.info. https://www.worlddata.info/africa/index.php

Tan, J. (2007). Breaking the "Bamboo Curtain" and the "Glass Ceiling": The Experience of Women Entrepreneurs in High-Tech Industries in an Emerging Market. *Journal of Business Ethics*, *80*(3), 547–564. doi:10.100710551-007-9454-9

Thaddeus, E. (2012b, season-04). Perspectives: Entrepreneurship Development & Growth of Enterprises in Nigeria.

The Startup VC Team. (2020, December 17). *Women Entrepreneurship in Latin America?* The StartupVC. https://www.thestartupvc.com/startup-news/women-entrepreneurship-in-latin-america/

Umar, M., Ali, S. A., & Sial, M. H. (2022). Exploring Women Entrepreneurship Prospects, Challenges, and Barriers in Pakistan. *International Journal of E-Entrepreneurship and Innovation*, *12*(1), 1–17. doi:10.4018/IJEEI.290823

Verheul, I., Stel, A. V., & Thurik, R. (2006). Explaining female and male entrepreneurship at the country level. *Entrepreneurship &Amp. Région et Développement*, *18*(2), 151–183. doi:10.1080/08985620500532053

Vinze, M. D. (1987). Women Entrepreneurs in India. In *A Socio-Economic Study of Delhi 1975-85*. South Asia Books.

Waseem, A. (2018). Female Entrepreneurship and Economic Growth: An Institutional Theory Analysis. *Pakistan Journal of Gender Studies, 16*. Academia. https://www.academia.edu/50993645/Female_Entrepreneurship_And_Economic_Growth_An_Institutional_Theory_Analysis

Welsh, D. H., Memili, E., & Kaciak, E. (2016). An empirical analysis of the impact of family moral support on Turkish women entrepreneurs. *Journal of Innovation &Amp. Knowledge (Beverly Hills, Calif.)*, *1*(1), 3–12. doi:10.1016/j.jik.2016.01.012

Wiriya, P. (2022, September 28). *Growth Impact of Women Entrepreneurs in India & Importance of Financial Independence*. Kinara Capital. https://kinaracapital.com/financial-independence-and-growth-impact-of-women-entrepreneurs-in-india/

Woetzel, J., Madgavkar, A., Ellingrud, K., Labaye, E., Devillard, S., Kutcher, E., Manyika, J., Dobbs, R., & Krishnan, M. (2022, April 12). *How advancing women's equality can add $12 trillion to global growth.* McKinsey & Company. https://www.mckinsey.com/featured-insights/employment-and-growth/how-advancing-womens-equality-can-add-12-trillion-to-gl
obal-growth

Women Entrepreneurship and Leadership. (2022, November 15). European Institute of Innovation & Technology (EIT). https://eit.europa.eu/our-activities/entrepreneurship/women-entrepreneurship-and-leadership

Women entrepreneurship is soaring in the US, a new survey finds. (2022, September 23). World Economic Forum. https://www.weforum.org/agenda/2022/07/women-entrepreneurs-gusto-gender/

Woolley, A., & Malone, T. (2011). What makes a team smarter? More women. *Harvard Business Review, 89*(6), 32. PMID:21714385

World Bank. (2012). Female Entrepreneurship: Program Guidelines and Case Studies. Washington DC

World Bank Group. (2022, October 17). *Defying Global Turmoil, Poverty Rates Fall Across Central Asia*. World Bank. https://www.worldbank.org/en/news/press-release/2022/10/17/defying-global-turmoil-poverty-rates-fall-across-central-asia

Yunis, M., Hashim, H., & Anderson, A. (2018). Enablers and Constraints of Female Entrepreneurship in Khyber Pukhtunkhawa, Pakistan: Institutional and Feminist Perspectives. *Sustainability, 11*(1), 27. doi:10.3390u11010027

Zgheib, P. (2018). Multi-level framework of push-pull entrepreneurship: Comparing American and Lebanese women. *International Journal of Entrepreneurial Behavior &Amp. Research, 24*(3), 768–786. doi:10.1108/IJEBR-12-2015-0314

Chapter 7
Female Entrepreneurs and Employees Among the Economy:
Selected Indicators From Turkey

Kenan Aydın
Istanbul Gelisim University, Turkey

Tugba Kantarcı
Tekirdag Namık Kemal University, Turkey

Seda Yildirim
Tekirdag Namık Kemal University, Turkey

ABSTRACT

Female entrepreneurs and employees are so important for the economy. Especially, sustainable development encourages more female empowerment in the world. When considering the economic support of female entrepreneurs and employees for GDP in a specific country, the number of each female entrepreneur will be so valuable. On the other side, the sustainability of enterprises should also be considered. The Covid-19 pandemic affected many employees and entrepreneurs negatively, and the global economy has fallen into a big crisis. Rates of economic growth and employment all declined due to the Covid-19 crises globally. This study aims to explore female entrepreneurs and employees among Turkish economy by investigating recorded statistics for Covid-19 period and post-Covid-19 period in Türkiye. It is thought to give a brief framework for the importance of female entrepreneurs and employees for economic growth and also sustainable development.

DOI: 10.4018/978-1-6684-7669-7.ch007

INTRODUCTION

Equality in education, employment, wages, etc. is a main theme within sustainable development goals. 2030 Sustainable Development Goals includes specific goals as "Goal 4; Goal 5; Goal 8 and Goal 10" to support reducing inequalities between women and men in the long term (United Nations Department of Economic and Social Affairs Sustainable Development, n.d.). Women's employment is among the priority issues in every economy and the absence of women's employment is seen as a factor that hinders sustainable development (Yıldırım et al., 2019). The desired goal in sustainable development is to achieve a development by providing the balance between "economy, social and environmental" issues (Munasinghe, 2002; Yıldırım and Yıldırım, 2020). Therefore, the lack and scarcity of women's employment and the low and inadequate female entrepreneurship are indicators of an imbalance in the economy (Erdogan et al., 2012).

Entrepreneurship, on the other hand, plays an important driving role in terms of employment and economic development with its social welfare effect. Entrepreneurship can be handled differently in each country due to cultural and developmental differences (Acs et al., 2011). Nevertheless, it is emphasized that entrepreneurship should be supported in achieving sustainable development and the gender gap should be reduced. Women's entrepreneurship is an important factor in economic growth in terms of both its employment-creating effect and more women's participation in business life (social welfare). The low or lack of female entrepreneurship will bring negative returns in a country or economy in the long run (Jamali, 2009). The rise of entrepreneurship in a country can solve some social problems and support economic development, allowing the country to enter a balanced development and growth process. In the literature, the relationships and effects between entrepreneurship, gender equality and economic growth have been frequently examined. The conclusion of the studies is that it can be said that it is beneficial for countries to achieve economic growth by providing equality (Aparicio et al., 2022). Encouraging women's entrepreneurship, especially in developing countries, will support economic and social development more rapidly. In some studies, it has been observed that female entrepreneurship has positive effects on the rate of increase, general household welfare and consumption. Because, entrepreneurship provides women with economic confidence (Panda, 2018). Supporting women's entrepreneurship will also be an effective factor in reducing poverty (Kobeissi, 2010). However, since the difficulties and obstacles faced by women entrepreneurs vary from country to country, country-specific analyzes may yield more useful results.

Since the 1950s, important changes have been observed in the positions of women entrepreneurs and the position of women in politics. From a theoretical point of view, academic research on women's entrepreneurship in the literature is carried out worldwide. While studies conducted in the 70s and 80s focused on gender-focused research; Feminist theories gained weight in research in the 90s. (Minniti and Naude, 2010). Today, women's employment and women's entrepreneurship are mainly discussed in the context of economic and social development in economic development studies and sustainability studies. For example, Yıldırım et al. (2019) examined the impact of education on women's careers in terms of sustainable development for Türkiye, and it was seen in the study that the higher the education level, the more positively women's careers were affected. In a study on role conflict of women entrepreneurs in Sub-Saharan Africa, it was seen that factors such as "negotiation, commitment to the entrepreneurial role, commitment to social roles, pleasing everyone, seeking social support and getting outside support" affect the role conflict of women entrepreneurs. Developing support programs that develop and strengthen the personal resources of women entrepreneurs may be a more effective strategy (Hundera et al., 2019).

Looking at the global picture of women's entrepreneurship, the following can be said (Kuadli, 2022): Many women have started their own businesses and achieved financial independence in order to get rid of social constraints. In the last 20 years, female entrepreneur statistics have shown that the number of female business owners has increased by 114%. For example; More than 46% of private businesses in Ghana are owned by women. 36% of small businesses worldwide are owned by women entrepreneurs. In the USA, 1.3 million women entrepreneurs operate in California, and there are more than 860,000 women entrepreneur-owned businesses in Texas. The World Bank states that there is a significant increase in developing countries. Accordingly, it is stated that there is at least one female employer/entrepreneur in 8-10 million small and medium-sized enterprises in the world. Some of the barriers faced by women entrepreneurs in developing economies are lack of access to finance and restrictions on owning or managing property (World Economic Forum, 2022).

Türkiye is an important country when considering its position among OECD countries and EU countries in the long term. Türkiye is a developing country and has an advantage of human capital. If the human capital is efficiently monitored and managed, economic growth and sustainable development can be achieved more efficiently. This study aims to present recent indicators on female entrepreneurs and female workers in Türkiye. In Turkish literature, there are many studies investigating the relationship between female employment and economic growth. For example, Serel and Özdemir examined the relationship between female employment and economic growth in Türkiye for the period of 200:1-2013:4. They determined that female employment contributed economic growth positively and pointed out the importance of female employment in Türkiye. Günsoy and Özsoy (2012) determined that education was an important motive for female employment and the balance between male and female employment decreased the poverty in Türkiye. Pata (2018) studied female employment and economic growth in Türkiye for the period of 1988-2015, he determined that female employment had no significant effect on agriculture sector and trade sector. On the other side, female employment spurred economic growth through service sector in Türkiye in the related years. Türlüoğlu (2018) determined that female employment contributed economic growth positively in Türkiye for the period of 1999-2017. Kasa and Alptekin (2015) found that female employment influenced economic growth positively in Türkiye. Zeren and Savrul (2018) studied factors influencing female employment in Türkiye for the period of 1991 and 2014. They determined that economic growth, unemployment rate and urbanization are the factors affecting the female employment rate. Çolak (2021) investigated gender inequality and economic growth in Türkiye. She found that economic growth could decrease the inequality of wages between women and men through education level. Tütüncü and Zengin (2020) studied female employment and economic growth in E7 countries for the period of 1991-2016. They said determining that there was a statistically significant long- and short-term relationship between female employment and economic growth in E7 countries showed the importance of female employment.

INDICATORS FOR FEMALE ENTREPRENEURS AMONG OECD COUNTRIES

This part will present indicators for female entrepreneurship from OECD countries as:

Table 1 shows each country from OECD for female entrepreneurship between 2019 and 2021. In 2019, the share of self-employed in services for female entrepreneurship was higher than other areas in OECD countries. In addition, the share of self-employed in services was higher rates among OECD countries by 2020.

Table 1. Indicators of female entrepreneurship in OECD (2019-2021; percentage)

Indicator	2019		2020		2021	
	Share of self-employed in manufacturing	Share of self-employed in services	Share of self-employed in manufacturing	Share of self-employed in services	Share of self-employed in manufacturing	Share of self-employed in services
Austria	4,1	89,1	3,1	90,4	..	..
Belgium	1,5	91,2	1,9	90,6	2,0	90,9
Canada	6,5	90,5	6,1	91,0	..	..
Czech Republic	3,6	86,2	-	87,5	..	..
Denmark	8,6	73,7	8,8	61,5	..	..
Estonia	3,6	77,4	4,3	77,6	..	..
Finland	4,7	84,5	4,5	85,8	..	..
France	4,1	91,2	4,3	83,2	..	..
Germany	2,9	61,8	2,9	65,4	..	..
Greece	5,5	79,2	5,3	80,9	..	..
Hungary	..	47,8	-	54,2	..	..
Iceland	..	72,9	..	65,8	..	..
Ireland	5,3	88,3	5,3	88,6	..	..
Italy	11,2	83,2	9,6	85,3	7,7	88,0
Japan	..	61,9	..	64,0	..	..
Luxembourg	..	..	..	..	..	..
Mexico	2,0	83,5	2,2	85,9	..	..
Netherlands	6,0	77,1	5,6	76,9	4,7	75,2
New Zealand	..	75,2	..	63,7	..	..
Norway	4,3	56,2	4,8	55,2	..	..
Poland	7,3	77,7	5,5	76,7	..	..
Portugal	7,5	79,9	7,1	84,3	..	..
Slovak Republic	9,2	72,2	8,0	74,1	..	..
Slovenia	5,2	85,5	4,9	86,9	..	..
Spain	4,8	86,1	5,4	85,6	..	..
Sweden	5,3	78,9	5,5	78,7	..	..
Switzerland	19,9	55,3	..	..	..	..
Türkiye	3,4	92,2	..	..	..	..
United Kingdom	..	..	..	..	..	..
Non-OECD Economies	South Africa					

Source: OECD.Stat, (t.y.a)

Table 2 shows the share of women inventors among OECD countries between 2015 and 2019. Looking at Table 2, it can be said that there has been a significant decrease in the ratio of female investors in OECD countries compared to the following years (from 2015 to 2019). On the other hand, there has been an increase in female investor rates in Türkiye, Denmark, Estonia, Greece, Austria and Portugal.

Table 2. Share of women inventors in OECD (2015-2019; percentage)

Country	2015	2016	2017	2018	2019
Australia	12,6	12,7	13,5	13,1	13,3
Austria	6,4	6,4	6,4	5,3	5,2
Belgium	13,8	14,7	15,2	13,4	12,3
Canada	12,6	12,6	12,6	11,5	11,4
Chile	24,9	25,6	22,5	17,4	13,2
Colombia	26,9	27,1	22,4	21,7	16,8
Czech Republic	10,1	9,7	9,7	7,5	6,8
Denmark	11,2	11,2	11,4	13,0	13,7
Estonia	15,3	12,9	16,4	15,1	16,2
Finland	10,8	10,9	11,0	8,8	8,1
France	14,4	14,3	13,7	12,2	11,3
Germany	8,2	8,2	7,9	7,0	6,5
Greece	21,8	22,2	22,1	20,6	21,5
Hungary	9,4	9,7	9,3	8,6	6,9
Iceland	14,4	16,8	16,1	10,8	..
Ireland	12,7	13,5	13,2	12,3	11,6
Israel	13,6	13,3	12,3	11,1	10,1
Italy	11,5	11,3	11,1	9,3	8,1
Japan	7,9	8,1	8,3	8,2	8,1
Lithuania	22,5	22,7	24,5	19,2	16,3
Luxembourg	9,4	10,0	9,4	9,9	9,4
Mexico	13,2	12,2	11,2	10,7	9,7
Netherlands	10,7	10,8	10,8	10,3	10,1
New Zealand	12,2	13,3	12,5	8,5	5,5
Norway	9,8	9,5	8,7	8,2	7,9
Poland	16,1	14,3	13,5	12,1	11,7
Portugal	27,7	26,8	26,2	25,7	26,6
Slovak Republic	8,2	10,1	8,7	8,4	6,8
Slovenia	14,3	9,9	12,0	8,3	8,4
Spain	20,4	20,9	20,1	17,0	14,6
Sweden	9,4	10,1	10,2	8,7	7,7
Switzerland	10,8	11,0	10,7	9,3	8,5
Türkiye	15,8	13,4	13,2	14,1	16,0
United Kingdom	11,7	12,0	11,7	11,0	10,5
United States	12,6	12,9	13,2	12,7	12,4

Source: OECD.Stat, (t.y.b)

Table 3 shows positive business status by sex among OECD countries in 2019. While in most countries the job position of men is higher than that of women, in some countries the job position of women is higher than that of men.

Table 3. Positive business status and outlook by sex in OECD (2019; percentage)

Indicator	2019			
	Positive current business status		Positive outlook on business	
	Men	Women	Men	Women
Australia	57,7	56,6	68,0	78,0
Austria	70,8	58,9	78,0	62,8
Belgium	65,6	73,9	71,5	77,8
Canada	65,7	66,2	78,9	77,9
Chile	53,4	62,1	81,9	79,2
Colombia	64,8	63,3	85,2	91,2
Costa Rica	61,0	56,2	75,2	78,0
Czech Republic	63,8	66,5	73,0	73,8
Denmark	71,4	73,4	75,3	81,9
Finland	62,7	53,4	73,0	64,5
France	61,3	50,3	69,8	66,2
Germany	68,7	60,3	74,8	64,7
Greece	49,4	51,5	56,1	56,2
Hungary	68,6	65,4	78,1	73,7
Ireland	59,1	68,9	74,9	78,0
Israel	54,6	52,2	73,6	70,5
Italy	63,7	58,6	62,5	59,7
Japan	39,8	27,4	42,1	39,4
Korea	52,6	55,2	52,3	63,0
Lithuania	60,5	64,6	75,7	81,4
Mexico	67,9	67,7	87,6	89,9
Netherlands	68,0	68,4	76,0	79,3
New Zealand	66,8	64,5	81,3	75,5
Norway	66,8	62,5	75,5	65,4
Poland	76,2	71,0	83,2	78,5
Portugal	76,1	60,8	92,1	87,4
Slovak Republic	68,6	65,2	83,7	77,7
Slovenia	59,2	62,2	77,2	79,8
Spain	68,1	53,3	82,1	61,4
Sweden	67,8	77,1	74,2	79,8
Switzerland	71,8	69,1	79,3	77,8
Türkiye	72,9	71,6	68,6	67,8
United Kingdom	63,9	62,9	69,6	79,8
United States	72,9	62,5	79,2	83,1

Source: OECD.Stat, (t.y.c)

Table 4. Share of the population who report borrowing money to start a business by sex

Countries	2017	
	Men	Women
Australia	41,0	35,6
Austria	21,0	18,4
Belgium	35,6	29,9
Canada	34,5	37,2
Chile	12,2	8,7
Czech Republic	19,9	19,3
Denmark	43,1	39,1
Estonia	24,3	25,6
Finland	36,8	34,3
France	30,2	28,9
Germany	23,4	18,9
Greece	10,8	9,3
Hungary	14,3	14,5
Ireland	28,2	27,0
Israel	35,6	35,7
Italy	22,2	11,6
Japan	20,0	14,7
Korea	30,1	22,1
Luxembourg	38,9	37,2
Mexico	4,8	3,9
Netherlands	48,2	44,6
New Zealand	31,8	33,2
Norway	57,3	51,4
Poland	16,7	14,2
Portugal	25,0	23,5
Slovak Republic	30,9	23,0
Slovenia	16,5	17,2
Spain	41,2	30,3
Sweden	50,4	46,2
Switzerland	31,8	28,0
Türkiye	11,0	10,9
United Kingdom	27,4	25,9
United States	36,3	31,6

Source: OECD.Stat, (t.y.d)

Table 4 shows the share of the population who report borrowing money to start a business by sex among OECD countries. In 2017, it can be said that men generally borrowed more when starting a business than women.

FEMALE ENTREPRENEURS AND EMPLOYEES IN TÜRKİYE

Historically, the position of women in Türkiye has been handled socially and economically at a more advanced level than many other countries in the world (Acar, 2019). However, cultural factors and family responsibilities may cause women to take less part employment in Türkiye (Tahtalıoğlu, 2016; Durmaz, 2016; Soysal 2010). At this point, significant progress has been made in Türkiye recently. Especially, from the perspective of sustainable development, women's right to equal education, equal employment and equal pay is on the agenda of policy makers as an important goal (UN News Centre, 2017). In this section, it is aimed to present women entrepreneurship and female employee information in line with the data obtained from TURKSTAT's website. Using various indicators, it is planned to give an up-to-date economic profile on women's entrepreneurship and the situation of women workers in Türkiye.

It would be useful to compile some data regarding the place of women in social and economic life in Türkiye. First of all, the information of male and female population in Türkiye is presented in Table 5:

Table 5. Population by gender and 2020-2021

Age group	Total		Male		Female	
	2020	2021	2020	2021	2020	2021
0-4	6 121 707	5 913 609	3 140 172	3 033 029	2 981 535	2 880 580
5-9	6 526 593	6 624 202	3 349 253	3 398 812	3 177 340	3 225 390
10-14	6 419 937	6 438 152	3 294 985	3 304 851	3 124 952	3 133 301
15-19	6 230 114	6 229 709	3 201 588	3 203 519	3 028 526	3 026 190
20-24	6 663 636	6 741 580	3 408 434	3 445 410	3 255 202	3 296 170
25-29	6 370 954	6 476 899	3 240 543	3 296 919	3 130 411	3 179 980
30-34	6 318 894	6 341 787	3 199 710	3 212 668	3 119 184	3 129 119
35-39	6 473 583	6 386 208	3 270 512	3 228 063	3 203 071	3 158 145
40-44	6 235 110	6 547 162	3 145 645	3 294 071	3 089 465	3 253 091
45-49	5 563 666	5 662 261	2 788 035	2 838 766	2 775 631	2 823 495
50-54	4 584 632	4 754 484	2 325 190	2 403 726	2 259 442	2 350 758
55-59	4 577 587	4 707 180	2 273 088	2 337 304	2 304 499	2 369 876
60-64	3 574 394	3 611 916	1 764 938	1 776 254	1 809 456	1 835 662
65-69	2 938 715	3 156 448	1 399 052	1 508 990	1 539 663	1 647 458
70-74	2 131 705	2 175 024	960 742	982 573	1 170 963	1 192 451
75-79	1 355 346	1 392 718	583 671	598 307	771 675	794 411
80-84	861 199	861 409	339 767	340 568	521 432	520 841
85-89	466 748	456 548	177 532	169 807	289 216	286 741
90+	199 842	202 977	53 128	54 464	146 714	148 513
Total	83 614 362	84 680 273	41 915 985	42 428 101	41 698 377	42 252 172

Source: TURKSTAT, (2022a)

As showing by Table 5, it can be said that the male population in Türkiye is more than the female population in 2021. Although the difference is small, the male population is more than the female population. On the other hand, as the population ages, the proportion of women is higher than that of men.

Table 6 shows the share of formal education by sex among Türkiye between 2011 and 2020. According to the current education status data in Türkiye, the rate of men's education status is higher than that of women's education status.

Table 6. Formal education completed by gender (Population aged 25 years and over), 2011-2020

Year	Illiterate	Literate without diploma	Primary school	Primary education	Junior high school and equivalent	High school and equivalent	Higher education	Master	Doctorate (Phd)
Total									
2011	7,2	6,3	36,7	11,1	6,9	19,0	11,5	1,0	0,3
2012	6,3	6,8	35,8	11,7	6,7	19,4	12,1	1,0	0,3
2013	5,9	6,8	34,6	12,4	6,5	18,9	13,3	1,2	0,4
2014	5,7	6,5	32,9	11,8	7,9	19,4	14,2	1,3	0,4
2015	5,5	6,2	31,9	11,5	7,8	19,7	15,6	1,4	0,4
2016	5,1	5,9	29,6	12,7	8,7	19,7	16,5	1,4	0,4
2017	4,8	5,7	28,6	13,4	8,4	19,9	16,8	1,8	0,4
2018	4,5	5,4	26,5	14,4	8,8	20,5	17,5	2,0	0,4
2019	4,1	4,9	25,0	11,4	12,5	21,4	18,2	2,2	0,4
2020	3,8	4,7	24,1	10,8	13,2	21,6	19,2	2,2	0,4
Male									
2011	2,5	4,0	32,6	13,8	8,5	23,2	13,9	1,2	0,4
2012	2,1	4,1	31,5	14,4	8,3	23,6	14,5	1,2	0,4
2013	2,0	4,1	30,2	15,2	8,0	23,0	15,7	1,4	0,4
2014	1,9	3,8	28,4	14,3	9,6	23,6	16,5	1,5	0,4
2015	1,8	3,5	27,5	13,7	9,6	23,7	18,1	1,6	0,4
2016	1,6	3,2	25,1	15,1	10,3	23,6	18,8	1,7	0,4
2017	1,5	3,0	24,1	15,8	10,0	23,9	19,0	2,1	0,5
2018	1,3	2,7	22,0	16,7	10,3	24,6	19,6	2,3	0,5
2019	1,2	2,4	20,5	13,1	14,3	25,4	20,1	2,4	0,5
2020	1,0	2,2	19,6	12,5	15,0	25,6	21,1	2,5	0,5
Female									
2011	11,8	8,5	40,7	8,4	5,3	15,0	9,1	0,8	0,2
2012	10,3	9,4	40,0	9,0	5,2	15,3	9,8	0,8	0,2
2013	9,7	9,5	38,9	9,7	5,1	14,9	11,0	1,0	0,3
2014	9,4	9,2	37,2	9,5	6,2	15,3	11,9	1,0	0,3
2015	9,1	8,9	36,2	9,3	6,0	15,7	13,3	1,2	0,3
2016	8,6	8,6	33,9	10,4	7,1	15,8	14,2	1,2	0,3
2017	8,1	8,3	33,0	11,1	6,9	16,0	14,7	1,6	0,3
2018	7,6	8,0	30,9	12,2	7,3	16,5	15,5	1,7	0,3
2019	6,9	7,4	29,4	9,7	10,7	17,5	16,3	1,9	0,3
2020	6,5	7,1	28,5	9,2	11,4	17,7	17,3	1,9	0,4

Source: TURKSTAT, (2022b)

Looking at the results of the household labor force survey, the total employment rate of people aged 15 and over in Türkiye in 2020 was found to be 42.8%. The rate of women in total employment was recorded as 26.3% and the rate of men as 59.8% (see Table 7).

Table 7. Labor force participation rate

Year	Gender	Total	Illiterate	Less than high school	High school	Vocational high school	Higher education
2019	Total	53,0	18,2	48,3	54,2	65,1	79,3
	Male	72,0	32,1	68,1	71,3	80,8	85,8
	Female	34,4	15,4	28,0	34,1	42,2	71,5
2020	Total	49,3	14,7	44,0	49,5	61,6	75,0
	Male	68,2	26,4	63,4	66,4	77,9	83,3
	Female	30,9	12,4	24,1	29,9	37,0	65,6

Source: TURKSTAT, (2022c)

Table 8 shows employment rate by sex and educational level among Türkiye for 2019 and 2020. When we look at the employment rates by education level and gender in Türkiye, the employment rates of men are higher than women at all levels of education.

Table 8. Employment rate by sex and educational level

Year	Gender	Total	Illiterate	Less than high school	High school	Vocational high school	Higher education
2019	Total	45,7	16,6	41,9	45,5	55,2	68,4
	Male	63,1	26,6	59,1	61,8	71,5	77,0
	Female	28,7	14,5	24,2	26,3	31,3	58,3
2020	Total	42,8	13,4	38,4	41,8	52,7	65,4
	Male	59,8	21,9	55,1	57,3	68,9	74,9
	Female	26,3	11,7	21,3	23,8	28,3	54,6

Source: TURKSTAT, (2022d)

Table 9 shows unemployment rate by sex and educational level among Türkiye. When we look at the unemployment rate by education level and gender in Türkiye, overall unemployment rates for men are higher than for women.

Table 9. Unemployment rate by sex and educational level

Year	Gender	Total	Illiterate	Less than high school	High school	Vocational high school	Higher education
2019	Total	13,7	9,2	13,2	16,1	15,3	13,7
	Male	12,4	17,2	13,1	13,3	11,5	10,3
	Female	16,5	5,8	13,4	22,8	25,8	18,5
2020	Total	13,2	9,1	12,7	15,6	14,4	12,8
	Male	12,3	17,0	13,1	13,7	11,5	10,1
	Female	15,0	5,6	11,6	20,3	23,5	16,8

Source: TURKSTAT, (2022e)

In Table 10, part-time employment rates are shown by gender. According to the latest data, the part-time employment rate of women in Türkiye was 19.5%. It is seen that women are employed part-time more than men.

Table 10. The Percent of employed working part-time by sex, 2014-2020 (15+ age)

Year	Total	Male	Female
2014	11,7	7,1	22,6
2015	10,9	6,7	20,6
2016	10,3	6,5	19,1
2017	10,5	6,6	19,1
2018	10,9	7,1	19,1
2019	10,4	7,1	17,4
2020	12,4	9,3	19,5

Source: TURKSTAT, (2022f)

The employment rates of women and men with children under the age of 3 in the household are shown in Table 11. In total, the employment rate of women in the 25-49 age group with children under the age of 3 was recorded as 25.2%. The employment rate of men with children under the age of 3 from 2014 to 2020 is higher than that of women.

Table 11. Employment rate of persons aged 25-49 with a child under age 3 living in the household

Year	Total	Male	Female
2014	59,8	90,2	24,3
2015	59,7	90,4	24,3
2016	59,4	89,2	25,4
2017	61,0	90,3	27,4
2018	60,5	90,4	26,5
2019	58,7	87,3	26,7
2020	56,8	85,5	25,2

Source: TURKSTAT, (2022g)

Table 12 shows the ratios of women and men employed in a childless household for the years 2014 to 2020. Accordingly, the employment rates of male childless households are higher than females.

Table 12. Employment rate of persons aged 25-49 with no children living in the household

Year	Total	Male	Female
2014	65,4	77,3	48,7
2015	66,6	78,1	50,1
2016	67,2	78,1	51,3
2017	68,1	78,4	53,0
2018	68,0	78,1	53,4
2019	66,0	75,1	52,8
2020	63,1	71,5	50,7

Source: TURKSTAT, (2022h)

Table 13 shows the rate of satisfaction of women with time spent on commuting to work between 2013 and 2021. It has been observed that 63.5% of women in business life are satisfied with the time spent commuting to and from work.

Table 13. Satisfaction with time spent on commuting to work (%), 2013-2021

Female	2013	2014	2015	2016	2017	2018	2019	2020	2021
Very satisfied	4,7	4,5	5,3	5,0	4,6	4,6	5,6	9,3	3,9
Satisfied	62,9	60,9	59,9	64,6	63,7	63,1	63,0	55,2	59,6
Neither satisfied nor unsatisfied	11,2	12,7	14,9	12,7	12,3	11,3	13,7	19,0	14,6
Not satisfied	17,2	17,0	15,9	15,2	16,3	17,7	14,6	12,6	16,6
Not satisfied at all	4,1	5,0	4,1	2,4	3,0	3,3	3,2	3,8	5,4

Source: TURKSTAT, (2022i)

In Table 14, the ratios of women and men to be ambassadors are given for the years 1982-2021. Accordingly, the rate of female ambassadors in 2021 was 26.5%.

Table 14. Number and proportion of ambassadors by sex, 1982-2021

Year	Total	Male	Female
1982	**102**	101	1
1990	**125**	124	1
1996	**168**	165	3
2000	**174**	166	8
2001	**194**	182	12
2002	**202**	188	14
2003	**193**	178	15
2004	**188**	170	18
2005	**199**	180	19
2006	**193**	174	19
2007	**160**	145	15
2008	**157**	140	17
2009	**157**	140	17
2010	**190**	169	21
2011	**193**	170	23
2012	**189**	167	22
2013	**214**	188	26
2014	**230**	198	32
2015	**239**	202	37
2016	**244**	201	43
2017	**249**	198	51
2018	**253**	197	56
2019	**254**	194	60
2020	**260**	195	65
2021	**275**	202	73

Source: TURKSTAT, (2022j)

Table 15 shows the ratio of female MPs. In 2021, the rate of female MPs was 17.4%. According to the data of the Turkish Grand National Assembly; As of the end of 2021, the number of female deputies among 582 deputies was 101 and the number of male deputies was 481.

Table 15. Number of representatives and proportion of representation of the Assembly by sex, 1935-2021

Year	Total number of representative	Male	Proportion of representation (%)	Female	Proportion of representation (%)
1935	399	381	95,5	18	4,5
1939	429	413	96,3	16	3,7
1943	455	439	96,5	16	3,5
1946	465	456	98,1	9	1,9
1950	487	484	99,4	3	0,6
1954	541	537	99,3	4	0,7
1957	610	602	98,7	8	1,3
1961	450	447	99,3	3	0,7
1965	450	442	98,2	8	1,8
1969	450	445	98,9	5	1,1
1973	450	444	98,7	6	1,3
1977	450	446	99,1	4	0,9
1983	399	387	97,0	12	3,0
1987	450	444	98,7	6	1,3
1991	450	442	98,2	8	1,8
1995	550	537	97,6	13	2,4
1999	550	527	95,8	23	4,2
2002	550	526	95,6	24	4,4
2007	550	500	90,9	50	9,1
2011	550	471	85,6	79	14,4
2012	548	469	85,6	79	14,4
2013	548	469	85,6	79	14,4
2014	535	458	85,6	77	14,4
2015	550	469	85,3	81	14,7
2016	550	469	85,3	81	14,7
2017	539	464	86,1	75	13,9
2018	600	496	82,7	104	17,3
2019	589	487	82,7	102	17,3
2020	584	483	82,7	101	17,3
2021	582	481	82,6	101	17,4

Source: TURKSTAT, (2022k)

Table 16 shows the number of men and women working in higher education for the years 1995-2021. Accordingly, the rate of female professors among the professors assigned in 2021 was 32.4%.

Table 16. Number of teaching staff in higher education by sex and academic title, 1995-2021

Year and Gender	Total	Professor	Associate professor	Doctor instructor	Assistant professor	Instructor	Language instructo	Specialist	Research assistant	Translato	Education and training planner
Male											
1995-1996	33 779	5 331	2 555	-	4 642	4 918	1 867	1 100	13 334	8	24
1996-1997	35 977	5 645	2 690	-	5 089	5 306	1 963	1 214	14 044	9	17
1997-1998	37 336	5 909	2 899	-	5 422	5 408	2 133	1 271	14 277	7	10
1998-1999	39 303	6 042	3 166	-	5 909	5 561	2 397	1 245	14 952	10	21
1999-2000	42 105	6 391	3 468	-	6 650	6 177	2 330	1 287	15 771	11	20
2000-2001	43 519	6 623	3 644	-	7 376	6 648	2 347	1 293	15 563	9	16
2001-2002	45 136	7 179	3 822	-	8 052	7 018	2 395	1 332	15 322	8	8
2002-2003	47 885	7 641	3 643	-	8 863	7 944	2 456	1 371	15 945	8	14
2003-2004	48 946	8 079	3 559	-	9 461	7 901	2 414	1 324	16 186	4	18
2004-2005	50 662	8 361	3 728	-	9 957	8 802	2 582	1 431	15 759	9	33
2005-2006	51 927	8 692	3 956	-	10 268	8 957	2 672	1 520	15 834	10	18
2006-2007	54 242	9 309	4 244	-	10 592	9 092	2 722	1 705	16 539	8	31
2007-2008	58 914	9 788	4 690	-	11 888	9 385	2 907	1 796	18 434	4	22
2008-2009	59 643	9 916	5 034	-	12 082	9 685	2 936	1 692	18 274	5	19
2009-2010	62 296	10 533	5 333	-	12 791	10 063	3 123	1 733	18 666	6	48
2010-2011	65 896	11 241	5 751	-	14 012	10 676	3 273	1 791	19 066	8	78
2011-2012	69 959	12 054	6 303	-	15 777	11 643	3 352	1 650	19 137	8	35
2012-2013	76 347	12 800	7 420	-	17 219	12 598	3 612	1 768	20 877	9	44
2013-2014	81 504	14 265	8 479	-	19 157	11 588	3 809	1 883	22 306	5	12
2014-2015	84 780	14 751	9 292	-	20 152	11 957	3 902	1 919	22 790	7	10
2015-2016	88 590	15 790	9 738	-	21 087	12 278	3 954	1 968	23 759	7	9
2016-2017	84 958	15 602	8 921	-	20 185	12 056	3 653	1 903	22 607	7	24
2017-2018	87 863	16 944	8 845	21 588	-	17 678	-	-	22 808	-	-

Continued on following page

Table 16. Continued

Year and Gender	Total	Professor	Associate professor	Doctor instructor	Assistant professor	Instructor	Language instructo	Specialist	Research assistant	Translato	Education and training planner
2018-2019	91 834	18 097	9 349	22 352	-	18 170	-	-	23 866	-	-
2019-2020	95 807	19 407	9 996	22 892	-	18 692	-	-	24 820	-	-
2020-2021	98 218	20 648	10 643	22 867	-	18 933	-	-	25 127	-	-
Female											
1995-1996	16 480	1 388	1 119	-	1 713	1 998	2 237	764	7 238	13	10
1996-1997	17 828	1 521	1 151	-	1 907	2 218	2 370	819	7 823	10	9
1997-1998	19 065	1 674	1 243	-	2 133	2 549	2 450	854	8 148	9	5
1998-1999	20 826	1 790	1 321	-	2 380	2 738	2 796	932	8 853	9	7
1999-2000	23 099	1 970	1 444	-	2 746	3 282	3 023	981	9 635	8	10
2000-2001	24 361	2 181	1 605	-	3 031	3 492	3 043	978	10 017	10	4
2001-2002	26 154	2 350	1 754	-	3 368	3 958	3 121	977	10 611	9	6
2002-2003	28 205	2 546	1 758	-	3 758	4 427	3 235	981	11 481	13	6
2003-2004	29 858	2 785	1 739	-	4 094	4 878	3 123	981	12 244	8	6
2004-2005	31 434	3 020	1 728	-	4 504	5 262	3 382	1 013	12 512	7	6
2005-2006	32 858	3 149	1 813	-	4 861	5 396	3 630	1 075	12 917	11	6
2006-2007	35 087	3 464	1 906	-	5 252	5 536	3 750	1 196	13 958	12	13
2007-2008	39 852	3 706	2 177	-	6 186	5 907	4 185	1 320	16 350	14	7
2008-2009	40 861	3 746	2 326	-	6 456	6 067	4 384	1 341	16 518	13	10
2009-2010	43 131	4 038	2 494	-	6 992	6 375	4 685	1 402	17 111	12	22
2010-2011	45 599	4 288	2 735	-	7 705	6 844	4 917	1 466	17 603	15	26
2011-2012	48 880	4 729	2 954	-	8 982	7 370	5 197	1 500	18 112	16	20
2012-2013	54 306	5 007	3 542	-	10 166	8 222	5 638	1 628	20 062	18	23
2013-2014	60 933	5 740	4 360	-	12 188	8 883	6 181	1 789	21 768	14	10
2014-2015	64 123	6 128	4 848	-	13 171	9 161	6 337	1 843	22 609	15	11

Continued on following page

Table 16. Continued

Year and Gender	Total	Professor	Associate professor	Doctor instructor	Assistant professor	Instructor	Language instructo	Specialist	Research assistant	Translato	Education and training planner
2015-2016	67 578	6 626	5 285	-	14 214	9 574	6 341	1 897	23 617	14	10
2016-2017	66 805	6 933	5 282	-	14 467	9 367	6 146	1 871	22 714	13	12
2017-2018	70 235	7 696	5 611	15 932	-	17 806	-	-	23 190	-	-
2018-2019	74 391	8 356	6 102	17 112	-	18 291	-	-	24 530	-	-
2019-2020	78 687	9 107	6 668	18 106	-	18 959	-	-	25 847	-	-
2020-2021	81 467	9 914	7 135	18 641	-	19 356	-	-	26 421	-	-

Source: TURKSTAT, (2022l)

Table 17 shows male and female employees by managerial level. In 2020, the rate of women in managerial positions was 19.3%. Men are more likely to be in managerial positions than women.

Table 17. Proportion of individuals in senior and middle management positions by sex, 2012-2020

Year	Total	Male	Female
2012	**100,0**	85,6	14,4
2013	**100,0**	83,4	16,6
2014	**100,0**	84,5	15,5
2015	**100,0**	85,6	14,4
2016	**100,0**	83,3	16,7
2017	**100,0**	82,7	17,3
2018	**100,0**	83,7	16,3
2019	**100,0**	82,5	17,5
2020	**100,0**	80,7	19,3

Source: TURKSTAT, (2022m)

In Table 18, the average wage information for seasonal workers is given separately for men and women. Although there are deficiencies in the information on wages paid to women, it can be said that male seasonal workers receive higher wages than women.

Table 18. Average daily wages of seasonal agricultural workers and the average monthly wages of permanent agricultural workers by province

	Daily wages of seasonal agricultural workers		Monthly wages of permanent agricultural workers	
Provinces	Female	Male	Female	Male
Ankara	105	106	c	3 827
Antalya	109	152	2 727	2 797
Aydın	104	157	c	3 560
Balıkesir	101	151	2655	3 719
Bursa	118	158	-	4 222
Çanakkale	106	151	-	c
Denizli	106	145	-	3 600
Edirne	129	172	-	3 405
Eskişehir	106	124	c	3 852
Gaziantep	122	153	-	c
Giresun	163	191	-	-
Hatay	75	107	-	3 300
Isparta	121	142	-	-
Mersin	96	114	-	2 961
İzmir	102	144	3 114	4 422
Konya	104	185	-	3 791
Malatya	100	106	-	3 000
Manisa	121	156	-	3 250
Kahramanmaraş	113	143	-	-
Ordu	157	164	-	c
Sakarya	134	157	-	-
Samsun	130	140	-	-
Zonguldak	130	133	-	-
Ardahan		220	-	2 774
Kilis	93	123	-	-
Osmaniye	90	139	-	c
Düzce	135	145	-	-

Source: TURKSTAT, (2022n

Considering the monthly wages paid to permanent agricultural workers in agricultural enterprises for 2021, İzmir was the province with the highest payment, with 4 422 TL for male workers and 3 114 TL for female workers. The lowest wages were in Ardahan with 2 774 TL for male workers and in Balıkesir with 2 655 TL for female workers (TURKSTAT, 2022o).

Table 19 shows the daily wages paid to men and women employed in selected agricultural products. Accordingly, the daily wages paid to men are seen to be higher in some product categories than women.

Table 19. Average daily wages of seasonal agricultural workers by selected activities, 2020-2021 (TL)

Activities	2020		2021	
	Female	Male	Female	Male
Other services about soil preparation	93	125	100	144
Seeding services	96	128	110	154
Seedling planting services	87	90	102	99
Hoeing services (weed clearance is included)	85	89	102	105
Irrigation of agricultural products services (ditch digging, flooding, sprinkling etc.)	100	131	136	159
Fertilizing services	136	137	166	163
Building an agricultural irrigation system services	-	108	-	117
Pruning and care of fruit trees and vineyards and related services	99	125	124	153
Other services of seeding, planting and caring of agricultural products	85	88	99	102
Agricultural spraying services	-	125	-	145
Harvest services (reap, pulling up, shaking down, mowing, tying etc.)	102	113	124	136
Thresing services	89	93	106	112
Drying services after harvest	117	157	148	190

Source: TURKSTAT, (2022n)

As seen in Table 20, the rate of private property employer enterprises owned by women was 19.3% in 2018. The ratio of employer enterprises, whose legal status is individual property and whose owner is women, has tended to increase over the years. The size group with the highest proportion of female-owned sole proprietorship enterprises was recorded as enterprises with 1-4 employees (TURKSTAT, 2020a).

Table 20. Rate of enterprises owned by females by size (number of employee), 2016-2018

Year	Total	Size group					
		1-4	5-9	10-19	20-49	50-99	100 +
2016	18,7	19,7	13,9	12,3	11,6	10,5	13,2
2017	18,9	19,7	13,8	12,0	11,9	10,0	10,8
2018	19,3	20,1	14,2	12,3	12,1	9,7	10,8

Source: TURKSTAT (2020b)

Figure 1. Share of women inventors in Türkiye
(OECD.Stat)

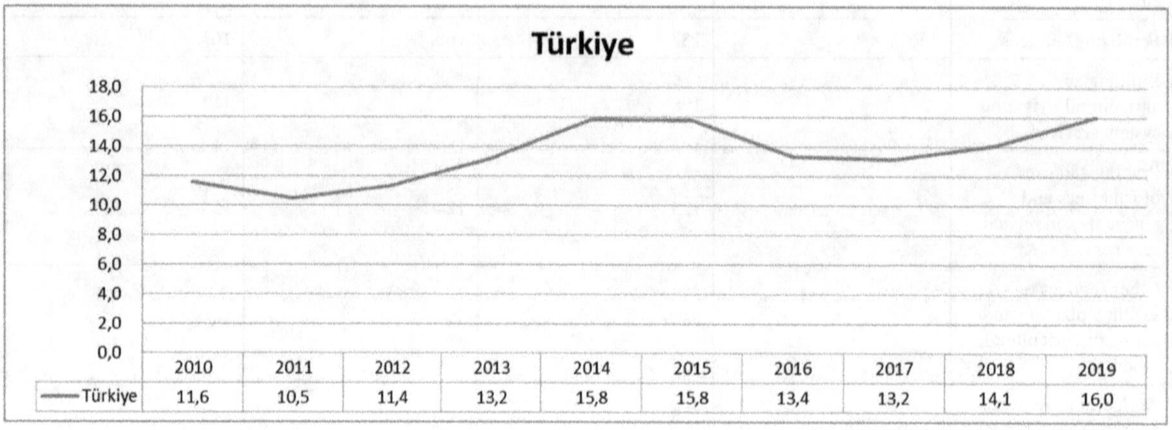

As seen by Figure 1, the share of women investors has increased from 2010 to 2019 in Türkiye. This is a good result for supporting women in employment in Türkiye.

SOLUTIONS AND RECOMMENDATIONS

This study aims to give a brief framework for female entrepreneurship in Türkiye. As being a developing country and a member of OECD, Türkiye tries to achieve 2030 Sustainable Development Goals and supports female employment and female entrepreneurship. Gender equity is an important goal and it aims to provide equity between women and men in education, employment and other issues. This study recommends supporting female entrepreneurship to achieve 2030 Sustainable Development Goals and so economic growth more efficiently.

FUTURE RESEARCH DIRECTIONS

This study gives recent indicators for female entrepreneurship in Türkiye. This study can suggest future researches to investigate female entrepreneurship for developing countries by empirical methods. This study used secondary data based on TURKSTAT (Turkish Statistical Institute)'s official web site. Different secondary data or reports can give different results. The study can list some suggestions for future studies as below:

- The future studies can focus on exploring the wage policies in developing countries whether there is a difference between women and men.
- The future studies can focus on examining the importance of working and coordination between Mediterranean countries in the long term.
- There will be helpful when there are empirical studies.
- New measurements can be developed to determine the level of female entrepreneurship in a global scope.

CONCLUSION

Achieving 2030 Sustainable Development Goals (2030SDGs) was accepted member countries of United Nations. 2030 SDGs includes 17 main goals and these goals aim to provide economic growth by ensuring social development and environmental quality (Yıldırım et al., 2016; Yıldırım and Yıldırım, 2020; Yildirim, 2022; Yıldırım and Kantarcı, 2022; Yildirim, 2023). Supporting female entrepreneurship and female employment will support economic growth and social development in a country. Accordingly, countries should give more attention to support female entrepreneurship in the long term. There are various incentive and support programs and policies in Türkiye. Small enterprises and women entrepreneurs who do manual labor can also be supported financially by KOSGEB institution. Although there has been an improvement in women's employment and entrepreneurship in Türkiye as of 2015, these figures may decrease due to the effects of the Covid-19 crisis. However, since Türkiye is a country that gives importance to women's initiative and women's labor, support continues within state policies. Researches on women's employment show that education has a positive effect on women's employment and supports economic development and growth. As a developing country, Turkey's support for women's employment and women's education together will ensure the achievement of sustainable development in the long run. Considering that women will achieve better careers with higher education levels, it would be beneficial to implement relevant strategies in education policy. It is thought that by supporting women's employment and women's entrepreneurship, crisis times can be overcome more successfully with a strong economy.

ACKNOWLEDGMENT

Turkish references are translated into English.

REFERENCES

Acar, H. (2019). Women in Turkish Culture and State Tradition. *İnsan ve İnsan Journal of Science, Culture. Art and Thought*, *6*(21), 395–411.

Acs, Z. J., Bardasi, E., Estrin, S., & Svejnar, J. (2011). Introduction to special issue of Small Business Economics on female entrepreneurship in developed and developing economies. *Small Business Economics*, *37*(4), 393–396. doi:10.100711187-011-9372-1

Aparicio, S., Audretsch, D., Noguera, M., & Urbano, D. (2022). Can female entrepreneurs boost social mobility in developing countries? An institutional analysis. *Technological Forecasting and Social Change*, *175*, 121401. doi:10.1016/j.techfore.2021.121401

Çolak, Z. (2021). Econometric Analysis on Gender Inequality and Economic Growth Relationship in Turkey, *MANAS. The Journal of Social Studies*, *10*(2), 1094–1105.

Durmaz, Ş. (2016). Women and Their Challenges in Labor Market. *Ahi Evran University Institute of Social Sciences Journal*, 2(3), 37-60. https://dergipark.org.tr/en/pub/aeusbed/issue/26794/282028

Erdogan, S., Yıldırım, D. C., & Tosuner, Ö. (2012). The Effect of Gender Inequality in Education on Health:Evidence from Turkey. *Educational Sciences: Theory and Practice*, *12*(3), 1860–1866.

Günsoy, G., & Özsoy, C. (2012). VAR Analysis of Woman Labor Force, Education and Growth Relations in Turkey. *Finans Politik & Ekonomik Yorumlar*, *49*(568), 23–42.

Hundera, M., Duysters, G., Naudé, W., & Dijkhuizen, J. (2019). How do female entrepreneurs in developing countries cope with role conflict? *International Journal of Gender and Entrepreneurship*, *11*(2), 120–145. doi:10.1108/IJGE-12-2018-0138

Jamali, D. (2009). Constraints and opportunities facing women entrepreneurs in developing countries: A relational perspective. *Gender in Management*, *24*(4), 232–251. doi:10.1108/17542410910961532

Kasa, H., & Alptekin, V. (2015). The Effect of Female Labor Force to Growth in Turkey. *Sosyal Bilimler Meslek Yüksekokulu Dergisi*, *18*(1), 1–24.

Kobeissi, N. (2010). Gender factors and female entrepreneurship: International evidence and policy implications. *Journal of International Entrepreneurship*, *8*(1), 1–35. doi:10.100710843-010-0045-y

Kuadli, J. (2022). *Women Entrepreneurs Statistics*. Legal Jobs. https://legaljobs.io/blog/women-entrepreneurs-statistics/#:~:text=How%20many%20female%20entrepreneurs%20are,in%20the%20l ast%2020%20years

Minniti, M., & Naudé, W. (2010). What Do We Know About the Patterns and Determinants of Female Entrepreneurship Across Countries? [EJDR]. *European Journal of Development Research*, *22*(3), 277–293. doi:10.1057/ejdr.2010.17

Munasinghe, M. (2002). The Sustainomics Trans-disciplinary Meta-framework for making Development more Sustainable: Applications to energy issues. *International Journal of Sustainable Development*, *4*(2), 6–54. doi:10.1504/IJSD.2002.002563

OECD. (2022). *Indicators of female entrepreneurship*. OECD. https://stats.oecd.org/index.aspx?queryid=83119

OECD. (2022). *Share of women inventors*. OECD. https://stats.oecd.org/index.aspx?queryid=83119

OECD. (2022). *Positive business status and outlook by sex*. OECD. https://stats.oecd.org/index.aspx?queryid=83119

OECD. (2022). *Share of the population who report borrowing money to start a business by sex*, Entrepreneurship. OECD. https://stats.oecd.org/index.aspx?queryid=83119

Panda, S. (2018). Constraints faced by women entrepreneurs in developing countries: Review and ranking. *Gender in Management*, *33*(4), 315–331. doi:10.1108/GM-01-2017-0003

Pata, U. K. (2018). The Relationship Between Female Employment and Economic Growth In Turkey: A Sectoral Analysis With Symmetric And Asymmetric Causality Tests, *International Journal of Economics and Administrative Studies. Year*, *2018*(21), 135–150.

Serel, H., & Özdemir, S. (2017, September). Female Employment and Economic Growth Relations In Turkey. *Journal of Management and Economics Research, Vol*, *15*(3), 132–148.

Soysal, A. (2010). Women Entrepreneurs in Turkey: An Assessment in the Context of Difficulties and Opportunities. *Ankara University SBF Journal*, *65*(01), 83–114.

Tahtalıoğlu, H. (2016). The Effects Of Glass Ceiling Syndrome On Women In Higher Education Institutions In Turkey.*Niğde Üniversitesi İktisadi ve İdari Bilimler Fakültesi Dergisi (Academic Review of Economics and Administrative Sciences). Year*, *9*(2), 89–105.

TURKSTAT. (2020). *Entrepreneurship, 2016-2018*, Number: 33664, Retrieved October 10, 2022, from https://data.tuik.gov.tr/Bulten/Index?p=Girisimcilik-2016-2018-33664

TURKSTAT. (2020b). *Rate of enterprises owned by females by size (number of employee), 2016-2018*. Entrepreneurship. https://data.tuik.gov.tr/Bulten/Index?p=Girisimcilik-2016-2018-33664

TURKSTAT. (2022a). *Population by sex and age group, 2020, 2021*. Women in Statistics. https://data.tuik.gov.tr/Bulten/Index?p=Women-in-Statistics-2021-45635

TURKSTAT. (2022b). *Formal education completed by sex, 2010-2020* Women in Statistics. https://data.tuik.gov.tr/Bulten/Index?p=Women-in-Statistics-2021-45635

TURKSTAT. (2022c). *Labour force status by sex and educational level, 2019, 2020*. Women in Statistics, 2021. https://data.tuik.gov.tr/Bulten/Index?p=Women-in-Statistics-2021-45635

TURKSTAT. (2022f). *Proportion of employed working part-time by sex, 2014-2020.* Women in Statistics. https://data.tuik.gov.tr/Bulten/Index?p=Women-in-Statistics-2021-45635

TURKSTAT. (2022g). *Employment rate of persons aged 25-49 with a child under age 3 living in the household and with no children living in the household by sex, 2014-2020.* Women in Statistics.https://data.tuik.gov.tr/Bulten/Index?p=Women-in-Statistics-2021-45635

TURKSTAT. (2022i). *Satisfaction with time spent on commuting to work, 2013-2021*, 2014-2020. Women in Statistics. https://data.tuik.gov.tr/Bulten/Index?p=Women-in-Statistics-2021-45635

TURKSTAT. (2022j). *Number and proportion of ambassadors by sex, 1982, 1990, 1996, 2000-2021.* Women in Statistics. https://data.tuik.gov.tr/Bulten/Index?p=Women-in-Statistics-2021-45635

TURKSTAT. (2022m). *Proportion of individuals in senior and middle management positions by sex, 2012-2020.* Women in Statistics. https://data.tuik.gov.tr/Bulten/Index?p=Women-in-Statistics-2021-45635

TURKSTAT. (2022n), *Average Daily Wages of Seasonal Agricultural Workers and the Average Monthly Wages of Permanent Agricultural Workers by Province (TL),* Agricultural Holdings Labour Wage Structure. https://data.tuik.gov.tr/Bulten/Index?p=Agricultural-Holdings-Labour-Wage-Structure-2020-2021-45783

Türlüoğlu, E. (2018). Women Employment And Growth Relationship: Var Model Analysis, Eurasian [EJRSE]. *Journal of Researches in Social and Economics*, *5*(9), 59–68.

Tütüncü, A., & Zengin, H. (2020). The Relationship Between Women Employment and Economic Growth In E7 Countries, *Int. Journal of Management Economics and Business*, *16*(1), 1–16.

UN News Centre. (2017). *UN and partners launch initiative to reach equal pay for women at work.* UN. https://www.un.org/sustainabledevelopment/blog/2017/09/un-and-partners-launch-initiative-to-reach-equal-pay-for-women-at-work/

United Nations Department of Economic and Social Affairs Sustainable Development. (n.d.). *Do you know all 17 SDGs?* UN. https://sdgs.un.org/goals

World Economic Forum. (2022), *Here's what women's entrepreneurship looks like around the world.* WEF. https://www.weforum.org/agenda/2022/07/women-entrepreneurs-gusto-gender/

Yildirim, S. (2022). The Consumer Role for Sustainable Development: How Consumers Contribute Sustainable Development Goals. In I. Management Association (Eds.), Research Anthology on Measuring and Achieving Sustainable Development Goals (pp. 872-888). IGI Global. doi:10.4018/978-1-6684-3885-5.ch047

Yildirim, S. (2023). Greenwashing: a rapid escape from sustainability or a slow transition? *LBS Journal of Management & Research*. doi:10.1108/LBSJMR-11-2022-0077

Yıldırım, S., & Kantarcı, T. (2022). A Review on Sustainability Policies of Businesses: Recycling and Waste Reduction. *Journal of Recycling Economy & Sustainability Policy*, *1*(1), 1–9. https://respjournal.com/index.php/pub/article/view/1

Yıldırım, S., & Yıldırım, D. Ç. (2020). Achieving Sustainable Development Through a Green Economy Approach. In S. Patti & G. Trizzino (Eds.), *Advanced Integrated Approaches to Environmental Economics and Policy: Emerging Research and Opportunities* (pp. 1–22). IGI Global. doi:10.4018/978-1-5225-9562-5.ch001

Yıldırım, S., Yıldırım, D. Ç., & Çoltu, S. (2019). The Role of Education in Women's Career Life in Emerging Economies: A Case of Turkey. In E. Pereira, & P. Paoloni (Ed.), Handbook of Research on Women in Management and the Global Labor Market (pp. 46-62). IGI Global.

Yıldırım, S., Yıldırım, D. Ç., & Gedikli, A. (2016). Sustainable Consumption Trends in the World in the Context of Green Economy and Sustainability. In M. Erdoğdu, T. Arun, & I. Ahmad (Eds.), *Handbook of Research on Green Economic Development Initiatives and Strategies* (pp. 65–84). IGI Global. doi:10.4018/978-1-5225-0440-5.ch004

Zeren, F., & Savrul, B. K. (2018). Evaluating the Hidden Cointegration Relationships Among Female Labor Force Participation Rate Economic Growth, Unemployment Rate and Urbanization Rate. *The Journal of American Science*, *15*(30), 87–103.

ADDITIONAL READING

Erdogan, S., Yıldırım, D. C., & Tosuner, Ö. (2012). The Effect of Gender Inequality in Education on Health:Evidence from Turkey. *Educational Sciences: Theory and Practice*, *12*(3), 1860–1866.

United Nations Department of Economic and Social Affairs Sustainable Development. (n.d.). *Do you know all 17 SDGs?* UN. https://sdgs.un.org/goals

Yıldırım, S., Yıldırım, D. Ç., & Çoltu, S. (2019). The Role of Education in Women's Career Life in Emerging Economies: A Case of Turkey. In E. Pereira, & P. Paoloni (Ed.), Handbook of Research on Women in Management and the Global Labor Market (pp. 46-62). IGI Global.

KEY WORDS AND DEFINITIONS

2030 Sustainable Development Goals: Sustainable Development Goals with 17 main goals which was launched by the UN in 2015.

Female Entrepreneurship: An entrepreneurship which is owned and operated by female.

OECD: Organisation for Economic Co-operation and Development.

Sustainable Development: A development approach which focuses on achieving a balance between economic growth, social development, and environmental quality.

TURKSTAT: Turkish Statistical Institute.

Chapter 8
Enhancements of Women's Entrepreneurship:
A Theme-Based Study

Kruthika S.
CHRIST University (Deemed), India

Amin Mohammed Arifulla
CHRIST University (Deemed), India

Pooja Jain
CHRIST University (Deemed), India

ABSTRACT

Woman entrepreneurs are defined as a group of women who initiate, organize, and run a business concern, from a situation where a woman was not even allowed to get out of their home, to today, running most of the successful brands of the world, contributing a major part to the economic growth, and breaking the stereotypes by providing a reality check to the male dominance. There has been a wide range of public policies enrolled out to facilitate and encourage the growth of women's entrepreneurship. A few such policies from India have proved to be successful, which will be outlined in this book chapter. From the past times of not gaining adequate recognition for their support, women have emerged successful in overcoming hardships such as lack of visibility, lack of training and educative support about public policies provided by governments to women entrepreneurs, fewer opportunities, and walking out of the social stigma.

INTRODUCTION

Entrepreneurship is the deliberate taking of risks and ongoing process of innovational activities that entails the discovery, assessment, and exploitation of opportunities, judgement of the possibilities, and making decisions in a known state of uncertainty within the context of a rapidly changing environment.

DOI: 10.4018/978-1-6684-7669-7.ch008

The importance of entrepreneurship in the global economy increased as a result of changes in employee qualifications, job duties, and psychological contracts in the employment field. Entrepreneurship is a multilevel and complex phenomenon. In order to spread new or existing knowledge and innovative ideas that might not otherwise be used and realised for the benefit of all, entrepreneurship contributes to economic growth. (Audretsch, Keilbach, & Lehmann, 2006)

in today's era, Entrepreneurial activities activities have a upper hand playing a critical role in the development of societies (Herrington & Kew, 2017). Therefore, various stakeholders including the governments, non-profit organization, researchers, and individuals are more interested in facilitating the development of supportive woman entrepreneurial ecosystems.

As small businesses are vital for the participation of female entrepreneurs to this sector takes enormous significance in the economic development of any emerging country. Women have successfully led small-scale projects all around the world. However, despite a rise in the number of female entrepreneurs in recent years, male entrepreneurs are more active, and significant variations can be seen across different national contexts. (Shinnar, 2012).

The act of starting a firm that gives a woman economic independence is referred to as women entrepreneurship. The continuous economic growth and social advancement are significantly influenced by female entrepreneurs. The act of starting a firm, which gives women economic independence, is the gender gap in female entrepreneurship. The continuous economic growth and social advancement are significantly influenced by female entrepreneurs. The disparity between men and women in terms of the number of people engaged in entrepreneurial activity, the reasons behind starting or running a firm, the industry they choose, and the performance and growth of their companies is known as the gender gap in entrepreneurship.

Women entrepreneurship must be molded properly with entrepreneurial traits and skills to meet the changes in trends, challenges global markets and also be competent enough to sustain and strive for excellence in the entrepreneurial arena (Devi, 2012)

India is now placed 52nd out of 57 countries in the most recent Mastercard Index of Women Entrepreneurs (MIWE). According to the report, India's "underlying conditions" for women entrepreneurs are less favourable than those in other nations with high index scores. The survey also shows that due to cultural bias, women in India are less likely to be business owners. Not only that, but women who really own firms are less likely to expand them and more likely to close them down due to a lack of funding. Additionally, it has been suggested that India should work on raising the number of women who enrol in postsecondary education, expanding access to financial loans for female entrepreneurs, and other initiatives to support women's entrepreneurship in the nation (The Mastercard Index of Women Entrepreneurs, 2022) because of cultural bias. Not just that, women who actually own businesses are less likely to grow their business and are more prone to shutting down because of lack of financing. In addition to this, it has been suggested that India needs to work on increasing women enrolment in postsecondary education, increasing access to financial loans to women entrepreneurs and single window clearances, tax breaks and other measures to promote women entrepreneurship in the country (The Mastercard Index of Women Entrepreneurs, 2022).

Studying female entrepreneurship advances our knowledge of entrepreneurship and human behaviour in general and enables researchers to pose questions that shed light on a variety of topics, including the reasons behind women's behaviour as well as the connections between entrepreneurship and wealth creation, employment, the accumulation of human capital, labour market dynamics, and many other topics. Across all the ethnicity groups in the United States, the rate of new business formation by women has recently greatly surpassed the rate of new business formation by men (CWBR, 2004). States (CWBR, 2004).

Venture creation can offer women more flexibility in work schedules, avoiding work-family conflicts (Kirkwood and Tootell, 2008; Thebaud, 2015; Rembulan et al., 2016).

Women are involving and entering into business and establishing different types of industries. The Government of India and Andhra Pradesh have been encouraging women to take up industrial establishments. Several financial corporations are funding for establishment of industries. Hence, women started establishing industries and collaborating self and economic development and coming out with flying colours. Despite playing a significant role in Indian society, women's entrepreneurial potential has not been fully realised because of their lower social status. Their role has only been explicitly acknowledged since the Fifth Five Year Plan (1974–1988), when the focus shifted from women's welfare to women's development and empowerment. (Devi, 2012)

(Agrawal, P. K. Ghosh) reducing impediments to women's entrepreneurship would necessitate a shift in society's mentality—one that willingly supports and empowers women. Joint efforts by the public and the government can help to promote such an attitude. The educated and liberal-minded should work with local government organizations as volunteers to run programmes and campaigns that inform people about the value of women's entrepreneurship and the advantages it would bring to the family, community, and country. Such a strategy would result in long-lasting societal improvements, (Neha Singh, Sanjeev Kumar)- When starting their businesses and in times of crisis, such as the COVID-19 pandemic, low-budget/very small-scale women entrepreneurs face both general and gender-specific challenges in the areas of the market, (Sucheta Agarwal and Usha Lenka).

A study conducted by the Center for Women's Business Research in 2009 measures the economic impact of the eight million women-owned businesses in the U.S. The estimated economic impact was $3 trillion annually that translated into the creation and/or maintenance of more than 23 million jobs – 16% of all jobs in the U.S market. This report makes an interesting statement that illustrates the importance of female entrepreneurship in the world's strongest economy: "If U.S. women-owned businesses were their own country, they would have the 5th largest GDP in the world, trailing closely behind Germany, and ahead of countries including France, United Kingdom and Italy" (Center for Women's Business Research 2009).

Most entrepreneurship research on individual-level male entrepreneurs' entrepreneurial actions have been the subject of analysis. Previous studies have expressly indicated that there is no discernible difference between male and female entrepreneurs (Carter, 2000; Carter and Cannon, 1992). The focus of several further studies was on examining the gender variations in entrepreneurship. According to several research, women entrepreneurs differ from men in terms of their traits, backgrounds, motivations, entrepreneurial skills, and challenges they face. Additionally, research have shown that when managing commercial firms, men and women employ various organisational structures and management techniques (Hisrich and Brush, 1984; Zapalska, 1997; Bird and Brush, 2002; Klyver and Grant, 2010; We now understand that across the world, far fewer women than men own and run businesses (Devine, 1994a, b; Georgellis and Wall, 2005; Kim, 2007).

This could be as a result of the fact that women start fewer firms than men do, or that women fail more frequently than men. There is some data to suggest that, after accounting for aspects like business size and sectoral distribution, women's failure rates do not differ considerably from men's (Kalleberg and Leicht, 1991; Perry, 2002; Kepler and Shane, 2007). Therefore, the fact that fewer women than men start businesses must account for at least some of the gender gap. Evidence to date indicates that a number of factors help to account for observed variances in entrepreneurial behaviour across genders, and that these variations have important macroeconomic ramifications (Minniti et al, 2006).

Maybe there are socioeconomic differences between men and women that would vanish if we took into account things like education, wealth, family status, and employment. Indeed, a large body of empirical research demonstrates the existence of such differences (Cowling and Taylor, 2001; Blanchflower, 2004; Minniti et al, 2005). We now know that significantly fewer women than men own and manage businesses worldwide (Devine, 1994a, b; Georgellis and Wall, 2005; Kim, 2007). This could be because women fail more often than men or because fewer women than men start businesses to begin with, or both. Some evidence exists that, after correcting for factors such as size of the business and sectoral distribution, women's failure rates are not significantly different from those of men (Kalleberg and Leicht, 1991; Perry, 2002; Kepler and Shane, 2007). Thus, at least a portion of the difference between genders must be due to the fact that fewer women than men start businesses. Evidence to date suggests that a variety of reasons contribute to explaining observed differences in entrepreneurial behaviour across gender and that such differences have significant implications at the macroeconomic level (Minniti et al, 2006).

Perhaps women and men have different socioeconomic characteristics and, if we were to correct for factors such as education, wealth, family and work status, those differences would disappear. Indeed, quite a bit of empirical evidence shows that such differences do exist (Cowling and Taylor, 2001; Blanchflower, 2004; Minniti et al, 2005).

The two main business endeavours that women launch is conventional and social. The development of traditional businesses for profit has been the subject of much of the study on gender disparities in entrepreneurship (Ahl, 2006). However, focus has shifted from start-ups to major corporations on the empowering of female entrepreneurship through social entrepreneurship (Johnstone-Louis, 2017). The "multiplier effect" that female entrepreneurs may have on communities and children is acknowledged by both types of businesses (Elborgh-Woytek, 2013).

Emirati males are about the 30 per cent more likely than their female counterparts there to be early-stage entrepreneurs. In addition, the rate of early-stage 7.6% of female business owners are female, compared to 11.8% of male business owners (El-Sokari et al., 2013). Males are significantly more affected than females by the rising post-modern values in the Arab world, which suggests that males will likely gain significantly more from their entrepreneurial behavior. Although Emirati society has undergone a significant amount of modernization, it is still characterised as traditional and patriarchal and is influenced by conventional Arab practises (Naguib and Jamali, 2015)(Ahmad, 2011).

The Indian government has started a number of policies and development initiatives to encourage women to start their own businesses and become financially independent as well as contribute to the nation's economic expansion. The study shows that the Indian government has implemented a number of policies and development initiatives to foster an entrepreneurial spirit among women groups, making them not only self-sufficient monetarily but also contributing to the expansion of the economy (Subhadip Roy,Dina Banerjee) A more in-depth research reveals societal forces that are opposed to the entrepreneur during the initiation period, but that the social environment becomes more favorable as the entrepreneurship develops. The findings support the idea that entrepreneurship is a kind of independence with stages such as seeking autonomy, authoring and declaring (Nidhi Goel and Pankaj Madan) - According to the study's findings, financial inclusion has a statistically significant effect on women's entrepreneurship. It gives women a platform that aids them in starting a new business

Types of women entrepreneur: · Women in organized & unorganized sector · Women in traditional & modern industries · Women in urban & rural areas (H. S, 2021)

Women are coming forth to the business arena with ideas to start small and medium enterprises. They are willing to be inspired by role models-the experience of other women in the business arena. The role of women entrepreneurs is especially relevant in the situation of large-scale unemployment that the country faces. The modern large-scale industry cannot absorb much of labor as it is capital intensive. The small-scale industry plays an important role absorbing around 80% of the employment. (H. S, 2021).

The role of Women entrepreneurs in In order to encourage women's entrepreneurship, efforts are being made to recognise and value economic development. These recommendations make it clear that there is a need for the following in the region in order to grow and promote women's entrepreneurship (H. S, 2021).

This stereotyped and male-centered vision discourages some women from participating in business activities, which could also have a consequence on people who interact with women at the community level, creating an additional barrier (Langowitz & Morgan, 2003)

Culture greatly influences the way in which entrepreneurs develop their business initiatives, referring to prejudices, social roles and a stereotyped vision of the gender (for example, women are seen as incompatible with the business because it is too emotional and less rational in making decisions) that contribute to a men-cenetred vision of entrepreneurship conclusion that the prejudices women face in business are the result of gender stereotypes. (Langowitz & Morgan, 2003).

These variables, which are connected to a nation's various views on the place of women in society, help to explain why there are disparities in attitudes toward entrepreneurship as well as some psychological characteristics that affect entrepreneurial intention: Men have greater degrees of self-efficacy, self-confidence, independence, appetite for risk, and autonomy than women do. (Langowitz, & Minniti, 2007).

Various entrepreneurship characteristics have been identified over time. Gürol and Ahsan (2006, p. 28) have identified three distinct factors that influence entrepreneurial behaviour: individual, social and environmental. Social factors include aspects pertaining to personal and family background, stage of career and early life experiences, while environmental factors may include aspects such as wealth, timing of opportunities, market conditions and so forth. The third factor relates to individual features with a focus on personality characteristics. Entrialgo, Fernandez and Vazques (2000, p. 427) identify control, the need for achievement, tolerance and the capacity to cope with ambiguity as entrepreneurial determinants;

CHALLENGES

Over half of adult women have completed postsecondary education, such as a university degree, and the nation received a perfect score on the Women, Business, and Law Index from the World Bank. Causality. the analysis done in this paper identifies five of the 14 barriers as causal. They are as follows: lack of education, experience and training opportunities; spatial mobility and lack of family support; lack of institutional support; lack of entrepreneurial management; and problem in acquiring financial resources. Women entrepreneurs, scholars and policymakers will gain greater understanding through this causal framework of barriers. Knowledge and containment of these barriers will help in fostering a more conducive environment for enabling more women to attempt entrepreneurship.

Amidst Pandemic, the patriarchal society has reinvented itself in numerous is still being dependent on the situation. Women entrepreneurs differ completely from each other, and their entrepreneurship could be differentiated into different assistance provided by male society work.

There are many barriers to female entrepreneurship, but previous research has given them all equal weight. We believe that prioritization helps us understand better. Therefore, we begin by identifying barriers from previous research and examining causal relationships between them. A framework based on causal relationships between disorders has been proposed. To establish this causality, the methodology of the Decision-Making Test and Evaluation Laboratory (DEMATEL) was used. Our analysis identified 5 out of 14 failures as the root cause. they are:

Lack of education, experience and training opportunities. Lack of spatial mobility and family support. lack of institutional support; lack of entrepreneurship; and funding problems. Entrepreneurs, scientists and policymakers will be better able to understand the causal framework of this barrier. Knowing and breaking down these barriers will help create a more conducive environment that allows more women to become entrepreneurs.

Within COVID-19, patriarchal structures have been reframed in new ways with contextual patriarchal scope and modalities. Each female entrepreneur is different, and based on the degree and level of male support in society, female entrepreneurs can be divided into four types. In the first type of entrepreneurship, the woman nominally runs the business and the male family makes all decisions. In the second type, a woman owns the company but shares decision-making authority with her male colleagues. In the third type, a single woman owns the business and makes all decisions herself. While there are many ways to categorize women entrepreneurs, this study focuses on national, family, social, and entrepreneurial perspectives. Sanjeev Kumar

Rastogi, M., Baral, R. and Banu, J. (2022), "What does it take to be a woman entrepreneur? Explorations from India"

successful entrepreneurs are opportunity-driven and they focus on innovation, service, generation of wealth and employment. Support from family, especially from fathers or husbands, is as important as the entrepreneurial drive, skills, and abilities of an entrepreneur. Success for them is being happy, thriving work, having a happy family, having a great work-life balance and the satisfaction to have served society apart from being independent (economically/ financially). Among India's societal and cultural realities, women have to conquer many hurdles (both implicit and explicit) in their way concerning the societal attitudes toward women stepping out of the home boundaries and traditional gender role expectations. The silver line is societal attitudes are changing, especially in urban India. There are enough support and encouragement from the family, which helps these women pursue their passion and eventually become a successful leader.

What does it take to be a woman entrepreneur? Explorations from India

Among India's societal and cultural realities, women have to conquer many hurdles (both implicit and explicit) in their way concerning the societal attitudes toward women stepping out of the home boundaries and traditional gender role expectations. The silver line is societal attitudes are changing, especially in urban India. There are enough support and encouragement from the family, which helps these women pursue their passion and eventually become a successful leader

Mansi Rastogi, Rupashree Baral and Jasmine Banu

Comparative Study

Recent evidence showed that prevalence rates of the female entrepreneurship tend to be relatively higher in developing than in developed countries (Minniti, Allen, & Langowitz, 2006). This has traditionally been explained by the fact that in developing economies, women face higher barriers to entry in the formal labor market and have to resort to entrepreneurship as a way out of unemployment and, often, out of poverty.

In the process of entrepreneurship in developing countries, females have been assigned a special role because they stand to benefit from entrepreneurship as the poorer and discriminated against gender, but also because they are seen as a critical driver of entrepreneurship in light of their unique role in the household, and in light of the rise in female-headed households across the developing world (Horrell, Krishnan, & ', 2007).

The second reason for the rise of interest in female entrepreneurship in developing countries is owing to the rapid increase in the number and proportion of female entrepreneurs in the developing world (Kevane & Wydick, 2001), and the insight that female-led micro- and small enterprises (MSEs) can have a more significant impact on overall household welfare and consumption than male-led MSEs. Women entrepreneurs and heads of household tend to spend more on household health, nutrition and education than men, and tend to employ proportionately more females than male-headed firms (Nichter & Goldmark, 2009).

One of the main lines of inquiry in the literature has been that hegemonic masculinity and gender stereotypes may deter female entrepreneurs (Gupta et al., 2008, 2009; Hechavarria and Ingram, 2016). Existing research reveals that socially ingrained gender stereotypes have a role in the variations between men and women's entrepreneurial aptitude (DeBruin et al., 2007; Eagly and Karau, 2002; Greene et al., 2013; Gupta et al., 2008). The extent to which these attitudes and preconceptions may prevent women from pursuing entrepreneurship has been the subject of extensive research.

Through the use of myths, society generally promotes prejudice against women who have the traits while it supports some women who possess the collective traits linked to social entrepreneurship (gentleness, sensitivity, affection, sympathy, etc.). Although not all antecedents influencing the creation of new ventures are included in this list, existing research indicates that these constructs will have a significant impact.

According to Minniti, gender disparities in entrepreneurial behaviour are remarkably constant across national boundaries, and males often participate at participation rates that are 50% greater than those of women. Her research also indicates that, presumably because many women start businesses out of necessity, gender differences in start-up activity are wider in middle-income nations and tend to be reduced in lower-income ones. Surprisingly, compared to women in middle- and high-income countries, women in poorer countries tend to be less fearful of failure and more self-confident about their abilities (skills and knowledge) to become entrepreneurs (Minniti, Allen, & Langowitz, 2006).

Terjesen and Amorós' investigation of the variation in female startup rates between nations should be expanded upon. They start by pointing out that, despite the fact that a growing body of research has concentrated on the differences in start-up rates between countries at various levels of development and with different structural features (as in the paper by Minniti) (Minniti, Allen, & Langowitz, 2006), it is also true that there is still a significant gender gap among nations with similar levels of national wealth, and that economic factors do not fully explain observed gender patterns of start-up activity.

Their paper's major goal is to explain the gender disparity in startup activity in nations with comparable economic development levels by taking non-economic factors like culture and institutions into account. The authors are especially interested in determining how "gendered institutions" or "gender culture" affect a person's decision to launch a new business, whether they are a man or a woman.

There are various outcome differences between male and female entrepreneurs. They can be categorized in various ways under different subheadings such as size, sector, location, productivity and profitability, growth, survival and failure collectively termed under economic outcomes. As per Eliana Carranza, Chandra Dhakal and Inessa Love, (Carranza, Dhakal, & Love, 2018) state that most of the studies found that women entrepreneurs run small scale businesses in terms of sales, assets and number of employees. There could have been many reasons why female-run businesses are smaller. For instance, limited access to business networks or an unattractive location (in a home) limit their customer base and sales. Reduced endowments of assets also result in smaller business size at start-up. Credit restrictions also limit the possibility for growth and expansion.

Strong sector-specific effects cause female business owners to locate their operations in traditionally female-dominated industries. Both industrialized and developing nations have noticed this influence. Sectors where women choose to work are less lucrative than those where men predominate. if or not they are run by women, the businesses in these sectors typically have a smaller overall footprint. For example, in the U.S, 80% of the small businesses are in the service sector (U.S. Small Business Administration, 2010).

While allowing women more flexible in caring for the children, a home-based location makes it more and more difficult In order to promote women's entrepreneurial activity and improve women's entrepreneurial success, it is important to understand how female entrepreneurs vary from their male counterparts, what particular obstacles they experience, and how to overcome these obstacles. We also point out gaps in the body of knowledge and offer directions for further investigation. For the women to focus on their business and not be distracted by home and child-rearing responsibilities. Women's entrepreneurs' businesses are more often located in their homes or nearby homes (Bosma & Harding, 2006). In developing nations, 80 percent or more of "homeworkers"—defined as industrial workers who operate from home—are women, according to a statistics report from the International Labor Organization (ILO) from 2004.

The types of businesses that women work for can help to explain some of the performance gaps. Particularly, the size and industry of the company frequently account for the majority of performance variations. Male-dominated industries offer substantial returns to all workers. Women still earn more than males in non-female-dominated industries, despite the fact that they make less money overall.

Although male-owned firm exit rates are typically higher than those of female-owned firms globally, not all firm exits result in failure. (Fairlie & Robb, 2009).The gender of the entrepreneur was no longer proven to be a major indicator of survival when pure business failures were examined independently.

According to Kantor (2002), the concept of success must include empowerment so that people can increase their position and authority in their homes, workplaces, and communities. This factor is particularly significant in cultural contexts when women's economic options are constrained. 7 The choices women make about their businesses should, in principle, be motivated by the desire to maximise profits and be unrelated to other decisions they make, such as how many hours to work or how much of the profits to reinvest in the company vs spend on personal consumption. In other words, utility maximisation should come after the problem of profit maximisation.

This suggests that women do not clearly distinguish their personal and professional life as much as men do. However, the majority of research to date has relied on a masculine model, evaluating company success with the presumption that the enterprise is a distinct economic entity created primarily to generate profit through competitive advantage. (Brush,, Carter, Gatewood, Greene, & Hart, 2004).

The level at which results should be measured—that is, whether the emphasis should be on individual or family/household outcomes—is another crucial factor that is frequently ignored. It is likely that households reallocate resources to maximize overall household outcomes at the price of less-than-ideal individual outcomes. While women's individual goals may be established at the household level, the majority of literature focuses on individual outcomes.

Eliana Carranza, Chandra Dhakal and Inessa Love state that there are four drivers of differences in the performance of women and men as entrepreneurs. (Carranza, Dhakal, & Love, 2018)

CHOICES AND PREFERENCES

Two categories of elements that affect people's decisions to become entrepreneurs were first recognized in the literature. A "pull" element is characterized by seizing an opportunity, such a novel company concept. The "push" factors refer to an unfavorable circumstance, such as a lack of employment opportunities, a lack of fulfilment, or a lack of flexibility in a current position. In essence, when the first option (like a wage job) is not available, the push factors capture the economic necessity and the second-best option.

Female-owned firms experience lesser growth. A key topic is whether women choose to have lesser growth based on their priorities and preferences, or if their decision is constrained by the context in which they work and the kinds of enterprises they decide to start.

Entrepreneurs' expectations for and actual growth are influenced by their reasons for starting their own businesses. According to some research, women who are "drawn" into entrepreneurship (i.e., by opportunity) have higher growth goals than those who are "pushed" into it by necessity (Morris et al., 2016). (Morris et al, 2006).

Risk is an important element of any entrepreneurial activity. Risk tolerance is important as a bridge the gap between opportunity recognition and entrepreneurial enactment (Marlow and Carter, 2004).

Mathews and Moser (1996) measured prospective interest in self-employment among college graduates in the U.S. and found that men are more interested in starting their own business than women. Interestingly, after 5 years as 15 employees, the difference between men's and women's interest in self-employment increased even further.

Women tend to focus more on meaningful work and place less importance on earning income. For example, a study in North Ireland concluded that women did not display "classic" entrepreneurial values, in particular rejecting risk-taking and profit motivation (MacNabb et al., 1993). Men and women also differ in their concept of what defines success. For women "success" means having control over their own destinies, building ongoing relationships with clients, and doing something fulfilling. Men described success in terms of achieving goals (Romano, 1994).

Endowments

Women have fewer assets than men for a variety of reasons. First, there is less possibility to build up money and other assets due to salary discrimination and fewer years spent working (due to pregnancy, childbirth, and child care). Second, it's commonplace for assets to be registered in a husband's name in many societies, both socially and legally.

Firm success is heavily influenced by human resources, including the expertise and abilities of business leaders. There is still a gender imbalance in education in many developing nations, particularly at the secondary level. Families frequently invest less in their daughters' education and training than in their sons, which limits the human capital that women may contribute to self-employment.

In many situations, women tend to rely more on their extended families than do males. social media. Such networks could have both benefits and drawbacks. On the one hand, family and close friends can help the business owner, such as by giving the funding required to launch the business, providing child-care assistance, or providing encouragement. Alternatively, they might drain the resources away from the company and impede its expansion.

External Constraints

The World Bank's report Women, Business and the Law, 2018 identifies many countries where laws restrict women's economic activities (World Bank Group, 2018). For example, 104 countries have laws preventing women from working in certain jobs, 59 countries have no laws to restrict sexual harassment in the workplace, and in 18 countries, husbands can legally prevent their wives from working. In Nigeria, Chad, and Guinea-Bissau, civil law does not allow women to open bank accounts without their husband's permission, and in Equatorial Guinea, women need their husbands' permission to sign a contract.

Many social norms include patrilineage where descent, and often resources, flow through males (Christopher Baughn, Chua and Neupert, 2006). The previous section described legal restrictions on asset ownership. Even if the legal system is not explicitly discriminatory against women, the social norms and traditions, especially in rural areas, can still prohibit women from owning property (see Borghi-Doku, 2002; Dowuona-Hammond, 2008).

Many cultures do not take women's business activities as "serious" because business is often considered a male's role. Jamali (2009) found that one of three obstacles mentioned by Lebanese women entrepreneurs was the negative societal attitude toward women entrepreneurs. Brush and Hisrich (1991)

It has frequently been noted that companies operated by women rely less on outside funding than companies run by men.

However, as with any equilibrium conclusion, it is not immediately clear whether this outcome is a result of the decisions women make or discriminatory behaviour on the part of financial institutions (i.e., the supply side, which is an external restriction) (i.e. the demand side, which is an internal constraint). The former will be covered in this section, while the latter will be covered in a subsequent one.

It is then important not to discount the severity of financial constraints even if the evidence suggests that conditional on small business size there is no discrimination. One of the reasons for gender discrimination on the job market is different cultural expectations for men and women. For instance, social standards may define which careers are suitable for women, which can result in labor markets that are divided based on gender. Vertical or horizontal segregation is also possible. Women are concentrated in different jobs than males in horizontal segregation.

Women's participation in entrepreneurship can be impacted in two different ways by gender imbalance in the workplace. On the one hand, more inequality may result in fewer women participating in the labor force as wage workers, leaving them without the confidence, knowledge, and experience necessary to launch their own enterprises.

There is evidence that the social pressure to redistribute is higher for women. For example, a study of women entrepreneurs in Madagascar found that the share of ethnic groups in the neighbourhood significantly increased the inefficiency of female entrepreneurs when they were home-based (Nordman and Vaillant, 2014).

Self-perceptions and lack of confidence have real consequences. The perception of having insufficient skills to start a new business was found to have a negative effect independent of institutional settings, culture, and overall level of entrepreneurial activities (Langowitz and Minniti, 2007).

Roper and Scott (2009) found that in the UK women are around 7.4 percent more likely to perceive financial barriers to business start-up than men, which has a disproportionate effect on women's start-up decisions. Greer and Green (2003) found that women business owners are less likely to use their bank as a source of financial advice and are reluctant to respond to that advice.

Women entrepreneurs may experience an environment that is more hostile than those which men do, or they may believe that the environment is more hostile when it is not. The former circumstance is discussed in the section on external constraints, whereas the latter possibility is discussed here.

Growth and Empowerment

Women entrepreneurs are out taking the world and the stereotypes we see are coming to a decline and sooner will be an end. For a seed to flourish, there are external and internal requirements need to garner the support. Hence, for empowering women entrepreneurs, the support of the country and the public policies of the government provide a huge backbone.

(Cooper, 2022) As per Cooper in her blog, William Russell, she states that the most female friendly countries that provide maximum support are:

1. Iceland
2. Finland
3. Ireland
4. Belgium
5. Denmark
6. Canada
7. France
8. Norway
9. Sweden
10. Lithuania

From the above list said, the top three countries making to the top charts are Iceland, Finland and Ireland. Iceland with a female empowerment score of 7.64 on a 10-point scale is well known for its progressive views and welcoming culture. More than half of adult women have achieved tertiary education such as a university degree, and the country scored full marks in the World Bank's *Women, Business and Law Index*. Following Iceland is Finland which has a female empowerment score of 7.62. Finland has achieved excellent representation for women in its government, with 50% of all ministerial positions being occupied by women. It has also had one of the highest numbers of elected female leaders, with four different women leading the country at one time or another.

Ireland has been ranked as the third best having a Female empowerment score of 7.22. It also received a perfect score in the World Bank's *Women, Business and Law Index*, combined with a relatively low gender wage gap of 7.99% and a very competitive 182 days of paid maternity leave for new mothers.

The study focuses on the existence of government initiatives expressly designed to assist women business owners in India, working with her MSME and the National Small Industries Corporation (NSIC).

In particular during the COVID-19 epidemic, it sought to study the primary challenges and opportunities experienced by women beginning and operating a business in Delhi. FREP 1,2 206 the Swa-Shakti Project, Rural Women's Development and Empowerment, Rashtriya Mahila Kosh, Priyadarshini, and Women's Empowerment and Livelihood have all been launched by the Indian government. Other initiatives include the National Mission for Empowerment of Women, Leadership Development of Minority Women, Integrated Scheme for Women Empowerment, Prime Minister's Rozgar Yojna (PMRY), and the Rural Women's Development and Empowerment.

(Sanjeev Kumar) Successful entrepreneurs are opportunity oriented and focus on innovation, service, wealth creation and employment. The support of family members, especially fathers and husbands, is as important as the entrepreneur's motivation, skills, and abilities. Success for her means being independent (financially/financially), being happy, having a successful career, having a happy family, and having a good work-life balance. But it also means the satisfaction of having contributed to something you've maintained so far. The Indian government has launched a number of initiatives aimed at empowering women through policy and entrepreneurship, including the National Mission for Empowerment of Women, Leadership Development of Minority Women, Integrated Scheme for Women Empowerment, Prime Minister's Rozgar Yojna (PMRY), the Swa-Shakti Project, Rural Women's Development and Empowerment, Rashtriya Mahila Kosh, Priyadarshani, and Women's Empowerment and Livelihood. The PMRY was established by the central government in 1993 to encourage women's self-employment by offering loans up to one lakh for businesses and two lakhs for industrial and agricultural operations.

Making women the best versions of themselves is the fundamental goal of women's empowerment. We will provide opportunities and facilities that every woman deserves as part of empowerment, and throughout the process, there is no mention of men. Increasing the status of women through education, knowledge, literacy, and training as well as acknowledging women's perspectives, making an effort to find them, and through the various societal issues, women's empowerment empowers and enables them to make decisions that have a significant impact on their lives. They might be given the chance to redefine gender roles and other kinds of responsibilities, giving them more flexibility to achieve their ambitions.

market. Since then, both developed and developing nations have adopted common policies and programmes promoting women's entrepreneurship. Women still encounter obstacles despite significant advances in assisting them to overcome obstacles to starting their own businesses and working for themselves, necessitating continuing public policy action (European Union, 2017).

The objectives of most entrepreneurship policies are to increase the ease of doing business (e.g., by dismantling legal and legislative barriers), and to facilitate access to resources requisite to start-up and firm growth (Acs. & Virgill, 2011).

Six common interventions include access to financing, government policies, taxes and bureaucracy, government programs, school-level entrepreneurship education and training, post-school entrepreneurship education and training, R&D transfer, access to commercial and professional infrastructure, internal market dynamics, internal market burdens, access to infrastructure, and social and cultural norms (Global Entrepreneurship Monitor – GEM, 2015). GEM 2015 also reports that there are significant differences in policy support across the entrepreneurial ecosystems of the 60 economies surveyed. Innovation-driven economies were deemed to be strongest with respect to government support (Acs. & Virgill, 2011).

The framework incorporates three pillars:

The regulative pillar contains mandated specifications including laws, governance and monitoring systems. This pillar is derived from a rational economic model of behavior (North, 1994) concerning rules, sanctions and conformity.8 Specifically, this study seeks to understand how regulatory policies and rules encourage and/or discourage women's entrepreneurship. The normative pillar concerns values, expectations and standards, such as roles, repertoire of action and conventions. This pillar underlies understanding motivation for, or resistance to, entrepreneurial behavior within different country contexts. The cultural-cognitive pillar denotes predispositions and symbolic value as a model for individual behavior regarding the individual acceptance of entrepreneurship. The review of literature suggests that examination of public policies that seek to address gender barriers for women entrepreneurs must consider factors that shape women's work experience, including government laws, governance, regulatory and monitoring mechanisms – the focus of this study. In the next section, the common methodological approach employed by the Global WEP team to analyze sample documents of the 13 countries is described. (Acts. & Virgill, 2011)

(Rodríguez, Rojo, Gento, & Albiñana, 2022) state that women's social and economic participation in the work environment has advanced substantially in the last few decades, several new policy approaches to supporting women in entrepreneurship are starting to emerge (OECD, 2017), specially during the Covid-19 pandemic (European Commission, 2020a).

The OECD guidelines highlighted also state that to achieve the objective, Sect. 2 of OECD will examine the current increasing interest in the role of women in entrepreneurial activity by policymakers and scholars (Wassem, 2018). Section 3 will explain the difference between necessity-driven entrepreneurship and opportunity-driven entrepreneurship and will consider the reasons for starting a business among females. This distinction is important because by understanding the real reasons why women decide to start a business, more efficient economic policies can be designed to promote their activity.

It has been shown that necessity-driven entrepreneurs are more likely to lack entrepreneurial skills, experience, and high levels of education (Block & Wagner, 2010). Human capital is an important factor in identifying more and better opportunities and promoting entrepreneurship (Marques, 2017). Although all these assessments can be applied to both men and women, the way in which they may make use of stocks of human capital to identify opportunities may differ (DeTienne & Chandler, 2007) Human capital is an important determinant for females to engage in entrepreneurship and has been extensively used to predict female propensity towards entrepreneurship (Wassem, 2018).

Higher-income level countries have auspicious economic conditions that offer more entrepreneurial opportunities for women. They can benefit from stronger institutions, along with easy access to human and monetary capital. Therefore, women in high-income level countries enter opportunity-driven entrepreneurship due to frustration in career advancement (Lerner & Malach-Pines, 2011), because of their need for achievement, or their desire for independence, self-efficacy, and self-reliance (Wassem, 2018).

A few studies have found that actually estimate the economic impact of women's entrepreneurship. These studies define women's entrepreneurship as firms owned and managed by women. In Canada, The Prime Minister's Task Force on Women Entrepreneurs (2003) has assembled statistics from Statistics Canada on women entrepreneurs. They find that there is more than 821 000 Canadian women entrepreneurs and they contribute to an excess of CAD 18 However, average annual sales for women-owned firms are significantly lower. In 2000, women-owned SMEs averaged CAD 311 289 in sales, compared with 654 294 in sales for firms owned by men. In the US, the latest analyses from the US Census Bureau estimate that women-owned and managed firms represent 28% of the 23 million firms (amounting to 6.4 million), and they provide employment for 9.2 million people. That represents 9% of all employed in the private sector. Women-owned and managed businesses having annual turnover of at least Euro 16 620 number 522 000, represent 18% of the total in this group, and provide jobs for 2 million employees (Günterberg & Wolter, 2004).

Significant schemes in India those specifically introduced for women for providing special benefits to women Trade Related Entrepreneurship Assistance and Development Scheme for Women (TREAD) It is with the objective of encouraging women in starting their own ventures, government launched a Scheme, namely, (TREAD) Trade Related Entrepreneurship Assistance and Development during the 11thPlan. The scheme envisaged economic empowerment of 297 women through the development of their entrepreneurial skills in non-farm activities (SUBATHRA).

Across the documents, the main contributions to women's entrepreneurship policy were: (a) affirmation of research highlighting gender differences; (b) gender-related challenges confronting women entrepreneurs; and/or (c) need for dedicated entrepreneurship policy support for women. For example, some profiled the challenges faced by women entrepreneurs, or drew attention to male-female differences in terms of entrepreneurial characteristics and behaviors (e.g., attitude to risk, motivation, growth orientation, access to capital). Some documents focused on differences in sector representation (such as STEM, health, education or the informal sector) (Acs. & Virgill, 2011).

A results-oriented approach would involve employing teaching methods that encourage or foster the entrepreneurial spirit, i.e., taking responsibility, learning-by-doing, group work, interactivity, problem-solving and the acceptance of error as a learning experience. A paradigm shift in the ultimate objective of education should end up creating a multiplier effect: entrepreneurship is not only nurtured, but education is used as a means of increasing open-mindedness and reducing general negative societal attitudes towards female entrepreneurship. It is not an overstatement to say that higher educated people are less likely to disregard women as entrepreneurs. In market economies where the private sector has a strong voice, employers' organizations can use their lobbying role to push forward such reforms to the educational system (Hookoomsing & Essoo, 2003).

(Hookoomsing & Essoo, 2003) state that it should not be forgotten that entrepreneurial activity is inseparable from the socio-economic and cultural context in which it is grounded. The process of motivating the entrepreneurial spirit in women and transforming them into successful entrepreneurs must necessarily respect the essential values in society. Entrepreneurship should thus be seen as a means of enhancing women's life in a holistic way, at a personal level, at the family level, and in the context of the community and society in general

The Philippines offers an example of how to create a broad-based and mutually reinforcing policy infrastructure in support of women's entrepreneurship. Using a dual-pronged approach, the Government of the Philippines has prioritized women's entrepreneurship by enacting gender-specific laws and strategies, as well as mainstreaming gender concerns into broader statutes and regulations regarding MSMEs. (The Asian Foundation, 2018)

A cluster is described as a group of enterprises, normally twenty or more producing the same/similar products/services. The Cluster Development Programme being implemented envisages diagnostic study of identified clusters of traditional skill-based MSEs to identify suitable technologies and their providers and to facilitate adoption of available technology meeting the specific needs of the end-users (SUBATHRA).

CONCLUSION

Women's entrepreneurship is a mark of economic growth for a country it is always important that a woman has the independence to make her own choices be it life or pursuing her passion, turning them into business, crossing up all the hurdles with both professional and private life juggling both roles equally is truly tremendously appreciable.

Entrepreneurs is defined as a group of women who initiates, organize and run a business concern from a situation where a woman was not even allowed to get out of their homes to today running most of the successful brands of the world, contributing a major part to the economic growth and breaking the stereotypes by providing a reality check to the male dominance. There has been a wide range of Public policies enrolled out to facilitate and encourage the growth of women`s entrepreneurship. From the past times of not gaining adequate recognition for their support, women have emerged successful in overcoming hardships such as lack of visibility, lack of training and educative support about public policies provided by governments to women entrepreneurs, and fewer opportunities and walking out of the social stigma.

Entrepreneurial activity is a calculated risk-taking and continuing process of innovation activities that embody discovery, evaluation, and exploitation of opportunities, the judgment of the possibilities, and making decisions in an identified uncertainty within a rapidly changing environment by using the spill over of knowledge and creating value out of this knowledge. Entrepreneurship As small businesses are vital for any developing country's economic progression, female entrepreneurs contribution to this sector assumes great significance. However, regardless of an upturn in the number of female entrepreneurs in recent years, entrepreneurial movement among males is greater, and noteworthy differences are evident across national settings.

Women entrepreneurship is "an act of owning a business which makes women economically independent." Female entrepreneurs play an important role in sustained economic development and social progress. The gender gap in entrepreneurship is defined as the difference between men and women in terms of numbers engaged in entrepreneurial activity, motives to start or run a business, industry choice, and business performance and growth. It is evident that women entrepreneurs contribute immensely to improved poverty levels, increased per capita income, and employment creation. The recent Mastercard Index of Women Entrepreneurs (MIWE) has ranked India in 52nd position among 57 nations.

Studying female entrepreneurship contributes to our understanding of entrepreneurship and human behavior in general and allows researchers to ask questions that shed light not only on why women behave the way they do but also on the linkages between entrepreneurship and wealth creation, employment, human capital accumulation, labor market dynamics, and many others.

Due to the advancement of technology, modernization, industrialization, urbanization, expansion of education, and government-sponsored development initiatives, the business environment in India is changing day by day. In such circumstances, women' s work opportunities significantly rose. The stereotype of constrained, housebound women in India is gradually changing. Even after experiencing numerous obstacles, Indian women are currently working to achieve economic independence. The government has introduced a number of facilities, discounts, and incentives specifically for female entrepreneurs. It is possible to take general actions to promote and advance female entrepreneurship. Due to the fact that even illiterate women are capable of starting, maintaining, and managing their own businesses in a fairly organized way. the correct kind of family aid, The government and society may integrate these roti-making women entrepreneurs into the national economy so they can advance the economy of the country. India has promising futures for women's entrepreneurship in this era of digitalization, globalization, and start-up booms. Women entrepreneurs come from all backgrounds and regions of the country. Women roles have evolved over the past few decades and are currently moving in the direction of much-needed development. In today industry 4.0, women can provide creative answers to problems and make wise decisions. By delivering creative solutions, women entrepreneurs have generated numerous new jobs, both for themselves and for others. Women entrepreneurs are outperforming and beyond market expectations in several enterprises. Women have achieved great success not just in the fields of health, aviation, law, science, space exploration, the military, and law enforcement but also in business and industry. Women' s status in society and the function of entrepreneurship in the same society are both topics covered by entrepreneurship. Women entrepreneurs had to overcome numerous challenges, particularly those related to family duties, in order to access the same opportunities as males. These challenges were present specifically in the marketing of their products. Women may also encounter challenges in some nations when it comes to owning property and signing contracts. Improving the status of women in society and among independent women depends on increased female involvement in the labor field. The entry of women into micro-businesses will be promoted and made worse in particular. By participating in entrepreneurship effectively and competently, women can achieve great things. Women are equipped with the fundamental indigenous knowledge and talent, Women status in society and the function of entrepreneurship in the same society are both topics covered by entrepreneurship. Women entrepreneurs had to overcome numerous challenges, particularly those related to family duties, in order to access the same opportunities as males. These challenges were present specifically in the marketing of their products. Women may also encounter challenges in some nations when it comes to owning property and signing contracts. Improving the status of women in society and among independent women depends on increased female involvement in the labor field. The entry of women into micro-businesses will be promoted and made worse in particular. By participating in entrepreneurship effectively and competently, women can achieve great things. The women are equipped with the fundamental indigenous knowledge, talent, and resources to create and run a business. What is required now is knowledge of loan accessibility, certification procedures for various funding institutions, awareness of government assistance programs, drive, technical talent, and support from family, the government, and other organizations.

Women empowerment is thus promoted by and brought to create and run a business. What is required now is knowledge of loan accessibility, certification procedures for various funding institutions, awareness of government assistance programs, drive, technical talent, and support from family, the government, and other organizations. Women empowerment is thus, promoted by and brought about by female businesses we hope that this chapter provides the readers and budding woman entrepreneurs to be more powered and the world gets enriched with knowledge.

REFERENCES

Afshan, G., Shahid, S., & Tunio, M. N. (2021). Learning experiences of women entrepreneurs amidst COVID-19. *International Journal of Gender.* doi:10.1108/IJSE-07-2017-0298

Agarwal, S., & Lenka, U. (2018). Why research is needed in women entrepreneurship in India: A viewpoint. *International Journal of Social Economics*, *45*(7), 1042–1057. doi:10.1108/IJSE-07-2017-0298

Agarwal, S., & Lenka, U. (2018b). Why research is needed in women entrepreneurship in India: A viewpoint. *International Journal of Social Economics*, *45*(7), 1042–1057. doi:10.1108/IJSE-07-2017-0298

Ascher, J. (2012). Female Entrepreneurship – An Appropriate Response to Gender Discrimination. *Journal of Entrepreneurship. Management and Innovation*, *8*(4), 97–114. doi:10.7341/2012847

Brush, C. G. (1992). Research on Women Business Owners: Past Trends, a New Perspective and Future Directions. *Entrepreneurship Theory and Practice*, *16*(4), 5–30. doi:10.1177/104225879201600401

Bulanova, O., Isaksen, E. J., & Kolvereid, L. (2016). Growth aspirations among women entrepreneurs in high growth firms. *Baltic Journal of Management*, *11*(2), 187–206. doi:10.1108/BJM-11-2014-0204

Cardella, G. M., Hernández-Sánchez, B. R., & Sánchez-García, J. C. (2020). Women Entrepreneurship: A Systematic Review to Outline the Boundaries of Scientific Literature. *Frontiers in Psychology*, *11*, 1557. doi:10.3389/fpsyg.2020.01557 PMID:32765357

Eliana Carranza, Chandra Shekhar Dhakal, & Inessa Love. (2018). Female Entrepreneurs: How and Why are They Different? *Worldbank.*

Chhabra, S., Raghunathan, R., & Rao, N. M. (2020). The antecedents of entrepreneurial intention among women entrepreneurs in India. *Asia Pacific Journal of Innovation and Entrepreneurship*, *14*(1), 76–92. doi:10.1108/APJIE-06-2019-0034

Datta, P. B., & Gailey, R. (2012). Empowering Women through Social Entrepreneurship: Case Study of a Women's Cooperative in India. *Entrepreneurship Theory and Practice*, *36*(3), 569–587. doi:10.1111/j.1540-6520.2012.00505.x

Gaweł, A., & Mroczek-Dąbrowska, K. (2021). Gender pay gap in explaining female entrepreneurship – industry perspective of selected European countries. *International Journal of Manpower*, *43*(9), 42–59. doi:10.1108/IJM-12-2020-0554

Gupta, N., & Etzkowitz, H. (2021). Women founders in a high-tech incubator: Negotiating entrepreneurial identity in the Indian socio-cultural context. *International Journal of Gender and Entrepreneurship*, *13*(4), 353–372. doi:10.1108/IJGE-11-2020-0181

Jabeen, F., & Faisal, M. N. (2018). Imperatives for improving entrepreneurial behavior among females in the UAE. *Gender in Management*, *33*(3), 234–252. doi:10.1108/GM-03-2016-0042

Jamali, D. (2009). Constraints and opportunities facing women entrepreneurs in developing countries. *Gender in Management*, *24*(4), 232–251. doi:10.1108/17542410910961532

Kumar, S., & Singh, N. (2021). Entrepreneurial prospects and challenges for women amidst COVID-19: A case study of Delhi, India. *Fulbright Review of Economics and Policy*, *1*(2), 205–226. doi:10.1108/FREP-09-2021-0057

Levitt, P., & Schiller, N. G. (2004). Conceptualizing Simultaneity: A Transnational Social Field Perspective on Society. *The International Migration Review*, *38*(3), 1002–1039. doi:10.1111/j.1747-7379.2004.tb00227.x

Llados-Masllorens, J., & Ruiz-Dotras, E. (2021). Are women's entrepreneurial intentions and motivations influenced by financial skills? *International Journal of Gender and Entrepreneurship*, *14*(1), 69–94. doi:10.1108/IJGE-01-2021-0017

Minniti, M., & Naudé, W. (2010). What Do We Know About the Patterns and Determinants of Female Entrepreneurship Across Countries? *European Journal of Development Research*, *22*(3), 277–293. doi:10.1057/ejdr.2010.17

Mitchell, L. (2011). Overcoming the Gender Gap: Women Entrepreneurs as Economic Drivers. SSRN *Electronic Journal*. doi:10.2139/ssrn.1934906

Mitchell, L. (2011b). Overcoming the Gender Gap: Women Entrepreneurs as Economic Drivers. SSRN *Electronic Journal*. doi:10.2139/ssrn.1934906

MuldoonJ.LucyC.LidzyS. (2019).

Parimala Devi, B. (2014). Problems and Prospects of Women Entrepreneurship in India. [IJSR]. *International Journal of Scientific Research*.

Raghuvanshi, J., Agrawal, R., & Ghosh, P. K. (2017). Analysis of Barriers to Women Entrepreneurship: The DEMATEL Approach. *The Journal of Entrepreneurship*, *26*(2), 220–238. doi:10.1177/0971355717708848

Ramesh, D. B. (2018). Problems and perspective of women entrepreneurship in india. *IJRAR*, *5*(Issue 1). https://www.ijrar.org/papers/IJRAR19D1059.pdf

Xavier, S. R., Ahmad, S. Z., Nor, L. M., & Yusof, M. (2012). Women Entrepreneurs: Making A Change from Employment to Small and Medium Business Ownership. *Procedia Economics and Finance*, *4*, 321–334. doi:10.1016/S2212-5671(12)00347-4

Chapter 9
Double Burden and Gender Disparity:
Women Diamond Miners Contribute to the Family Economy

Nana Noviana Nadarsyah
Regional Research and Development Agency, Banjarbaru, Indonesia

ABSTRACT

Gender issues are problems that often occur in social life in society by separating definitions based on biological and physical characteristics. A discriminatory culture limits women in their roles, including their human rights to make choices. This role is due to the distribution and allocation of power as well as the division of labor in the family, but in fact, there is no division of labor in fulfilling the family economy. In terms of family economic downturn, gender disparity no longer applies. A woman is not only responsible as a housewife but also works to fulfill the family's economy.

INTRODUCTION

The problem of gender is a problem that often occurs in society, where gender is associated with structural differences in every aspect of social life. Stoller, (1968) first introduced the term gender to separate definitions that are socio-cultural in nature from definitions based on biological physical characteristics. In Indonesia, there is still a discriminatory culture that applies, so gender equality and gender justice are hampered in their implementation, including gender equality in the health sector. Gender limits women in their roles, including their human rights to make choices. Women are not only faced with choices in determining a life partner, education choices, health choices, the right to get information, and the choice to be happy in the household.

It can be seen that the number of early marriages (married before the age of 16 years) is almost found in all provinces in Indonesia. Around 10% of young women between the ages of 15 and 19 have their

DOI: 10.4018/978-1-6684-7669-7.ch009

first child. Most adolescents do not have accurate knowledge about reproductive health and sexuality and do not have access to reproductive health services and information, including contraception.

A high education is deemed necessary for women, because a high level of education allows them to improve their standard of living and make decisions regarding their own health issues. Reproductive rights are regulated in the Human Rights Law in articles 49, paragraph 2 and 3. Protection of women's reproductive rights this is an effort with the aim of providing guarantees and comfort in all aspects of life for women, including the economic aspect. Women have an important role in the economy. One of the activities carried out by women in an effort to strengthen the economy is diamond mining. They have a share in family income, although they often do not get recognition. This traditional diamond mining activity is in great demand by the Banjar community, especially the Kepumpung village community (Noviana, 2016).

The community hopes that this diamond mining activity will be able to lift the community's economy, but in reality, this mining activity is not able to lift the economy of the miners' families but, on the contrary, has a negative impact on both the environment and their health.

METHODOLOGY

The approach used in this study is a qualitative approach with an ethnographic type of research. The researcher explores in depth the female diamond miners both at work and not, and examines the impact of diamond mining on women's health and local values that arise in various interactions, especially the economy carried out by the diamond mining community. The location of this study is in Cempaka Village, Banjarbaru City, South Kalimantan. This location was chosen because this is where there is traditional diamond mining (people's mining) and local miners who live and work around the mining area.

There are two types of data extracted in this study, namely primary and secondary data. Primary data comes from female miners who work in the local diamond mining community. In addition, data is also collected from local residents, community leaders, and, if possible, from mining land owners or investors.

Secondary data extracted from this study was collected from data on environmental conditions and socio-economic conditions of the residents who work as diamond miners at the study site.

The data collection procedures used were interviews, observations, and documentation. Interviews were conducted on the main subject of the study, namely the female diamond miners. In addition, interviews were also conducted with parties directly or indirectly involved in mining activities, such as local community leaders, communities around the mining area, miners' families, and village officials.

There are two types of data extracted in this study, namely primary and secondary data. Primary data comes from female miners who work in the local diamond mining community. In addition, data is also collected from local residents, community leaders, and, if possible, from mining land owners or investors.

Secondary data extracted from this study was collected from data on environmental conditions and socio-economic conditions of the residents who work as diamond miners at the study site.

The data collection procedures used were interviews, observations, and documentation. Interviews were conducted on the main subject of the study, namely the female diamond miners. In addition, interviews were also conducted with parties directly or indirectly involved in mining activities, such as local community leaders, communities around the mining area, miners' families, and village officials.

Collecting Data (Logging the Data)

According to Creswell, the qualitative research data collection procedure involves four types of strategies, namely qualitative observation, qualitative interviews, qualitative documents, and qualitative audio and visual materials. Therefore, the researcher in collecting the research data used data collection methods, namely: interviews, observations, documentation, and audio and visual materials.

THE GENDER DISPARITY OF FEMALE MINERS IN SUPPORTING THE FAMILY ECONOMY

Norms and values in society determine the gender roles that underlie responsibility, power, and behavior. Based on the scientist Plato, women are viewed in terms of physical and spiritual strength. A woman's mentality is weaker than a man's, but the mental differences that women have do not cause a weakening of women's talents. Broverman, a feminist figure, said that humans, both male and female, were created to have certain biological (natural) characteristics (Fakih, 2008). The opinion of feminists is that women in the concept of gender have different inherent characteristics as a form of gender stereotypes. In the Women's Studies Encyclopedia, it is explained that gender is a cultural concept that seeks to make a difference (distinction) in terms of roles, behavior, mentality, and emotional characteristics between men and women who develop in society.

Gender roles or roles based on gender are a way of assessing society's making boundaries about what it means to be a woman and what it means to be a man. These boundaries arise because they are based on the biological condition of a woman, as well as restrictions on women's rights, so they have a great impact on women. People assume that because a person is born with a certain gender, he must think, feel, and act in a certain way. However, other activities in the community may not be the same. This is due to differences in legal and religious customs. It also depends on the level of education, ethnicity, and in general, This is in line with Caplan's opinion in the cultural construction of sexuality that behavioral differences between men and women are not just biological, but mediated through social and cultural processes.

In the anthropology of social relations, a man can provide protection, income, sex, etc. On the other hand, he also received service in a number of situations. Inequality measured only externally can lead to gender bias. Inequality in the social sphere does not make women sit idly by watching the slump in the family economy. Women try to help the family economy by being simple diamond miners. Why are women no longer considered weak in a state of economic downturn? Men are still asked to do menial jobs like cleaning diamonds. This is the dilemma faced by women. Gender roles do not apply when the family economy slumps.

According to Allport, (1964), the most important aspect of the family structure is the position of family members because of the distribution and allocation of power as well as the division of labor in the family. The fact that happened in this village is that there is no division of labor in fulfilling the family economy. Women also contribute to working as diamond miners in order to lift the family out of the economic downturn. Basically, women are only biologically different from men, but in their role in the social and cultural order prevailing in society, they are equal to men. The role of women in efforts to improve the family economy is an effort to support inclusive economic growth. Because in an effort to increase inclusive economic growth, the participation of all elements of society is needed. This is in line with research conducted by the Asian Development Bank (ADB) in the 2016 Economic Working Paper study with the topic "A Model of Gender Inequality and Economic Growth," conveying the conclusion that increasing gender equity contributes significantly to economic growth. Therefore, efforts to increase economic growth need to be based on justice and gender equality.

THE DOUBLE BURDEN OF FEMALE MINERS IN SUPPORTING THE FAMILY ECONOMY

The role of women in the public sector in this modern and democratic era still considers that women are second class citizens, even as complements. Actually, the involvement of women in the public area is more as workers to meet the demands of the family's economic needs. So the role of women is very complex, namely not only being a wife but also being a mother who is responsible for her children and workers to meet the needs of the family. The diamond mining activity carried out by the women of Kepumpung village was carried out in a simple way to raise the family's economic status. With the demands of women's complex roles, the women in this village do diamond mining, but this can have a negative effect on women's reproductive conditions.

Community mining is mining that has been passed down from generation to generation by the community or local residents, either individually or in groups with traditional management. Hilton, 2005. This diamond mining depends on the lives of the small people, which is done traditionally from generation to generation. As is the case in the Cempaka sub-district, it is a sub-city where one of its functions is as a mining center. In this case, women in diamond mining activities play an important role in improving the family economy. One of the activities carried out by women in an effort to strengthen the economy is by mining diamonds. They have a share in family income even though they often do not get recognition.

Diamond mining is a good opportunity for women to help the household economy, but without realizing it, diamond mining can cause problems in the reproductive system. Therefore, the role of women in participating in efforts to improve the family economy contributes to improving family welfare. Despite the fact that diamond mining activities do not make a significant contribution to improving the economy of the Cempaka sub-district community. In the context of poverty, the existence of people's diamond mining in the Cempaka area is not able to raise the economic status of the local community.

In addition, women's education is low but does not hinder women's desire to continue to struggle to improve the family economy for the welfare of the family. The low level of education causes them to carry out mining with minimal formal education because this does not require a high level of formal education. The dual role of women in the family does not weaken women's ability to continue to struggle, and this is proof that women are not as weak as they appear physically. Even though it is a result of the family's economic pressure and the low level of education, there is a lack of understanding of the negative impacts of diamond mining, which will have an impact in the future.

CONCLUSION AND RECOMMENDATIONS

Conclusion

Gender disparities in an area vary depending on the values and norms that pass in society. In terms of family economic downturn, gender disparity no longer applies. A woman is not only responsible as a housewife but also works to provide for the family economy.

The role of women is no longer as a complement but also the main role in improving the family economy, despite the fact that it often does not get recognition. However, this role is very meaningful in supporting inclusive economic growth because, in an effort to increase inclusive economic growth, the participation of all elements of society is required.

Suggestion

This policy formulation needs to be combined with applicable actions from the aspect of economic institutions so that efforts to reduce poverty and improve the quality of life for diamond mining communities in Cempaka District, Banjarbaru City, can be realized.

In this context, efforts are needed to transform knowledge and efforts to empower them through the formation of independence and creativity to cultivate their natural surroundings. Besides that, it also needs to be studied further in order to systematically formulate policies that can be applied to the empowerment of the mining community.

Figure 1. Man shown in dug out structure

Figure 2. Man shown holding basket

REFERENCES

Caplan, P. (1987). *Cultural Construction of Sexuality*. Tavictock Publication.

Indonesian Ministry of Health. (2005). *Reproductive Health National Policy and Strategy in Indonesia.*

Inter-agency Working Group on Reproductive Health in Crises. (2010). *Inter-Institutional Field Handbook Reproductive Health in emergency situations.* IWGRHC.

Lloyd, C. B., & Mensch, B. S. (2008). Marriage and childbirth as factors in dropping out from school: An analysis of DHS data from sub-Saharan Africa. *Population Studies, 62*(1), 1–13. doi:10.1080/00324720701810840 PMID:18278669

Ministry of Health Republic of Indonesia. (2008). *Communication, Information, Education (KIE).* Reproductive Health for Health Officers at Basic Services.

National Research Council, Institute of Medicine (NRC/IOM). (2005). *Growing up global: The changing transitions to adulthood in developing countries.* NRC/IOM.

Noviana, N. (2015). Female Reproduction Rights in Remote Area: Gender Perspective. Proceedings in *International ASEAN Forum On Ict For Sustainable Rural Development And Knowledge Cross-Fertilization 2015.*

Noviana, N. (2016). *Konsep HIV/AIDS Seksualitas dan Kesehatan Reproduksi.* Trans Info Media.

Noviana, N., & Rahmattullah, M. (2016). Reproduction health of female diamond miners in cempaka subdistrict, banjarbaru. Advancing inclusive rural development and transformation in a challenging environment, p.538.

Robert, J. (1968). *Stoller. Sex and Gender: On the Development of Masculinity and Femininity* (Vol. 2). Science House.

Sahay, S. (2011). Assessment of the ability of the health management information system in India to use information for action [Doctoral dissertation, HISP India].

Tierney, H. (1995). *Women's Studies Encyclopedia*. Green Word Press.

KEY TERMS AND DEFINITIONS

Double Burden: The role of women is no longer as a complement but also the main role in the family, both in the implementation of the household and in improving the family economy.

Family Economy: the conditions and efforts made to meet the needs of family members in order to achieve family welfare.

Female Diamond Miner: is a woman or man who performs diamond-seeking activities by making holes and spraying water in the traditional way.

Gender Disparity: the biological differences between women and men that underlie power and responsibility, both in terms of norms and morals that apply in society

Chapter 10
Masculine Presentation of Women's Entrepreneurship

Kazım Tolga Gürel
Independent Researcher, Turkey

Dilek Şen
Independent Researcher, Turkey

ABSTRACT

In this study, news on women's entrepreneurship will be selected from Turkish newspapers. Turkey, with its geopolitical location in the middle of two continents and its political regime, is an important example due to its capitalisation since the 19th century when it started to integrate into the capitalist economy. Since it is a country that maintains heteronormative patterns where these norms are protected, glorified, and pumped by the state, a lot of data will be available in terms of news on the masculinized presentation of the female entrepreneur. In this study, news selected from social media and published newspapers will be subjected to content analysis and the findings obtained as a result of this analysis will be interpreted. Some of the sample news will be selected and subjected to qualitative data analysis and more findings will be interpreted. 198 news items selected from newspapers with mainstream and right-conservative ideology will be analyzed.

INTRODUCTION

For a long period of history, women have been excluded from the spheres of business and money management. The women who have gained this chance at governance are women who fit the qualities of masculine power. Women such as Cleopatra, queen of Egypt, and Elizabeth I, queen of England, perpetuate male hegemony (Essex, 2022; Ehrenreich, 2010). Such women are symbols of dominant forms of masculinity. They have more power than men outside of dominant masculinity (Millet, 2016). We characterize this power as "male". Because masculinity is not a phenomenon related to the biological penis. Masculinity is about possessing certain qualities of power. All genders that possess these quali-

DOI: 10.4018/978-1-6684-7669-7.ch010

ties are masculine. In this sense, women entrepreneurs are masculinized and therefore transformed into "strong" and entrepreneurial beings desired by capitalist power.

Intelligence and entrepreneurship are two of the most important phenomena of modern times. The concept that makes a person in harmony with the environment and himself/herself is not intelligence but emotion. Emotional empathy is the real power of man (Zerzan, 2004). Civilization has glorified intelligence today more than ever before. Qualities such as entrepreneurship, strength, courage, speed and practicality have become important intelligence indicators. Power has always been associated with masculine qualities, and the person who has power, regardless of gender, is male, sick and harmful to the world (Solanas, 2019).

In this study, ideas will be generated through the presentation of the female entrepreneur. It will be shown how women's entrepreneurship is constructed in the news, one of the narrative genres of modernism. Turkey is one of the first countries where women's rights were recognized. In 1930, women were elected to municipalities and in 1934 they participated in parliamentary elections. Mustafa Kemal Atatürk, the founder of the Republic of Turkey, attached great importance to the equality of men and women, even though he could be criticized on some points. In order to establish a modernist Turkey, he controlled the party he founded. He made room for women in his party under his control, supported the equality of women and men in social environments, and granted women various rights. However, Islamist and right-wing conservative governments have changed this over time, especially after his death. Many gains have been lost by the AKP government in the last two decades. Unfortunately, due to the reproduction of the male-dominated social structure, especially with the AKP government, Turkey provides good examples of the masculine presentation of the female entrepreneur.

1. Power is Male

The social paradigm constitutes the criteria that determine the superiority of a group or a subject over others. In other words, the causes of differences may be biological, but the causes of networks of domination are ideology and power. Although power is imposed on subjects from the outside, this imposition lasts moment by moment from the birth of the subject until its death. Therefore, it creates the immanent conditions of being a subject. It establishes it in a structure with all indicators. It envelops the subject's tendencies and genetic qualities like a mold. It seeps into these tendencies and shapes them. Subjects poured into this mold identify with it at every moment.

Identity is formed through the constant repetition of practices (Butler, 2014; Benhabib, 2015). Every identity has to repeat and renew itself through various ritual repetitions. Otherwise, the identity disintegrates. Male sexual identity is not independent of these expressions. Just like other identities, it is doomed to certain rituals and repetitions to exist.

Identity draws on the grammar of everyday life. In other words, daily communication takes place because ordinary people have a shared cultural context that forms the basis for why they feel an affinity for a certain identity and for other members who share this identity. Identities are fluid and multiple. They are fluid in that, over time new interpretations of an identity may emerge (Banerjee,2003).

Identities are formed through the constant filling in of patterns of behavior. The value of female identity is ambiguous and fixed through its allegorization (Spivak, 1989). The initial sign of making a subject a man is a penis. The penis seen at birth is the initial sign of a series of attributions to the subject (Lacan, 2020). These many attribution groups are multifunctional tendency groups/grids such as dominance, influence, direction, and entrepreneurship, which circulate like an energy network between factors, transforming every point they touch and shaping themselves as they are touched.

Alexander refers to this as the transition. In his article, in which he explains how black masculine identity transitions towards white masculine identity through repetitive performative behaviors, he shows that identity is constantly reproduced through repetitive life practices such as speech patterns, hairstyles, clothes, etc. and that gender stereotypes are transitive and fluid with each other. Masculine power produces gender stereotypes through these transitions (Alexander, 2004).

From a Laclauian perspective, populist patterns exclude certain attitudes and behavioral patterns and construct identities both in the social sphere and through political apparatuses. Many apparatuses, from politics to the media, are effective, and hegemony is reproduced precisely in this way. Power imposes a populist set of behaviors and attitudes on subjects through specific patterns. In social life, the distinction between the emotional and the rational maintain exclusionary practices against those who step outside the mold of identities and challenge the status quo (Eklundh, 2020).

Nelson argues that the importance of geography is overlooked in constructing power through performative acts, that geographical culture is still essential in the masculinization of gender and the cultivation of individuals, and that Butler does not sufficiently address this issue in performative acts. She emphasizes that while power masculinizes all identities, the influence of geography on culture is essential and sets the boundaries in this regard (Nelson, 2010).

Butler (2014, p. 50) argues that gender is constructed through complex patterns of power and is not innate. For her, sexual identity is "more than biological determination, it is the construction of the subjects of society through performative acts". Gender and biological sex are the total acts of acting and doing and are constructed through the constant repetition of all these. In this sense, biological and social gender is produced from the same point, and both are fictions: There is no gender (Butler, 2014).

What is man if there is no gender? He is a totality of character ultimately burdened with the oppressive face of power. Nietzsche, who inverted many acts read as power, showed their true roots by embarking on the archaeology of emotions that seem ordinary and are thought to be easily understood. According to him, all life practices and all acts are the wills to power (Nietzsche, 2010). "Man" as an identity can be read as the pinnacle of the will to power. He is a machine destined to subjugate and reconstruct (O'Connell, 2018). It is because he cannot give birth. There is no production in his nature. Therefore, he is prone to neuroticization. It is always incomplete because it cannot give birth. It becomes conscious of a lack in itself; it exists with a lack (Firestone, 2019).

"Power", like all material entities in the universe, is abstract energy (Einstein, 2021; Hawkins, 2016)), but it takes shape at every point in the concrete. Just like this, in social spheres, power produces a similar form and takes shape everywhere in attitudes, behaviors and relations with the matter. Since it also produces consciousness, it is in every moment. It is in the perception of the moment. It infiltrates all identities and reproduces itself through power in every identity. According to Foucault, power does not originate from a different point outside the field where it is exercised but is directly inherent in the fields of its exercise. According to Foucault, power should be understood as a multiplicity of power relations. In other words, it is necessary to understand the movement that transforms, strengthens and reverses these relations through struggles and confrontations. It is essential to understand the bases that these power relations find in each other in such a way as to form a chain or a system, or on the contrary, differences and oppositions that isolate them from each other. To understand the strategies whose general line or institutional concretization develops in the state apparatus and social hegemony. But this is not because it has the privilege of clustering everything under the roof of its invincible unity. It is because it reproduces at every moment, point, or connection between one point and another. Power is everywhere. It is everywhere, not because it encompasses everything, but because it comes from everywhere. Moreover, with all its continuous, repetitive, inanimate, self-reproducing everything, power emerges from all these mobilities. It is a general conclusion that supports each of them and returns to stabilize them (Foucault, 2010, pp.71-72).

The agitating title that power is male is now slowly materializing into reality. The statements are written so far, Donovan's assertion that "every aspect of life shows that patriarchy is one of the most important components of power" supports the title "power is male". (Donovan, 1997). One of the most critical facts strengthening this argument is that the capitalist understanding of colonialism resembles the relationship forms of patriarchy. Many analyses of colonialism shed light on gender and feminism studies (Spivak, 2020; Butler, Spivak, 2010). Considering the question of identity and the practices of power and resistance, some relationships and similarities exist between colonialism and gender-related policies. Recognizing these similarities, anti-colonial theorists and opinion leaders have also considered the situation of those subalternates by dominant forms of masculinity when generating ideas against the apparatuses of power. According to Sancar (2011, p. 21), the critique of colonialism has shown that the development of the capitalist class societies of the West was simultaneous with the colonization of the East and that in this process, class differences, as well as racial and gender differences, were constructed together. Post-colonial theorists argue that colonialism and Orientalism construct representations of masculinity as well as representations of women.

The adoption of gender-related roles and values is inherent in the practices of power. As Wittig (2013, p. 83) emphasizes, all differences constructed concepts of sexual difference and opposition are differences created by the political, economic, and ideological order. These differences are created by a certain hegemony.

People's egos are constructed throughout their lives by interacting with other people and the material world (micro-channels of power). This self is not a given and fixed set of personality traits; it is constantly changing, with or without awareness. In modern societies, people spend hours in front of screens, reading newspapers, looking at magazines, and surfing the internet. These experiences obviously influence people's relationships and how they position themselves in society (Gauntlett, 2008).

As a result of the subject's identification of her/his self with a sexual identity under the domination of a certain gender paradigm, her/his self and behavior can also be categorized. In other words, as in Simon de Beauvoir's (2010) famous statement "one is not born a woman, one becomes a woman", being a man or a woman is a social construction that is learned during socialization processes. Evans and Williams (2013) argue that gender cannot simply be treated as a difference between subjects in society; they are different subjects constructed by the socio-cultural structure. Badiou and Zizek, on the other hand, speak of the representation of universal humanity by the very human, rich, white, heterosexual, male bourgeois figure who combines the dignity of humanity with the privileges of the elite (Badiou, Zizek, 2011, p.101).

Monique Wittig (2013) argues that sexual categorization is a construction from the ground up. According to Wittig, bodies that have been corrupted by a network of power are called "natural". However, the forms of men and women accepted today are not natural. To accept that there is a natural distinction between men and women is to naturalize the history of power and to accept the myth that men and women have always existed as if they were a historical construction. According to Wittig (2013), the category of gender is a political category that constructs society as heterosexual from the ground up.

Like Wittig, Butler believes that there is no biological sex. Based on Foucault's (2010) explanation of modern subjectivity based on sexuality and showing that this sexuality is constructed within a heteronormative framework, she argues that the division of human bodies into male and female is the fulfillment of the economic needs of heterosexuality (Butler, 2014).

The Power relations that enable masculine domination to have a multidimensional functioning that operates through economic arrangements, is embedded in emotional relations, and lives intertwined with language and meaning systems (Sancar, 2011, p. 21). It can be said that male-dominated culture, together with its relations and the objects it shapes, constitutes power over subjects. This power is engraved in consciousness through symbols. Human beings are born into the world of symbols and their maturation process passes through learning the meanings of symbols. Through symbols, through learning them, identity is acquired. Symbolic power is an almost magical form of power exercised directly on the bodies and without any physical force. But this magic can only work by drawing on predispositions that are buried deep within the body like springs of water. Symbolic power acts as a trigger that requires very little energy to cause the predispositions to gush forth like springs. It comes from the fact that a long process of consciousness and embodiment has already been carried out on people and they are subject to it (Bourdieu, 2015, p. 54).

Monique Wittig defines the domination of heterosexuality over the whole culture and the entities within it as living in heterosexuality. To live in society is to live in heterosexuality. When I question the term heterosexuality, I find myself in front of an object that does not exist, a fetish, a form of ideology that exists in the minds of people in a way that affects their entire lives, the way they behave, the way they act, the way they think. In other words, I am dealing with an object that is both real and imaginary at the same time (Wittig, 2013, p. 69).

Etymology contains many clues about gender. The word "erkek" in Turkish means "male". "Erk" means "power" in Turkish. This word, a combination of the words "Erk" and "ekmek", means one who sows power. Every being in the world who sows and spreads power, and therefore understands power as it is understood in today's relations, is a "man" regardless of genital organs.

2. THE POLITICAL ECONOMY OF THE SHARP GENDER SEGREGATION OF THE EARLY CAPITALIST PERIOD

The trend towards unisex was born out of the baby boom of the 1950s when stereotypes about gender were shattered. In the 1960s, the term 'unisex' was first used, initially by hairdressing salons to cater to boys and girls who wanted long, tousled hair equally. By the mid-1970s, gender non-differentiation was becoming a social phenomenon that permeated every aspect of American life. The 1970s was an era of freedom (Dai, Xia, Zhao, 2022). How did the concept of unisex become widespread in the 1970s? How and why did these gender stereotypes start to be overcome, especially in countries with an abundance of capital and accelerated by neo-liberal policies? To understand this, we need to look at the evolution of the capitalist economy.

When we speak of monopoly capitalism, it should not be assumed that it eliminates competition. There is no such thing. It means that this form of capitalism behaves in a completely different way, that it is no longer oriented towards price reductions through ever-increasing production, but rather applies the technique of sharing the market and determining market shares (Mandel, 1998:50). Thus, from the 19th century onwards, capitalism began to be exported to third-world countries that had not yet been capitalized, and these countries were capitalized through dictatorial practices from above. Over time, all countries were modernized by transforming them into investment areas for capital. The whole world has been interconnected by an economic network, and the tremors that occur in this network have reached a position that can affect the regions and even the whole structure in waves. Cultures tend to merge in the essence called "consumption" with the advertising waves of consumer culture. Adorno and Horkheimer warned about this in their work "Dialectics of Enlightenment":

"The materially considerable and socially paltry rise in the standard of living of the lower classes is reflected in the hypocritical propagation of intellect. Intellect's true concern is a negation of reification. It must perish when it is solidified into a cultural asset and handed out for consumption purposes. The flood of precise information and brand-new amusements make people smarter and more stupid at once (Adorno, Horkheimer, 2002, p.17)."

The economic crisis of 1929, structured by Fordism, exemplifies how a system of production that changes as technology permits can create an incalculable crisis. "The depression of the 1930s led to the transition of the industry from nineteenth-century production methods based on coal and steam to new technologies based on electricity, gas, and oil. At the Dagenham plant, which opened in 1931, Ford's company introduced mass production methods that would have a disruptive effect on much of the rest of the industry. These are known as "Fordism"." (Hall and Jacques, 1995:31) "Throughout the twentieth century, this revolutionary system of production would move from sector to sector, from processed food to furniture, from clothing to food, and even to shipbuilding after the Second World War." (Hall and Jacques, 1995:47)

In order for subjects are ergonomically utilized and integrated into capitalism, some mechanisms have to form an oligarchy. Many structures, from law to psychiatry to schooling, were established in previous centuries. The distinctive feature of the first half of the twentieth century is that the labor force was put to work with a much more intense technology of biopower. "The reason why the body is surrounded by relations of power and domination is largely due to the fact that it is a productive force. But in turn, the body can only be constituted as a labor force if it is placed in a relationship of subordination (where need is also a political tool that is carefully regulated, calculated, and used). The body can only become a useful force when it is both a productive body and a subordinated body. This subordination can only be achieved through either violence or ideology. It can be directly violent and physical, it can be forced against force, it can be directed against material elements. It can be non-violent: it can be calculated, organized, technically thought out, it can be subtle, and it can resort to neither arms nor terror, but still remain at the concrete level. This knowledge and domination constitute what can be called the political technology of the body." (Foucault, 2010:63)

Karl Marx's statement in his work "The German Ideology" that "it is not consciousness that determines life, but, on the contrary, the life that determines consciousness" (Marx, 1992:43) emphasizes that human beings are produced by life practices. Throughout the history of civilization, man has first been shaped by his environment and then attempted to shape his environment. The practices created by the twentieth-century economy produce today's human beings. "In the golden age of post-war world trade, which lasted from the 1950s to the early 70s, large Fordist factories produced standardized products for an ever-expanding circle of customers. In this way, capitalism went unchecked and there was a significant increase in the symbolic violence of individual life. In the post-war Northern world, one often finds 'standard' biographies. Male factory workers have been in the same workplace for thirty years or more. Their wives are usually housewives. Working wives are most likely to have part-time jobs. They have a 'normal' family with two children. A car, a telephone, a television, and two weeks of summer vacation are their greatest luxuries. Nowadays, 'standard' biographies have been replaced by 'optional' ones." (Ginsborg, 2010:103) Lifestyles are diversifying like the products of the postfordist mode of production, and Fordist factories are being replaced by offices and flexible production. Society itself is turning into a factory. While preferential lives replace standard lives, subjects have the means to repair themselves. Among these opportunities, magazine products stand out as the most consumed "self-production mechanism". The mechanism of self-production has spread to the whole of society. In this sense, it has transformed the whole society into a society of the spectacle, as Guy Debord puts it. "The spectacle is the moment when the commodity succeeds in completely occupying social life. It is not only the relationship with the commodity that is visible. Nothing other than the commodity can be seen: The world seen is now entirely the world of the commodity." (Debord, 2006)

How is it that this production affects ways of life in almost every part of the world, and how is it that power can turn the dominant gender regime into a global male order? The answers to this question can be said to reside in anthropology as well as in the current state of socio-political evolution. Therefore, it is important to explain this socio-political evolution within the limits of this study for the sake of clarity.

Foucault's emphasis on "biopower" rarely touches upon the relations between the so-called "state" apparatuses of capitalism that have spread worldwide and dominated all spheres of life. The most famous work that brings Foucault's thought to the field of international relations is Michael Hardt and Antonio Negri's "Empire". This work speaks of a new "network power" (Kelly, 2016).

In their work "Empire", Hardt and Negri (2003) argue that the age of imperialism has been overcome and the age of empire has entered. Imperialism is a structure based on territorial occupation. Empire, however, is a new socio-economic and socio-political structure that is not limited by territorial criteria and whose rule is endless. Hardt and Negri (2002, p. 21) explain empire as follows:

"The empire not only governs a territory and a population but also creates the world in which it lives. The empire does not simply regulate human relations, but directly seeks to dominate human nature. The object of the imperial rule is social life in its totality and therefore empire is the paradigmatic form of biopower."

At the point of socio-political evolution, which Hardt and Negri define as empire, this new system shapes the gender regime differently from region to region, just as products are produced according to the characteristics of geographical regions and cultures (glocalization). In each region, as far as possible, it transforms economic relations into an important supporter. Of course, this transformation and reproduction are passive and decentralized. Decentralization and the passive production of life can be said to be the most important characteristic of the empire. The empire has not yet transformed into a controlled society in all geographies. This transformation is closely related to capital accumulation. While at some points it continues in a mixed form with the technologies applied by the government in the past, in other words, in some geographies the characteristics of disciplinary society and control society continue in a combined form within complex relations; in some geographies where capitalist relations are developed and capital accumulation is high, the characteristics of control society come to the fore.

The decentralized system that is capable of the passive production of life, which Hardt and Negri call "Empire", is able to work out various strategies of exclusion and acceptance, based on economic profit, down to the finest details of life with the opportunities provided by technology and new disciplines. New disciplines such as statistics, demography, epidemiology, and biology make it possible to analyze life processes at the population level and to "manage" communities and individuals through practices of punishment, normalization, discipline, rehabilitation, and optimization (Lemke, p.20). Political economy as a strand of biopolitics encompasses dispositifs that extend all relations between forces. As in classical political economy and its critique, it encompasses the entire social structure, not just the relationship between capital and labor (Lazzarato, 2006, p.3).

Since masculine domination permeates all subjects living in society, especially in countries far from capital accumulation where old-type production technologies prevail, and the factory-farm environment constitutes the majority of production, it is not only men who show anger against others. Every subject within this domination has the potential to see women and homosexuality as a threat and to direct anger against the other towards the non-man. Masculine domination dominates not only men but also women. Hegemonic masculinity directly targets different forms of masculinity and men's lives. It initiates adolescents who aspire to be men into smoking, drugs and alcohol at a very early age. The perception of masculinity is the most critical factor among the reasons they become victims of violence because they aspire to violence and bullying (Yücel, 2013). The fact that "men have shorter lifespans than women" and that "men die at a much earlier age than women with increasing age" cannot be explained only by biology. Although men have larger hearts and lungs in proportion to their size and carry more oxygen in their blood, men's life statistics are much direr than women's. It is argued that this is because of how they perceive the world (Goldberg, 1994, p. 213). Hegemonic masculinity socializes men, just as it disciplines women, by establishing masculine domination that appears to be in their interests but is essentially masculine.

From a political economy perspective, the questions "Whose interests are protected by norms?" and "Which classes benefit from a gendered society?" are essential. The gender-based division is also embedded in the foundations of industrial organization and is intertwined with class contradictions. The early stages of capitalism are a system that operates for the benefit of the ruling class. However, at every point of its functioning, it establishes links with masculine relations of domination. Maximizing profit through mechanisms of exploitation is only possible through the production of consent and physical force exerted by a masculine power over the oppressed. Capitalism is, to some extent, constituted by the possibilities of power and profit created by gender relations (Connell, 2003, p. 161). Considering that production is tied to a gendered structure allows for more explicit recognition of differentiations within the workforce that are linked to sexual politics but operate within broad gender categories. Some of these differentiations are related to the marketing of sexuality itself, as in sex work or the entertainment industry. However, the issue is much broader. Examples include the creation of many professions, such as receptionist, airline stewardess and secretary, as a combination of specific technical skills loaded with particular femininity. Certain industries, especially clothing and theatre, are also linked to homosexuality (Connell, 2003, p. 159).

Pre-capitalist societies are based on gender. Over time, however, the political economy changes brought about by the evolution of relations of production and technology, combined with the strength of the impact of women's struggles. The harsh distinctions between men and women seen in pre-capitalist times began to soften. The emergence of a consumer society and the concentration of capital in a certain geographical area desexualizes that area. Sexual identities come closer to each other and the sharp lines between them fade. According to Illich (1996, p. 212), subsistence in modern times is a neutral term for this gendered existence. The societies in which gender domination is relatively broken are capitalist societies; their genderless subjects are individual producers.

An industrial society cannot exist without imposing certain unisex assumptions: That both sexes are created for the same work, perceive the same reality and have the same needs, except for some minor cosmetics. The subject on which economic theory is based is the 'sexless' man (Illich, 1996, p. 21).

Under capitalism, sexuality has become a productive force controlled and limited by the utility-driven domain of the parents' bedroom. There are various relationships between gender norms and hegemonic masculinity, which are intrinsically linked to this phenomenon, and the socio-economic conditions prevailing in a community. If there is any form of "power" (economic, political, scientific, religious, or military) in any society, "patriarchy" also persists (Özbudun, Demirer, 2000, p. 8). The patriarchal state can be seen not as the manifestation of a patriarchal essence but as the center of a resonant set of power relations and political processes in which patriarchal structure is both established and contested (Connell, 2003, p. 196).

Pre-capitalist societies are based on gender. Over time, however, the political economy changes brought about by the evolution of relations of production and technology, combined with the strength of the impact of women's struggles. The sharp distinctions between men and women seen in pre-capitalist times began to soften. The emergence of a consumer society and the concentration of capital in a specific geography desexualizes that region. Sexual identities come closer to each other, and the sharp lines between them fade. According to Illich (1996, p. 212), subsistence in modern times is a neutral term for this gendered existence. The societies where gender domination is relatively broken are advanced capitalist societies; their genderless subjects are individual producers.

Societies where trade has reached enormous dimensions, and consumer society has become widespread have diversified in terms of the liberation of sexual identities and especially their unification in the freedom of consumption. The flow of profits from economic niches to the center has become widespread, and diversity has been transformed into profit. Postmodern consumer society cannot exist without imposing certain unisex assumptions: Both sexes are made for the same work, perceive the same reality and have the exact needs, except for some minor cosmetics. The subject on which economic theory is based is the 'sexless' man (Illich, 1996, p. 21). Under capitalism, sexuality has become a productive force controlled and limited by the utility-driven domain of the parents' bedroom. There are various relationships between gender norms and hegemonic masculinity, which are intrinsically linked to this phenomenon, and the socio-economic conditions prevailing in a community. If there is any form of "power" (economic, political, scientific, religious, or military) in any society, "patriarchy" also persists (Özbudun, Demirer, 2000, p. 8). The patriarchal state can be seen not as the manifestation of a patriarchal essence but as the center of a rich set of power relations and political processes in which patriarchal structure is established and contested (Connell, 2003, p. 196).

3. QUEER APPROACHES TO "WOMEN ENTREPRENEURS"

Before the 1980s, when neoliberal policies accelerated, binary oppositions pervaded almost every aspect of life. It is a way of thinking and domination over multiplicity. Sharp distinctions such as good-bad, beautiful-ugly, solid-deficient, mobile-immobile, and male-female also provide a form of regulation. Constantly reading and interpreting the curtain called life through these binary opposites produces a specific historical process of the human mind. Since multiplicities are infinite, limitless and uncertain, opposites establish intelligent control and regulation. People are forced to enter this control due to socialization; the dialectical way of thinking formed by opposites has been questioned philosophically and scientifically for some time (Hardt, Negri, 2005).

Dialectical thoughtfulness, which bases the various multiplicities of the community on us-them duality and identities, cannot be seen because it organizes consciousness in socialization. Communities are composed of particular multiplicities. When multiplicities are identified through "us", they absorb the qualities of particular entities. The ideologically constructed concept of "us" is fiction. People belong authentically to spontaneous communities, but the constructed concept of "us" produces an alienating identity.

Julia Kristeva sensed the falsity of those, as mentioned earlier, "we" and saw that this alienation ignores diversity in the service of male domination. According to Kristeva (2012), there is no "woman"; there are "women". The female identity covers this diversity and closes the non-identical diversity of women.

Dividing the entrepreneur into males and females legitimizes and reinforces assigned genders. It assimilates LGBT+ entrepreneurs of other sexual identities into these assigned genders. Female entrepreneur, male entrepreneur, gay entrepreneur, transexual entrepreneur, lesbian entrepreneur... These identities can be extended indefinitely because gender diversity is limitless, and every category is social.

The fact that the process of occupational socialization extends over a long period makes the effects of the occupation much stronger in shaping the paradigmatic characteristics of the individual. In fact, beyond shaping its members' moral, social and psychological characteristics according to its characteristics and demands, the profession instils a particular worldview and mentality. It imposes certain character traits and outlooks on the world (Kwantes and Boglarsky, 2004: 337; Mucchielli, 1991: 53). When we examine the dichotomies utilized in the construction of the entrepreneurial woman, we notice that most identities emphasize the dichotomy of "what is and what is not". While the identity gathers the positive in its existence, it hides or ignores (deletes) the negative. Every identity is built on positive and negative binaries. While acting on "positive us" and "negative them", it blesses and glorifies the "us" that it equips with positives (Van Dijk, 1998). These dichotomies, which are mobilized through strong-weak, aggressive-lazy, sociable-social, innovative-fixed, intelligent-dumb, and successful-failure, reinforce the positive-negative judgments imposed by the system.

Parts of the common ground are also the general norms and values shared by members of a culture. Groups select some of these cultural values and organize them into their own ideology. Ideologies and their structures are also the cognitive core of a group's identity. They can be seen as a social self-schema of its members. Ideologies and the social representations organized by them control the social behavior (practices) of actors as group members (van Dijk, 2003). It can be argued that stereotypical adjectives and expressions are somehow produced through representations, influencing attitudes and behaviors. "People's actions and discourses are interrelated. In order to control actions, discourse must be kept under control" (van Dijk, 2010, p. 13). Discourses and representations are effective in the transmission and establishment of ideology. "When the relationship between ideology and discourse is analyzed, it is seen that ideologies are constructed, shared and hegemony is maintained through language" (Matheson, 2005, p. 6). According to Van Dijk, critically important discourses and representations have the potential to reproduce inequalities related to ethnicity, class, culture, race, and gender (Van Dijk, 1993, p. 250).

With which discourses is the woman entrepreneur covered up? Within which power centers is she structured while being represented? Where, with whom, through which adjectives and emphases does the news construct the female entrepreneur? What are the positive expressions it chooses among contrasts and what do they represent? Answering these questions and showing the background deciphers the dimensions and aims of ideological construction. The social representations that meet on common ground reveal the structure of this construction.

FINDINGS AND COMMENTS

In this study, the news published on social media by Yeni Şafak, Sabah, Hürriyet, Mynet, Milliyet, Posta, NTV, HaberTürk, CNNTürk, Dünya, Cumhuriyet, TRT were analyzed. News published between January 1, 2021, and 27.09.2022, covering a period of 21 months, were selected by random sampling method. This news was analyzed by content analysis research method and the data and findings were interpreted. Published news and photographs were analyzed qualitatively.

Despite this common goal, one of the many differences between quantitative and qualitative research is the data analysis process. The aim of data collection with the quantitative method is to express the problem of the research with numerical data. In other words, the answers given about the problem are realized by expressing the data numerically (Gönç-Şavran, 2018, p. 183).

The content analysis research technique used in this study was both quantitative and qualitative (mixed research method). In the first part of the findings and interpretation section, the data compiled from the news texts were expressed quantitatively; a description of a single variable was made, that is, the frequency distribution was analyzed. It is shown which professions and social representations of women entrepreneurs are more intensively covered in the news.

Whether the quantitative or qualitative method is preferred in the design of the research, the main purpose of the researcher in collecting data is to answer the research question. The main question of this study is how women entrepreneurs are represented within the framework of masculine messages. The categories looked at for these representations were formed as follows:

What is the intensity of the word "power" emphasized in the news reports? On which other words is the other intensity placed?

Table 1. The facts emphasized in the news

The fact emphasized in the news	Frequency	%
Power	102	51,5
Speed	35	18
Innovation	28	14
Pride of Womanhood	25	12,5
Competition	6	3
Raising Awareness/Consciousnes	2	1

According to Marx, "relations of power and control" based on the ownership of the means of production are reproduced throughout society. Those who hold economic power also rule that society. The basic positions and relations in society are class-based (Cuff, Sharrock, and Francis, 2013). In the theoretical part of the study, the relationship between power and masculinity was mentioned. Subjects are often inclined to read the equivalent of actions such as changing, influencing, directing, sustaining, or destroying as the phenomenon of "power". These actions, which have long functioned as male-producing practices, have also been producing female identity for some time. Butler (2014) emphasizes that performative acts, not biological determination, produce gender. As seen in Table 1, the representation of entrepreneurial women in the news is mostly based on the emphasis on "power". Representations are important because they can shape the way people perceive the world (Hall, 2017). The oppressive face of power is placed at the very center of the presentation of women's identity. Considering Donovan's (1997) emphasis that power is identified with patriarchy and that they produce each other, it can be understood that the same qualities are attributed to the female identity with this emphasis on representation. The representation of female identity is also based on patriarchy. The power networks that have been corrupting the man and turning him into a harmful machine for centuries have been targeting the female identity for some time. This situation is also reflected in news representations. In 102 of the 198 news items analyzed, the main emphasis was on power (f:102).

One of the most important phenomena of capitalism, as seen in scientific literature (dromology), is speed. In today's working process, time is controlled rather than "earned". Time is rendered non-subjective because of its programmability. Time is difficult to control. Achieving this requires the cooperation of the exploited subject. The best way is to make the subject control itself. Control should turn into self-control (L'Heuillet, 2020, pp.22-23). According to Virilio (2006), it is considered to be a predominant logic in the organization of urban spaces. In other words, modern society is not only based on economic transformations. Modern societies are constructed through a new logic of speed that includes political, military, spatial, and technological changes. According to Virilio, the modern age has brought about a model of society based on movement through the proliferation of speed-generating tools. As seen in Table 1, this phenomenon comes to the fore in 18% of the news items analyzed on women entrepreneurs. Regardless of gender, identity and race, all subjects are being kneaded in speed.In the analyzed news reports, the concept of "innovation" is covered immediately after the phenomenon of power and speed. Innovation can also be traced in the writings of early philosophers explaining what capitalism is. In Capital, Karl Marx repeats at many points that capitalism cannot exist without constantly reproducing the means of production and relations of production. It is also common to come across the phenomenon of "innovation" in news reports on economic concepts such as entrepreneurship and production. The "innovation" referred to here is the capitalist finding new ways to increase his capital. However, at many points in the news, the phenomenon of "innovation" is propagandized. There is not a new initiative. The phenomenon is covered in the news because of its positive effect on people. The frequency of Innovation in the analyzed news items is 14%.

What is the proportion of specific women entrepreneurs presented in the news? What is the rate of news items that are addressed holistically?

Table 2. Presentation of women entrepreneurs

General/Particular	Frequency (n)	%
General	146	74
Particular	52	26
Total	198	100

In the table 2, 198 news items are separated in terms of their coverage of women entrepreneurs and women with universal and particular representations. Generalizing "general" news items are those that do not cover a single or a group of women but address all women in general. The majority of the 146 news items coded as "general" (63%) were related to ministries, the presidency, or the spokespersons of the party in the government. Most of the news actors are people associated with state institutions (33%). The social representations that the general news items meet are nationalism (54%) and nationalism (48%). News constructed in this way transforms the news into a state apparatus that acts directly as propaganda.

Particular news, on the other hand, is produced as "special" news that affects and defines only the events or subjects within its borders. They describe the entrepreneurship of a group of women or a single woman. General news is news that generalizes the entrepreneurship that is the subject of the news by referring to all women without an event affecting a single actor or a group of actors (f:146). On the other hand, news about women entrepreneurs is not widespread by referring to a single person or group (f:52).

Which occupational groups are focused on more in the news? Through which professions are women entrepreneurs represented?

Table 3. News topic

News Topic	Frequency (n)	%
Kitchen	68	34.5
Support	43	22
Care&Health	19	9.5
Cleanliness	17	8.5
Marketing	11	5.5
Project Competition	13	6.5
Industry	13	6.5
Farmer	11	5.5
Congress	2	1
Art	1	0.5
Total	198	100

As seen Table 3. among the 198 news on women entrepreneurs analyzed, 58 news items were about support, project competition, and congress news. The remaining 140 news items cover the subject of the initiative and the related profession. Among the professions that are the subject of the initiative, the most frequently covered profession is cooking and kitchen-related issues (f:68). The prominence of professions related to the kitchen is a representation of women's confinement to the home in these news items. The basic tasks of housewifery, which has historically been the most intensive work done by women, come to the fore. Cooking, which is one of the basic tasks of housewifery, also appears in the news on women entrepreneurs. In a sense, a representation that closes women to the kitchen again is in effect. Women's identity is not processed through other professions in society. After the kitchen, the most intensively covered occupation is the care and health work (f:19). The third occupation, following these, is cleaning (f:17). The kitchen-care-cleaning triangle is reproduced even when it comes to entrepreneurship. When it comes to women's entrepreneurship, only 6.5% of the news items analyzed were related to the industry. The news on entrepreneurship related to art is only 1 out of 198 news items.

In which social representations are the news stories concentrated?

Table 4. Social representations in the news

Social Representation	Frequency (n)	%
Nationalism	93	47
Family	41	21
Gender Equality	30	15
Social Sharing	23	11,5
Integration with the World	6	3
Ecology	5	2,5
Total	198	100

Mainstream newspapers in Turkey construct news pumping nationalism in almost every news genre. Especially after the 2016 coup attempt, Recep Tayyip Erdoğan's government has produced such a nationalist attitude in all newspapers under its pressure. This effect of the right-wing conservative government is also evident when news on women entrepreneurs is analyzed. As seen Table 4. in the 198-women entrepreneur news analyzed, the most common social representation is nationalism with a rate of 47%. Immediately after nationalism, the family, which is the main area in which they want to confine women, is seen (21%). Although equality between men and women is emphasized in 15% of the news items, these are modern ideals disconnected from real practices. The government, unable to change the modern way of life that started in the last period of the Ottoman Empire and was laid on a solid foundation by Mustafa Kemal Atatürk and the republic he founded, uses these ideals in its discourse. But actual practice is different from these ideals. Erdoğan's government is a government that is destroying the equality between men and women, transforming the foundations of the republic, and slowly making changes to this end. This is the reason why in many news reports women are accompanied by older brothers, fathers, and husbands, and why women are presented with their children and in family contact. The right-wing conservative government has a problem with the independent representation of women. Since they control newspapers directly through corporate ownership, they also influence the news. The lowest rates of social representation phenomena are integration with the world (3%) and ecology (2.5%). It is precisely here that the hegemony of the Erdoğan government is once again in opposition to contemporary phenomena.

Table 5. Market type

Domestic market/foreign market	Frequency (n)	%
Foreign market	11	5,5
Domestic market	187	94,5
Total	198	100

The proportion of news items that relate to the domestic market is 94.5%. The percentage of news items reporting an initiative related to international trade is 5.5%.

Which institutions and organizations are mentioned in the news reports?

Table 6. Institutions mentioned in the news

Institutions Mentioned in the News	Frequency (n)	%
No Institution	23	11,5
Presidency	39	19,5
Ministry of Family	34	17
Bank	16	8
United Nations	2	1
Company	8	4
Ministry of Finance	19	11
Union of Chambers and Commodity Exchanges	9	4
EU	4	2
AKP	5	2,5
Municipality	5	2,5
State Support	34	17
Total	198	100

When the institutions mentioned in the news items are analyzed in Table 6, no institution is mentioned in 11.5% of the news items. The institution mentioned with the lowest rate is the United Nations (1%). The fact that it is followed by the European Union (2%) confirms the emphasis on the domestic market in the previous table. These are indicators of an economy that cannot integrate with the world as a result of wrong policies and the closure of women's enterprises to the domestic market.

The presidency is the most frequently mentioned institution in the news with 19.5%. The fact that the Republic of Turkey, which is a postmodern dictatorship with a veil of democracy and a law that remains on paper at many points, is today a postmodern dictatorship is also seen in the news on women's entrepreneurship. The news on women's entrepreneurship is aimed at government propaganda, sometimes featuring Emine Erdoğan, sometimes featuring presidential spokespersons, and sometimes featuring Recep Tayyip Erdoğan directly. The total percentage of news items (53.5%) featuring various state institutions (17%), the Ministry of Family (17%), the Ministry of Finance (17%), and Erdoğan's party, the AK Party (2.5%), is higher than the percentage of other institutions. The data shows that mainstream newspapers, which are the voice of the government in Turkey, have turned the news on women's entrepreneurship into government propaganda.

Based on which individuals and system phenomena are entrepreneurial women represented in the news?

Table 7. The person who supports the woman

The person who supported the woman	Frequency (n)	%
No Person in the News	53	26,5
Her children	17	9
President's Daughter	10	5
Her husband	34	17,5
Her father	11	5,5
Company	6	3
Her brother	10	5
President	22	11
Male partner	12	6
Family	23	11,5
Total	198	100

In the analyzed news articles, it is seen Table 7 that women entrepreneurs are not alone in the photographs and the news text but are represented together with other people. The number of news items in which the female entrepreneur is alone is 53 (26.5%). In 145 out of 198 news items, the woman or women are not alone (73.5%). Together with these women entrepreneurs who are not alone, the husband of the woman entrepreneur is the most represented (17.5%). Sometimes standing behind her in photographs, sometimes holding her hand, husbands are reported as supporting the women entrepreneur. Following the husbands, the phenomenon of "family" stands out in terms of support (11.5%). Interestingly, as shown in many other categories, the president is the third most prominent figure represented in the news as a supporter of women entrepreneurs. The control of the state, family, and husband triad over the female entrepreneur is evident in the analysis of the news items analyzed. The child, which is the most fundamental element that connects the woman to the family and enables her to identify with the family, is seen in 9% of the news items (f:17). The father (5.5%) and sometimes the elder brother (5%) come to the forefront with their support for the female entrepreneur.

Who is in the news photo?

Table 8. The person who is in the news

Who is in the news photo?	Frequency (n)	%
Women entrepreneurs	38	19
Government or company representative	17	8,5
Daughter of the President of the Republic	10	5
Her husband	34	18
Her father	11	5,5
Company representation	6	3
Her brother	10	5
President	22	11
Her children	15	7,5
Male partner	12	6
Her family	23	11,5
Total	198	100

As seen Table 8. in 38 of the news items analyzed, the female entrepreneur or entrepreneurs who are the actors of the news item and introduced are seen alone (19%). Representatives of the state or the company and news items photographed directly with the company emblem etc. make up 8.5% of the news items. The second most common people to appear with women entrepreneurs in photographs are the entrepreneur's husband (18%), the entrepreneur's family (11.5%), and the president (11%). The tripartite alliance seen in the previous tables remains intact in this table. The alliance of husband, family, and state is also seen in the representations in the photographs. These are followed by the state or company representative with 8.5% and the children of the entrepreneur with 7.5%. The male partner of the entrepreneur (6%), the entrepreneur's father (5.5%), and the entrepreneur's brother (5%) are also seen in the photographs.

What is the gender of a journalist?

Table 9. Distribution of the journalist on the basis of gender

The Gender of Journalist	Frekans (n)	%
Unknown	15	7.5
Agency	126	63.5
Female	7	3.5
Male	50	25.5
Total	198	100

This category, which was created based on the question "Do men write the news about women entrepreneurs?", was aimed to show from which gender perspective the news was created. Table 9 shows that the author of 15 of the 198 news items analyzed was not listed on the news website (7.5%). This is one of the indicators of the lawlessness and lack of seriousness of the Turkish media. It is not known which gender people wrote 126 of the news items. This is because these 126 news items are agency news and have the emblem or letters of the reporting agency at the bottom of the news item. Apart from all these news items, 57 news items were published with the name of the author (29%). However, only 7 of these news items published with the name of the author are written by women. The number of male journalists producing news on women entrepreneurs is 50 (25.5%).

These numbers show that the vast majority of the analyzed news items were produced with a male consciousness. It was emphasized that only 3.5% of the news items analyzed were produced by female journalists.

CONCLUSION

Newspaper news texts are often perceived as transparent and impartial structures that directly convey the truth by general followers who do not have expertise in media readership. When the fact that the language used by the news establishes its own reality in a legitimizing way is examined a little more closely and with scientific methods, it can be understood that it is actually a propaganda tool in many cases. Newspapers present news in line with patterns that legitimize the prevailing ideas of society. This is especially evident in countries like Turkey, where state propaganda insidiously prevails at every point. News texts play a role in the construction of various facets of social power. These texts have the function of regulating, legitimizing, and reproducing phenomena that constitute the main pillars of the system such as gender, power, hegemony, interest, social order, and official ideology.

Gender stereotypes structured by heteronormative values are one of the building blocks of the current form of patriarchal ideology, and this structure is further reinforced through representations in the media. Since media organizations also tend to reflect the general values of society, they reproduce patriarchal culture by using norms and codes that reproduce patriarchy in almost every type of program from news to television series, from mainstream movies to advertisements. Masculinity is an ideology that needs to be constantly reproduced to protect the advantages brought to it by the gender regime, to protect the comfort zones created by these advantages, and to draw its boundaries clearly. The phenomenon that Connell conceptualizes as "hegemonic masculinity" and "global gender regime", which is a power relationship independent of physiology and all sexual identities, and which Bourdieu calls "masculine domination", is produced both as a result of performative acts, as Butler emphasizes, and through discourses and language, as Foucault states. The media is one of the ideological institutions that reproduce the ideas and ideologies necessary for the continuity of the social organization based on gender difference that exists today. Heterosexual myths based on naturalization, de-historicization, and biologization preserve the constancy of assigned genders, and as a result of the strengthening of these constancies by combining them with norms based on race, class, and gender discrimination, they perceive those who are not themselves as threats and "other" those who are not themselves or who are positioned outside of "us".

Mass media have important ideological functions in the construction of modern nation-states, in the survival of these states, and in the maintenance of the hegemony of political power. It can be said that the means of communication have important effects in terms of bringing subjects together with various identities, intensifying some identities and the values that constitute these identities, and excluding others. To live in modern society is to live in a heteronormative culture. When the term heteronormativity is questioned, we are talking about a social fetish, a form of ideology that exists in the minds of people in a way that affects their entire lives, behaviors, ways of acting, and ways of thinking. It can be argued that this form of ideology infiltrates all messages as the products of the means of communication spread to society in supply-demand relations and become the dominant culture. It is seen that the power of communication tools is undeniable in the transformation of ideology, which Michel Foucault defines as "discursive formations", into the dominant culture.

Since institutions such as the family, the military, and the school convey values loaded with gender norms to subjects, many of those who produce the meanings/discourses in communication tools or news media and the followers of these messages produce social formations. These values, which are already established in their consciousness, are reproduced in tabloidized news. Without having the opportunity to question the issues in tabloidized news, they maintain their attitudes and thoughts on the subject as a part of daily life. The newspaper news they access maintains their existing patterns without making them think from a different angle.

This was also observed when the news on women entrepreneurs was analyzed. Most of the news items reinforce the triangle of state, husband, and family. It was observed that most of the writers of women entrepreneur news are men. In most of the news reports, it is not women entrepreneurs who are seen, but women who are defined in terms of gender equality or within the family and who need support.

The study focuses on Turkish society, but many countries have been shaped by a heteronormative social perception from the past to the present, and as a result, it is seen that women's actions are tried to be approximated to a masculine form. Especially when it comes to women entrepreneurs, the definitions of entrepreneurship are assimilated into power patterns such as power, competition, courage, and speed. The political system, which reproduces values that play an active role in the formation of social codes, makes heteronormative values dominant in the social atmosphere through institutions that reinforce gender roles in line with its dominant interests. The news produced in this atmosphere has also been influenced by masculine attitudes and qualities related to women's entrepreneurship, albeit at different levels. The professions of women entrepreneurs presented in the news are grouped under kitchen, care, cleaning, textile, and health. This is the woman who "feeds", "takes care of", "cleans", "dresses" and "takes care of the sick" in which women are positioned within patriarchal norms. In a new formation, the woman is one step different from the woman in the family and in the home who is presented as an entrepreneur. However, the main common ground in the news is mostly nationalism. While issues such as ecology, integration with the world, and collectivity are very much in the background, nationalism emerges as the main common ground and social representation. The president, the first lady, and the president's family members appear in many news items, and various representatives and ministries of the state are consistently seen in women entrepreneur news.

It can be said that the recent news on women entrepreneurs in Turkey is official ideology-oriented, nationalism-pumping, and male-oriented and attempts to preserve traditional female qualities even when it is about women entrepreneurs

REFERENCES

Adorno, T. W., & Horkheimer, M. (2002). *Dialectic of enlightenment* (E. Jephcott, Trans.). Stanford University Press.

Alexander, B. K. (2004). Passing, Cultural Performance, and Individual Agency: Performative Reflections on Black Masculine Identity. Sage Publications.

Badiou, A., & Zizek, S. (2011). *Bir idea olarak komünizm (Çev: Ahmet Ergenç ve Ebru Kılıç.).* Ayrıntı Yayınları.

Banerjee, S. (2003, March–April). Gender and nationalism: The masculinization of hinduism and female political participation in india. *Women's Studies International Forum, 26*(2), 167–179. doi:10.1016/S0277-5395(03)00019-0

Beauvoir, S. D. (2019). *İkinci cinsiyet, (Çev:Gülnur Acar Savran).* Koç Üniversitesi Yayınları.

Bourdieu, P. (2015). *Devlet üzerine. (Çev: A. Sümer).* İletişim Yayınları.

Butler, J. (2014). *Cinsiyet belası- feminizm ve kültürün altüst edilmesi. (Çev: B. Ertür).* Metis Yayınları.

Catherine, T. (2007). Kwantes, Cheryl A. Boglarsky (2004). Perceptions of organizational culture, leadership effectiveness and personal effectiveness across six countries [Elsevier.]. *Journal of International Management, 13*(2), 204–230. doi:10.1016/j.intman.2007.03.002

Connell, R. W. (2003). In M. Hussey (Ed.), *Schools and gender* (pp. 92–100). PrenticeHall.

Cuff, E. C., & Sharrock, W. W. ve Francis, D. W. (2013). Sosyolojide perspektifler. (Ü. Tatlıcan, Çev.). İstanbul: Say Yayınları.

Dai, H., Xia, T., & Zhao, S. (2022). Unisex Style: The History, Current Situation and Future. *Proceedings of the 2022 8th International Conference on Humanities and Social Science Research* (ICHSSR 2022). Atlantis Press SARL 10.2991/assehr.k.220504.205

Debord, G. (2006). *Gösteri Toplumu, Çev: Ayşen Ekmekçi, Okşan Taşkent.* Ayrıntı Yayınları.

Donovan, J. (1997). *Feminist teori. (Çev: A. Bora, M. Ağduk-Gevrek ve F. Sayılan).* İletişim Yayınları.

Ehrenreich, B. (2010). *Witches, Midwives, and Nurses: A History of Women Healers.* Feminist Press at CUNY.

Einstein, A. (2021). *İzafiyet Teorisi, (Çev: Gülen Aktaş).* Say Yayınları.

Eklundh, E. (2020). The Cultural Side of Populism and Rethinking Money, Rebuilding Community. *Excluding Emotions: The Performative Function of Populism, Partecipazione, and Conflitto, 13*(1).

Essex, K. (2022). *Kleopatra: Book 1: The Early Years.* Routledge.

Firestone, S. (2019). *Cinselliğin Diyalektiği, (Çev: Yurdanur Salman).* Payel Yayınları.

Foucault, M. (2000). *Kelimeler ve Şeyler (Mehmet Ali Kılıçbay).* Ayrıntı Yayınları.

Foucault, M. (2010). *Cinselliğin tarihi (Çev: H. U. Tanrıöver).* Ayrıntı Yayınları.

Gauntlett, D. (2008). *Media, genderandidentity: An introduction.* Routledge. doi:10.4324/9780203930014

Ginsborg, P. (2010). *Gündelik Hayat Politikaları, (Çev: Muhsin Önal Mengüşoğlu).* Açılım Kitap.

Goldberg, S. (1994). *The Inevitability of Patriarchy.* William Morrow and Company.

Hall, S. (2017). *Temsil, Anlam ve Dil. S. Hall içinde, Temsil: Kültürel Temsiller ve Anlamlandırma Uygulamaları. Dündar, İ. (Çev.).* Pinhan.

Hall, S., & Jacques, M. (1995). *Yeni Zamanlar*. Ayrıntı Yayınları.

Hardt, M., & Negri, A. (2002). *İmparatorluk. (Çev: A.Yılmaz)*. Ayrıntı Yayınları.

Hardt, M., & Negri, A. (2005). *Multitude: War and Democracy in the Age of Empire*. Penguin Books.

Helene, L'Heuillet, (2020). *Gecikmeye Övgü, Zaman Nereye Gitti?, (Çev:Şehsuvar Aktaş)*, İstanbul, YKY.

Illich, I. (1996). *Gender(Çev: A. fethi)*. Ayraç Yayınları.

Kelly, M. G. (2016). *Uluslararası biyopolitika: foucault, küreselleşme ve emperyalizm (Çev. U. Özmakas)*. Pharmakon Kitap.

Kristeva, J. (2012). *Kadın Dehası, (Çev: Zeynep Mertoğlu Onur)*. Pinhan Yayıncılık.

Lacan, J. (2020). *Fallusun Anlamı, (Çev: Saffet Murat Tura)*. Altıkırkbeş Yayınları.

Lazzarato, M. (2006).. . *Frombiopowertobiopolitics, TailoringBiotochnologies*, *2*(2), 11–20.

Lemke, T. (2016). *Biyopolitika. (Çev: U. Özmakas)*. İletişim Yayınları.

Mandel, E. (1998). *Marksist Ekonomi Kuramına Giriş, (Çev: Ali Ünlü)*. Toplumsal Dönüşüm Yayınları.

Marx, K. (1999). *Alman İdeolojisi, (Çev: sevim Belli)*. Sol Yayınları.

Millet, K. (2016). *Cinsel Politika, (Çev: Seçkin Selvi)*. Payel Yayınları.

Nelson, L. (2010). Bodies (and Spaces) do Matter: The limits of performativity, Gender, Place & Culture, *A Journal of Feminist Geography*, *6*(4).

Nietzsche, F. (2010). *Güç İstenci, (Çev: Nilüfer Epçeli)*. Say Yayınları.

O'Connell, M. (2018). *Makine Olmak, (Çev: Öznur Karakaş)*. Domingo Yayınları.

Özbudun, S., & Demirer, T. ve Demirer, Y. (2000). Kadın yazıları. Ankara: Ütopya Yayınevi.

Sancar, S. (2011). *Erkeklik: imkansız iktidar*. Metis Yayınları.

Solanas, V. (2019). *Erkek Doğrama Cemiyeti Manifestosu, (Çev: Ayşe Düzkan)*. Sel Yayıncılık.

Spivak, G. C. (1989). "Feminism and Deconstruction Again: Nogotiationg with Unacknowledged Masculinism. In C. Macdonald & T. Brennan (ed.) Between Feminism and Psychoanalysis. University of Nebraska Press.

Spivak, G.C. (2010). *Ulus-devlet Marşını Kim Söyler?, (Çev: Osman Akınhay)*. İstanbul, Agora kitaplığı.

Spivak, G. C. (2020). *Madun Konuşabilir mi? (Çev: Emre Koyuncu)*. Dipnot Yayınları.

Van Dijk, A. T. (2010). Söylem ve iktidar. A. Çavdar ve A. B. Yıldırım (Ed.), Nefret suçları ve nefret söylemi içinde (s. 9-44). İstanbul: Hrant Dink Vakfı Yayınları.

Van Dijk, T. (1998). *Ideology: a multidisciplinaryapproach. Londra*. Sage Publications.

Van Dijk, T. A. (2003). *Söylemin yapıları ve iktidarın yapıları. Mehmet Küçük (Der.), Medya iktidar ideoloji içinde*. Bilim ve Sanat Yayınları.

Virilio, P. (2006). Speed and Politics. Los Angeles: Semiotext(E)

Wittig, M. (2013). *Straight düşünce. (Çev: L. S. Darıcıoğlu ve P. Büyükbaş).* Sel Yayıncılık.

Zerzan, J. (2020). *Gelecekteki İlkel, (Çev: Cemal Atila).* Kaos Yayınları.

Chapter 11
Indian Women's Entrepreneurship:
A Study of Issues, Opportunities, and Development

Geeta Sachdeva
National Institute of Technology, Kurukshetra, India

ABSTRACT

In India, women-owned businesses are becoming more significant because of economic liberalization and globalization. The policy and institutional framework for fostering entrepreneurship, offering career education, and giving training has expanded the possibilities for women's economic empowerment. The demographics of business and the nation's economic growth have been altered because of the rising number of women entrepreneurs. In order to offer skill training, vocational education, and entrepreneurial development to the emerging labor force, the government of India has created various schemes for assisting women entrepreneurs. However, government is not only responsible for entrepreneurial development and skill training, but other stakeholders must also assume responsibility. Henceforth, the focus of the current chapter is on the difficulties that women company owners confront, how to resolve them, and an analysis of the government of India's business-related policies designed to support female entrepreneurs.

INTRODUCTION

The word "entrepreneur" comes from the French word "entreprender," that refers to someone who takes on the responsibility of organizing numerous resources & managing them to produce preferred outcomes & reap rewards. Our culture has always been dominated by men, and historically, women have not been recognized as equivalent companions and have been restricted to the four walls of the home. However, women have played a noteworthy part in the improvement of society and the country. Working women, particularly female entrepreneurs, contribute to the creativity, employment creation, and economic prosperity of a nation (Zeb & Ihsan, 2020). From last few years the ratio of women at

DOI: 10.4018/978-1-6684-7669-7.ch011

workplace is increasing especially female entrepreneurs worldwide (Staniewski & Awruk, 2019; Welsh et al., 2018). In India as well as the rest of the globe, half of the populace is made up of the women. In earlier times, they were restricted to the four walls of their homes where they used to carry out domestic duties in traditional society and were not allowed to go outside their homes to work. However, they have emerged from the four walls of their homes to assume significant positions in the national government and service industries in contemporary civilizations. The overwhelming body of evidence aids the fact that women have shined in politics, administration, social work, and other fields.

Women who start their own businesses are an alarming force to be taken into account in the corporate world. They do so not only to survive, but also to satiate their innermost drive for creativeness and to exhibit their skills. They are people that are willing to adopt inspiring tasks with a goal to accomplish their own goals & accomplish economic freedom. Several women have this quality; however, they do not realize their full potential since they were never given the chance to demonstrate it. Women are equally proficient at operating businesses, but they still trail behind. Despite their brilliance and ability, women are excluded from opportunities, information, and education. The status of women in India has seen substantial transformation during the last few millennia. India's history with women has been chaotic, going from having equivalent position with men in antiquity through the low moments of the mediaeval era to the championing of equal rights by numerous reformers. India has historically been a nation ruled by men, but this is changing. Indian women have expressed displeasure over the fact that they have been deferring to men's dictates for hundreds of years. Since women are getting more cognizant of their rights & responsibilities, they are no longer considered inferior to men. In every field, they are moving at the same pace as the men.

THEORETICAL FRAMEWORK

The expansion of entrepreneurship is the key factor in creating jobs worldwide. It is claimed that a number of variables, including entrepreneurial traits, resources, strategy, organizational structure, and systems, are influencing the new venture's growth and survival (Ferreira et al., 2012; Khan et al., 2019a, b). Entrepreneurial intentions that result in the development of new ventures are preceded by the economic opportunities and conditions. (Nair, 2020).

Entrepreneurship has mostly been a male phenomenon since its inception. The situation changed with time, though, and today's most prominent & inspiring entrepreneurs are women. Women's participation in entrepreneurship in India, however, remains very low, despite the fact that they are progressively backing to the country's financial development. Surprisingly, India, the second-most populated country in the world, partakes a women labor participation rate of only 26.97%, instead of that women constitute over half of its population—a high proportion when compared to many other nations (Saraswathy, 2019). India is a nation with a long past, vibrant philosophy, & rich traditions (Gupta & Gupta, 2008). Women are respected as the family's goddesses, but they nonetheless submit to men (Dubois,18211924). Every facet of traditional Indian culture was infused with inequality and hierarchical ideas, emphasizing the role of the male as the family's principal provider and decision-maker (Batra and Reio, 2016). Women were expected to take care of their families and young children while playing a supportive role (Thapar, 1981). As a result, Indian women frequently have fewer employment options than men. Women continue to face salary discrimination, the glass barrier, and sticky floors even after building a profession, making the path to success more challenging than that of their male colleagues (Agrawal, 2013; Kapil, 2019).

As a result, a number of push & pull forces encouraged women to pursue entrepreneurship as a career (Banu & Baral, 2021). Though, it is believed that men predominate in the field of entrepreneurship, and that men are more suited for it due to their masculine traits. Gender stereotypes have a huge impact on women's motivations and performance, which affects their willingness to launch their own firm (Prasad et al., 2013). The body of research in the Indian context has shown that young people's entrepreneurial intentions are significantly influenced by entrepreneurial education (Srivastava & Misra, 2017; Agarwal et al., 2020a).

Women Entrepreneurship Journey in India

The phrase "women entrepreneurs" & the idea of an entrepreneur were first popularized in the 19th century. Ancient India is where the growth of entrepreneurship began. In essence, being an entrepreneur involves organizing a business to engage in production and service endeavors, as well as recognizing investment opportunities and producing them.

In India, women are praised and exhorted in the names of Durga, Saraswati, Parvati, and Kali, but in reality, they are treated like abla (weak and dependent). Traditional societies continue to limit women to the four walls of the home, children, domestic duties & domiciliary rites. Few people ever got the chance to leave their homes and engage in economic activity.

Indian women used to own a variety of businesses in the middle of the 18th century, including small handloom businesses, retail stores, and more. More women started to break free from society's restrictions and enter the public eye in the 18th and 19th centuries. However, prior to the 20th century, females operated businesses as a means of generating additional revenue.

Although there were reforms made to mend the prestige of women in modern India during the British era, it wasn't until after independence that they began to experience privileges. According to the constitution, different provisions are introduced to elevate women and treat them similarly to men.

Women's participation and input were clearly evident in the early 20s. Businesswomen have become more prevalent, especially in the 1990s. Women stepped forward to use contemporary methods, make investments, identify a market segment, and generate significant employment or other.

The need for expanding women's entrepreneurship programs was highlighted in the Industrial Policy Resolution of 1991. As per 1981 Census Report, there were 1.5 lakh women who worked for themselves in India, making up 5.2% of all independent workers. "Women establish small-scale industries exclusively run by a female, there are more than 2, 95,680 business women claiming 11.2% of total 2.64 million entrepreneurs in the nation during 1995-96," according to Government of India reports.

Numerous factors, including urbanization, technological development, and women's educational standing, have changed their circumstances. It is encouraging to see that women are participating in economic development in all the spheres of business.

Females' position & responsibilities have rapidly changed. The completely house-trained women, whose only concern was for their families' wellbeing, awoke to take action. They have a robust desire to progress & this desire is regenerating their suppressed personality. Females are capable & skilled enough to manage the majority of positions.

Women are now more cognizant of their rights & are working in a variety of industries. They have built successful corporate empires of their own. They support the expansion of the economy and the improvement of their socioeconomic situation. As women's literacy rates rise in India, the share of females in the workforce is rising as well. Women entrepreneurs have received the proper attention from the Indian government, which has developed a number of programs to support their growth.

Entrepreneurship & Women

The factors that influence women's business are increasingly being evaluated globally (Parihar, 2017; Cavada et al., 2018). Sharma (2020) evaluated how women fit into the growth of society and highlighted the important contributions women have made to the socio-cultural and financial advancement of the country. The desire for female entrepreneurs to grow their businesses may be hampered by the predominant association of entrepreneurship with masculine notions of success (Ladge et al., 2019).

Noguera et al. (2015) examined the aspects that affect women entrepreneurship & found that informal factors likewise female networks & recognition of an entrepreneurial career are more important for female entrepreneurship than formal factors such as schooling, family context & differential of income level.

The Indian government has made significant financial investments and implemented a number of policies and programmes to support women entrepreneurs (Agarwal and Lenka, 2018). However, there is a substantial disparity when it comes to the underrepresentation of women in business. The hardship of Indian women in business forums is understandable given the Mastercard Index of Women Entrepreneurs' global standings, where India came in 52nd out of 57 nations (Mitter, 2018). Further evidence for this comes from the 2017 NASSCOM start-up ecosystem study, which shows that only 11% of Indian businesses are founded or co-founded by women. Only 8.05 million (13.76%) of the 58.5 million people were counted in the 2016 All India Report of the Sixth Economic Census. Though, the development of developing markets, industrialization, technical advancements & globalization—all of that are closely related to the economic performance of the nation—have led to cultural and demographic changes that have improved the situation for women in India.

In order to empower women locally, India is working toward a balanced growth of its economy, society, politics, and environment. The Government of India (GOI) prioritizes establishing equivalent privileges for women & girls at all levels through practical efforts like requiring compulsory education, capacity building, and creating awareness in order to meet one of the sustainable development goals (SDG-5, gender equality).

Indian Women's Entrepreneurship Situation India's Women Entrepreneurship Categories

1. Women in the Organized and Informal Sector
2. Women in traditional and contemporary fields of work
3. Women in rural and urban settings
4. The presence of women in both major and small industries.
5. Female entrepreneurs who are single

Statistics Showing the Growth of Women Entrepreneurs in India

Women-led startups have a 35% higher return on investment than those led by men, according to statistics, and 10-15% of tech startups have at least one female founder or co-founder. Women lead 10% of Indian startup unicorns. 20.37 percent of MSME owners are women. This accounts for 23.3% of the labor force.

LITERATURE REVIEW

Tambunan did a study on growth of female entrepreneurs in developing Asian countries (2009). The key focus of study was on female business owners in small and medium-sized businesses. Small & medium-sized firms (SMEs) that account for an average of more than 95% of all businesses across all industries, are growing more and more significant in developing Asian countries, according to this analysis. The survey also revealed that this region's underrepresentation of women entrepreneurs is a result of issues like low educational attainment, a lack of capital, and cultural or religious limitations.

Gupta et al. (2009) argued that both internal & external elements play a significant role in influencing entrepreneurial intentions amongst females while researching the characteristics of entrepreneurs. For instance, women are risk-averse by nature, which may prevent their entrepreneurial intentions from succeeding. According to Barragan et al. (2018), patriarchal structures and religious rules have also been important for entrepreneurship in societies where men are considered to be the only breadwinners and women are expected to take care of domestic duties. As a result, female entrepreneurs typically start their businesses with less money than their male counterparts, and their businesses are typically smaller than those held by men.

In 2000, Das conducted research on female SME owners in Tamil Nadu and Kerala, two states in India. The level of work-family conflict experienced by Indian female business owners was lower than that of their counterparts in western nations. Other Asian nations like Singapore and Indonesia exhibit similar patterns. Once more, statistics revealed that the percentage of businesses founded and run by female is far lower than those seen in western nations. Singh & Belwal (2008) describe the reasons and factors that encourages females to be entrepreneurs. In the context of India, he discussed the characteristics of their businesses as well as the challenges they faced. He claimed that social rejection of women entrepreneurs, the necessity to take care for one's family, gender discrimination, deficiency of networks & lenders' low primacy for lending to female business owners are the biggest obstacles to the growth of women's entrepreneurship. He recommended remedial actions likewise encouraging microbusinesses, releasing institutional constraints, projecting & pulling for growth and support of the winners, etc. The report urges the Indian government to ensure cooperation across its departments dealing with women, the economy, and social and welfare development.

PURPOSE OF THE STUDY

The present chapter endeavors to highlight the following mentioned objectives:

- Studying the characteristics of women business owners will help us better understand the challenges they face as they work to achieve success.
- To raise knowledge of the various potential programmes accessible to women entrepreneurs
- To come to findings and make recommendations

Exploring the origins of female entrepreneurs' intentions becomes crucial because it is widely believed that women entrepreneurship plays a substantial part in the overall progress of a nation. As per the Sixth Economic Census (2013), which was published by the Ministry of Statistics and Program Implementation, Government of India, only 14% of all entrepreneurs, or 8.05 million out of the 58.5 million entrepreneurs, are females, who make up about 49% of the people in India. There are roughly 13.45 million individuals working for female-owned businesses in the nation. In 2016, the Indian government unveiled a major effort with the goal of laying the groundwork for entrepreneurship and innovation in the nation. Even with, India being the third largest start-up nation, it still has only 5% of women start-up founders.

Over the past ten years, India has seen a significant increase in the number of start-ups & new businesses, bulk of which have been founded by males. Therefore, it is important to understand or predicting how a female becomes an entrepreneur is an evaluation of factors related to the growth of entrepreneurial intention amongst women.

This study could be helpful for numerous stakeholders in espousing a gender-based approach in executing all-encompassing entrepreneurial initiatives, given the government's current emphasis in the nation on supporting new ventures through numerous schemes. In a nation like India, the entrepreneurial environment is changing year after year. Numerous initiatives have been started with an emphasis on female entrepreneurship to offer all-around support to aspiring business owners. The coordinated efforts of numerous parties have helped to develop an ecosystem that is gender inclusive. However, both public and private parties need to exert a little more pressure to support female entrepreneurs.

Research Gap

Globally, entrepreneurship has been widely acknowledged for its contribution to innovation, social empowerment, economic prosperity, recovery, and societal advancement. It is widely acknowledged that encouraging female entrepreneurship is essential to a nation's overall development. However, in most developing economies, including India, women are significantly the ratio of women in entrepreneurship journey is rising globally. As per the GEM (2016) report on women's entrepreneurship, ten percent upsurge in totality of the entrepreneurial activity was found amongst women whereas narrowing the gender gap by 5 per cent over 2014. There is a rise in the demand for female entrepreneurship in developing economies as it offers a prospect for economic development, poverty mitigation & women's empowerment (Prasad, 2007).

This study concentrates on women's entrepreneurship in India because there is a lack of research in this area but there is potential for socioeconomic development.

CHALLENGES & ISSUES FACING INDIAN WOMEN

Women business owners face two distinct sets of issues: those that affect all entrepreneurs generally, and issues that are unique to women business owners.

The expansion of women's entrepreneurship has been constrained by the issues and limitations faced by these businesswomen. Women in India struggle mightily to advance in the business world. From the beginning of their business until it is operational, female entrepreneurs deal with a number of challenges. A woman entrepreneur faces many challenges simply by virtue of her gender. Every woman needs a favorable environment in order to instill entrepreneurial values and participate actively in company affairs. However, it can be difficult for Indian women to advance in business.

Expectations about one's own role. Women often act as obstacles to their own success and growth. Despite her tremendous success at work, a woman cannot escape the feeling of guilt when she miscarries to fulfil the anticipations of her job in the family sphere (Khandelwal & Sehgal, 2018; Sehgal & Khandelwal, 2020).

Chauvinism- It still controls the day. Males and females do not share the same rights. Before they may establish a business, the family patriarch must approve. Men have always related to entrepreneurship. They all impede the growth of female-owned businesses.

Education gap – In India, women behind men in terms of schooling by a wide margin. A majority of women—roughly 60% of them—are uneducated. Those who are educated acquire either less or inadequate education in comparison to their male counterparts due to untimely marriage, sons' greater education & poverty. The education required for women entrepreneurs to be aware of new breakthroughs in technology, production methods, marketing, and other government efforts that can be helpful to their success is lacking.

Socio-Cultural Barriers - Family and personal responsibilities can occasionally act as a significant obstacle for women entrepreneurs' success in the corporate world. Only little women have capability of managing both home & business proficiently, providing adequate time to perform all their accountabilities in priority.

Lack of business skills: Research shows that certain abilities, such as the ability to recognize opportunities, self-efficacy, networking, time management, creativity, social skills, and personality traits, are essential for any business to grow (Kerr et al., 2018). In their entrepreneurial journeys, women encounter significant obstacles, often ones that are unique (Chatterjee et al., 2018; Welsh et al., 2018).

Lack of knowledge of government policies and initiatives—most of women business owners today have little experience with actual government initiatives to promote women business owners (Agarwal and Lenka, 2017, 2018). While some people are unaware of these regulations, others are unable to access & utilize them (Shastri et al.,2019).

Market-related risks - The market's fierce rivalry and women's limited mobility make them dependent on middlemen. It can be very challenging for businesswomen to gain market share & get their goods well-liked and accepted by consumers. They could successfully take benefit of the media & internet services because they are not fully conscious of the shifting market environment circumstances.

Financial issues: Whether a business is large or little, finance is considered to be its "life blood." However, women business owners face two financial challenges. First off, women typically do not own property that can be used as collateral to get funding from outside sources. As a result, they have limited access to outside funding sources. Second, because banks believe that women can leave their businesses at any time, they view them as less creditworthy and discourage them from borrowing. Women business owners must therefore exclusively rely on their own savings. Women's businesses consequently fail as a result of a lack of funding.

Women's Entrepreneurial Skills are Viewed with Suspicion

Financial institutions do not have faith in women's entrepreneurship. Bankers used ludicrous and impractical securities to obtain loans for women business owners. Females still face more trouble getting credit, as per research by the United Nations Industrial Development Organization (UNIDO), often because of the prejudice of banks and unofficial lending organizations, "despite evidence indicating women's loan repayment rates are higher than men's."

Family Ties and Relationships are More Significant

Women of India put more value on relationships and family ties. Married women must strike a fair balance between work and home. Furthermore, family members' assistance to wedded females who are involved in business operations and management is crucial to a company's success.

Small Mobility

In comparison to male entrepreneurs, women are less likely to have the courage to travel during the day and at night, as well as between different areas and states. This demonstrates how little flexibility there is for women entrepreneurs to express themselves and move around.

Women in India lead protected lives and have low-risk reproductive capacity. They lack economic independence and have less education. All of these lessen their capacity to accept the risk associated in operating a business. A crucial requirement of a successful entrepreneur is the ability to take risks. In addition to the aforementioned issues, socioeconomic limitations, social attitudes, a lack of need for achievement, and inadequate infrastructure facilities prevent women from starting their own businesses.

GOVERNMENT'S ROLE IN FOSTERING WOMEN ENTREPRENEURS IN INDIA

Women's growth and development must be accelerated because their participation is crucial to the expansion of the entrepreneurial sector. A welcoming environment must be formed to empower females to actively take part in business activity. Government, non-Government, promotional, and regulatory organizations must step up and take an encouraging role in fostering women entrepreneurs in India. The Indian government has also initiated many programmes empowering females to initiate their own trades. These initiatives include the following: **The government created a separate chapter on the "Integration of women in development" in the seventh five-year plan with the following recommendation:**

- **Specific target group:** It was advocated that women be treated as a specific target group in all of the nation's main development initiatives.
- **Setting up training facilities:** The chapter makes the suggestion that facilities for women's vocational training be designed and expanded to better meet their evolving needs & abilities.
- **Creating new tools:** By using the right technology, tools, and procedures, efforts should be made to improve their productivity & efficiency.
- **Promoting support:** It was advised that the necessary support be given for marketing the goods created by female entrepreneurs.
- **Decision-making:** Including women in the decision-making process was also recommended.

PLANS FOR THE ENTREPRENEURSHIP DEVELOPMENT OF WOMEN

Only 10.11% of India's Micro and Small Enterprises are owned by women, and 9.46% of MSE enterprises are managed by women, according to the Third All India Census of Small-Scale Industries, which was performed in 2001-2002. This Ministry has developed a number of schemes that are specifically focused on the growth of women-owned businesses in India in order to promote women-owned businesses more actively in the MSE sector. Important programmes that were created in India exclusively for women to give them unique privileges.

Trade Related Entrepreneurship Assistance and Development Scheme for Women (TREAD) During the 11th Plan, the Indian government announced a program named as (TREAD) Trade Related Entrepreneurship Assistance and Development with the objective of boosting females to initiate their own trades. The plan envisioned economic empowerment of 297 women through the development of their entrepreneurial abilities in non-farm enterprises. The scheme is divided into three main components: the U.S. For the purpose of encouraging female entrepreneurs, the government of India has granted NGOs up to 30% of the entire project cost. The lending organization provides a loan to cover the remaining 70% of the project's total cost so that it can be used to carry out the planned activities.

Assistance with Managerial and Entrepreneurial Development

For current and potential business owners, MSME DIs regularly offer EDPs and MDPs for a fee. It is suggested that these recipients not be charged any fees but rather get a stipend of Rs. 500 per capita per month in order to encourage more entrepreneurs from the SC/ST, female, and physically challenged categories. Through specialized courses offered by MSME DIs, 50,000 entrepreneurs will receive training in IT, Fashion Technology, Agro & Food Processing, Catering, Biotechnology, Pharmaceuticals, etc. These Institutions must only provide 20% of their courses to women.

The MSME has developed a structure for female entrepreneurs to back small and micro manufacturing divisions possessed by females in their efforts to expand into foreign markets, to increase involvement of representatives of small & micro manufacturing enterprises under SIDOstall at international trade fairs/ exhibitions, and to increase export from such units. The 11th Plan is intended to include participation by female entrepreneurs in 25 international exhibitions.

Business loan from Bharatiya Mahila Bank (BMB): BMB was established on November 19, 2019, and on April 1, 2017, it merged with State Bank of India. Women who wanted to launch their own business are eligible for this financing. It provides business loans to female entrepreneurs with an interest rate of 10.15% and above for manufacturing businesses up to 20 Crores. Additionally, it provides Credit Guarantee Fund Trust for Micro and Small Enterprises (CGTMSE)-covered collateral-free loans up to Rs. 1 crore. The loans under this bank loan arrangement are to be returned in seven years.

Business Loan from Bharathiya Mahila Bank

This plan is meant for those females whose visions are big instead of lack of finance and other means. This bank provides funding of up to 20 crores to women entrepreneurs who desire to initiate manufacturing projects. There is no requirement for collateral if the requested loan amount is less than Rs. 1 crore.

Mudra Yojana Scheme

A program named Mudra Yojana is helpful for females who desire to initiate or cultivate their own small business. Women business owners are eligible to apply for loans between $5,000 and $10 lakh. It is perfect for opening up beauty salons, a small business, or a home-based operation. Even without any collateral or a guarantor, women are still eligible to apply for this loan.

Three categories make up the scheme:

Shishu is eligible for loans up to 50,000; Kishor is eligible for loans over 50,000 and up to 5 lakh; Tarun is eligible for loans over 5 lakh and up to 10 lakh. This program has helped many female-owned businesses because it is simple to use.

Cent Kalyani Scheme

The Central Bank of India's Cent Kaylani program is offered to women who seek to start or cultivate their small and medium-sized businesses (SMEs). Every other sort of business is eligible for loans under this program, with the exception of self-help groups, retail trade, educational institutions, and training facilities. Loans up to 100 lakhs are approved under this program without requiring any collateral or processing costs.

Women Entrepreneurship Platform (WEP)

This scheme has subsequent benefits:

- A program for early-stage enterprises to accelerate their growth.
- Mentorship and skill-building initiatives to learn about business and leadership
- Support with marketing
- Assistance in assuring adherence to rules and laws
- Resources and financial support
- A group and network of females with similar interests.

Annapurna Plan

With the help of this program, women will be able to open a catering business that will sell lunch kits, tiffin, and other culinary items. It provides loans up to Rs. 50,000. Utensils, other kitchen appliances, and other items can be purchased using the money provided as a loan under this program. The market rate and the relevant bank both influence the interest rate. The loan must be secured by a guarantor and can be repaid in three years (36 monthly installments). Women don't have to make EMI payments for the first month after the loan is granted.

Stree shakti Package

Women who own 50% or more of a company or enterprise and have participated in the Entrepreneurship Development Programmes (EDP) administered by state agencies are eligible for the Stree Shakti package. If the loan amount exceeds Rs. 2 lakh, the program additionally provides a 0.5% interest rate rebate. For loans up to Rs. 5 lakhs, there is no security requirement for small sector units.

Many more schemes are there which are offered by Government of India to assist female entrepreneurs.

Possibilities Developed by Associations

Self Help Groups (SHG), the Federation of Indian Women Entrepreneurs (FIWE), the Women's India Trust (WIT), the Small Industries Development Organization (SIDO), the National Bank for Agriculture and Rural Development (NABARD), the Self Employed Women's Association (SEWA), and the Association of Women Entrepreneurs of Karnataka are just a few of the associations that exist (AWAKE). Women entrepreneurs are actively being encouraged to start businesses in India by organizations like the International Centre for Entrepreneurship and Career Development, TiEStree Shakti (TSS), Tamilnadu Corporation for Development of Women Ltd. (TNCDW), Marketing Organization of Women Enterprises (MOOWES), Women Entrepreneurs Promotion Association (WEPA), Women Entrepreneurs Association of Tamil Nadu (WEAT), and WeoW by Google. Similar to this, the MSE cluster development program foots a sizeable chunk of the bill for projects involving businesses run and owned by women entrepreneurs. For MSEs owned and run by women, the Credit Guarantee Fund Scheme for Micro and Small Enterprises offers guarantees of up to 80%.

India's Consortium of Women Entrepreneurs (CWEI)

The Consortium of Women Entrepreneurs of India (CWEI) is a non-profit organization that was established in New Delhi in 1996 and is registered as a civil society. The Indian government has approved it. It collaborates closely with the Ministry of Rural Development in the Public Private Partnership to assist Indian families living below the poverty line. It is a member of the National Board of the Ministry of MSME. The following services are being provided by them:

They are serving as a launch pad for businesses established by women. It aids women in achieving significant economic empowerment. It is serving as a catalyst to increase women's access to natural resources. In the case of women-owned businesses, it entails offering technological assistance in the area of product creation and development. It offers quality assurance, marketing assistance, and technological support to women-owned businesses. It is educating female business owners about several government initiatives.

In conclusion, it can be said that women consortium is an organization that offers a wide range of services to women-owned businesses.

NEW OPPORTUNITIES ENCOURAGE WOMEN TO START THEIR OWN BUSINESSES.

E-Commerce & Female Opportunities

With so many new opportunities opening up for women, e-commerce is one such sector where notable and brilliant women have made their marks. With more women running their own businesses from home or while travelling, the e-commerce sector has become more accessible. Additionally, starting a firm outside of a typical career and selling distinctive things has gotten simpler. The development of e-commerce has undoubtedly lowered the threshold for starting a business. The ability to trade online has helped several small enterprises run by women get access to a new group of customers with little outlay of cash. Additionally, this amazing accomplishment empowers women around the nation.

STRATEGIES NECESSARY

The best method to support economic growth and global development is through empowering women to realize their "choices" and "opportunities" and investing in their "capabilities." The first step towards empowering women is to eradicate illiteracy. Even though it is steadily increasing, India's female literacy rate is still lower than that of men. Early marriage and childbirth are consequently more common in families with lower socioeconomic standing. The first step in advancing gender equality and empowering women is universal education and the eradication of gender gap in education.

The desire for self-actualization, achievement, hard work, and independence is sparked by education (Rita and Rajasekar, 2012). Economic security for women is a result of education, and this opens the door to other forms of women's empowerment, including social, psychological, technological, and political empowerment (Hans, and Sowjanya, 2015). The issue of "Skilling India" is receiving adequate attention. However, when addressing the issue of women's skill development, it is important to pay attention to the elements that impede it or, to put it another way, to promote enabling conditions for women's skill development (Nathan, 2018).

The following are some of the typical actions necessary to support female entrepreneurs:

- Promoting women from being housewives to being business managers by instilling the entrepreneurial spirit through "learning by doing" opportunities
- An extensive awareness campaign should be undertaken with the goal of educating women about the different business opportunities and niches available to them.
- Efforts should be made to raise the educational standards of women and systematize vocational training programs to develop managerial competencies so that they are prepared to adapt to changing times by utilizing the most up-to-date technological advantages that enable women to excel in decision-making.
- Hold international, national, local, and regional trade shows and industrial exhibits to assist women in connecting with other female businesses.
- Both small- and large-scale ventures should receive more working capital help from financial institutions. Soft loans and subsidies should be made available to businesswomen to encourage them to engage in industrial operations.
- Giving local SHGs priority when providing microcredit to female entrepreneurs is a good idea.
- Therefore, entrepreneurship is an economic activity and has a significant impact on the economic environment. India has plenty of natural and human resources, thus there is room for the growth of entrepreneurship, particularly among women entrepreneurs.

IDEAS FOR SOLVING THE ISSUES INDIAN WOMEN ENTREPRENEURS FACE

Although female entrepreneurship has been growing rapidly in recent years, there are still a number of particular difficulties that must be overcome. Women entrepreneurs have offered the following advice in response to the numerous "stumbling hurdles" they encounter in their careers:

Money cells: Many other finance cells can be available to offer women businesses quick financing. These specialized cells should offer financing to female business owners at low and concessional interest rates with simple repayment terms. Women officers and clerks should work in even these finance cells. It is important to make efforts to finance local initiatives.

Marketing Co-operatives: In order to support and develop female entrepreneurs, marketing cooperatives should be established. When procuring their needs, the government should give women business owners preference. These marketing partnerships will aid female business owners in getting fair rates for their goods. This will assist in cutting out middlemen.

Supply of raw materials: Women businesses should be given priority access to scarce and imported raw resources at reduced prices.

Education and awareness: Programs for education and awareness should be set up to alter the unfavorable social views regarding women. Elders' perspectives on the potential of females and their proper place in society need to be modified.

Facilities for training: Programmers for training and development are extremely important for the growth of enterprise. Special training programmes should be created so that women can benefit fully. To draw more and more women to the training centers, mobile training facilities, part-time training facilities, etc. Create a Blueprint: According to Wesman, one of the biggest problems she encounters with female entrepreneurs is that they frequently start their businesses out of the blue without a clear plan in place. They don't develop a clear plan or strategy because they appear to enter the business because it's something they enjoy doing, she claimed. All female business owners should create a business blueprint when they first start out that clearly outlines their product or service, their target market, and how the company will operate on a daily basis, according to Wesman. The precise duties of the business owner and staff should also be covered in this design, along with an estimate of the costs associated with operating the company for the first year.

Building a team: According to Wesman, many female business owners try to handle all part of the company by themselves, which is a surefire prescription for failure. It's critical for female company owners to surround themselves with a team of collaborators who each bring a unique set of skills and abilities to the table. Women don't think about teamwork and resourcefulness the same way men do since they believe they can handle everything on their own. Men in the professional environment are more likely to understand this than women, who are accustomed to multitasking.

Build Ties: According to Wesman, women frequently attempt to form relations with potential consumers that could lead towards disappointment. Because they sought to create a relationship with the customer, she claimed that when they are unable to close the transaction, they take it too personally. "Instead of taking a moment to reflect and ask yourself, "What did I learn from that sales experience?," or "How can I use this to better my next sales experience?" Wesman attributes this to the social conditioning of women, their discomfort with rivalry, and their need to be loved. Since you want to sell based on people liking you, you then take it very personally, Wesman added. She stated that although women should develop relationships, they shouldn't be afraid to be aggressive while making sales pitches.

Underpricing services: According to Wes Man, many women find it difficult to discuss pricing details because money can be a sensitive matter. Female business owners frequently undervalue their goods or services as a result of this unease. Wes man claimed, "It doesn't grasp what it genuinely costs to make a good or what it costs to supply a service." "Women undervalue themselves in the job, and becoming an entrepreneur is no different."

Hiding from cash flow problems: According to Wes man, women typically are less proactive when it comes to collecting money. However, managing cash flow and following up on outstanding money and payments is crucial to every successful organization. This is related to the idea that talking about money, thinking about money, or even collecting it is unladylike or unfeminine, she continued. Owners must confront such debtors head-on and collect what is owed.

Getting too close to employees: Wes Man remarked that while many small firms embrace the "family" mindset, female business owners are frequently especially guilty of doing so. She claimed, "They treat staff like family and friends." It's important to maintain strong work ties while without becoming overly intimate. It becomes more difficult to make judgments that are best for the company when a relationship reaches that extent, she said.

CONCLUSION

It can be concluded that things are better now because there are more women contributing in entrepreneurship at a significant rate. Economic efforts have promised Indian women equal chance in all domains, and legislation guaranteeing equal participation in the political process as well as equivalent prospects & rights in education & employment have been passed. But regrettably, only a small group of women—namely, women in the urban middle class—have profited from the government-sponsored development efforts. Nearly 45% of Indians are in the female sector. Effective action is now required to offer women entrepreneurial awareness, orientation, and skill development programmes. In order to encourage women's entrepreneurship, measures are being taken to highlight the importance of female entrepreneurs for economic development. A resurgence of entrepreneurship is urgently needed, with a focus on educating the female population and encouraging women to excel in the business world by educating them about their strengths, their significant roles in society, and the substantial contributions they could make to their industries & the whole economy. In order to adapt to changing trends, navigate the challenges of global markets, and pursue excellence in the entrepreneurial sphere, women entrepreneurs must be properly molded with entrepreneurial qualities & abilities.

With independence, Indian women were promised equal chance in all spheres, and legislation was passed ensuring their equal participation in political processes as well as equal opportunities and rights in education and employment. But regrettably, only a small group of women have profited from government-sponsored development initiatives. The bulk of them are still largely unaffected by change, and only a small group of urban middle class women have benefited from development efforts. Women are eager to start their own businesses and aid in the development of the country. Their importance is acknowledged, and actions are being taken to encourage female entrepreneurship. The need of the hour is for entrepreneurship to flourish again.

The government is endeavoring to close this breach with many programmes even though women-owned companies make 8–10% more income in comparison to male-owned companies of the same age in the same industries. Solitary 5% of women-owned businesses obtain venture capitalist subsidy, linked to 77% of male-owned businesses. The capability of women to succeed in business has always been outside question, but societal obstacles have always been considerable. With the sustenance of many programmes for assisting female entrepreneurs, we hope to fortify our country and make a truly free-market economy. Further, in order to meet changing trends and competitive global marketplaces, women entrepreneurs must be appropriately molded with entrepreneurial traits and talents. They must also be capable of sustaining and competing in the local economic environment.

REFERENCES

Agarwal, S., & Lenka, U. (2017). Does growth of ventures depend on competencies?: Selected cases from India. *International Journal of Entrepreneurship and Small Business*, *31*(2), 227–243. doi:10.1504/IJESB.2017.10004850

Agarwal, S., & Lenka, U. (2018). Why research is needed in women entrepreneurship in India: A viewpoint. *International Journal of Social Economics*, *45*(7), 1042–1057. doi:10.1108/IJSE-07-2017-0298

Agrawal, T. (2013). Are there glass-ceiling and sticky-floor effects in India? An empirical examination. *Oxford Development Studies*, *41*(3), 322–342. doi:10.1080/13600818.2013.804499

Banu, J., Baral, R., Agarwal, U. A., & Rastogi, M. (2021). Role of socio-cultural factors in shaping entrepreneurial decision and behavior: an Indian perspective. In U. Guelich, A. Bullough, T. Manolova, & L. Schjoedt (Eds.), *Women's Entrepreneurship and Culture: Socio-Cultural Context, Traditional Family Roles and Self-Determination*. Edward Elgar Publishing. doi:10.4337/9781789905045.00015

Baporikar, N. (2007). *Entrepreneurship development & project management*. Himalaya publication house.

Barragan, S., Erogul, M. S., & Essers, C. (2018). 'Strategic (dis) obedience': Female entrepreneurs reflecting on and acting upon patriarchal practices. *Gender, Work and Organization*, *25*(5), 575–592. doi:10.1111/gwao.12258

Batra, R., & Reio, T. G. Jr. (2016). Gender inequality issues in India. *Advances in Developing Human Resources*, *18*(1), 88–101. doi:10.1177/1523422316630651

Cavada, M.C., Bobek, V., Skoko, H., & Maček, A. (2018). Cultural foundations of female entrepreneurship in Mexico: challenges and opportunities", *Naše Gospodarstvo/Our Economy*, *64*(1), 28-40.

Census, E. (2013). *6th Economic Census*. Ministry of Statistics & Programme Implementation, Government of India.

Charumathi, B. (1998). Women entrepreneur's challenges and prospects. In C. Swarajya Lakshmi (Ed.), *Development of Women Entrepreneurship in India: Problems and Prospects*. Discovery Publishing House.

Chatterjee, N., Das, N., & Srivastava, N. K. (2018). A structural model assessing key factors affecting women's entrepreneurial success. *Journal of Entrepreneurship in Emerging Economies*, *11*(1), 122–151. doi:10.1108/JEEE-08-2016-0030

Damwad, (2007). *Women Entrepreneurship – A Nordic Perspective*. Nordic Innovation Centre.

Das, M. (2000). Women Entrepreneurs from India: Problems, Motivations and Success Factors. *Journal of Small Business and Entrepreneurship*, *15*(4), 67–81. doi:10.1080/08276331.2000.10593294

Dubois, A. J. A. (1924). *Hindu Manners, Customs, and Ceremonies, Beauchamp, H.K. (edited and corrected)*. Clarendon Press.

Walokar, S. K. & Deepak, M. (2001). *Opportunities, Performance and Problems.* Himalaya Publishing House. https://vakilsearch.com/blog/7-indian-government-initiatives-to-help-women-entrepreneurs-smash-the-glass-ceiling/ http://www.dcmsme.gov.in/publications/women_schemes.pdf,

Gordon, E., & Natarajan, K. (2007). Entrepreneurship development. Himalaya 300 publication house.

Gupta, K. R., & Gupta, J. R. (2008). Indian Economy, Atlantic Publishers & Dist, New Delhi.Ladge, J., Eddleston, K.A. and Sugiyama, K. (2019), "Am I an entrepreneur? How imposter fears hinder women entrepreneurs' business growth. *Business Horizons*, *62*(5), 615–624.

Kerr, S. Kerr, W., & Xu, T. (2018). Personality Traits of Entrepreneurs: A Review of Recent Literature. Foundations and Trends in Entrepreneurship. doi:10.1561/0300000080

Khandelwal & Sehgal. (2018). Exploring work-family interface for Indian women entrepreneurs. Gender in Management: An International Journal, 33. doi:10.1108/GM-04-2016-0075

Ladge, J., Eddleston, K. A., & Sugiyama, K. (2019). Am I an entrepreneur? How imposter fears hinder women entrepreneurs' business growth. *Business Horizons*, *62*(5), 615–624. doi:10.1016/j.bushor.2019.05.001

Mitter, S. (2018). India isn't doing great in nurturing women entrepreneurs, finds survey. *Your Story.* https://yourstory.com/2018/03/india-isnt-great-nurturing-women-entrepreneurs-finds-survey/

Nathan, F. (2018). Returns to Microcredit, Cash Grants and Training for Male and Female Micro entrepreneurs in Uganda. *World Development*, *105*, 189–200. doi:10.1016/j.worlddev.2017.12.027

Noguera, M., Alvarez, C., Merigó, J. M., & Urbano, D. (2015). Determinants of female entrepreneurship in Spain: An institutional approach. *Computational & Mathematical Organization Theory*, *21*(4), 341–355. doi:10.100710588-015-9186-9

Parihar, S. (2017). Entrepreneurial intent: Exploring the roles of gender and family business background. *International Journal of Marketing and Business Communication*, *6*(4), 28–37.

Prasad, V. K., Naidu, G. M., Murthy, B. K., Winkel, D. E., & Ehrhardt, K. (2013). Women entrepreneurs and business venture growth: An examination of the influence of human and social capital resources in an Indian context. *Journal of Small Business and Entrepreneurship*, *26*(4), 341–364. doi:10.1080/08276331.2013.821758

Rita, C., & Rajasekar, D. (2012). Role of women in Independent India: An assessment. *Southern Economist*, *51*(11), 7–9.

Saraswathy, M. (2019). Women's day 2019: labor force participation of females is still an Achilles heel for India. *Money Control.* www.moneycontrol.com/news/business/economy/womens-day-2019-labour-force-participation-of-females-is-still-an-achilles-heel-for-india-3623061.html

Sehgal & Khandelwal. (2020). Work–family interface of women entrepreneurs: evidence from India. *South Asian Journal of Business Studies*, . doi:10.1108/SAJBS-11-2019-0213

Sharma, P. (2020). Women entrepreneurship in India: The socio-economic context. *Materials Today: Proceedings*. s doi:10.1016/j.matpr.2020.09.437

Shastri, S., Shastri, S., & Pareek, A. (2019). Motivations and challenges of women entrepreneurs: Experiences of small businesses in Jaipur city of Rajasthan. *The International Journal of Sociology and Social Policy*, *39*(5/6), 338–355. doi:10.1108/IJSSP-09-2018-0146

Shetty, Sowjanya and Hans, V. Basil, Role of Education in Women Empowerment and Development: Issues and Impact (September 26, 2015). Available at SSRN: https://ssrn.com/abstract=2665898 or doi:10.2139/ssrn.2665898

Singh, G., & Belwal, R. (2008). Entrepreneurship and SMEs in Ethiopia. *Gender in Management*, *23*(2), 120–136. doi:10.1108/17542410810858321

Srivastava, S., & Misra, R. (2017). Exploring antecedents of entrepreneurial intentions of young women in India: A multi-method analysis. *Journal of Entrepreneurship in Emerging Economies*, *9*(2), 181–206. doi:10.1108/JEEE-04-2016-0012

Staniewski, M. W., & Awruk, K. (2019). Entrepreneurial success and achievement motivation – a preliminary report on a validation study of the questionnaire of entrepreneurial success. *Journal of Business Research*, *101*, 433–440. doi:10.1016/j.jbusres.2019.01.073

Tambunan, T. (2009). Women entrepreneurship in Asian developing countries: Their development and main constraints, Journal of Development and Agricultural Economics: Vol. 1. *(2), Page No. 027-040. the glass ceiling*. Sage.

Thapar, R. (1981). Ideology and the interpretation of early Indian history. *Social Sciences Information. Information Sur les Sciences Sociales*, *20*(2), 239–258. doi:10.1177/053901848102000201

Welsh, D. H. B., Kaciak, E., & Shamah, R. (2018). Determinants of women entrepreneurs' firm performance in a hostile environment. *Journal of Business Research*, *88*, 481–491. doi:10.1016/j.jbusres.2017.12.015

Zeb, A., & Ihsan, A. (2020). Innovation and the entrepreneurial performance in women-owned small and medium-sized enterprises in Pakistan. *Women's Studies International Forum*, *79*, 102342. doi:10.1016/j.wsif.2020.102342

Compilation of References

Abdul Jalil, M. M., Mohd, F., Man, M., Ali, N., & Muhamad, S. (2019). Social media application usage and women entrepreneurship achievement through e-business model: Case of Setiu wetland. *ACM International Conference Proceeding Series, Part F1479*, (pp. 505–509). ACM. 10.1145/3316615.3316709

Abor, J., & Quartey, P. (2010). Issues in SME development in Ghana and South Africa. *International Research Journal of Finance and Economics, 39*, https://www.eurojournals.com/finance.htm

Aboutaleb, G. A. (2020). *Social Media Potentials in Supporting Women Entrepreneurship: The Case of Egypt*. The American University in Cairo.

Acar, H. (2019). Women in Turkish Culture and State Tradition. *İnsan ve İnsan Journal of Science, Culture. Art and Thought*, *6*(21), 395–411.

Acs, Z. (2006). How Is Entrepreneurship Good for Economic Growth? *Innovations: Technology, Governance, Globalization*, *1*(1), 97–107. doi:10.1162/itgg.2006.1.1.97

Acs, Z. J., Bardasi, E., Estrin, S., & Svejnar, J. (2011). Introduction to special issue of Small Business Economics on female entrepreneurship in developed and developing economies. *Small Business Economics*, *37*(4), 393–396. doi:10.100711187-011-9372-1

Adams, R. B., & Funk, P. (2012). Beyond the glass ceiling: Does gender matter? *Management Science*, *58*(2), 219–235. doi:10.1287/mnsc.1110.1452

Adams, R. B., & Kirchmaier, T. (2016). Women on boards in finance and STEM industries. *The American Economic Review*, *106*(5), 277–281. doi:10.1257/aer.p20161034

Adorno, T. W., & Horkheimer, M. (2002). *Dialectic of enlightenment* (E. Jephcott, Trans.). Stanford University Press.

Africa: First female entrepreneurs in the high-tech sector as new role models. (2018, September 28). Roland Berger. https://www.rolandberger.com/en/Insights/Publications/Africa-First-female-entrepreneurs-in-the-high-tech-sector-as-new-role-models.html

Afshan, G., Shahid, S., & Tunio, M. N. (2021). Learning experiences of women entrepreneurs amidst COVID-19. *International Journal of Gender*. doi:10.1108/IJSE-07-2017-0298

Agarwal, S., & Lenka, U. (2015). Study on work-life balance of women entrepreneurs – review and research agenda. *Industrial and Commercial Training*, *47*(7), 356–362. doi:10.1108/ICT-01-2015-0006

Agarwal, S., & Lenka, U. (2017). Does growth of ventures depend on competencies?: Selected cases from India. *International Journal of Entrepreneurship and Small Business*, *31*(2), 227–243. doi:10.1504/IJESB.2017.10004850

Agarwal, S., & Lenka, U. (2018). Why research is needed in women entrepreneurship in India: A viewpoint. *International Journal of Social Economics*, *45*(7), 1042–1057. doi:10.1108/IJSE-07-2017-0298

Agrawal, A., Gandhi, P., & Khare, P. (2021). Women empowerment through entrepreneurship: Case study of a social entrepreneurial intervention in rural India. *The International Journal of Organizational Analysis*. doi:10.1108/IJOA-03-2021-2659

Agrawal, T. (2013). Are there glass-ceiling and sticky-floor effects in India? An empirical examination. *Oxford Development Studies*, *41*(3), 322–342. doi:10.1080/13600818.2013.804499

Ahrens, A., Bhati, P. P., Zascerinska, J., Zascerinskis, M., Aleksejeva, A., & Abjalkiene, I. (2021). Engineering Master Students' Views on Digital Entrepreneurship in a Host European Country. In *Environment. Technologies. Resources: Proceedings of the International Scientific and Practical Conference* (Vol. 2, pp. 225-231). Research Gate.

Akter, M., Rahman, M., & Radicic, D. (2022). Gender-Aware Framework in International Entrepreneurship: How Far Developed?—A Systematic Literature Review. *Sustainability (Switzerland)*, *14*(22), 15326. doi:10.3390u142215326

Alam, S. S., Jani, M. F. M., & Omar, N. A. (2011). An Empirical Study of Success Factors of Women Entrepreneurs in Southern Region in Malaysia. *International Journal of Economics and Finance*, *3*(2). doi:10.5539/ijef.v3n2p166

Al-Dmour, R. H., & Abuhammad, H. (2021). The extent of use of social media networks by the female entrepreneurs in Jordan: Empirical study. *International Journal of Business and Globalisation*, *29*(3), 406–427. doi:10.1504/IJBG.2021.118684

Alecchi, B. A. (2020). Toward Realizing the Potential of Latin America's Women Entrepreneurs: An Analysis of Barriers and Challenges. *Latin American Research Review*, *55*(3), 496–514. doi:10.25222/larr.108

Alegre, I., Kislenko, S., & Berbegal-Mirabent, J. (2017). Organized chaos: Mapping the definitions of social entrepreneurship. *Journal of Social Entrepreneurship*, *8*(2), 248–264. doi:10.1080/19420676.2017.1371631

Alessa, A. A., Alotaibie, T. M., Elmoez, Z., & Alhamad, H. E. (2021). Impact of COVID-19 on Entrepreneurship and Consumer Behaviour: A Case Study in Saudi Arabia. *Journal of Asian Finance Economics and Business*, *8*(5), 201–210. doi:10.13106/jafeb.2021.vol8.no5.0201

Alexander, B. K. (2004). Passing, Cultural Performance, and Individual Agency: Performative Reflections on Black Masculine Identity. Sage Publications.

Ali, J., Shabir, S., & Shaikh, A. (2021). Exploring antecedents of entrepreneurial intentions among females in an emerging economy. *International Journal of Social Economics, 48(7), 1044-1059.*, *48*(7), 1044–1059.

Ali, J., Jabeen, Z., & Burhan, M. (2023). Measuring factors influencing entrepreneurial intention across gender in India: Evidence from Global Entrepreneurship Monitor (GEM) Database. *Journal of Research in Marketing and Entrepreneurship*, *25*(1), 63–82. doi:10.1108/JRME-08-2021-0105

Allahar, H. (2015). Female Entrepreneurship: The Experience of Latin America and the Caribbean. *European Academic Research*, *2*(10), 12739–12762. https://www.researchgate.net/publication/279191666_Female_Entrepreneurship_The_Experience_of_Latin_America_and_the_Caribbean#fullTextFileContent

Alonso-Galicia, P. E., Fernández-Pérez, V., Rodríguez-Ariza, L., & del Mar Fuentes-Fuentes, M. (2015). Entrepreneurial cognitions in academia: Exploring gender differences. *Journal of Managerial Psychology*, *30*(6), 630–644. doi:10.1108/JMP-08-2013-0262

Alvarez, C., Urbano, D., Coduras, A., & Ruiz-Navarro, J. (2011). Environmental conditions and entrepreneurial activity: A regional comparison in Spain. *Journal of Small Business and Enterprise Development, 18*(1), 120–140. doi:10.1108/14626001111106460

Åmo, B. W. (2014). Antecedents, prevalence and manifestations of social entrepreneurship. *International Journal of Entrepreneurial Venturing, 6*(2), 162–178. doi:10.1504/IJEV.2014.062750

Amrita, K., Garg, C. P., & Singh, S. (2018). Modelling the critical success factors of women entrepreneurship using fuzzy AHP framework. *Journal of Entrepreneurship in Emerging Economies, 10*(1), 81–116. doi:10.1108/JEEE-03-2017-0017

Anderson, J. C., & Gerbing, D. W. (1988). Structural equation modeling in practice: A review and recommended two-step approach. *Psychological Bulletin, 103*(3), 411–423. doi:10.1037/0033-2909.103.3.411

Anggadwita, G., Mulyaningsih, H. D., Ramadani, V., & Arwiyah, M. Y. (2015). Women entrepreneurship in Islamic perspective: A driver for social change. *International Journal of Business and Globalisation, 15*(3), 389–404. doi:10.1504/IJBG.2015.071914

Anggadwita, G., Ramadani, V., Permatasari, A., & Alamanda, D. T. (2021). Key determinants of women's entrepreneurial intentions in encouraging social empowerment. *Service Business, 15*(2), 309–334. doi:10.100711628-021-00444-x

Anwar, M., Bingley, S., & Burgess, S. (2018). Understanding ICT strategy of women small business owners in developing countries: Linking social media use, business strategy and well-being. *ACIS 2018 Proceedings.* IEEE.

Aparicio, S., Audretsch, D., Noguera, M., & Urbano, D. (2022). Can female entrepreneurs boost social mobility in developing countries? An institutional analysis. *Technological Forecasting and Social Change, 175*, 121401. doi:10.1016/j.techfore.2021.121401

Arasti, Z., Panahi, S. M. S., Zarei, B., & Rezaee, S. O. (2012). A Qualitative Study on Individual Factors Affecting Iranian Women Entrepreneurs' Growth Orientation. *International Business Research, 5*(3). Advance online publication. doi:10.5539/ibr.v5n3p81

Ascher, J. (2012). Female Entrepreneurship – An Appropriate Response to Gender Discrimination. *Journal of Entrepreneurship. Management and Innovation, 8*(4), 97–114. doi:10.7341/2012847

Austin, J., Stevenson, H., & Wei–Skillern, J. (2006). Social and commercial entrepreneurship: Same, different, or both? *Entrepreneurship Theory and Practice, 30*(1), 1–22. doi:10.1111/j.1540-6520.2006.00107.x

Autio, E., Nambisan, S., Thomas, L. D., & Wright, M. (2018). Digital affordances, spatial affordances, and the genesis of entrepreneurial ecosystems. *Strategic Entrepreneurship Journal, 12*(1), 72–95. doi:10.1002ej.1266

Aylward, E. (2007). *Traditional and Non-Traditional Female Entrepreneurs: An Exploration into what Influences their Selection of Industry Sector* [Masters Thesis, Waterford Institute of Technology].

Ayob, A. H. (2018). Diversity, trust and social entrepreneurship. *Journal of Social Entrepreneurship, 9*(1), 1–12. doi:10.1080/19420676.2017.1399433

Bacigalupo, M., Kampylis, P., Punie, Y., & Van den Brande, G. (2016). *EntreComp: The Entrepreneurship Competence Framework.* Publication Office of the European Union. doi:10.2791/593884

Bacq, S., Hartog, C., & Hoogendoorn, B. (2013). A quantitative comparison of social and commercial entrepreneurship: Toward a more nuanced understanding of social entrepreneurship organizations in context. *Journal of Social Entrepreneurship, 4*(1), 40–68. doi:10.1080/19420676.2012.758653

Bacq, S., & Janssen, F. (2011). The multiple faces of social entrepreneurship: A review of definitional issues based on geographical and thematic criteria. *Entrepreneurship and Regional Development, 23*(5–6), 373–403. doi:10.1080/08985626.2011.577242

Badiou, A., & Zizek, S. (2011). *Bir idea olarak komünizm (Çev: Ahmet Ergenç ve Ebru Kılıç.).* Ayrıntı Yayınları.

Baldarelli, M. G., Del Baldo, M., & Vignini, S. (2016). *Pink accounting in Italy: Cultural perspectives over discrimination and/or lack of interest.* Meditari Accountancy Research.

Banerjee, S. (2003, March–April). Gender and nationalism: The masculinization of hinduism and female political participation in india. *Women's Studies International Forum, 26*(2), 167–179. doi:10.1016/S0277-5395(03)00019-0

Banu, J., Baral, R., Agarwal, U. A., & Rastogi, M. (2021). Role of socio-cultural factors in shaping entrepreneurial decision and behavior: an Indian perspective. In U. Guelich, A. Bullough, T. Manolova, & L. Schjoedt (Eds.), *Women's Entrepreneurship and Culture: Socio-Cultural Context, Traditional Family Roles and Self-Determination*. Edward Elgar Publishing. doi:10.4337/9781789905045.00015

Baporikar, N. (2007). *Entrepreneurship development & project management*. Himalaya publication house.

Baranik, L. E., Gorman, B., & Wales, W. J. (2018). What Makes Muslim Women Entrepreneurs Successful? A Field Study Examining Religiosity and Social Capital in Tunisia. *Sex Roles, 78*(3–4), 208–219. doi:10.100711199-017-0790-7

Barot, H. (2015, January). Entrepreneurship - A Key to Success. *International Journal of Business and Management, 3*(1), 163–165.

Barragan, S., Erogul, M. S., & Essers, C. (2018). 'Strategic (dis) obedience': Female entrepreneurs reflecting on and acting upon patriarchal practices. *Gender, Work and Organization, 25*(5), 575–592. doi:10.1111/gwao.12258

Basaffar, A. A., Niehm, L. S., & Bosselman, R. (2018). Saudi Arabian women in entrepreneurship: Challenges, opportunities and potential. *Journal of Developmental Entrepreneurship, 23*(2), 1850013. doi:10.1142/S1084946718500139

Batjargal, B., Webb, J. W., Tsui, A., Arregle, J. L., Hitt, M. A., & Miller, T. (2019). The moderating influence of national culture on female and male entrepreneurs' social network size and new venture growth. *Cross Cultural & Strategic Management, 26*(4), 490–521. doi:10.1108/CCSM-04-2018-0057

Batra, R., & Reio, T. G. Jr. (2016). Gender inequality issues in India. *Advances in Developing Human Resources, 18*(1), 88–101. doi:10.1177/1523422316630651

Baulch, E., & Pramiyanti, A. (2018). Hijabers on Instagram: Using Visual Social Media to Construct the Ideal Muslim Woman. *Social Media + Society, 4*(4). doi:10.1177/2056305118800308

Beauvoir, S. D. (2019). *İkinci cinsiyet, (Çev:Gülnur Acar Savran).* Koç Üniversitesi Yayınları.

Bedarkar, M. M., Mishra, M., & Khatwani, R. A. (2020). Leveraging social media in facilitating women entrepreneurs in India: A case study of pune ladies (PULA). *International Journal of E-Entrepreneurship and Innovation, 10*(2), 76–90. doi:10.4018/IJEEI.2020070105

Bello, H. S. (2019). Female Entrepreneurship in the African Fashion Industry: A Review of Its Determinants and Characteristics. *Palgrave Studies of Entrepreneurship in Africa*, 99–113. doi:10.1007/978-3-319-91265-3_5

Bennett, R., & Dann, S. (2000). The Changing Experience of Australian Female Entrepreneurs. *Gender, Work &Amp. Organization, 7*(2), 75–83. doi:10.1111/1468-0432.00095

Bernardino, S., Santos, J. F., & Ribeiro, J. C. (2018). Social entrepreneur and gender: What's personality got to do with it? *International Journal of Gender and Entrepreneurship, 10*(1), 61–82. doi:10.1108/IJGE-07-2017-0040

Bharadwaj, A., Sawy, O. A. E., Pavlou, P. A., & Venkatraman, N. (2013). Digital business strategy: Toward a next generation of insights. *Management Information Systems Quarterly, 37*(2), 471–482. doi:10.25300/MISQ/2013/37:2.3

Bhatti, M. A., Al Doghan, M. A., Saat, S. A. M., Juhari, A. S., & Alshagawi, M. (2021). Entrepreneurial intentions among women: Does entrepreneurial training and education matters? (Pre- and post-evaluation of psychological attributes and its effects on entrepreneurial intention). *Journal of Small Business and Enterprise Development, 28*(2), 167–184. doi:10.1108/JSBED-09-2019-0305

Bianchi, M., Parisi, V., & Salvatore, R. (2016). Female entrepreneurs: Motivations and constraints. An Italian regional study. *International Journal of Gender and Entrepreneurship, 8*(3), 198–220. doi:10.1108/IJGE-08-2015-0029

Billson, B. (2022, March 14). *"Disappointing": Why it's easier for men to grow a business than women in Australia*. Kochie's Business Builders. https://www.kochiesbusinessbuilders.com.au/disappointing-why-its-easier-for-men-to-grow-a-business-than-women-in-austral ia/

Birley, S. (1987). Female entrepreneurs: Are they really any different? *Journal of Small Business Management, 27*(1), 32.

Bogenhold, D. (2004). Entrepreneurship: Multiple meanings and consequences. *International Journal of Entrepreneurship and Innovation Management, 4*(1), 3. doi:10.1504/IJEIM.2004.004496

Borquist, B. R., & de Bruin, A. (2019). Values and women-led social entrepreneurship. *International Journal of Gender and Entrepreneurship, 11*(2), 146–165. doi:10.1108/IJGE-08-2018-0093

Bourdieu, P. (2015). *Devlet üzerine. (Çev: A. Sümer)*. İletişim Yayınları.

Brahem, M., & Boussema, S. (2022). Social media entrepreneurship as an opportunity for women: The case of Facebook-commerce. *International Journal of Entrepreneurship and Innovation*. doi:10.1177/14657503211066010

Bridges, S., & Mann, S. (2019). Sexual orientation, legal partnerships and wages in Britain. *Work, Employment and Society, 33*(6), 1020–1038. doi:10.1177/0950017019873265

Brixiová, Z., Kangoye, T., & Said, M. (2020). Training, human capital, and gender gaps in entrepreneurial performance. In Economic Modelling, 85.. doi:10.1016/j.econmod.2019.11.006

Brixiová, Z., Kangoye, T., & Tregenna, F. (2020). Enterprising Women in Southern Africa: When Does Land Ownership Matter? *Journal of Family and Economic Issues, 41*(1), 37–51. doi:10.100710834-020-09663-2

Brush, C. G. (1992). Research on Women Business Owners: Past Trends, a New Perspective and Future Directions. *Entrepreneurship Theory and Practice, 16*(4), 5–30. doi:10.1177/104225879201600401

Brush, C. G., De Bruin, A., & Welter, F. (2009). A gender-aware framework for women's entrepreneurship. *International Journal of Gender and Entrepreneurship, 1*(1), 8–24. doi:10.1108/17566260910942318

Brydges, T., & Hracs, B. J. (2019). What motivates millennials? How intersectionality shapes the working lives of female entrepreneurs in Canada's fashion industry. *Gender, Place &Amp. Culture (Québec), 26*(4), 510–532. doi:10.1080/0966369X.2018.1552558

Brydges, T., & Sjöholm, J. (2019). Becoming a personal style blogger: Changing configurations and spatialities of aesthetic labour in the fashion industry. *International Journal of Cultural Studies, 22*(1), 119–139. doi:10.1177/1367877917752404

Bui, H. T., Kuan, A., & Chu, T. T. (2018). Female entrepreneurship in patriarchal society: Motivation and challenges. *Journal of Small Business &Amp. Entrepreneurship, 30*(4), 325–343. doi:10.1080/08276331.2018.1435841

Bukstein, D., & Gandelman, N. (2019). Glass ceilings in research: Evidence from a national program in Uruguay. *Research Policy, 48*(6), 1550–1563. doi:10.1016/j.respol.2019.03.007

Bulanova, O., Isaksen, E. J., & Kolvereid, L. (2016). Growth aspirations among women entrepreneurs in high growth firms. *Baltic Journal of Management, 11*(2), 187–206. doi:10.1108/BJM-11-2014-0204

Bullough, A., Guelich, U., Manolova, T. S., & Schjoedt, L. (2022). Women's entrepreneurship and culture: Gender role expectations and identities, societal culture, and the entrepreneurial environment. *Small Business Economics, 58*(2), 985–996. doi:10.100711187-020-00429-6

Burke, A. E., FitzRoy, F. R., & Nolan, M. A. (2002). Self-employment wealth and job creation: The roles of gender, non-pecuniary motivation and entrepreneurial ability. *Small Business Economics, 19*(3), 255–270. doi:10.1023/A:1019698607772

Butler, J. (2014). *Cinsiyet belası- feminizm ve kültürün altüst edilmesi. (Çev: B. Ertür).* Metis Yayınları.

Buttner, E. H. (1993). Female entrepreneurs: How far have they come? *Business Horizons, 36*(2), 59–65. doi:10.1016/S0007-6813(05)80039-4

Calderon, Iacovone, & Juarez. (2014). *Opportunity vs Necessity: Understanding the Heterogeneity of Female Micro-Entrepreneurs.* World Bank. https://www.worldbank.org/content/dam/Worldbank/Event/DEC/ABCDE/ABCDE-2015/378.%20Gabriela%20Calderon.pdf

Camacho, S., & Barrios, A. (2021). Social commerce affordances for female entrepreneurship: The case of Facebook. *Electronic Markets.* doi:10.100712525-021-00487-y

Caplan, P. (1987). *Cultural Construction of Sexuality.* Tavictock Publication.

Caporale, C. (2022). Soffitto di cristallo. In *Italia a che punto siamo?* Business Community.

Cardella, G. M., Hernández-Sánchez, B. R., & Sánchez-García, J. C. (2020). Women Entrepreneurship: A Systematic Review to Outline the Boundaries of Scientific Literature. *Frontiers in Psychology, 11*(July), 1–18. doi:10.3389/fpsyg.2020.01557 PMID:32765357

Casado-Díaz, J. M., Driha, O., & Simón, H. (2022). The gender wage gap in hospitality: New evidence from Spain. *Cornell Hospitality Quarterly, 63*(3), 399–417. doi:10.1177/1938965520971273

Castelló-Sirvent, F., & Pinazo-Dallenbach, P. (2021). Corruption shock in Mexico: FsQCA analysis of entrepreneurial intention in university students. *Mathematics, 9*(14), 1702. doi:10.3390/math9141702

Catford, J. (1998). Social entrepreneurs are vital for health promotion - But they need supportive environments too. *Health Promotion International, 13*(2), 95–97. doi:10.1093/heapro/13.2.95

Catherine, T. (2007). Kwantes, Cheryl A. Boglarsky (2004). Perceptions of organizational culture, leadership effectiveness and personal effectiveness across six countries [Elsevier.]. *Journal of International Management, 13*(2), 204–230. doi:10.1016/j.intman.2007.03.002

Ćatić-Kajtazović, E., Glavaš, J., & Kljajić-Dervić, M. (2022). The effects of creativity supported at the university on entrepreneurial behavior. *Ekonomski Vjesnik, 35*(1), 31–44. doi:10.51680/ev.35.1.3

Cavada, M. C., Bobek, V., Skoko, H., & Maček, A. (2018). Cultural Foundations of Female Entrepreneurship in Mexico: Challenges and Opportunities. *Naše Gospodarstvo/Our Economy, 64*(1), 28–40. doi:10.2478/ngoe-2018-0004

Cavada, M.C., Bobek, V., Skoko, H., & Maček, A. (2018). Cultural foundations of female entrepreneurship in Mexico: challenges and opportunities", *Naše Gospodarstvo/Our Economy, 64*(1), 28-40.

Cavallo, A., Ghezzi, A., Dell'Era, C., & Pellizzoni, E. (2019). Fostering digital entrepreneurship from startup to scaleup: The role of venture capital funds and angel groups. *Technological Forecasting and Social Change*, *145*, 24–35. doi:10.1016/j.techfore.2019.04.022

Census, E. (2013). *6th Economic Census*. Ministry of Statistics & Programme Implementation, Government of India.

Certo, T., & Miller, T. L. (2008). Social entrepreneurship: Key issues and concepts. *Business Horizons*, *51*(4), 267–271. doi:10.1016/j.bushor.2008.02.009

Cesaroni, F. M., Paola, D., & Paola, P. (2017). Women in business and social media: Implications for female entrepreneurship in emerging countries. *African Journal of Business Management*, *11*(14), 316–326. doi:10.5897/AJBM2017.8281

Chaker, H., & Zouaoui, S. (2022). Meeting the Challenge of Entrepreneurship with social media: The Case of Tunisian Women Entrepreneurs. *Journal of Entrepreneurship and Innovation in Emerging Economies*, *9*(1), 33–61. doi:10.1177/23939575221138439

Chakraborty, U., & Biswal, S. K. (2021). Psychological empowerment of women entrepreneurs: A netnographic study on twitter. *Management Research Review*. doi:10.1108/MRR-01-2021-0046

Chant, S. (2014). Exploring the "feminisation of poverty" in relation to women's work and home-based enterprise in slums of the Global South. *International Journal of Gender and Entrepreneurship*, *6*(3), 296–316. doi:10.1108/IJGE-09-2012-0035

Charumathi, B. (1998). Women entrepreneur's challenges and prospects. In C. Swarajya Lakshmi (Ed.), *Development of Women Entrepreneurship in India:Problems and Prospects*. Discovery Publishing House.

Chatterjee, N., Das, N., & Srivastava, N. K. (2018). A structural model assessing key factors affecting women's entrepreneurial success. *Journal of Entrepreneurship in Emerging Economies*, *11*(1), 122–151. doi:10.1108/JEEE-08-2016-0030

Chaudhry,I.S.,&Paquibut,R.Y.(2021).WomenEmpowermentthroughMicropreneurshipinOnlineBusinessesintheSultanateof Oman.*AcademyofEntrepreneurshipJournal*,*27*(1),1–14.https://www.scopus.com/inward/record.uri?eid=2-s2.0-85103106690&partnerID=40&md5=74db46e6d48a8ebf3a99fdfa2a24d862

Chaudhuri, S., Agrawal, A. K., Chatterjee, S., & Hussain, Z. (2022). Examining the role of gender on family business entrepreneurial intention: influence of government support and technology usage. *Journal of Family Business Management*.

Chhabra, S., Raghunathan, R., & Rao, N. M. (2020). The antecedents of entrepreneurial intention among women entrepreneurs in India. *Asia Pacific Journal of Innovation and Entrepreneurship*, *14*(1), 76–92. doi:10.1108/APJIE-06-2019-0034

Chipfunde, D., Yahaya, S. N., & Othman, N. A. (2021). The determinants influencing the performance of women entrepreneurs in malaysia: A conceptual framework. *Estudios de Economía Aplicada*, *39*(4). doi:10.25115/eea.v39i4.4577

Choi, S. (2019). Breaking through the glass ceiling: Social capital matters for women's career success? *International Public Management Journal*, *22*(2), 295–320. doi:10.1080/10967494.2018.1425225

Cho, Y., Park, J., Han, S. J., Sung, M., & Park, C. (2020). Women entrepreneurs in South Korea: Motivations, challenges, and career success. *European Journal of Training and Development*, *45*(2/3), 97–119. doi:10.1108/EJTD-03-2020-0039

Ciruela-Lorenzo, A. M., González-Sánchez, A., & Plaza-Angulo, J. J. (2020). An exploratory study on social entrepreneurship, empowerment and peace process. The case of Colombian women victims of the armed conflict. *Sustainability*, *12*(24), 10425. doi:10.3390u122410425

Clark, A., & Tomos, F. (2020). Entrepreneurial learning and the success of Welsh businesswomen. *Journal Women's Entrepreneurship and Education*, *2020*(1–2), 87–102. doi:10.28934/jwee20.12.pp87-102

Cobo, M. J., López-Herrera, A. G., Herrera-Viedma, E., & Herrera, F. (2011). Science Mapping Software Tools: Review, Analysis, and Cooperative Study Among Tools. *Journal of the American Society for Information Science and Technology, 62*(7), 1382–1402. doi:10.1002/asi.21525

Cockburn, C. (1991). *In the way of women: Men's resistance to sex equality in organizations.* Macmillan Education, Ltd. doi:10.1007/978-1-349-21571-3

Çolak, Z. (2021). Econometric Analysis on Gender Inequality and Economic Growth Relationship in Turkey, *MANAS. The Journal of Social Studies, 10*(2), 1094–1105.

Colombo, M. G., & Delmastro, M. (2001). Technology-based entrepreneurs: Does the internet make a difference? *Small Business Economics, 16*(3), 177–190. doi:10.1023/A:1011127205758

Connell, R. W. (2003). In M. Hussey (Ed.), *Schools and gender* (pp. 92–100). PrenticeHall.

Connor, R. F., & Bent-Goodley, T. B. (2016). Zanzibari social entrepreneurs and poverty alleviation strategies: Understanding efforts to build local community sustainability. *Journal of Community Practice, 24*(3), 302–318. doi:10.1080/10705422.2016.1201784

Cooper, A. C., & Artz, K. W. (1995). Determinants of satisfaction for entrepreneurs. *Journal of Business Venturing, 10*(6), 439–457. doi:10.1016/0883-9026(95)00083-K

Council of European Professional Informatics Societies (CEPIS). (n.d.). *Terms of Reference for the Information Society Group.* CEPIS. https://cepis.org/app/uploads/2020/01/13.TermsofReferenceforInformationSocietyGroup1-1.pdf

Cover, L. (2021, June 17). *7 statistics that prove the importance of social media marketing in business.* Sprout Social.

Cromie, S. (1987). Motivations of aspiring male and female entrepreneurs. *Journal of Organizational Behavior, 8*(3), 251–261. doi:10.1002/job.4030080306

Cuff, E. C., & Sharrock, W. W. ve Francis, D. W. (2013). Sosyolojide perspektifler. (Ü. Tatlıcan, Çev.). İstanbul: Say Yayınları.

Da Fonseca, A. L. A., & Campos, R. D. (2021). The cultural intertwining of consumption and entrepreneurship: A selective review of qualitative studies. *Journal of Business Research, 135*, 149–162. doi:10.1016/j.jbusres.2021.06.032

Dacin, M. T., Dacin, P. A., & Tracey, P. (2011). Social entrepreneurship: A critique and future directions. *Organization Science, 22*(5), 1203–1213. doi:10.1287/orsc.1100.0620

Dacin, P. A., Dacin, M. T., & Matear, M. (2010). Social entrepreneurship: Why we don't need a new theory and how we move forward from here. *The Academy of Management Perspectives, 24*(3), 37–57. doi:10.5465/AMP.2010.52842950

Dai, H., Xia, T., & Zhao, S. (2022). Unisex Style: The History, Current Situation and Future. *Proceedings of the 2022 8th International Conference on Humanities and Social Science Research* (ICHSSR 2022). Atlantis Press SARL 10.2991/assehr.k.220504.205

Dam, L. B., & Pillai, D. (2021). Crafting Virtual Community of Indigenous Entrepreneurs: Case in Social Entrepreneurship. *South Asian Journal of Business and Management Cases.* doi:10.1177/2277977921991916

Damwad, (2007). *Women Entrepreneurship – A Nordic Perspective.* Nordic Innovation Centre.

Danish, A. Y., & Smith, H. L. (2012). Female entrepreneurship in Saudi Arabia: Opportunities and challenges. *International Journal of Gender and Entrepreneurship, 4*(3), 216–235. doi:10.1108/17566261211264136

Das, M. (2000). Women Entrepreneurs from India: Problems, Motivations and Success Factors. *Journal of Small Business and Entrepreneurship, 15*(4), 67–81. doi:10.1080/08276331.2000.10593294

Datta, P. B., & Gailey, R. (2012). Empowering women through social entrepreneurship: Case study of a women's cooperative in India. *Entrepreneurship Theory and Practice, 36*(3), 569–587. doi:10.1111/j.1540-6520.2012.00505.x

Davidson, E., & Vaast, E. (2010). Digital entrepreneurship and its socio-material enactment. In *43rd Hawaii International Conference on System Sciences* (pp. 1–10). IEEE.

Dawson, C., & Henley, A. (2012). "Push" versus "pull" entrepreneurship: An ambiguous distinction? *International Journal of Entrepreneurial Behavior &Amp. Research, 18*(6), 697–719. doi:10.1108/13552551211268139

Dawson, C., & Henley, A. (2015). Gender, risk, and venture creation intentions. *Journal of Small Business Management, 53*(2), 501–515. doi:10.1111/jsbm.12080

de Siles, L. E. (2011, May 6). *Female Entrepreneurship Theory: A Multidisciplinary Review of Resources*. SSRN. https://papers.ssrn.com/sol3/papers.cfm?abstract_id=1833385

Debord, G. (2006). *Gösteri Toplumu, Çev: Ayşen Ekmekçi, Okşan Taşkent*. Ayrıntı Yayınları.

Debroux, P. (2016). *Female Entrepreneurship in East and South-East Asia: Opportunities and Challenges (Chandos Asian Studies Series)* (1st ed.). Chandos Publishing.

Deng, S., Wang, X., & Alon, I. (2011). Framework for female entrepreneurship in China. *International Journal of Business and Emerging Markets, 3*(1), 3. doi:10.1504/IJBEM.2011.037682

Dhanamalar, M., Preethi, S., & Yuvashree, S. (2020). Impact of digitization on women's empowerment: A study of rural and urban regions in India. *Journal of International Women's Studies, 21*(5), 107–112.

Dickel, P., & Eckardt, G. (2021). Who wants to be a social entrepreneur? The role of gender and sustainability orientation. *Journal of Small Business Management, 59*(1), 196–218. doi:10.1080/00472778.2019.1704489

Dimov, D. (2016). Toward a design science of entrepreneurship. In *Models of start-up thinking and action: Theoretical, empirical, and pedagogical approaches* (Vol. 18, pp. 1–31). Emerald Group Publishing Limited.

Dixit, A. R., Malik, N., Seth, M., & Sethi, D. (2023). The role of social entrepreneurial leadership and benchmarking in women empowerment. *Benchmarking, 30*(1), 180–195. doi:10.1108/BIJ-08-2021-0493

Dobón, S. R., & Soriano, D. R. (2008). Exploring alternative approaches in service industries: The role of entrepreneurship. *Service Industries Journal, 28*(7), 877–882. doi:10.1080/02642060701846879

Domazet, I. (2018). Improving competitiveness and economic development through FDI. In *Developmental State and Millennium Development Goals: country experiences* (pp. 169–189). World Scientific Publishing Co. doi:10.1142/9789813235281_0008

Donovan, J. (1997). *Feminist teori. (Çev: A. Bora, M. Ağduk-Gevrek ve F. Sayılan)*. İletişim Yayınları.

Dubois, A. J. A. (1924). *Hindu Manners, Customs, and Ceremonies, Beauchamp, H.K. (edited and corrected)*. Clarendon Press.

Durmaz, Ş. (2016). Women and Their Challenges in Labor Market. *Ahi Evran University Institute of Social Sciences Journal, 2*(3), 37-60. https://dergipark.org.tr/en/pub/aeusbed/issue/26794/282028

Dutta, N., & Mallick, S. (2018). Enabling Women Entrepreneurs: Exploring Factors That Mitigate the Negative Impact of Fertility Rates on Female Entrepreneurship. *Kyklos, 71*(3), 402–432. doi:10.1111/kykl.12175

Dye, K., & Golnaraghi, G. (2015). Organizational benefits through diversity management. The Oxford Handbook of Diversity in Organizations, 255.

Eagly, A. H., & Carli, L. L. (2003). The female leadership advantage: An evaluation of the evidence. *The Leadership Quarterly*, *14*(6), 807–834. doi:10.1016/j.leaqua.2003.09.004

Echchabi, A., Omar, M. M. S., & Ayedh, A. M. (2020). Entrepreneurial intention among female university students in Oman. *Journal for International Business and Entrepreneurship Development*, *12*(4), 280–297. doi:10.1504/JIBED.2020.110251

Ehrenreich, B. (2010). *Witches, Midwives, and Nurses: A History of Women Healers*. Feminist Press at CUNY.

Einstein, A. (2021). *İzafiyet Teorisi, (Çev: Gülen Aktaş)*. Say Yayınları.

Eklundh, E. (2020). The Cultural Side of Populism and Rethinking Money, Rebuilding Community. *Excluding Emotions: The Performative Function of Populism, Partecipazione, and Conflitto, 13*(1).

Elam, A. B., Brush, C. G., Greene, P. G., Baumer, B., Dean, M., & Heavlow, R. (2019). *Global Entrepreneurship Monitor 2018/2019 Women's Entrepreneurship Report*. Babson College: Smith College and the Global Entrepreneurship Research Association.

Eliana Carranza, Chandra Shekhar Dhakal, & Inessa Love. (2018). Female Entrepreneurs: How and Why are They Different? *Worldbank*.

Enterprises. (2023). A report of the Strategic Policy Forum on Digital Entrepreneurship. *Europea*. http://ec.europa.eu/DocsRoom/documents/9462/attachments/1/translations/en/renditions/native

Entrialgo, M., & Iglesias, V. (2018). Are the Intentions to Entrepreneurship of Men and Women Shaped Differently? the Impact of Entrepreneurial Role-Model Exposure and Entrepreneurship Education. *Entrepreneurship Research Journal*, *8*(1). doi:10.1515/erj-2017-0013

Erdogan, S., Yıldırım, D. C., & Tosuner, Ö. (2012). The Effect of Gender Inequality in Education on Health:Evidence from Turkey. *Educational Sciences: Theory and Practice*, *12*(3), 1860–1866.

Essex, K. (2022). *Kleopatra: Book 1: The Early Years*. Routledge.

EU Science Hub - European Commission. (2020). *Learning And Skills for The Digital Era*. EC. https://ec.europa.eu/jrc/en/research-topic/learning-and-skills

European Commission. (2015). *Digital Transformation of European Industry and European Commission*. EC.

European Commission. (2020). *The Entrepreneurship 2020 Action Plan - Internal Market, Industry, Entrepreneurship and SMEs*. EC. https://ec.europa.eu/growth/smes/promoting-entrepreneurship/action-plan_en

Fachrunnisa, O., Adhiatma, A., Lukman, N., & Ab Majid, M. N. (2020). Towards SMEs' digital transformation: The role of agile leadership and strategic flexibility. *Journal of Small Business Strategy*, *30*(3), 65–85. https://libjournals.mtsu.edu/index.php/jsbs/article/view/1610

Faiza, S., Saeed, L., & Muhammad, A. (2022). Institutions and Women Entrepreneurship: The Mediating Role of Women Entrepreneurial Self Efficacy and Ethical Decision Making. *Journal of Asian Finance*, *9*(6), 33–0044. doi:10.13106/jafeb.2022.vol9.no6.033

Farrokhnia, M., Pijeira-Díaz, H. J., Noroozi, O., & Hatami, J. (2019). Computer-supported collaborative concept mapping: The effects of different instructional designs on conceptual understanding and knowledge co-construction. *Computers & Education, 142*, 103640. doi:10.1016/j.compedu.2019.103640

Fayolle, A., & Gailly, B. (2013). The Impact of Entrepreneurship Education on Entrepreneurial Attitudes and Intention: Hysteresis and Persistence. *Journal of Small Business Management, 53*(1), 75–93. doi:10.1111/jsbm.12065

Fazalbhoy, S. (2014). Women Entrepreneurship as the Way for Economic Development. *Annual Research Journal of Symbiosis Centre for Management Studies, 2*(1), 117–127. https://www.scmspune.ac.in/chapter/pdf/Chapter%2010.pdf

Fernandes, C. E., Pereira, M., & Madeira, M. J. (2020). Fashion design entrepreneurship: A qualitative approach. In Textiles, Identity, and Innovation: In Touch (1st ed.). CRC Press. doi:10.1201/9780429286872-23

Fernandes, C., Ferreira, J. J., Veiga, P. M., Kraus, S., & Dabić, M. (2022). Digital entrepreneurship platforms: Mapping the field and looking towards a holistic approach. *Technology in Society, 70*(February), 101979. doi:10.1016/j.techsoc.2022.101979

Ferreira, J., Fernandes, C., & Ratten, V. (2019). The effects of technology transfers and institutional factors on economic growth: Evidence from Europe and Oceania. *The Journal of Technology Transfer, 44*(5), 1505–1528. doi:10.100710961-019-09730-3

Firestone, S. (2019). *Cinselliğin Diyalektiği, (Çev: Yurdanur Salman).* Payel Yayınları.

Folberg A.M. (2016). *Preferences for organizations that emphasize interpersonal relationships or entrepreneurship among Arab-and Jewish-Israeli women: The roles of culture, goal orientation, and traditionalism.* University of North Carolina.

Forson, C., & Özbilgin, M. (2003). Dot-Com Women Entrepreneurs in the UK. *International Journal of Entrepreneurship and Innovation, 4*(1), 13–24. doi:10.5367/000000003101299366

Foucault, M. (2000). *Kelimeler ve Şeyler (Mehmet Ali Kılıçbay).* Ayrıntı Yayınları.

Foucault, M. (2010). *Cinselliğin tarihi (Çev: H. U. Tanrıöver).* Ayrıntı Yayınları.

Frankel, S., Cuevas, L., Lim, H., & Benjamin, S. (2021). Exploring Tattooed Presentation on YouTube: A Case Study of Kat von D. *Fashion Theory, 0*(0), 1–21. doi:10.1080/1362704X.2021.1882769

Gagnon, S., Augustin, T., & Cuckier, W. (2021). Interplay for change in equality, diversity and inclusion studies. *Human Relations*, 00187267211002239.

Galvez, L., & Fernández, P. (2007). Female Entrepreneurship in Spain during the Nineteenth and Twentieth Centuries. *Business History Review, 81*(3), 495–515. doi:10.1017/S0007680500036692

Gasparyan, A. Y., Ayvazyan, L., & Kitas, G. D. (2013). Multidisciplinary bibliographic databases. *Journal of Korean Medical Science, 28*(9), 1270–1275. doi:10.3346/jkms.2013.28.9.1270 PMID:24015029

Gauntlett, D. (2008). *Media, genderandidentity: An introduction.* Routledge. doi:10.4324/9780203930014

Gaweł, A., & Mroczek-Dąbrowska, K. (2021). Gender pay gap in explaining female entrepreneurship – industry perspective of selected European countries. *International Journal of Manpower, 43*(9), 42–59. doi:10.1108/IJM-12-2020-0554

Ghouse, S., McElwee, G., Meaton, J., & Durrah, O. (2017). Barriers to rural women entrepreneurs in Oman. *International Journal of Entrepreneurial Behaviour & Research, 23*(6), 998–1016. doi:10.1108/IJEBR-02-2017-0070

Gilbert, J. A., Stead, B. A., & Ivancevich, J. M. (1999). Diversity management: A new organizational paradigm. *Journal of Business Ethics, 21*(1), 61–76. doi:10.1023/A:1005907602028

Ginalski, S. (2021). Who runs the firm? A long-term analysis of gender inequality on Swiss corporate boards. *Enterprise and Society*, *22*(1), 183–211. doi:10.1017/eso.2019.64

Ginsborg, P. (2010). *Gündelik Hayat Politikaları, (Çev: Muhsin Önal Mengüşoğlu)*. Açılım Kitap.

Girotra, K., Terwiesch, C., & Ulrich, K. T. (2010). Idea Generation and the Quality of the Best Idea. *Management Science*, *56*(4), 591–605. doi:10.1287/mnsc.1090.1144

Global Entrepreneurship Monitor Releases New Research Highlighting Women's Entrepreneurship Trends Across the Globe. (n.d.). GEM Global Entrepreneurship Monitor. https://www.gemconsortium.org/reports/womens-entrepreneurship

Global Entrepreneurship Monitor. (2022). *Global Entrepreneurship Monitor 2021/2022 Global Report Opportunity Amid Disruption Global Entrepreneurship Monitor 2021/2022 Global Report Key GEM Definitions and Abbreviations 6*. http://www.witchwoodhouse.comBBRDesignhttps://bbrdesign.co.uk

Goldberg, S. (1994). *The Inevitability of Patriarchy*. William Morrow and Company.

Gomes, S., Santos, T., Sousa, M., Oliveira, J. C., Oliveira, M., & Lopes, J. M. (2022). Entrepreneurial intention among women: A case study in the Portuguese academy. *Strategic Change*, *31*(2), 197–209. doi:10.1002/jsc.2489

Gordon, E., & Natarajan, K. (2007). Entrepreneurship development. Himalaya 300 publication house.

Gramm, V., Torre, C. D., & Membretti, A. (2020). Farms in progress-providing childcare services as a means of empowering women farmers in South Tyrol, Italy. *Sustainability*, *12*(2), 467. doi:10.3390u12020467

Grant, M. J., & Booth, A. (2009). A typology of reviews: An analysis of 14 review types and associated methodologies. *Health Information and Libraries Journal*, *26*(2), 91–108. doi:10.1111/j.1471-1842.2009.00848.x PMID:19490148

Griffiths, M. D., Gundry, L. K., & Kickul, J. R. (2013). The socio-political, economic, and cultural determinants of social entrepreneurship activity An empirical examination. *Journal of Small Business and Enterprise Development*, *20*(2), 1462–6004. doi:10.1108/14626001311326761

Grimes, M. G., Gehman, J., & Cao, K. (2018). Positively deviant: Identity work through B Corporation certification. *Journal of Business Venturing*, *33*(2), 130–148. doi:10.1016/j.jbusvent.2017.12.001

Growth and Stability in the Middle East and North Africa -- Economic Overview. (n.d.). IMF. https://www.imf.org/external/pubs/ft/mena/04econ.htm

Günsoy, G., & Özsoy, C. (2012). VAR Analysis of Woman Labor Force, Education and Growth Relations in Turkey. *Finans Politik & Ekonomik Yorumlar*, *49*(568), 23–42.

Gupta, K. R., & Gupta, J. R. (2008). Indian Economy, Atlantic Publishers & Dist, New Delhi.Ladge, J., Eddleston, K.A. and Sugiyama, K. (2019), "Am I an entrepreneur? How imposter fears hinder women entrepreneurs' business growth. *Business Horizons*, *62*(5), 615–624.

Gupta, N., & Etzkowitz, H. (2021). Women founders in a high-tech incubator: Negotiating entrepreneurial identity in the Indian socio-cultural context. *International Journal of Gender and Entrepreneurship*, *13*(4), 353–372. doi:10.1108/IJGE-11-2020-0181

Gupta, P., Chauhan, S., Paul, J., & Jaiswal, M. P. (2020). Social entrepreneurship research: A review and future research agenda. *Journal of Business Research*, *113*, 209–229. doi:10.1016/j.jbusres.2020.03.032

Gupta, V. K., Wieland, A. M., & Turban, D. B. (2019). Gender characterizations in entrepreneurship: A multi-level investigation of sex-role stereotypes about high-growth, commercial, and social entrepreneurs. *Journal of Small Business Management*, *57*(1), 131–153. doi:10.1111/jsbm.12495

Halkias, D., Nwajiuba, C., Harkiolakis, N., & Caracatsanis, S. M. (2011). Challenges facing women entrepreneurs in Nigeria. *Management Research Review*, *34*(2), 221–235. doi:10.1108/01409171111102821

Hallak, R., Assaker, G., & Lee, C. (2015). Tourism Entrepreneurship Performance: The Effects of Place Identity, Self-Efficacy, and Gender. *Journal of Travel Research*, *54*(1), 36–51. doi:10.1177/0047287513513170

Hall, S. (2017). *Temsil, Anlam ve Dil. S. Hall içinde, Temsil: Kültürel Temsiller ve Anlamlandırma Uygulamaları. Dündar, İ. (Çev.)*. Pinhan.

Hall, S., & Jacques, M. (1995). *Yeni Zamanlar*. Ayrıntı Yayınları.

Hansen, H., & Rand, J. (2014). The Myth of Female Credit Discrimination in African Manufacturing. *The Journal of Development Studies*, *50*(1), 81–96. doi:10.1080/00220388.2013.849337

Hardt, M., & Negri, A. (2002). *İmparatorluk. (Çev: A.Yılmaz)*. Ayrıntı Yayınları.

Hardt, M., & Negri, A. (2005). *Multitude: War and Democracy in the Age of Empire*. Penguin Books.

Hartman, R. L., & Barber, E. G. (2020). Women in the workforce: The effect of gender on occupational self-efficacy, work engagement and career aspirations. *Gender in Management*, *35*(1), 92–118. doi:10.1108/GM-04-2019-0062

Hashim, S., Naldi, L., & Markowska, M. (2021). "The royal award goes to ... ": Legitimacy processes for female-led family ventures .... *Journal of Family Business Strategy*, *12*(3), 100358. doi:10.1016/j.jfbs.2020.100358

Haslam, S. A., & Ryan, M. K. (2008). The road to the glass cliff: Differences in the perceived suitability of men and women for leadership positions in succeeding and failing organizations. *The Leadership Quarterly*, *19*(5), 530–546. doi:10.1016/j.leaqua.2008.07.011

Hassanzadeh, M., Hatami, J., Latifi, S., Farrokhnia, M. R., & Saheb, T. (2016, September). Teaching science for understanding: The positive impact of simultaneous concept mapping and computer simulations. In *International Conference on Concept Mapping* (pp. 192-202). Springer, Cham.10.1007/978-3-319-45501-3_15

Haugh, H. M., & Talwar, A. (2016). Linking social entrepreneurship and social change: The mediating role of empowerment. *Journal of Business Ethics*, *133*(4), 643–658. doi:10.100710551-014-2449-4

Hechavarría, D. M., & Brieger, S. A. (2022). Practice rather than preach: Cultural practices and female social entrepreneurship. *Small Business Economics*, *58*(2), 1131–1151. doi:10.100711187-020-00437-6

Hechavarría, D. M., Terjesen, S. A., Ingram, A. E., Renko, M., Justo, R., & Elam, A. (2017). Taking care of business: The impact of culture and gender on entrepreneurs' blended value creation goals. *Small Business Economics*, *48*(1), 225–257. doi:10.100711187-016-9747-4

Heidari, E., Salimi, G., & Mehrvarz, M. (2020). The influence of online social networks and online social capital on constructing a new graduate students' professional identity. *Interactive Learning Environments*, 1–18. doi:10.1080/10494820.2020.1769682

Helene, L'Heuillet, (2020). *Gecikmeye Övgü, Zaman Nereye Gitti?, (Çev:Şehsuvar Aktaş)*, İstanbul, YKY.

Henfridsson, O., & Yoo, Y. (2014). The liminality of trajectory shifts in institutional entrepreneurship. *Organization Science*, *25*(3), 932–950. doi:10.1287/orsc.2013.0883

Henry, C. (2009). Women and the creative industries: Exploring the popular appeal. *Creative Industries Journal, 2*(2), 143–160. doi:10.1386/cij.2.2.143/1

Hidalgo, G., Monticelli, J. M., & Bortolaso, I. V. (2021). Social capital as a driver of social entrepreneurship. *Journal of Social Entrepreneurship*, 1–24. doi:10.1080/19420676.2021.1951819

Hietschold, N., & Voegtlin, C. (2022). Blinded by a social cause? Differences in cognitive Biases between social and commercial entrepreneurs. *Journal of Social Entrepreneurship, 13*(3), 431–452. doi:10.1080/19420676.2021.1880466

Hossain, M., & Rahman, M. F. (2018). Social Media and the Creation of Entrepreneurial Opportunity for Women. *Management, 8*(4), 99–108. doi:10.5923/j.mm.20180804.02

Hota, P. K., Subramanian, B., & Narayanamurthy, G. (2020). Mapping the intellectual structure of social entrepreneurship research: A citation/co-citation analysis. *Journal of Business Ethics, 166*(1), 89–114. doi:10.100710551-019-04129-4

How women are transforming the Arab world's start-up scene. (2020, February 7). World Economic Forum. https://www.weforum.org/agenda/2018/07/start-up-middle-east-arab-women-transforming-entrepreneurship/

Huang, Y., Li, P., Wang, J., & Li, K. (2022). Innovativeness and entrepreneurial performance of female entrepreneurs. *Journal of Innovation and Knowledge, 7*(4), 100257. doi:10.1016/j.jik.2022.100257

Hundera, M., Duysters, G., Naudé, W., & Dijkhuizen, J. (2019). How do female entrepreneurs in developing countries cope with role conflict? *International Journal of Gender and Entrepreneurship, 11*(2), 120–145. doi:10.1108/IJGE-12-2018-0138

Ibáñez, M. J. (2022). Social entrepreneurship review: A gap in the Latin American context. *Management Research, 20*(1), 6–24. doi:10.1108/MRJIAM-09-2021-1232

Ilgaz, Z. (2022, June 23). 8 Qualities to Drive Your Success as a Female. *Entrepreneur.* https://www.entrepreneur.com/leadership/8-qualities-female-entrepreneurs-need-to-succeed/428136

Illich, I. (1996). *Gender(Çev: A. fethi).* Ayraç Yayınları.

Indonesian Ministry of Health. (2005). *Reproductive Health National Policy and Strategy in Indonesia.*

Inter-agency Working Group on Reproductive Health in Crises. (2010). *Inter-Institutional Field Handbook Reproductive Health in emergency situations.* IWGRHC.

International Labor Organization. (2018). *Women in Business and Management: Gaining Momentum in Eastern Europe and Central Asia.* International Labor Office. https://www.ilo.org/wcmsp5/groups/public/---ed_dialogue/---act_emp/documents/publication/wcms_624225.pdf

Isa, F. M., Jaganathan, M., Ahmdon, M. A. S., & Ibrahim, H. M. (2019). Malaysian Women Entrepreneurs: Some Emerging Issues and Challenges of Entering Global Market. *International Journal of Academic Research in Business & Social Sciences, 8*(12). doi:10.6007/IJARBSS/v8-i12/5261

Isaga, N. (2019). Start-up motives and challenges facing female entrepreneurs in Tanzania. *International Journal of Gender and Entrepreneurship, 11*(2), 102–119. doi:10.1108/IJGE-02-2018-0010

Ivanovic, Dj., Simovic, V., Domazet, I., & Antonijević, M. (2021). Average Matching Levels for Two DigComp Competence Areas of the Female Entrepreneurs in Serbia. *Journal of Women's Entrepreneurship and Education., 3-4*, 42–60.

Jaafar, M., Othman, R., & Jalali, A. (2014). Main Determinations of Female Entrepreneurs in the Construction Industry in Malaysia. *Project Management Journal, 45*(1), 76–86. doi:10.1002/pmj.21391

Jabeen, F., & Faisal, M. N. (2018). Imperatives for improving entrepreneurial behavior among females in the UAE. *Gender in Management, 33*(3), 234–252. doi:10.1108/GM-03-2016-0042

Jamali, D. (2009). Constraints and opportunities facing women entrepreneurs in developing countries: A relational perspective. *Gender in Management, 24*(4), 232–251. doi:10.1108/17542410910961532

Jarrodi, H., Byrne, J., & Bureau, S. (2019). A political ideology lens on social entrepreneurship motivations. *Entrepreneurship and Regional Development, 31*(7–8), 583–604. doi:10.1080/08985626.2019.1596353

Jha, P., Makkad, M., & Mittal, S. (2018). Performance-oriented factors for women entrepreneurs–a scale development perspective. *Journal of Entrepreneurship in Emerging Economies, 10*(329–360), 148–167.

Jha, P., & Alam, M. M. (2022). Antecedents of women entrepreneurs' performance: An empirical perspective. *Management Decision, 60*(1), 86–122. doi:10.1108/MD-07-2020-0849

Jia, H., Xu, Z., Lin, S., & Jiang, F. (2021). Does persistence make you healthy? An empirical study on female entrepreneurs from China. *BMC Women's Health, 21*(1), 327. Advance online publication. doi:10.118612905-021-01471-6 PMID:34496817

Jiménez-Zarco, A. I., Clemente-Almendros, J. A., González-González, I., & Aracil-Jordà, J. (2021). Female Micro-Entrepreneurs and Social Networks: Diagnostic Analysis of the Influence of Social-Media Marketing Strategies on Brand Financial Performance. *Frontiers in Psychology, 12*, 630058. doi:10.3389/fpsyg.2021.630058 PMID:33912108

Jose, S. (2018). Strategic use of digital promotion strategies among female emigrant entrepreneurs in UAE. *International Journal of Emerging Markets, 13*(6), 1699–1718. doi:10.1108/IJoEM-10-2016-0268

Jost, J. T., & Amodio, D. M. (2012). Political ideology as motivated social cognition: Behavioral and neuroscientific evidence. *Motivation and Emotion, 36*(1), 55–64. doi:10.100711031-011-9260-7

Kabeer, N. (1999). Resources, agency, achievements: Reflections on the measurement of women's empowerment. *Development and Change, 30*(3), 435–464. doi:10.1111/1467-7660.00125

Kamberidou, I. (2013). Women entrepreneurs: 'we cannot have change unless we have men in the room.'. *Journal of Innovation and Entrepreneurship, 2*(1), 6. doi:10.1186/2192-5372-2-6

Kamberidou, I. (2020). "Distinguished" women entrepreneurs in the digital economy and the multitasking whirlpool. *Journal of Innovation and Entrepreneurship, 9*(1), 3. doi:10.118613731-020-0114-y

Kantor, P. (2002). Gender, microenterprise success and cultural context: The case of South Asia. *Entrepreneurship Theory and Practice, 26*(4), 131–143. doi:10.1177/104225870202600408

Kao, R. W. (1993). Defining Entrepreneurship: Past, Present and? *Creativity and Innovation Management, 2*(1), 69–70. doi:10.1111/j.1467-8691.1993.tb00073.x

Karatas, M. (2017). Diversity Dimensions of Entrepreneurship: Addressing Multiple Strands of Diversity in Entrepreneurship Research. In *Management and Diversity*. Emerald Publishing Limited. doi:10.1108/S2051-233320160000004011

Kargwell, S. (2021). The impact of horizontal revolution on small and medium size enterprises owned by women: The context of the UAE. *International Journal of Entrepreneurship and Small Business, 44*(3), 256–273. doi:10.1504/IJESB.2021.119230

Kasa, H., & Alptekin, V. (2015). The Effect of Female Labor Force to Growth in Turkey. *Sosyal Bilimler Meslek Yüksekokulu Dergisi, 18*(1), 1–24.

Kedmenec, I., Rebernik, M., & Perić, J. (2015). The impact of individual characteristics on intentions to pursue social entrepreneurship. *Ekonomski Pregled, 66*(2), 119–137. https://www.researchgate.net/publication/279494290

Kelly, M. G. (2016). *Uluslararası biyopolitika: foucault, küreselleşme ve emperyalizm (Çev. U. Özmakas)*. Pharmakon Kitap.

Kepler, E., & Shane, S. (2007). *Are Male and Female Entrepreneurs Really That Different*. Research Papers in Economics.

Kerr, S. Kerr, W., & Xu, T. (2018). Personality Traits of Entrepreneurs: A Review of Recent Literature. Foundations and Trends in Entrepreneurship. doi:10.1561/0300000080

Kessler, M. M. (1963). Bibliographic coupling between scientific papers. *American Documentation, 14*(1), 10–25. doi:10.1002/asi.5090140103

Kézai, P. K., & Szombathelyi, M. K. (2021). Factors Effecting Female Startuppers in Hungary. *Economia e Sociologia, 14*(4), 186–203. doi:10.14254/2071-789X.2021/14-4/11

Khandelwal & Sehgal. (2018). Exploring work-family interface for Indian women entrepreneurs. Gender in Management: An International Journal, 33. doi:10.1108/GM-04-2016-0075

Kimbu, A. N., & Ngoasong, M. Z. (2016). Women as vectors of social entrepreneurship. *Annals of Tourism Research, 60*, 63–79. doi:10.1016/j.annals.2016.06.002

Kimjeon, J., & Davidsson, P. (2022). External enablers of entrepreneurship: A review and agenda for accumulation of strategically actionable knowledge. *Entrepreneurship Theory and Practice, 46*(3), 643–687. doi:10.1177/10422587211010673

Kluzer, S., & Pujol Priego, L. (2018). DigComp into Action - Get inspired, make it happen. S. In: Carretero, Y. Punie, R. Vuorikari, M. Cabrera, and O'Keefe, W. (Eds.). JRC Science for Policy Report, EUR 29115 EN. Publications Office of the European Union. doi:10.2760/112945

Kobeissi, N. (2010). Gender factors and female entrepreneurship: International evidence and policy implications. *Journal of International Entrepreneurship, 8*(1), 1–35. doi:10.100710843-010-0045-y

Kong, H., & Kim, H. (2022). Does National Gender Equality Matter? Gender Difference in the Relationship between Entrepreneurial Human Capital and Entrepreneurial Intention. *Sustainability (Switzerland), 14*(2), 928. Advance online publication. doi:10.3390u14020928

Kovačić, Z. (1994). *Multivarijaciona analiza*. Beograd: Ekonomski fakultet

Kristeva, J. (2012). *Kadın Dehası, (Çev: Zeynep Mertoğlu Onur)*. Pinhan Yayıncılık.

Krueger, D. (2000). Characteristics Of The Female Entrepreneur. *Journal of Business and Entrepreneurship, 12*(1), 87-0_12. https://christuniversity.knimbus.com/loginAndLaunch?docUrl=?url=https://www.proquest.com/scholarly-journals/characterist ics-female-entrepreneur/docview/214235108/se-2

Kruse, P., Wach, D., Costa, S., & Moriano, J. A. (2019). Values Matter, Don't They?–Combining Theory of Planned Behavior and Personal Values as Predictors of Social Entrepreneurial Intention. *Journal of Social Entrepreneurship, 10*(1), 55–83. doi:10.1080/19420676.2018.1541003

Kuadli, J. (2022). *Women Entrepreneurs Statistics*. Legal Jobs. https://legaljobs.io/blog/women-entrepreneurs-statistics/#:~:text=How%20many%20female%20entrepreneurs%20are,in%20the%20l
ast%2020%20years

Kumar, A. (2013). Women entrepreneurs in a masculine society: Inclusive strategy for sustainable outcomes. *The International Journal of Organizational Analysis*, *21*(3), 373–384. doi:10.1108/IJOA-01-2013-0636

Kumari, G., & Eguruze, E. S. (2022). Positive deviance traits and social entrepreneurship for women empowerment amid COVID-19. *IIM Kozhikode Society & Management Review*, *11*(1), 109–125. doi:10.1177/22779752211030697

Kumar, S., & Singh, N. (2021). Entrepreneurial prospects and challenges for women amidst COVID-19: A case study of Delhi, India. *Fulbright Review of Economics and Policy*, *1*(2), 205–226. doi:10.1108/FREP-09-2021-0057

Kurczewska, A., & Białek, J. (2014). Is the interplay between self-efficacy and entrepreneurial intention gender-dependent? *Argumenta Oeconomica*, *33*(2), 23–38. doi:10.15611/aoe.2014.2.02

Kuzminska, O., Mazorchuk, M., Morze, N., Pavlenko, V., & Prohorov, A. (2019). Study of Digital Competence of the Students and Teachers in Ukraine. *14th International Conference, ICTERI 2018*, Kyiv, Ukraine. 10.1007/978-3-030-13929-2_8

Kwong, C., Jones-Evans, D., & Thompson, P. (2012). Differences in perceptions of access to finance between potential male and female entrepreneurs. *International Journal of Entrepreneurial Behavior &Amp. Research*, *18*(1), 75–97. doi:10.1108/13552551211201385

Lacan, J. (2020). *Fallusun Anlamı, (Çev: Saffet Murat Tura)*. Altıkırkbeş Yayınları.

Ladge, J., Eddleston, K. A., & Sugiyama, K. (2019). Am I an entrepreneur? How imposter fears hinder women entrepreneurs' business growth. *Business Horizons*, *62*(5), 615–624. doi:10.1016/j.bushor.2019.05.001

Lambert, J. (2016). Cultural diversity as a mechanism for innovation: Workplace diversity and the absorptive capacity framework.

Lasprogata, G. A., & Cotten, M. N. (2003). Contemplating "enterprise": The business and legal challenges of social entrepreneurship. *American Business Law Journal*, *41*(1), 67–114. doi:10.1111/j.1744-1714.2003.tb00002.x

Latif, M., & Ali, S. (2021). Managerial ties as determinant of social entrepreneurial intentions: Does gender make a difference? *Journal of Public Affairs*, *21*(2), e2183. doi:10.1002/pa.2183

Lazzarato, M. (2006)... *Frombiopowertobiopolitics, TailoringBiotochnologies*, *2*(2), 11–20.

Lemke, T. (2016). *Biyopolitika. (Çev: U. Özmakas)*. İletişim Yayınları.

Lerner, M., Brush, C., & Hisrich, R. (1997). Israeli women entrepreneurs: An examination of factors affecting performance. *Journal of Business Venturing*, *12*(4), 315–339. doi:10.1016/S0883-9026(96)00061-4

Levitt, P., & Schiller, N. G. (2004). Conceptualizing Simultaneity: A Transnational Social Field Perspective on Society. *The International Migration Review*, *38*(3), 1002–1039. doi:10.1111/j.1747-7379.2004.tb00227.x

Liberati, A., Altman, D. G., Tetzlaff, J., Mulrow, C., Gøtzsche, P. C., Ioannidis, J. P. A., Clarke, M., Devereaux, P. J., Kleijnen, J., & Moher, D. (2009). The PRISMA statement for reporting systematic reviews and meta-analyses of studies that evaluate health care interventions: Explanation and elaboration. *Journal of Clinical Epidemiology*, *6*(7), 1–28. doi:10.1016/j.jclinepi.2009.06.006 PMID:19631507

Li, L., Su, F., Zhang, W., & Mao, J. Y. (2018). Digital transformation by SME entrepreneurs: A capability perspective. *Information Systems Journal*, *28*(6), 1129–1157. doi:10.1111/isj.12153

Litt, E. (2013). Measuring users' internet skills: A review of past assessments and a look toward the future. *New Media & Society, 15*(4), 612–630. doi:10.1177/1461444813475424

Llados-Masllorens, J., & Ruiz-Dotras, E. (2022). Are women's entrepreneurial intentions and motivations influenced by financial skills? *International Journal of Gender and Entrepreneurship, 14*(1), 69–94. doi:10.1108/IJGE-01-2021-0017

Lloyd, C. B., & Mensch, B. S. (2008). Marriage and childbirth as factors in dropping out from school: An analysis of DHS data from sub-Saharan Africa. *Population Studies, 62*(1), 1–13. doi:10.1080/00324720701810840 PMID:18278669

Lock, R., & Smith, H. L. (2016). The impact of female entrepreneurship on economic growth in Kenya. *International Journal of Gender and Entrepreneurship, 8*(1), 90–96. doi:10.1108/IJGE-11-2015-0040

Lockyer, J., & George, S. (2012). What women want: Barriers to female entrepreneurship in the West Midlands. *International Journal of Gender and Entrepreneurship, 4*(2), 179–195. doi:10.1108/17566261211234661

López-Meneses, E., Sirignano, F. M., Vázquez-Cano, E., & Ramírez-Hurtado, J. M. (2020). University students' digital competence in three areas of the DigCom 2.1 model: A comparative study at three European universities. *Australasian Journal of Educational Technology*, 69–88. doi:10.14742/ajet.5583

Loukil, N., Yousfi, O., & Yerbanga, R. W. K. (2019). Does gender diversity on boards reduce information asymmetry problems? Empirical evidence from the French market. *Journal of Family Business Management.*

Luc, P. T. (2022). The relationships between Big-Five personality traits and social entrepreneurship intention. *Cogent Business & Management, 9*(1), 2137950. doi:10.1080/23311975.2022.2137950

Lumpkin, G. T., Moss, T. W., Gras, D. M., Kato, S., & Amezcua, A. S. (2013). Entrepreneurial processes in social contexts: How are they different, if at all? *Small Business Economics, 40*(3), 761–783. doi:10.100711187-011-9399-3

Maida, A., & Weber, A. (2022). Female leadership and gender gap within firms: Evidence from an Italian board reform. *Industrial & Labor Relations Review, 75*(2), 488–515. doi:10.1177/0019793920961995

Mair, J., & Martí, I. (2006). Social entrepreneurship research: A source of explanation, prediction, and delight. *Journal of World Business, 41*(1), 36–44. doi:10.1016/j.jwb.2005.09.002

Mamodu, C., Moses, C., Ekeagbara, J., & Peter, D. (2019). Effects Of Instagram Marketing on Female Entrepreneurial Performance in Lagos Nigeria: An Exploratory Study. *Covenant Journal of Entrepreneurship, 3*(2), 60–75. https://journals.covenantuniversity.edu.ng/index.php/cjoe

Manager Italia. (2021). Rapporto Donna. *Manager Italia.* https://www.manageritalia.it/resources/manageritalia-rapporto-donne-manager-2020-marzo-2021.pdf

Mandel, E. (1998). *Marksist Ekonomi Kuramına Giriş, (Çev: Ali Ünlü).* Toplumsal Dönüşüm Yayınları.

Manzanera-Román S., Brändle G. (2016). Abilities and skills as factors explaining the differences in women entrepreneurship. *Suma de negocios, 7*(15), 38-46.

Marchiori, D., & Franco, M. (2020). Knowledge transfer in the context of inter-organizational networks: Foundations and intellectual structures. *Journal of Innovation and Knowledge, 5*(2), 130–139. doi:10.1016/j.jik.2019.02.001

Marlow, S., & Patton, D. (2005). All credit to men? Entrepreneurship, finance, and gender. *Entrepreneurship Theory and Practice, 29*(6), 717–735. doi:10.1111/j.1540-6520.2005.00105.x

Martinc, M. (2018). *The Digital Competency Wheel.* LearnPatch. https://learnpatch.com/2018/12/the-digital-competencywheel/

Martinez Dy, A., Martin, L., & Marlow, S. (2018). Emancipation through digital entrepreneurship? A critical realist analysis. *Organization, 25*(5), 585–608. doi:10.1177/1350508418777891

Martini, U., Malacarne, K., Pederzolli Giovanazzi, S., & Buffa, F. (2020). Sustainable tourism development in rural and marginal areas and opportunities for female entrepreneurship: Lessons from an exploratory study. *Worldwide Hospitality and Tourism Themes, 12*(4), 421–430. doi:10.1108/WHATT-05-2020-0023

Martins, L. L., & Parsons, C. K. (2007). Effects of gender diversity management on perceptions of organizational attractiveness: The role of individual differences in attitudes and beliefs. *The Journal of Applied Psychology, 92*(3), 865–875. doi:10.1037/0021-9010.92.3.865 PMID:17484566

Marx, K. (1999). *Alman İdeolojisi, (Çev: sevim Belli).* Sol Yayınları.

Mastercard. (2022). The Mastercard Index of Women Entrepreneurs.

Meeralam, E. A., & Adeinat, I. (2022). Understanding the role of universities in fostering female entrepreneurship in the emerging ecosystem. *Gender in Management, 37*(3), 388–404. doi:10.1108/GM-02-2021-0041

Mehtap, S., Caputo, A., & Pellegrini, M. M. (2016). Encouraging Female Entrepreneurship in Jordan: Environmental Factors, Obstacles and Challenges. *Entrepreneurship and Management in an Islamic Context*, 207–225. doi:10.1007/978-3-319-39679-8_13

Mehtap, S., Ozmenekse, L., & Caputo, A. (2019). "I'm a stay-at-home businesswoman": An insight into informal entrepreneurship in Jordan. *Journal of Entrepreneurship in Emerging Economies, 11*(1), 44–65. doi:10.1108/JEEE-10-2017-0080

Melissa, E., Hamidati, A., Saraswati, M. S., & Flor, A. (2015). The internet and indonesian women entrepreneurs: Examining the impact of social media on women empowerment. In *Impact of Information Society Research in the Global South* (pp. 203–222). Springer Singapore, doi:10.1007/978-981-287-381-1_11

Melissa, E., Hamidati, A., Saraswati, M. S., & Flor, A. G. (2013). Investigating the potentials of social media to support women entrepreneurship in Indonesian urban areas. *ACM International Conference Proceeding Series,* (pp. 92–95). ACM. 10.1145/2517899.2517921

Merza, Z. (2019). The role and importance of social media on women entrepreneurship. SSRN *Electronic Journal.* doi:10.2139/ssrn.3408414

Meutia, & Ismail, T. (2012). The development of entrepreneurial social competence and business network to improve competitive advantage and business performance of small medium sized enterprises: A case study of batik industry in Indonesia. *Procedia - Social and Behavioral Sciences, 65*, 46–51. doi:10.1016/j.sbspro.2012.11.089

Milanov, H., Justo, R., & Bradley, S. W. (2015). Making the most of group relationships: The role of gender and boundary effects in microcredit groups. *Journal of Business Venturing, 30*(6), 822–838. doi:10.1016/j.jbusvent.2015.04.001

Millet, K. (2016). *Cinsel Politika, (Çev: Seçkin Selvi).* Payel Yayınları.

Miniesy, R., Elshahawy, E., & Fakhreldin, H. (2021). Social media's impact on the empowerment of women and youth male entrepreneurs in Egypt. *International Journal of Gender and Entrepreneurship.* doi:10.1108/IJGE-06-2021-0085

Ministry of Health Republic of Indonesia. (2008). *Communication, Information, Education (KIE).* Reproductive Health for Health Officers at Basic Services.

Minniti, M., & Naude, W. (2010). What do we know about the patterns and determinants of female entrepreneurship across countries? *European Journal of Development Research, 22*(3), 277–293. doi:10.1057/ejdr.2010.17

Miranda, F. J., Sergio, A. C., & Jesús, R. (2017). Academic Entrepreneurial Intention. *International Journal of Gender and Entrepreneurship, 9*(1), 66–86. doi:10.1108/IJGE-10-2016-0037

Mishra, O., Sharma, R., & Agrawal, B. (2020). Facilitating women prosperity with higher purpose at Vyomini. *South Asian Journal of Business and Management Cases, 9*(2), 198–207. doi:10.1177/2277977920905820

Mitchell, L. (2011). Overcoming the Gender Gap: Women Entrepreneurs as Economic Drivers. SSRN *Electronic Journal*. doi:10.2139/ssrn.1934906

Mitter, S. (2018). India isn't doing great in nurturing women entrepreneurs, finds survey. *Your Story*. https://yourstory.com/2018/03/india-isnt-great-nurturing-women-entrepreneurs-finds-survey/

Mounzer, L. (2022, March 8). *Overview of Female Entrepreneurship in the Middle East and North Africa Region*. Wilson Center.

Mrkonjić, E. (2022, July 7). *Women Entrepreneurs Statistics: Equality in 2022*. Writer's Block Live. https://writersblocklive.com/blog/women-entrepreneurs-statistics/

MuldoonJ.LucyC.LidzyS. (2019).

Mulkowe, E., & Korir, J. (2016). Social Media and Entrepreneurship: Tools, Benefits, and Challenges. A Case Study of Women Online Entrepreneurs on Kilimani Mums Marketplace on Facebook. *International Journal of Humanities and Social Science, 6*(8), 248–256.

Munasinghe, M. (2002). The Sustainomics Trans-disciplinary Meta-framework for making Development more Sustainable: Applications to energy issues. *International Journal of Sustainable Development, 4*(2), 6–54. doi:10.1504/IJSD.2002.002563

Muntean, S. C., & Ozkazanc-Pan, B. (2016). Feminist perspectives on social entrepreneurship: Critique and new directions. *International Journal of Gender and Entrepreneurship, 8*(3), 221–241. doi:10.1108/IJGE-10-2014-0034

Muravyev, A., Talavera, O., & Schäfer, D. (2009). Entrepreneurs' gender and financial constraints: Evidence from international data. *Journal of Comparative Economics, 37*(2), 270–286. doi:10.1016/j.jce.2008.12.001

Murphy, P. J., Ferreira, J. J., Fernandes, C. I., & do Paço, A. (2021). Blended value and female entrepreneurial performance: Social and economic aspects of education and technology transfer. *The International Entrepreneurship and Management Journal, 17*(2), 759–777. doi:10.100711365-019-00620-6

Myers, B. (1998). *Women entrepreneurs: key messages*. Purdue.

Nair, S. R. (2020). The link between women entrepreneurship, innovation and stakeholder engagement: A review. *Journal of Business Research, 119*, 283–290. doi:10.1016/j.jbusres.2019.06.038

Nambisan, S. (2017). Digital entrepreneurship: Toward a digital technology perspective of entrepreneurship. *Entrepreneurship Theory and Practice, 41*(6), 1029–1055. doi:10.1111/etap.12254

Nathan, F. (2018). Returns to Microcredit, Cash Grants and Training for Male and Female Micro entrepreneurs in Uganda. *World Development, 105*, 189–200. doi:10.1016/j.worlddev.2017.12.027

National Research Council, Institute of Medicine (NRC/IOM). (2005). *Growing up global: The changing transitions to adulthood in developing countries*. NRC/IOM.

Nawaser, K., Khaksar, S. M. S., Shaksian, F., & Afshar Jahanshahi, A. (2011). Motivational and Legal Barriers of Entrepreneurship Development. *International Journal of Business and Management*, *6*(11). doi:10.5539/ijbm.v6n11p112

Ndubisi, N. O., & Kahraman, C. (2005). Malaysian women entrepreneurs: Understanding the ICT usage behaviors and drivers. *Journal of Enterprise Information Management*, *18*(6), 721–739. doi:10.1108/17410390510628418

Nekhili, M., Gull, A. A., Chtioui, T., & Radhouane, I. (2020). Gender-diverse boards and audit fees: What difference does gender quota legislation make? *Journal of Business Finance & Accounting*, *47*(1-2), 52–99. doi:10.1111/jbfa.12409

Nelson, L. (2010). Bodies (and Spaces) do Matter: The limits of performativity, Gender, Place & Culture, *A Journal of Feminist Geography*, *6*(4).

Nga, J. K. H., & Shamuganathan, G. (2010). The influence of personality traits and demographic factors on social entrepreneurship start up intentions. *Journal of Business Ethics*, *95*(2), 259–282. doi:10.100710551-009-0358-8

Ngoasong, M. Z. (2017). Digital entrepreneurship in a resource-scarce context: A focus on entrepreneurial digital competencies. *Journal of Small Business and Enterprise Development*, *25*(3), 483–500. doi:10.1108/JSBED-01-2017-0014

Nicolás, C., & Rubio, A. (2016). Social enterprise: Gender gap and economic development. *European Journal of Management and Business Economics*, *25*(2), 56–62. doi:10.1016/j.redeen.2015.11.001

Nietzsche, F. (2010). *Güç İstenci, (Çev: Nilüfer Epçeli).* Say Yayınları.

Nissan, E., Carrasco, I., & Castaño, M. S. (2012). Women entrepreneurship, innovation, and internationalization. In *Women's entrepreneurship and economics* (pp. 125–142). Springer. doi:10.1007/978-1-4614-1293-9_9

Noguera, M., Alvarez, C., Merigó, J. M., & Urbano, D. (2015). Determinants of female entrepreneurship in Spain: An institutional approach. *Computational & Mathematical Organization Theory*, *21*(4), 341–355. doi:10.100710588-015-9186-9

Noguera, M., Alvarez, C., Ribeiro, D., & Urbano, D. (2013). Sociocultural factors and female entrepreneurship in the innovative service sector in Catalonia: A qualitative analysis. In J. J. M. Ferreira, M. Raposo, R. Rutten, & A. Varga (Eds.), *Cooperation, Clusters, and Knowledge Transfer, Advances in Spatial Science* (Vol. 79, pp. 141–162). Springer Berlin., doi:10.1007/978-3-642-33194-7_8

Noguera, M., Álvarez, C., & Urbano, D. (2013). Socio-cultural factors and female entrepreneurship. *The International Entrepreneurship and Management Journal*, *9*(9), 183–198. doi:10.100711365-013-0251-x

Noroozi, O., Biemans, H., & Mulder, M. (2016). Relations between scripted online peer feedback processes and quality of the written argumentative essay. *The Internet and Higher Education*, *31*, 20–31. doi:10.1016/j.iheduc.2016.05.002

Noviana, N. (2015). Female Reproduction Rights in Remote Area: Gender Perspective. Proceedings in *International ASEAN Forum On Ict For Sustainable Rural Development And Knowledge Cross-Fertilization 2015.*

Noviana, N., & Rahmattullah, M. (2016). Reproduction health of female diamond miners in cempaka subdistrict, banjarbaru. Advancing inclusive rural development and transformation in a challenging environment, p.538.

Noviana, N. (2016). *Konsep HIV/AIDS Seksualitas dan Kesehatan Reproduksi.* Trans Info Media.

O'Connell, M. (2018). *Makine Olmak, (Çev: Öznur Karakaş).* Domingo Yayınları.

O'Connor, D. O., & Voos, H. (1981). Empirical laws, theory construction and bibliometrics. *Library Trends*, *30*(1), 9–20.

OECD. (2022). *Indicators of female entrepreneurship.* OECD. https://stats.oecd.org/index.aspx?queryid=83119

OECD. (2022). *Positive business status and outlook by sex.* OECD. https://stats.oecd.org/index.aspx?queryid=83119

OECD. (2022). *Share of the population who report borrowing money to start a business by sex*, Entrepreneurship. OECD. https://stats.oecd.org/index.aspx?queryid=83119

OECD. (2022). *Share of women inventors*. OECD. https://stats.oecd.org/index.aspx?queryid=83119

Ojala, A. (2016). Business models and opportunity creation: How IT entrepreneurs create and develop business models under uncertainty. *Information Systems Journal*, *26*(5), 451–476. doi:10.1111/isj.12078

Olamide, A., & Ogbechie, R. (2021). Social capital and business performance: A study of female-owned SMEs in the Nigerian informal sector. *Small Enterprise Research*, *28*(2), 190–205. doi:10.1080/13215906.2021.1901140

Olson, S. F., & Currie, H. M. (1992). Female Entrepreneurs: Personal Value Systems and Business Strategies in a Male-Dominated Industry. *Journal of Small Business Management*, *30*(1). https://www.proquest.com/docview/221006040/abstract/18AF1B10320A46E9PQ/1?accountid=38885

Olsson, A. K., & Bernhard, I. (2020a). Keeping up the pace of digitalization in small businesses–Women entrepreneurs' knowledge and use of social media. *International Journal of Entrepreneurial Behaviour & Research*, *27*(2), 378–396. doi:10.1108/IJEBR-10-2019-0615

Omar, S. S. (2015). The entrepreneurial network of Muslim women entrepreneurs: The study of multiple-cases of small businesses in the southern region of Malaysia. *International Journal of Economics and Financial Issues*, *5*(1), 106–115.

Oppedal Berge, L. I., & Garcia Pires, A. J. (2020). Gender, formality, and entrepreneurial success. *Small Business Economics*, *55*(4), 881–900. doi:10.100711187-019-00163-8

Özbudun, S., & Demirer, T. ve Demirer, Y. (2000). Kadın yazıları. Ankara: Ütopya Yayınevi.

Ozturk, M. B., & Tatli, A. (2016). Gender identity inclusion in the workplace: Broadening diversity management research and practice through the case of transgender employees in the UK. *International Journal of Human Resource Management*, *27*(8), 781–802. doi:10.1080/09585192.2015.1042902

Palalic, R., Ramadani, V., & Dana, L. P. (2017). Entrepreneurship in Bosnia and Herzegovina: Focus on gender. *European Business Review*, *29*(4), 476–496. doi:10.1108/EBR-05-2016-0071

Panda, S. (2018). Constraints faced by women entrepreneurs in developing countries: Review and ranking. *Gender in Management*, *33*(4), 315–331. doi:10.1108/GM-01-2017-0003

Pareek, P., & Bagrecha, C. (2018). An analysis of the financial challenges faced by women entrepreneurs. *International Journal of Scientific and Engineering Research*, *9*(10), 2229–5518. https://www.researchgate.net/publication/362429718_An_analysis_of_the_financial_challenges_faced_by_women_entrepreneurs

Pareek, P., & Bagrecha, C. (2018b). Socio – Personal Challenges Faced by Indian Women Entrepreneur. *International Journal of Management Studies*, *V*(4(8)), 38. doi:10.18843/ijms/v5i4(8)/05

Pareja-Cano, B., Valor, C., & Benito, A. (2020). How social enterprises nurture empowerment: A grounded theoretical model of social change. *Journal of Social Entrepreneurship*, 1–21. doi:10.1080/19420676.2020.1821753

Parihar, S. (2017). Entrepreneurial intent: Exploring the roles of gender and family business background. *International Journal of Marketing and Business Communication*, *6*(4), 28–37.

Parimala Devi, B. (2014). Problems and Prospects of Women Entrepreneurship in India. [IJSR]. *International Journal of Scientific Research.*

Pastore, P., & Tommaso, S. (2016). Women on corporate boards. The case of 'gender quotas' in Italy. *Corporate Ownership and Control*, *13*(4), 132–155. doi:10.22495/cocv13i4p13

Pata, U. K. (2018). The Relationship Between Female Employment and Economic Growth In Turkey: A Sectoral Analysis With Symmetric And Asymmetric Causality Tests, *International Journal of Economics and Administrative Studies. Year, 2018*(21), 135–150.

Patterson, L., & Benuyenah, V. (2021). The real losers during times of economic crisis: Evidence of the Korean gender pay gap. *International Journal of Manpower, 42*(7), 1238–1256. doi:10.1108/IJM-02-2020-0045

Pavlović, D., Bjelica, D., & Domazet, I. (2019). What Characteristics in the Youth Labor Market of Serbia Are Likely to Result in Employment? *Stanovnistvo, 57*(2), 35–47. doi:10.2298/STNV190823006P

Pelegrini, G. C., & Moraes, G. H. S. M. D. (2022). Does gender matter? A university ecosystem, self-efficacy and entrepreneurial intention analysis in Brazilian universities. *Gender in Management, 37*(2), 271–286. doi:10.1108/GM-01-2021-0007

Perekrestova, V. (2022). Normative coherence through social entrepreneurship: Fostering women's empowerment in Myanmar. *Development Policy Review, 40*(S1), e12627. doi:10.1111/dpr.12627

Perez-Quintana, A., Hormiga, E., Martori, J. C., & Madariaga, R. (2017). The influence of sex and gender-role orientation in the decision to become an entrepreneur. *International Journal of Gender and Entrepreneurship, 9*(1), 8–30. doi:10.1108/IJGE-12-2015-0047

Piazzalunga, D., & Di Tommaso, M. L. (2019). The increase of the gender wage gap in Italy during the 2008-2012 economic crisis. *The Journal of Economic Inequality, 17*(2), 171–193. doi:10.100710888-018-9396-8

Pistrui, D., & Sreih, J. F. (2010). Islam, entrepreneurship and business values in the Middle East. *International Journal of Entrepreneurship and Innovation Management, 12*(1), 107. doi:10.1504/IJEIM.2010.033170

Plazibat, I., & Renko, S. (2020). Social Media as a Channel for Boosting Female Entrepreneurship in Retailing. In T. Kovačević & I. Akrap (Eds.), *Contemporary issues in economy & technology* (pp. 84–97). University of Split.

Pless, N., & Maak, T. (2004). Building an inclusive diversity culture: Principles, processes and practice. *Journal of Business Ethics, 54*(2), 129–147. doi:10.100710551-004-9465-8

Prasad, V. K., Naidu, G. M., Murthy, B. K., Winkel, D. E., & Ehrhardt, K. (2013). Women entrepreneurs and business venture growth: An examination of the influence of human and social capital resources in an Indian context. *Journal of Small Business and Entrepreneurship, 26*(4), 341–364. doi:10.1080/08276331.2013.821758

Prendes-Espinosa, P., Solano-Fernández, I. M., & García-Tudela, P. A. (2021). EmDigital to promote digital entrepreneurship: The relation with open innovation. *Journal of Open Innovation, 7*(1), 63. doi:10.3390/joitmc7010063

Qader, A. A., Zhang, J., Ashraf, S. F., Syed, N., Omhand, K., & Nazir, M. (2022). Capabilities and Opportunities: Linking Knowledge Management Practices of Textile-Based SMEs on Sustainable Entrepreneurship and Organizational Performance in China. *Sustainability (Switzerland), 14*(4), 2219. doi:10.3390u14042219

Qazi, Z., Qazi, W., Raza, S. A., & Yousufi, S. Q. (2022). Investigating Women's Entrepreneurial Intention: The Moderating Role of Family Support. *ASR: CMU Journal of Social Sciences and Humanities, 9*(1). Advance online publication. doi:10.12982/CMUJASR.2022.003

Quader, M. S. (2012). A characteristic model of successful women entrepreneurs in the UK. *Journal of Services Research, 12n*, 1.

Quagrainie, F. A. (2016). Institutional approach and competitive behaviours of informal Ghanaian women entrepreneurs. *International Journal of Entrepreneurship and Small Business, 28*(2–3), 323–338. doi:10.1504/IJESB.2016.076648

Québec Ministère de l'Éducation et de l'Enseignement supérieur, (2019). *Digital Competency Framework*. Québec Ministère de l'Éducation et de l'Enseignement. http://www.education.gouv.qc.ca/fileadmin/site_web/documents/ministere/Cadre-reference-competence-num-AN.pdf

Raevskaya, A. A., Anastasia, A., & Tatarko, A. N. (2022). What makes a family work: Current problems of family psychology and psychotherapy. *Psychology in Russia-State of the Art, 15*(3), 3–20. doi:10.11621/pir.2022.0301 PMID:36699141

Raghuvanshi, J., Agrawal, R., & Ghosh, P. K. (2017). Analysis of Barriers to Women Entrepreneurship: The DEMATEL Approach. *The Journal of Entrepreneurship, 26*(2), 220–238. doi:10.1177/0971355717708848

Ragins, B. R., Townsend, B., & Mattis, M. (1998). Gender gap in the executive suite: CEOs and female executives report on breaking the glass ceiling. *The Academy of Management Perspectives, 12*(1), 28–42. doi:10.5465/ame.1998.254976

Rahman, R. S. A. R. A., Kutty, F. M., & Othman, N. (2019). Gender and family background as antecedents on the social entrepreneurial strategic domain of university students. *International Journal of Innovation. Creativity and Change, 7*(6), 336–346.

Rahmatullah, M., & Zaman, F. (2014). Female Entrepreneurship in Bangladesh: Constraints, Motivation and Success. *Bangladesh e-Journal of Sociology, 11*(2), 65–77. https://www.academia.edu/22377887/Motivational_factors_and_the_constraints_of_women_entrepreneurship_development_in_Bangladesh

Ramesh, D. B. (2018). Problems and perspective of women entrepreneurship in india. *IJRAR, 5*(Issue 1). https://www.ijrar.org/papers/IJRAR19D1059.pdf

Republic Bureau of Statistics (2020). *Statistical Release. Statistics of social activities, Serbia, Number 166*. RBS.

Rey-Martí, A., Tur Porcar, A., & Mas-Tur, A. (2015). Linking female entrepreneurs' motivation to business survival. *Journal of Business Research, 68*(4), 810–814. doi:10.1016/j.jbusres.2014.11.033

Ridgeway, C. L. (2001). Gender, status, and leadership. *The Journal of Social Issues, 57*(4), 637–655. doi:10.1111/0022-4537.00233

Riedo, V., Kraiczy, N. D., & Hack, A. (2019). Applying person-environment fit theory to identify personality differences between prospective social and commercial entrepreneurs: An explorative study. *Journal of Small Business Management, 57*(3), 989–1007. doi:10.1111/jsbm.12377

Risman, B. J. (2004). Gender as a social structure: Theory wrestling with activism. *Gender & Society, 18*(4), 429–450. doi:10.1177/0891243204265349

Rita, C., & Rajasekar, D. (2012). Role of women in Independent India: An assessment. *Southern Economist, 51*(11), 7–9.

Roberson, Q. M. (2006). Disentangling the meanings of diversity and inclusion in organizations. *Group & Organization Management, 31*(2), 212–236. doi:10.1177/1059601104273064

Robert, J. (1968). *Stoller. Sex and Gender: On the Development of Masculinity and Femininity* (Vol. 2). Science House.

Roberto, F., Rey, A., Maglio, R., & Agliata, F. (2020). The academic "glass-ceiling": Investigating the increase of female academicians in Italy. *The International Journal of Organizational Analysis, 28*(5), 1031–1054. doi:10.1108/IJOA-06-2019-1779

Robichaud, Y., Cachon, J.-C., & McGraw, E. (2014). Why Are Female-Owned Businesses Smaller? An Empirical Study in Canada and the United States. *Journal of Management Policy and Practice*, *16*(1). http://www.m.www.na-businesspress.com/JMPP/RobichaudY_Web16_1_.pdf

Rodie, A. R., & Martin, C. L. (2001). Competing in the service sector - The entrepreneurial challenge. *International Journal of Entrepreneurial Behavior &Amp. Research*, *7*(1), 5–21. doi:10.1108/13552550110385718

Rosca, E., Agarwal, N., & Brem, A. (2020). Women entrepreneurs as agents of change: A comparative analysis of social entrepreneurship processes in emerging markets. *Technological Forecasting and Social Change*, *157*, 120067. doi:10.1016/j.techfore.2020.120067

Rouse, J., Treanor, L., & Fleck, E. (2013). The gendering of entrepreneurship: Theoretical and empirical insights. *International Journal of Entrepreneurial Behaviour & Research*, *19*(5), 452–459. doi:10.1108/IJEBR-06-2013-0083

Rudhumbu, N., du Plessis, E. E., & Maphosa, C. (2020). Challenges and opportunities for women entrepreneurs in Botswana: Revisiting the role of entrepreneurship education. *Journal of International Education in Business*, *13*(2), 183–201. doi:10.1108/JIEB-12-2019-0058

Ryan, M. K., & Haslam, S. A. (2005). The glass cliff: Evidence that women are over-represented in precarious leadership positions. *British Journal of Management*, *16*(2), 81–90. doi:10.1111/j.1467-8551.2005.00433.x

Ryzin, G. G., Grossman, S., DiPadova-Stocks, L., & Bergrud, E. (2009). Portrait of the social entrepreneur: Statistical evidence from a US panel. *Voluntas*, *20*(2), 129–140. doi:10.100711266-009-9081-4

Sahay, S. (2011). Assessment of the ability of the health management information system in India to use information for action [Doctoral dissertation, HISP India].

Samuelsson, P., & Witell, L. (2022). Social entrepreneurs in service: Motivations and types. *Journal of Services Marketing*, *36*(9), 27–40. doi:10.1108/JSM-08-2017-0274

Sancar, S. (2011). *Erkeklik: imkansız iktidar*. Metis Yayınları.

Sánchez-Algarra, P., & Anguera, M. T. (2013). Qualitative/quantitative integration in the inductive observational study of interactive behaviour: Impact of recording and coding among predominating perspectives. *Quality & Quantity*, *47*(2), 1237–1257. doi:10.100711135-012-9764-6

Sandberg, W. R., & Hofer, C. W. (1987). Improving new venture performance: The role of strategy, industry structure, and the entrepreneur. *Journal of Business Venturing*, *2*(1), 5–28. doi:10.1016/0883-9026(87)90016-4

Santos, G., Marques, C. S., & Ferreira, J. (2021). The influence of embeddedness on entrepreneurship, innovation and strategy: A gender perspective in the agri-food sector. *Sustainability (Switzerland)*, *13*(16), 9384. doi:10.3390u13169384

Saraswathy, M. (2019). Women's day 2019: labor force participation of females is still an Achilles heel for India. *Money Control*. www.moneycontrol.com/news/business/economy/womens-day-2019-labour-force-participation-of-females-is-still-an-achilles-he
el-for-india-3623061.html

Sarfaraz, L., Faghih, N., & Majd, A. (2014). The relationship between women entrepreneurship and gender equality. *Journal of Global Entrepreneurship Research*, *2*(1), 6. doi:10.1186/2251-7316-2-6

Sarpong, D., Nyuur, R., & Torbor, M. K. (2021). Careers of commercially successful female entrepreneurs in context of underdeveloped markets and weak institutions. *International Journal of Entrepreneurial Behaviour & Research*. doi:10.1108/IJEBR-06-2021-0526

Saxon, R., & Gillin, M. (2004). *Female entrepreneurship in Australia.* Swinburne University of Technology. https://researchbank.swinburne.edu.au/file/f6045220-08ee-4c62-9b1b-409764424687/1/PDF%20%28Published%20version%29.pdf

Schaffer, N. (2022, December). *55 Compelling Social Media Marketing Statistics You Need To Know For 2023.* Sprout Social.

Schmidt, S., Bohnenberger, M. C., Nodari, C. H., & Da Silva, M. D. J. S. (2022). Gender, entrepreneurial behaviour and firm performance of Brazilian students: Integrating economic and behavioral perspectives. *Heliyon, 8*(1), e08750. doi:10.1016/j.heliyon.2022.e08750 PMID:35059525

Scholarios, D., & Taylor, P. (2011). Beneath the glass ceiling: Explaining gendered role segmentation in call centres. *Human Relations, 64*(10), 1291–1319. doi:10.1177/0018726711416265

Schumpeter, J. (1942). *Capitalism, socialism and democracy.* Harper & Row.

Scuotto, V., & Morellato, M. (2013). Entrepreneurial Knowledge and Digital Competence: Journal of the Knowledge Economy, 4(3), 293-303. Springer. doi:10.100713132-013-0155-6

Sebora, T. C., Lee, S. M., & Sukasame, N. (2009). Critical success factors for e-commerce entrepreneurship: An empirical study of Thailand. *Small Business Economics, 32*(3), 303–316. doi:10.100711187-007-9091-9

Secundo, G., del Vecchio, P., & Mele, G. (2021). Social media for entrepreneurship: Myth or reality? A structured literature review and a future research agenda. *International Journal of Entrepreneurial Behaviour & Research, 27*(1), 149–177. doi:10.1108/IJEBR-07-2020-0453

Secundo, G., Rippa, P., & Cerchione, R. (2020). Digital Academic Entrepreneurship: A structured literature review and avenue for a research agenda. *Technological Forecasting and Social Change, 157*, 120118. doi:10.1016/j.techfore.2020.120118

Sehgal & Khandelwal. (2020). Work–family interface of women entrepreneurs: evidence from India. *South Asian Journal of Business Studies*, . doi:10.1108/SAJBS-11-2019-0213

Seo, K., Dodson, S., Harandi, N. M., Roberson, N., Fels, S., & Roll, I. (2021). Active learning with online video: The impact of learning context on engagement. *Computers & Education, 165*, 104132. doi:10.1016/j.compedu.2021.104132

Serel, H., & Özdemir, S. (2017, September). Female Employment and Economic Growth Relations In Turkey. *Journal of Management and Economics Research, Vol, 15*(3), 132–148.

Shahedul, Q. M. (2012). A Characteristic Model of Successful Women Entrepreneurs in the UK. *Journal of Services Research, 12*(1), 89–113. https://www.proquest.com/docview/1019285931?fromopenview=true&pq-origsite=gscholar

Shah, H., & Saurabh, P. (2015). Women Entrepreneurs in Developing Nations: Growth and Replication Strategies and Their Impact on Poverty Alleviation. *Technology Innovation Management Review, 5*(8), 34–43. doi:10.22215/timreview/921

Shahin, M., Ilic, O., Gonsalvez, C., & Whittle, J. (2021). The impact of a STEM-based entrepreneurship program on the entrepreneurial intention of secondary school female students. *The International Entrepreneurship and Management Journal, 17*(4), 1867–1898. doi:10.100711365-020-00713-7

Shahzad, F., Abbas, A., Fateh, A., Kasim, R. S. R., Akram, K., & Ashraf, S. F. (2021). Late-Night Use of social media and Cognitive Engagement of Female Entrepreneurs: A Stressor–Strain–Outcome Perspective. *SAGE Open, 11*(3). doi:10.1177/21582440211037652

Sharma, P. (2020). Women entrepreneurship in India: The socio-economic context. *Materials Today: Proceedings*. s doi:10.1016/j.matpr.2020.09.437

Sharma, S., & Kumar, A. (2021). Can social enterprises create holistic women empowerment? *Journal of Women's Entrepreneurship and Education*, *2021*(3–4), 96–112. doi:10.28934/JWEE21.34.PP96-112

Shastri, S., Shastri, S., & Pareek, A. (2019). Motivations and challenges of women entrepreneurs: Experiences of small businesses in Jaipur city of Rajasthan. *The International Journal of Sociology and Social Policy*, *39*(5/6), 338–355. doi:10.1108/IJSSP-09-2018-0146

Shaw, K. L. (2006). Re-creating identity in exile: Hybridity and gender in the works of Assia Djebar, Leïla Sebbar, and Malika Mokeddem. T. U. of Alabama, Ed..

Shen, J., Chanda, A., D'netto, B., & Monga, M. (2009). Managing diversity through human resource management: An international perspective and conceptual framework. *International Journal of Human Resource Management*, *20*(2), 235–251. doi:10.1080/09585190802670516

Shetty, Sowjanya and Hans, V. Basil, Role of Education in Women Empowerment and Development: Issues and Impact (September 26, 2015). Available at SSRN: https://ssrn.com/abstract=2665898 or doi:10.2139/ssrn.2665898

Sidratulmunthah, H., Hussain, S., & Imran Malik, M. (2018). Towards nurturing the entrepreneurial intentions of neglected female business students of Pakistan through proactive personality, self-efficacy and university support factors. *Asia Pacific Journal of Innovation and Entrepreneurship*, *12*(3), 363–378. doi:10.1108/APJIE-03-2018-0015

Simović, V., & Domazet, I. (2021). An overview of the frameworks for measuring the digital competences of college students: A European perspective. In T. Neimann (ed.) Stagnancy Issues and Change Initiatives for Global Education in the Digital Age. IGI Global Publishing House. doi:10.4018/978-1- 7998-4993-3.ch012

Simović, V., et al., (2022) Identification of Opportunities as the Component of Digital Entrepreneurial Competences of University Students: A pilot study in Kuwait and Serbia. In: *ICEEG 2022: 2022 6th International Conference on E-Commerce, E-Business and E-Government*. Association for Computing Machinery. 10.1145/3537693.3537724

Singh, G., & Belwal, R. (2008). Entrepreneurship and SMEs in Ethiopia. *Gender in Management*, *23*(2), 120–136. doi:10.1108/17542410810858321

Singh, V., Terjesen, S., & Vinnicombe, S. (2008). Newly appointed directors in the boardroom: How do women and men differ? *European Management Journal*, *26*(1), 48–58. doi:10.1016/j.emj.2007.10.002

Skov, A. (2016). The Digital Competence Wheel. *Digital Competence*. https://digital-competence.eu/.

Smollan, R., & Singh, S. (2021). How social entrepreneurs respond to enterprise failure. *Journal of Social Entrepreneurship*, *0*(0), 1–25. doi:10.1080/19420676.2021.1890189

Solanas, V. (2019). *Erkek Doğrama Cemiyeti Manifestosu, (Çev: Ayşe Düzkan)*. Sel Yayıncılık.

Songini, L., & Gnan, L. (2014). The glass ceiling in SMEs and its impact on firm managerialisation: A comparison between family and non-family SMEs.

Sospeter, N. G. (2012). Challenges Facing Women Entrepreneurs in the Construction Industry in Tanzania. *Journal of Business and Economics*, *7*(11). Advance online publication. doi:10.15341/jbe(2155-7950)/11.07.2016/016

Soysal, A. (2010). Women Entrepreneurs in Turkey: An Assessment in the Context of Difficulties and Opportunities. *Ankara University SBF Journal*, *65*(01), 83–114.

Spivak, G. C. (1989). "Feminism and Deconstruction Again: Nogotiationg with Unacknowledged Masculinism. In C. Macdonald & T. Brennan (ed.) Between Feminism and Psychoanalysis. University of Nebraska Press.

Spivak, G.C. (2010). *Ulus-devlet Marşını Kim Söyler?, (Çev: Osman Akınhay).* İstanbul, Agora kitaplığı.

Spivak, G. C. (2020). *Madun Konuşabilir mi? (Çev: Emre Koyuncu).* Dipnot Yayınları.

Sriram, V., & Mersha, T. (2010). Stimulating entrepreneurship in Africa. *World Journal of Entrepreneurship, Management and Sustainable Development*, *6*(4), 257–272. doi:10.1108/20425961201000020

Srivastava, S., & Misra, R. (2017). Exploring antecedents of entrepreneurial intentions of young women in India: A multimethod analysis. *Journal of Entrepreneurship in Emerging Economies*, *9*(2), 181–206. doi:10.1108/JEEE-04-2016-0012

Staniewski, M. W., & Awruk, K. (2019). Entrepreneurial success and achievement motivation – a preliminary report on a validation study of the questionnaire of entrepreneurial success. *Journal of Business Research*, *101*, 433–440. doi:10.1016/j.jbusres.2019.01.073

Statistics and data of all countries in Africa. (n.d.). Worlddata.info. https://www.worlddata.info/africa/index.php

Steel, G. (2021). Going global – going digital. Diaspora networks and female online entrepreneurship in Khartoum, Sudan. *Geoforum*, *120*(July 2019), 22–29. doi:10.1016/j.geoforum.2021.01.003

Steel, G. (2017). Navigating (im)mobility: Female entrepreneurship and social media in Khartoum. *Africa*, *87*(2), 233–252. doi:10.1017/S0001972016000930

Steininger, D. M. (2019). Linking information systems and entrepreneurship: A review and agenda for IT-associated and digital entrepreneurship research. *Information Systems Journal*, *29*(2), 363–407. doi:10.1111/isj.12206

Stone, A. (2004). Essentialism and Anti-Essentialism in Feminist Philosophy. *JMP*, *1*(2), 135–153.

Strategic Direction. (2019). Getting the most out of Facebook and WhatsApp: social media strategies by female entrepreneurs in the UAE. *Strategic Direction*, *35*(4), 18–20. doi:10.1108/SD-01-2019-0008

Sułkowski, Ł., Bogacz-Wojtanowska, E., Wrona, S., Jędrzejczyk-Kozioł, A., Góral, E., & Mormul, K. (2019). Unsustainable power distribution? women leaders in Polish academia. *Economia e Sociologia*, *12*(3), 162–180. doi:10.14254/2071-789X.2019/12-3/11

Swartz, E., Amatucci, F. M., & Coleman, S. (2016). Using a multiple method and mixed mode approach to examine women entrepreneur negotiating styles. *International Journal of Gender and Entrepreneurship*, *8*(1), 48–68. doi:10.1108/IJGE-09-2013-0060

Sweida, G. L., Sherman, C. L., Duranso, C. M. W., & Berkley, R. A. (2022). Lawns And Lemonade: Exploring The Relationship Between Gendered Childpreneur Activities, Adult Entrepreneurial Intentions And Industry Preference. *Journal of Developmental Entrepreneurship*, *27*(02), 2250010. doi:10.1142/S1084946722500108

Tahtalıoğlu, H. (2016). The Effects Of Glass Ceiling Syndrome On Women In Higher Education Institutions In Turkey. *Niğde Üniversitesi İktisadi ve İdari Bilimler Fakültesi Dergisi (Academic Review of Economics and Administrative Sciences). Year*, *9*(2), 89–105.

Tambunan, T. (2009). Women entrepreneurship in Asian developing countries: Their development and main constraints, Journal of Development and Agricultural Economics: Vol. 1. *(2), Page No. 027-040.the glass ceiling*. Sage.

Tan, J. (2007). Breaking the "Bamboo Curtain" and the "Glass Ceiling": The Experience of Women Entrepreneurs in High-Tech Industries in an Emerging Market. *Journal of Business Ethics*, *80*(3), 547–564. doi:10.100710551-007-9454-9

Tan, L. P., Le, A. N. H., & Xuan, L. P. (2020). A systematic literature review on social entrepreneurial intention. *Journal of Social Entrepreneurship, 11*(3), 241–256. doi:10.1080/19420676.2019.1640770

Terjesen, S., Bosma, N., & Stam, E. (2016). Advancing public policy for high-growth, female, and social entrepreneurs. *Public Administration Review, 76*(2), 230–239. doi:10.1111/puar.12472

Thaddeus, E. (2012b, season-04). Perspectives: Entrepreneurship Development & Growth of Enterprises in Nigeria.

Thapar, R. (1981). Ideology and the interpretation of early Indian history. *Social Sciences Information. Information Sur les Sciences Sociales, 20*(2), 239–258. doi:10.1177/053901848102000201

The European Parliament. (2006). Recommendation of the European Parliament and of the Council. EP. https://eur-lex.europa.eu/legal-content/EN/TXT/?uri=celex%3A32006H0962.

The Startup VC Team. (2020, December 17). *Women Entrepreneurship in Latin America?* The StartupVC. https://www.thestartupvc.com/startup-news/women-entrepreneurship-in-latin-america/

Thébaud, S. (2015). Business as Plan B: Institutional Foundations of Gender Inequality in Entrepreneurship across 24 Industrialized Countries. *Administrative Science Quarterly, 60*(4), 671–711. doi:10.1177/0001839215591627

Tierney, H. (1995). *Women's Studies Encyclopedia*. Green Word Press.

Tiwari, P., Bhat, A. K., & Tikoria, J. (2017). An empirical analysis of the factors affecting social entrepreneurial intentions. *Journal of Global Entrepreneurship Research, 7*(1), 1–25. doi:10.118640497-017-0067-1

Toma, G. A. (2022). Social entrepreneurship: A conceptual taxonomy. *Journal of Community Positive Practices, 22*(1), 60–76. doi:10.35782/JCPP.2022.1.04

Tranfield, D., Denyer, D., & Smart, P. (2003). Towards a Methodology for Developing Evidence-Informed Management Knowledge by Means of Systematic Review* Introduction: The need for an evidence- informed approach. *British Journal of Management, 14*(3), 207–222. doi:10.1111/1467-8551.00375

Tripathy, K. K., Paliwal, M., & Singh, A. (2022). Women's social entrepreneurship and livelihood innovation: An exploratory study from India. *Service Business, 16*(4), 863–881. doi:10.100711628-022-00493-w

Tuite, A. (2021). Gendered Entrepreneurialism and the Labour of Online Consumption in the Independent Fashion Sector. *Fashion Theory, 25*(3), 419–438. doi:10.1080/1362704X.2019.1633831

TURKSTAT. (2020). *Entrepreneurship, 2016-2018*, Number: 33664, Retrieved October 10, 2022, from https://data.tuik.gov.tr/Bulten/Index?p=Girisimcilik-2016-2018-33664

TURKSTAT. (2020b). *Rate of enterprises owned by females by size (number of employee), 2016-2018*. Entrepreneurship. https://data.tuik.gov.tr/Bulten/Index?p=Girisimcilik-2016-2018-33664

TURKSTAT. (2022a). *Population by sex and age group, 2020, 2021*. Women in Statistics. https://data.tuik.gov.tr/Bulten/Index?p=Women-in-Statistics-2021-45635

TURKSTAT. (2022b). *Formal education completed by sex, 2010-2020* Women in Statistics. https://data.tuik.gov.tr/Bulten/Index?p=Women-in-Statistics-2021-45635

TURKSTAT. (2022c). *Labour force status by sex and educational level, 2019, 2020.* Women in Statistics, 2021. https://data.tuik.gov.tr/Bulten/Index?p=Women-in-Statistics-2021-45635

TURKSTAT. (2022f). *Proportion of employed working part-time by sex, 2014-2020.* Women in Statistics. https://data.tuik.gov.tr/Bulten/Index?p=Women-in-Statistics-2021-45635

TURKSTAT. (2022g). *Employment rate of persons aged 25-49 with a child under age 3 living in the household and with no children living in the household by sex, 2014-2020.* Women in Statistics.https://data.tuik.gov.tr/Bulten/Index?p=Women-in-Statistics-2021-45635

TURKSTAT. (2022i). *Satisfaction with time spent on commuting to work, 2013-2021*, 2014-2020. Women in Statistics. https://data.tuik.gov.tr/Bulten/Index?p=Women-in-Statistics-2021-45635

TURKSTAT. (2022j). *Number and proportion of ambassadors by sex, 1982, 1990, 1996, 2000-2021.* Women in Statistics. https://data.tuik.gov.tr/Bulten/Index?p=Women-in-Statistics-2021-45635

TURKSTAT. (2022m). *Proportion of individuals in senior and middle management positions by sex, 2012-2020.* Women in Statistics. https://data.tuik.gov.tr/Bulten/Index?p=Women-in-Statistics-2021-45635

TURKSTAT. (2022n), *Average Daily Wages of Seasonal Agricultural Workers and the Average Monthly Wages of Permanent Agricultural Workers by Province (TL),* Agricultural Holdings Labour Wage Structure. https://data.tuik.gov.tr/Bulten/Index?p=Agricultural-Holdings-Labour-Wage-Structure-2020-2021-45783

Türlüoğlu, E. (2018). Women Employment And Growth Relationship: Var Model Analysis, Eurasian [EJRSE]. *Journal of Researches in Social and Economics*, *5*(9), 59–68.

Tur-Porcar, A., Mas-Tur, A., & Belso, J. A. (2017). Barriers to women entrepreneurship. Different methods, different results? *Quality & Quantity*, *51*(5), 2019–2034. doi:10.100711135-016-0343-0

Tütüncü, A., & Zengin, H. (2020). The Relationship Between Women Employment and Economic Growth In E7 Countries, *Int. Journal of Management Economics and Business*, *16*(1), 1–16.

Tyrowicz, J., Terjesen, S., & Mazurek, J. (2020). All on board? New evidence on board gender diversity from a large panel of European firms. *European Management Journal*, *38*(4), 634–645. doi:10.1016/j.emj.2020.01.001

Umar, M., Ali, S. A., & Sial, M. H. (2022). Exploring Women Entrepreneurship Prospects, Challenges, and Barriers in Pakistan. *International Journal of E-Entrepreneurship and Innovation*, *12*(1), 1–17. doi:10.4018/IJEEI.290823

UN News Centre. (2017). *UN and partners launch initiative to reach equal pay for women at work*. UN. https://www.un.org/sustainabledevelopment/blog/2017/09/un-and-partners-launch-initiative-to-reach-equal-pay-for-women-at-work/

UNESCO Sustainable Development Goals. (n/d). *Sustainable Goals.* UNESCO. http://uis.unesco.org/en/country/kw#slideoutmenu Accessed on November 23, 2022.

United Nations Department of Economic and Social Affairs Sustainable Development. (n.d.). *Do you know all 17 SDGs?* UN. https://sdgs.un.org/goals

Urbancová, H., Hudáková, M., & Fajčíková, A. (2020). Diversity management as a tool of sustainability of competitive advantage. *Sustainability, 12*(12), 5020. doi:10.3390u12125020

Valacich, J., & Schneider, C. (2018). *Information systems today: Managing in the digital world* (8th ed.). Pearson.

Van Deursen, A., & van Dijk, J. (2009). Improving digital skills for the use of online public information and services. *Government Information Quarterly, 26*(2), 333–340. doi:10.1016/j.giq.2008.11.002

Van Dijk, A. T. (2010). Söylem ve iktidar. A. Çavdar ve A. B. Yıldırım (Ed.), Nefret suçları ve nefret söylemi içinde (s. 9-44). İstanbul: Hrant Dink Vakfı Yayınları.

Van Dijk, T. (1998). *Ideology: a multidisciplinaryapproach. Londra.* Sage Publications.

Van Dijk, T. A. (2003). *Söylemin yapıları ve iktidarın yapıları. Mehmet Küçük (Der.), Medya iktidar ideoloji içinde.* Bilim ve Sanat Yayınları.

van Eck, N. J., & Waltman, L. (2010). Software survey: VOSviewer, a computer program for bibliometric mapping. *Scientometrics, 84*(2), 523–538. doi:10.100711192-009-0146-3 PMID:20585380

Van Emmerik, H., Euwema, M. C., & Wendt, H. (2008). Leadership behaviors around the world: The relative importance of gender versus cultural background. *International Journal of Cross Cultural Management, 8*(3), 297–315. doi:10.1177/1470595808096671

Van Welsum, D. (2016). *Enabling Digital Entrepreneurs.* World Bank Group. doi:10.1596/23646

Verheul, I., van Stel, A., & Thurik, R. (2006). Explaining female and male entrepreneurship at the country level. *Entrepreneurship and Regional Development, 18*(2), 151–183. doi:10.1080/08985620500532053

Vial, G. (2021). Understanding digital transformation: A review and a research agenda. *Managing Digital Transformation*, 13-66. doi:10.1016/j.jsis.2019.01.003

Vinze, M. D. (1987). Women Entrepreneurs in India. In *A Socio-Economic Study of Delhi 1975-85.* South Asia Books.

Virilio, P. (2006). Speed and Politics. Los Angeles: Semiotext(E)

Vivakaran, M., & Maraimalai, N. (2017). Feminist pedagogy and social media: A study on their integration and effectiveness in training budding women entrepreneurs. *Gender and Education, 29*(7), 869–889. doi:10.1080/09540253.2016.1225008

Vodă, A. I., Haller, A. P., Anichiti, A., & Butnaru, G. I. (2020). Testing entrepreneurial intention determinants in post-transition economies. *Sustainability (Switzerland), 12*(24), 1–28. doi:10.3390u122410370

Voronkova, O., Nikishkin, V., Frolova, I., Matveeva, E., Murzagalina, G., & Kalykova, E. (2019). Importance of the process of teaching the basics of social entrepreneurship for the sustainable development of society. *Entrepreneurship and Sustainability Issues, 7*(2), 1048–1058. doi:10.9770/jesi.2019.7.2(18)

Vuorikari, R., Punie, Y., Carretero Gomez S., & Van den Brande, G. (2016). *DigComp 2.0: The Digital Competence Framework for Citizens. Update Phase 1: The Conceptual Reference Model.* Luxembourg Publication Office of the European Union. doi:. doi:10.2791/11517

Walby, S., Armstrong, J., & Strid, S. (2012). Intersectionality: Multiple inequalities in social theory. In Sociology, 46(2), 224–240)s SAGE Publications Ltd. doi:10.1177/0038038511416164

Walokar, S. K. & Deepak, M. (2001). *Opportunities, Performance and Problems*. Himalaya Publishing House. https://vakilsearch.com/blog/7-indian-government-initiatives-to-help-women-entrepreneurs-smash-the-glass-ceiling/ http://www.dcmsme.gov.in/publications/women_schemes.pdf,

Wang, W. (2022). Toward economic growth and value creation through social entrepreneurship: Modelling the mediating role of innovation. *Frontiers in Psychology*, *13*, 914700. doi:10.3389/fpsyg.2022.914700 PMID:35783796

Waqar, A., Jamil, M., Firdause, A., & Fadzil, M. (2020). Comprehensive review of social entrepreneurship: Developing the conceptual framework for describing the phenomenon of social new venture creation. *International Journal of Scientific & Technology Research*, *9*(4), 1987–1995.

Waseem, A. (2018). Female Entrepreneurship and Economic Growth: An Institutional Theory Analysis. *Pakistan Journal of Gender Studies, 16*. Academia. https://www.academia.edu/50993645/Female_Entrepreneurship_And_Economic_Growth_An_Institutional_Theory_Analysis

Weerawardena, J., & Sullivan Mort, G. (2006). Investigating social entrepreneurship: A multidimensional model. *Journal of World Business, 41*(1), 21–35. doi:10.1016/j.jwb.2005.09.001

Welsh, D. H. B., Kaciak, E., & Shamah, R. (2018). Determinants of women entrepreneurs' firm performance in a hostile environment. *Journal of Business Research, 88*, 481–491. doi:10.1016/j.jbusres.2017.12.015

Welsh, D. H., Memili, E., & Kaciak, E. (2016). An empirical analysis of the impact of family moral support on Turkish women entrepreneurs. *Journal of Innovation &Amp. Knowledge (Beverly Hills, Calif.)*, *1*(1), 3–12. doi:10.1016/j.jik.2016.01.012

Wilson, F., Kickul, J., & Marlino, D. (2007). Gender, entrepreneurial self–efficacy, and entrepreneurial career intentions: Implications for entrepreneurship education. *Entrepreneurship Theory and Practice*, *31*(3), 387–406. doi:10.1111/j.1540-6520.2007.00179.x

Winkler, R., Söllner, M., & Leimeister, J. M. (2021). Enhancing problem-solving skills with smart personal assistant technology. *Computers & Education, 165*, 104148. doi:10.1016/j.compedu.2021.104148

Wiriya, P. (2022, September 28). *Growth Impact of Women Entrepreneurs in India & Importance of Financial Independence*. Kinara Capital. https://kinaracapital.com/financial-independence-and-growth-impact-of-women-entrepreneurs-in-india/

Wittig, M. (2013). *Straight düşünce. (Çev: L. S. Darıcıoğlu ve P. Büyükbaş)*. Sel Yayıncılık.

Woetzel, J., Madgavkar, A., Ellingrud, K., Labaye, E., Devillard, S., Kutcher, E., Manyika, J., Dobbs, R., & Krishnan, M. (2022, April 12). *How advancing women's equality can add $12 trillion to global growth.* McKinsey & Company. https://www.mckinsey.com/featured-insights/employment-and-growth/how-advancing-womens-equality-can-add-12-trillion-to-gl
obal-growth

Women Entrepreneurship and Leadership. (2022, November 15). European Institute of Innovation & Technology (EIT). https://eit.europa.eu/our-activities/entrepreneurship/women-entrepreneurship-and-leadership

Women entrepreneurship is soaring in the US, a new survey finds. (2022, September 23). World Economic Forum. https://www.weforum.org/agenda/2022/07/women-entrepreneurs-gusto-gender/

Woolley, A., & Malone, T. (2011). What makes a team smarter? More women. *Harvard Business Review*, *89*(6), 32. PMID:21714385

World Bank Group. (2022, October 17). *Defying Global Turmoil, Poverty Rates Fall Across Central Asia*. World Bank. https://www.worldbank.org/en/news/press-release/2022/10/17/defying-global-turmoil-poverty-rates-fall-across-central-asia

World Bank. (2012). Female Entrepreneurship: Program Guidelines and Case Studies. Washington DC

World Economic Forum. (2022), *Here's what women's entrepreneurship looks like around the world*. WEF. https://www.weforum.org/agenda/2022/07/women-entrepreneurs-gusto-gender/

Xavier, S. R., Ahmad, S. Z., Nor, L. M., & Yusof, M. (2012). Women Entrepreneurs: Making A Change from Employment to Small and Medium Business Ownership. *Procedia Economics and Finance*, *4*, 321–334. doi:10.1016/S2212-5671(12)00347-4

Yadav, V., & Unni, J. (2016). Women entrepreneurship: Research review and future directions. *Journal of Global Entrepreneurship Research*, *6*(1), 1–18. doi:10.118640497-016-0055-x

Yamini, R., Soloveva, D., & Peng, X. (2022). What inspires social entrepreneurship? The role of prosocial motivation, intrinsic motivation, and gender in forming social entrepreneurial intention. *Entrepreneurship Research Journal*, *12*(2), 71–105. doi:10.1515/erj-2019-0129

Yang, S., Kher, R., & Newbert, S. L. (2020). What signals matter for social startups? It depends: The influence of gender role congruity on social impact accelerator selection decisions. *Journal of Business Venturing*, *35*(2), 105932. doi:10.1016/j.jbusvent.2019.03.001

Yap, C. S., Keling, W., & Ho, P. L. (2022). Determinants of entrepreneurial performance of rural indigenous women entrepreneurs in Sarawak, Malaysia. *Gender in Management: An International Journal.*.

Yildirim, S. (2022). The Consumer Role for Sustainable Development: How Consumers Contribute Sustainable Development Goals. In I. Management Association (Eds.), Research Anthology on Measuring and Achieving Sustainable Development Goals (pp. 872-888). IGI Global. doi:10.4018/978-1-6684-3885-5.ch047

Yildirim, S. (2023). Greenwashing: a rapid escape from sustainability or a slow transition? *LBS Journal of Management & Research*. doi:10.1108/LBSJMR-11-2022-0077

Yıldırım, S., Yıldırım, D. Ç., & Çoltu, S. (2019). The Role of Education in Women's Career Life in Emerging Economies: A Case of Turkey. In E. Pereira, & P. Paoloni (Ed.), Handbook of Research on Women in Management and the Global Labor Market (pp. 46-62). IGI Global.

Yıldırım, S., & Kantarcı, T. (2022). A Review on Sustainability Policies of Businesses: Recycling and Waste Reduction. *Journal of Recycling Economy & Sustainability Policy*, *1*(1), 1–9. https://respjournal.com/index.php/pub/article/view/1

Yıldırım, S., & Yıldırım, D. Ç. (2020). Achieving Sustainable Development Through a Green Economy Approach. In S. Patti & G. Trizzino (Eds.), *Advanced Integrated Approaches to Environmental Economics and Policy: Emerging Research and Opportunities* (pp. 1–22). IGI Global. doi:10.4018/978-1-5225-9562-5.ch001

Yıldırım, S., Yıldırım, D. Ç., & Gedikli, A. (2016). Sustainable Consumption Trends in the World in the Context of Green Economy and Sustainability. In M. Erdoğdu, T. Arun, & I. Ahmad (Eds.), *Handbook of Research on Green Economic Development Initiatives and Strategies* (pp. 65–84). IGI Global. doi:10.4018/978-1-5225-0440-5.ch004

Yoopetch, C. (2021). Women empowerment, attitude toward risk-taking and entrepreneurial intention in the hospitality industry. *International Journal of Culture, Tourism and Hospitality Research, 15*(1), 59–76. doi:10.1108/IJCTHR-01-2020-0016

Yoo, Y., Henfridsson, O., & Lyytinen, K. (2010). Research commentary—The new organizing logic of digital innovation: An agenda for information systems research. *Information Systems Research, 21*(4), 724–735. doi:10.1287/isre.1100.0322

Yunis, M., Hashim, H., & Anderson, A. (2018). Enablers and Constraints of Female Entrepreneurship in Khyber Pukhtunkhawa, Pakistan: Institutional and Feminist Perspectives. *Sustainability, 11*(1), 27. doi:10.3390u11010027

Zaheer, H., Breyer, Y., & Dumay, J. (2019). Digital entrepreneurship: An interdisciplinary structured literature review and research agenda. *Technological Forecasting and Social Change, 148*, 119735. doi:10.1016/j.techfore.2019.119735

Zahra, S. A., Gedajlovic, E., Neubaum, D. O., & Shulman, J. M. (2009). A typology of social entrepreneurs: Motives, search processes and ethical challenges. *Journal of Business Venturing, 24*(5), 519–532. doi:10.1016/j.jbusvent.2008.04.007

Zainuddin, A., Ahmad, J., Puteh, F., Chandran, S. D., Hassim, A. A., & Ismail, T. N. T. (2017). The 21st century challenges among women entrepreneurs: Revisiting the literature. *Advanced Science Letters, 23*(8), 7845–7848. doi:10.1166/asl.2017.9591

Zeb, A., & Ihsan, A. (2020). Innovation and the entrepreneurial performance in women-owned small and medium-sized enterprises in Pakistan. *Women's Studies International Forum, 79*, 102342. doi:10.1016/j.wsif.2020.102342

Zeren, F., & Savrul, B. K. (2018). Evaluating the Hidden Cointegration Relationships Among Female Labor Force Participation Rate Economic Growth, Unemployment Rate and Urbanization Rate. *The Journal of American Science, 15*(30), 87–103.

Zerzan, J. (2020). *Gelecekteki İlkel, (Çev: Cemal Atila)*. Kaos Yayınları.

Zgheib, P. (2018). Multi-level framework of push-pull entrepreneurship: Comparing American and Lebanese women. *International Journal of Entrepreneurial Behavior &Amp. Research, 24*(3), 768–786. doi:10.1108/IJEBR-12-2015-0314

Zhai, Y., Yang, K., Chen, L., Lin, H., Yu, M., & Jin, R. (2023). Digital entrepreneurship: Global maps and trends of research. *Journal of Business and Industrial Marketing, 38*(3), 637–655. doi:10.1108/JBIM-05-2021-0244

Zhang, J., & Zhou, N. (2021). The Family's Push and Pull on Female Entrepreneurship: Evidence in China. *Emerging Markets Finance & Trade, 57*(5), 1312–1332. doi:10.1080/1540496X.2019.1697671

Zhao, F., & Collier, A. (2016). *Digital Entrepreneurship: Research and Practice*. In the 9th Annual Conference of the EuroMed Academy of Business, Warsaw, Poland.

Zhu, X., Cooke, F. L., Chen, L., & Sun, C. (2022). How inclusive is workplace gender equality research in the Chinese context? Taking stock and looking ahead. *International Journal of Human Resource Management, 33*(1), 99–141. doi:10.1080/09585192.2021.1988680

About the Contributors

Ana Daniel is a Professor of Entrepreneurship and Innovation at the Department of Economics, Management, Industrial Engineering and Tourism (DEGEIT) at the University of Aveiro and a Researcher at the Research Unit in Governance Competitiveness and Public Policies (GOVCOPP), Portugal. As a researcher her main interests are on management issues related to innovation, entrepreneurship and entrepreneurial university, especially the dynamics that affect university-business collaboration, technology and knowledge transfer in order to stimulate socio-economic development. A number of publications have been produced in these areas, as well as several entrepreneurship prizes have been awarded due to her work in the development of technology-based spin-offs. She is/was principal investigator of several national and European funded projects. She is currently a partner in the RUNIN Marie Curie ITN on the role of universities in regional innovation, and Erasmus + project 'More Entrepreneurial Life at European Schools (MELES)'. She also reviewer of several scientific journals and member of the scientific board of the Portuguese conference in the field of entrepreneurship education.

Cristina Fernandes is Assistant Professor w/Habilitation at the University of Beira Interior (UBI), Portugal. She holds a PhD in Management from the University of Beira Interior. She is researcher at the NECE – Research Centre for Studies in Business Sciences at the University of Beira Interior and Centre for Corporate Entrepreneurship and Innovation at Loughborough University, UK. She is part of the editorial board of Management Decision; has several dozen scientific articles published in international journals including: Journal of Technology Transfer; Journal of Knowledge Management; R&D Management and Journal of Business Research. Actively participates in scientific meetings and international conferences on these topics, having been distinguished several times with awards for best article. Has participation in several international projects.

***

Amin Arifulla is pursuing a masters programme at Christ University.

Kenan Aydın is working at Istanbul Gelisim University and he is a dean of Faculty of Economics, Administration and Social Sciences at Istanbul Gelisim University.. He also worked at Kocaeli University and Yıldız Technical University. He studies on marketing, retailing, consumer behavior, marketing research and business administraion. He has several national and international papers and book.

Francesco Bifulco is Full Professor in Management at University of Naples Federico II. His main areas of interest are focused on branding enhancement, phygital journey, sustainable business models, innovation ecosystem, cultural heritage. He published papers and books about these themes on top journal and publisher. He chaired and participated sessions in international conferences. He led, as Scientific coordinator (University of Naples Federico II) in projects PON Research & Competitiveness Program (High-tech districts and related networks).

Francesco Carignani is a PhD student in Management at the Department of Economics, Management and Institutions at the University of Naples Federico II. He earned a Master's degree in Cultural Heritage Management. His main areas of interest are cultural management, social impact of culture, social innovation, audience development.

Ivana Domazet is Principal Research Fellow at the Institute of Economic Sciences and Associate Professor at the Faculty for Banking, Insurance and Finance, Union University. She teaches Marketing (undergraduate studies), Marketing Management, Marketing Strategy and Integrated Communications (postgraduate studies). Her scientific interests refer to: competitiveness, marketing research and strategy, communications, CRM and strategic management. She published a book in the field of competitiveness, market research, integrated marketing communications, as well as numerous papers related to the foregoing topics. She is Vice President and Board member of the Institute of Economics Sciences; Board member of the Institute of Social Sciences; member of the Scientific Society of Economists in Serbia (NDES); member of the Serbian Marketing Association. She was President of the Scientific Council at the Institute of Economic Sciences.

Catarina Fernandes is an Assistant Professor of Finance and Entrepreneurship at Polytechnic Institute of Braganca, Portugal and a researcher at CEF.UP – Center for Economics and Finance at University of Porto (UP), Portugal. She holds a Licenciatura in Management from ISEG – Lisbon School of Economics and Management, University of Lisbon, Portugal, a Master in Monetary and Financial Economics also from ISEG and a Ph.D in Finance from the Faculty of Economics, UP. Her research interests include Corporate Governance, Corporate Finance, Banking, Innovation and Entrepreneurship. Over the recent years, her work appeared in academic peer-reviewed journals, book chapters and proceedings.

João Ferreira is an Associate Professor at the University of Beira Interior (UBI), member of the Research Unit in Business Sciences (NECE-UBI), Portugal, and QUT Australian Centre for Entrepreneurship Research, Australia. He holds a PhD in Entrepreneurship and Small Business Management from the Autonomous University of Barcelona (UAB), Spain. He has edited or co-edited several books on strategy, innovation and entrepreneurship and published over 200 papers in premier international journals, including Technological Forecasting & Social Change, IEEE Transactions in Engineering Management, Journal of Business Research, R&D Management, Journal of Technology Transfer, Management Decision, Service Business, European Management Journal, Regional Studies, and many others. He is Senior Editor of the Journal of Small Business and Enterprise Development and Associate Editor of Management Decision, Journal of Management and Organization, Journal of Global Information Management, Journal of the Knowledge Economy and Revista de Administração de Empresas, and his research interests include strategy, competitiveness, and entrepreneurship.

Natália Figueiredo holds a PhD in Management at Faculty of Social and Human Sciences, University of Beira Interior (UBI), Portugal. She is a member of the research center NECE – Center for Studies in Business Sciences at the University of Beira Interior and a researcher of the research center CISeD – Center of Investigation in Digital Services, at the Polytechnic of Viseu. Degree in Management from Higher School of Technology of Viseu, Polytechnic Institute of Viseu, Portugal. Master's degree in management from ISCTE - University Institute of Lisbon, Portugal. Employee of Instituto Polytechnic of Viseu since 2000.

Ginu George has around 10+ years of academic and industry experience and is currently working as an Assistant Professor, Christ (Deemed to be University) teaching subjects like management, organizational behvaiour, HRM, and research methodology for undergraduate and postgraduate students. Completed Ph.D. in 2017 in the area of Employee Engagement. Her areas of interest are HRM, Marketing, and Organizational Behaviour. Research has always been a passion, and George has published papers in Scopus indexed, UGC, and ABDC journals, and also presented papers in various international and national journals.

Adriana Gradim is a Business Economics PhD student at the University of Aveiro (Portugal), where she took the undergraduate degree in Languages and Business Relations. Currently and a Master's Degree in Management. Adriana has several interests in the Management area, such as International Business and Marketing. She is also a research fellow at the same university.

Fabio Greco is an assistant professor in Management at University of Naples Federico II PhD in Management at University of Naples Federico II. Founder of a start-up and Academic Spin-off of Food delivery incubated in the Federico II certified university accelerator "Campania New Steel". The main research topics in which he is engaged are Entrepreneurship, Start-up Ecosystems, Management of cultural heritage, Food Economy.

Hartiningsih was born in Matabu, Central Kalimantan, on April 22, 1964. The author completed his master's degree in communication science management. The author is a researcher at the regional research and development agency in the province of South Kalimantan with media expertise and socio-cultural studies.

Gesualda Iodice is a PhD student in Management at the Department of Economics, Management and Institutions at the University of Naples Federico II. Since her Master's degree in Cultural Heritage Management she deals with research, benchmarking and strategic analysis in the cultural and creative sector. Her areas of specialisation concern the management of art and heritage, enhancement of the archeological incoming, innovative museum practises and stakeholder engagement

Teresa Jacob is a second-year Master of Commerce student from Christ University, Bangalore. She received a bachelor's degree in Commerce (Honors) from St. Francis Degree College affiliated to Osmania University, Hyderabad. Her interest in research and other academic pursuits have inspired her to opt for a Master's degree in Commerce. The areas that interest her are entrepreneurship, organizational behavior, HRM and so forth.

Tugba Kantarcı has a Phd Degree from Tekirdag Namık Kemal University in 2022. She is an expert in Economics. She studies on economic growth, innovation, employment, energy consumption and sustainable development. She has several papers published in international journals indexed by Web of Science and other quality indexes. She graduated from the Economics doctorate program of Tekirdag Namık Kemal University.

Nana Nadarsyah was born in Banjarmasin, January 10, 1977. The author currently works at the Regional Research and Development Agency of South Kalimantan Province as a researcher with public health expertise and is a Non-Permanent Lecturer at the Midwifery Academy. Previously, the author was assigned to work in health services both at the Puskesmas and at the Government Hospital. The author completed his Masters in Health Promotion at Diponegoro University, Semarang with a specialization in Reproductive Health and HIV / AIDS in 2012. In 2019 the author has completed his doctoral education in Public Administration at Diponegoro University, Semarang, Indonesia. In 2021 accept Scientific Research Awards from Research Culture Society (Scientific Research Association)

Lurdes Patrício is a Ph.D. candidate at the University of Beira Interior, Senior Technician, and Guest Assistant Teacher at the Escola Superior de Tecnologia e Gestão de Viseu - Instituto Politécnico de Viseu (ESTGV-IPV), a member of the Research Unit in Business Sciences (NECE-UBI), and of the Center for Research in Digital Services (CISED-IPV), Portugal. Her research interests include strategy and entrepreneurship.

Rui Pires is a Lecturer of Management Accounting and Pricing at the Instituto Politécnico de Bragança (IPB), Portugal. He holds a Licenciatura in Accounting and Administration from IPB, Portugal, and a Master in Accounting from the School of Economics and Management, University of Minho, Portugal. He is the author of publications in international academic peer-reviewed journals, book chapters, and proceedings at international academic conferences. His research interests focus on strategic management accounting, strategic decision-making process, strategic resources and capabilities, innovation and entrepreneurship.

Dilek Şen graduated from Marmara University, Department of Public Relations and Publicity and worked professionally in many different sectors. In 2011, she co-founded an occupational health and safety company in Bursa, one of Turkey's major industrial cities. She is a female employer and is about to complete her thesis on female workers and female employer profiles at Uludağ University, Department of Women's Studies. She is a civil society volunteer and moderator of reading clubs.

Vladimir Simovic is a Senior Research Fellow at the Institute of Economic Sciences and at Australian University, West Mishref, Kuwait. He is also Associate Professor at the Faculty for Banking, Insurance and Finance, Union University, Belgrade. Ever since 2012 he teaches courses Information systems and Management information systems to undergraduate students and Contemporary information technology to PhD students. The areas of his professional interests are in e-Business in general and more specifically in business information systems, IT entrepreneurship, Internet marketing and e-Learning. He is a member of a Scientific Council at the Institute of Economic Sciences.

Vismaya Thomas is a second-year Master of Commerce student from Christ University, Bangalore. She did her Bachelor of Commerce from Kristu Jayanti College, affiliated to Bangalore North University. Her budding inquisitiveness towards research and other academic pursuits has inspired her to opt for a Master's degree in Commerce. The areas that interest her are entrepreneurship, organizational behavior, behavioral finance, consumer behavior, business ethics, corporate governance, and so forth.

Seda Yıldırım currently works at Tekirdag Namık Kemal University in Turkey. She studies on sustainable development, 2030 sustainable development goals, sustainable consumption patterns, Islamic finance and banking, consumption patterns, environmental quality and food security. She won Emerald literati award- Outstanding Paper Award 2022. #LiteratiAwards.

Index

Ensure Quality Research is Introduced to the Academic Community

Become an Evaluator for IGI Global Authored Book Projects

The overall success of an authored book project is dependent on quality and timely manuscript evaluations.

Applications and Inquiries may be sent to:
development@igi-global.com

Applicants must have a doctorate (or equivalent degree) as well as publishing, research, and reviewing experience. Authored Book Evaluators are appointed for one-year terms and are expected to complete at least three evaluations per term. Upon successful completion of this term, evaluators can be considered for an additional term.

If you have a colleague that may be interested in this opportunity, we encourage you to share this information with them.

www.ingramcontent.com/pod-product-compliance
Lightning Source LLC
LaVergne TN
LVHW062156300926
849161LV00010B/2681